bach

nent

Other Titles in This Series

Also of Interest

*Available in paperback only.

Social Impact Assessment Series
C. P. Wolf, General Editor

A Systems Approach to Social Impact Assessment: Two Alaskan Case Studies
Lawrence A. Palinkas, Bruce Murray Harris, and John S. Petterson

This book provides two case studies that demonstrate the use of systems analysis to forecast the often far-reaching consequences of government policies and economic development for the social relations and cultural values of different communities. The case studies examine the potential effects of oil development in two rural Alaskan communities, comparing the impact of proposed oil-related activities with projected changes in the sociocultural and socioeconomic aspects of these communities under other sets of assumptions, such as the development of a local groundfish industry.

Each case study begins with an ethnographic description of the community, organized along the lines of a systems model, which is then used to assess the impact of development upon economic activities, political and social organizations, religion, education, health and social services, and recreation. The systems approach to social impact assessment is a commonly used decision-making tool, and the comparisons set forth in these two case studies will allow managers and policymakers to better tailor models to suit the needs of their inquiries.

Lawrence A. Palinkas and Bruce Murray Harris are executive directors of Impact Assessment, Inc., a research corporation specializing in applied social science. John S. Petterson is president of Impact Assessment, Inc.

A Systems Approach to Social Impact Assessment
Two Alaskan Case Studies

Lawrence A. Palinkas,
Bruce Murray Harris,
and John S. Petterson

Westview Press / Boulder and London

Social Impact Assessment Series

Copyright © 1985 by Westview Press, Inc.

Published in 1985 in the United States of America by Westview Press, Inc.,
5500 Central Avenue, Boulder, Colorado 80301; Frederick A. Praeger, Publisher

Library of Congress Cataloging in Publication Data
Palinkas, Lawrence A.
  A systems approach to social impact assessment.
  (Social impact assessment series; no. 15)
  Bibliography: p.
  1. Petroleum industry and trade--Social aspects--
Alaska--Case studies. 2. Cities and towns--Alaska--Case
studies. 3. Alaska--Rural conditions--Case studies.
I. Harris, Bruce Murray. II. Petterson, John S.
III. Title.
HD9567.A4P35   1985   303.4'09798   84-25631
ISBN 0-8133-7031-0

Composition for this book was provided by the authors
Printed and bound in the United States of America

10 9 8 7 6 5 4 3 2 1

Contents

Tables and Figures

Figures

Preface

Ever since the enactment of the National Environmental Policy Act in 1969 several quantitative models have been developed to assist managers, government officials, and researchers in conducting social impact assessments. Development in this field has been both rapid and focussed on economic and demographic indicators of change. Models range in scope and complexity from relatively simple accounting models of population, employment and income, to sophisticated computerized models of economic sector growth, migration, government revenues, social services, and income stratification. In comparison, there has been relatively little progress made in the development of qualitative models. This is unfortunate because of the need to incorporate qualitative data into the social impact assessment process and because of the relatively narrow range of social system components which are analyzed by quantitative models.

This book represents an effort at developing a qualitative model for use in social impact assessments. The systems approach described in this book and applied in two different case studies is not intended to replace the quantitative models widely used today, but rather it could be used as a supplement to these models. Our objective in using the systems approach was to explain the relationships among the various components of a community's socioeconomic and sociocultural systems. It was believed that in doing so, the forecasts generated from the quantitative models could be contextualized in the larger systemic view of the community. Aspects of socioeconomic and sociocultural systems, including values, religious organization, social networks, health care, and recreation, which are often excluded from social impact assessments, are included in this approach. Moreover, this particular model appeared to be ideally suited to the task of integrating quantitative and qualitative data in social impact assessments. Hence, the projections of economic and population growth typically given by the quantitative models are related to concepts such as political conflict, psychological stress, and patterns of subsistence exchange in this model.

Several weaknesses exist with this particular qualitative model, some which were uncovered by applying it in the two Alaskan case studies described below, and some which remain to be examined

by further testing and critical evaluation. The intent of this
book is to present the results of its initial application and to
open a dialogue which will generate criticism, feedback, and
eventual refinements, thus enhancing the model's validity and use
in other types of social impact studies.

The two social impact studies were conducted by Impact
Assessment, Inc. for the Social and Economic Studies Program of the
Minerals Management Service, Alaska OCS Region. Dr. Petterson
served as Project Manager and Principal Investigator for these
studies and provided overall supervision for the data collection
efforts in the field. Mr. Michael Downs conducted four months of
field data collection in Unalaska and provided most of the
primary data contained in Chapters Two and Three in this volume.
Dr. Harris conducted two months of field data collection and provided most of the information contained in Chapters Five and Six.
Data on regional relationships in the Aleutians were provided by
Beverly Holmes. The initial format for the systems model used to
describe and develop forecast scenarios for the communities of
Unalaska and Cold Bay was developed by Dr. Palinkas and applied in
a previous OCS study (Petterson, Palinkas and Harris 1982). The
model was later refined by Dr. Petterson and Dr. Harris to meet the
specific requirements of social impact assessments for rural
Alaskan communities.

The book itself is a condensation two technical reports, No.
92 (Petterson, Palinkas, Harris, Downs, and Holmes 1983) and No. 93
(Petterson, Harris, Palinkas, and Langdon 1983) prepared for the
Minerals Management Service. These reports have been further con-
densed by the staff of the MMS OCS Region and incorporated into
environmental impact statements for OCS Lease Sales.

Lawrence A. Palinkas
Bruce Murray Harris
John S. Petterson
La Jolla, California

Acknowledgments

While we bear sole responsibility for the information contained in the following pages and for the conclusions based on that information, we wish to recognize the efforts of the many individuals who helped to make this book a reality. Most of the research for this book was conducted as part of our work for the Social and Economic Studies Program, Minerals Management Service, Alaska OCS Region under contract nos. BLM AA852-CT2-35 and MMS 14-12-0001-29069. Karen Gibson, the Contracting Officer's Representative, and George Allen, the Project Inspector, played instrumental roles in providing the focus for our research, evaluating our data, methods of analysis, and forecast projections, and editing our technical reports. Ms. Gibson provided us with technical guidance and support while Mr. Allen supervised the methodological and analytical components of our work. Both of these individuals assisted us in a timely and professional manner.

The research described in this book is the product of a team effort conducted by the staff of Impact Assessment, Inc., a research corporation specializing in applied social science. Mr. Michael Downs, a Ph.D. candidate at the University of California, San Diego, spent four months of fieldwork in the community of Unalaska. The data collected in this endeavor provided the basis for the chapters on Unalaska contained in this book as well as his own doctoral dissertation on ethnicity and social change among Aleuts in Alaska. Ms Beverly Holmes, a longtime resident of the Aleutians region, provided invaluable information on social relations within the region. Dr. Steve Langdon of the University of Alaska, Anchorage, provided insight as well as information on the communities of the Alaska Peninsula surrounding the community of Cold Bay.

The data and the insights gained from our research in the communities of Unalaska and Cold Bay are as much the product of the residents of these communities are they are of our own efforts. There are individuals, too numerous to mention, to whom we owe a great deal of gratitude for the time and effort they devoted to making the field researchers feel welcome, providing housing and introductions to other local residents, and contributing to data collection efforts. In Unalaska, Mr. Jess Burton, the Mayor, Mr Richard Careaga, the Director of Planning, and Mr. Philemon xvi

Tutiakoff of the Ounalashka Corporation were particularly helpful.
The Mayor of Cold Bay, Mr. Monte Larsh, served as a key informant
on the history and current social structure of the community, and
has continued to keep us abreast of local developments.

F. G. Bailey served as a consultant for our research and
edited the technical reports which provided the basis for this
book. We are particularly indebted to Professor Bailey who served
as both mentor and colleague at the University of California, San
Diego, and who instructed us on the potential uses of systems
analysis in social research. The approach described in this book
is largely based on his own work on social change.

Finally, to our families and friends who endured our
enthusiasm as well as our hardships in completing this work, we
wish to express our heartfelt thanks.

Lawrence A. Palinkas
Bruce Murray Harris
John S. Petterson
La Jolla, California

1
Introduction

1.1 DEVELOPMENT AND ASSESSMENT

Whether in a positive or negative sense, development cannot fail but have some impact on someone, somewhere, and somehow. Scarce resources and the potential for fiscal mismanagement, destruction of the environment, and disruption of social networks and cultural traditions of small communities demand greater efficiency in decisionmaking by government and industry. This need has been repeatedly demonstrated by the rapid population growth and associated public service and social problems resulting from energy resource development in the rural areas of the United States (Albrecht 1978; Dixon 1978; Gilmore 1976; Murdock and Leistritz 1980).

In response to this need, the National Environmental Policy Act (NEPA) was passed in 1969, mandating that environmental impact statements be generated which "insure that environmental information is available to public officials and citizens before decisions are made and actions are taken" (U.S. Council on Environmental Quality 1978:2). This information has been used for a wide range of purposes, including the siting of project facilities, project management, public information and relations management, the evaluation of impacts for state licensing and permitting processes, public facility planning, impact mitigation analysis and planning, and project monitoring (Murdock, Leistritz, Hamm, and Hwang 1982:334).

An important component of these environmental impact statements has been the assessment of social impacts. A social impact assessment (SIA) entails the evaluation of the consequences of an existing development or program or the projected consequences of a proposed development or program that are likely to affect the social, economic, and cultural activities of a community or group of people. "The job of the SIA practitioner," as Freudenberg (1983:9) describes it, "is to assess, or to try to measure in advance, the impacts (a) project is likely to create in (a) particular setting. The impacts, in a nutshell, are the differences between what would happen with the project and what would have happened otherwise." The range of impacts assessed is quite extensive including: demographic structure, community facilities,

1

housing and real estate, employment opportunities, labor force participation rates, income, crime rates, morbidity and mortality, government and social services, mental health, social networks, attitudes, and values. Most practitioners agree that a thorough grounding in the social sciences and an interdisciplinary perspective are essential to conduct social impact assessments.

The tasks of assessing the impacts of recent policy decisions and managing the course of future social change are complex and fraught with numerous opportunities for miscalculation. The information collected must be accurate (valid) and the generalizations obtained must enable us to have reasonable expectations or project with some degree of accuracy the course of change over a specified time period. To meet these requirements, several models have been developed. "These models range from relatively simple techniques for extrapolating various social and economic indicators, in which the interrelations between dimensions are only casually examined, to very complex computerized models in which model dimensions are systematically interrelated and integrated" (Leistritz and Murdock 1981:xiii-xiv).

In the past decade, several computerized socioeconomic impact assessment models have been developed and used with varying degrees of success (Cluett, Mertaugh and Micklin 1977; Denver Research Institute 1979; Ford 1976; Huskey and Kerr 1980; Stenehjem 1978; Leistritz et al. 1978; Mountain West Research 1978). Although these models differ in input and output structures and computational methods, they typically provide quantified data on economic, demographic, public service, and social changes likely to occur under both baseline and impact conditions (Murdock and Leistritz 1980:243).

However, quantitative data and socioeconomic forecast models alone provide an incomplete picture of the likely consequences of proposed developments. Models which are based on very generalized principles of development and socioeconomic change often fail to reflect the unique historical and socioenvironmental context as well as the possibility of unanticipated changes in the project itself. At times the idiographic perspective which is vital to understanding and forecasting social change in one community is sacrificed in favor of a nomothetic perspective which emphasizes comparability of change situations.

Second, these models typically reflect the cultural beliefs and values of the observer but not necessarily of the observed. Assumptions are made in each of these models regarding the relationship between basic and support sectors of the economy, desirability of employment, patterns of saving, investment, and consumption, and incentives for migration, which are based on Euro-American values. In cross-cultural contexts, these assumptions often do not apply to the social and economic behavior of the community under investigation. For example, in a hybrid market-subsistence economy, there is an element of choice not present in a pure market economy. The fact that subsistence goods are available as alternatives to the cash economy means that the demand for market goods is not necessarily fixed at a certain level. In addition, labor force participation is different from what it would be in a pure market economy. The existence of subsistence activity as an option to participation in wage-labor, and the perceived relation of return and cost of participation in each activity, will affect levels of employment. Lastly, there is a "cultural cost" of market participation in a partially subsistence-based economy. Subsistence activity is a part of a social and cultural matrix which defines such activity as important for social relations, adaptation to an uncertain environment, and maintaining a sense of self. A set of values dictates that such activities are both necessary and rewarding for reasons other than economic gain. This means that the change to market participation, such as accepting a wage-labor position, is not a decision based on economic motives alone.

Finally, social impacts are readily observed in terms of the behavior of the community under observation. However, as the above example suggests, this behavior is also guided by systems of meaning. Several social impact studies have noted that attitudes and impacts are very much interrelated (Shields, Cowan and Bjornstad 1979; Finsterbusch 1980; Carley and Derrow 1980; Muth 1983); "people's attitudes can have a good deal of influence on the impacts that are created, and the expected (or unexpected) impacts can obviously have a great deal to do with people's attitudes towards a project" (Freudenberg 1983:11). The relationship between a proposed development and the social, economic and demographic changes assessed is largely determined by the systems of meaning and values of the affected population. A thorough understanding of these relationships usually requires the inclusion of qualitative data.

This does not mean that these aspects of a sociocultural system are unquantifiable. Several quantitative models have been employed with great success in assessing the impact of proposed development on values, attitudes, and behavior (Berger and Associates 1982; Campbell, Converse and Willard 1976). However, a need exists for the inclusion of qualitative data in the assessment process. We need to assess the impact of demographic and economic changes on values and beliefs as well as measure the degree to which these values and beliefs in turn influence the organization of social and economic activities and the course of future change.

These issues were confronted in the task of conducting two separate social impact assessments of proposed offshore oil development in Alaska. From the perspective the policymaker and manager, usually outsiders to the community under investigation, oil development is critical for several reasons, including the reduction of national dependence on foreign oil, the continued flow of state revenues derived from corporate taxation which are required to maintain essential government services, and the development of income and employment opportunities in rural areas. The prospect of discovery of large reserves of oil located on the outer continental shelf (OCS) of Alaska carries with it anticipation of huge profits among businessmen and large tax revenues among legislators.

These goals and concerns are not necessarily shared by local residents of rural Alaskan communities, however. These individuals are often more concerned with the increasing numbers of outsiders with different values and what impact new migrants associated with oil development will have on the quality of life as they strain existing facilities, compete for available land, and threaten traditional culture and identity. These individuals also are concerned with the impact of proposed development on existing natural resources which are currently used for both commercial and subsistence purposes. The prospect of disruption of fisheries by oil spills, energy projects, and construction activities is viewed as threatening not only to economic activity, but to a way of life by local residents and hence something not to be desired.

These conflicting concerns were evident when conducting social impact assessments in two rural Alaskan communities, Unalaska and Cold Bay. Both of these communities could potentially be affected by oil-development activities in the North Aleutian Shelf Region of Alaska. However, these two communities greatly differ with respect to their history, the composition of their population, their cultural traditions, and their social structure. The utilization of a generalized model to project the likely consequences of oil-related and other economic development in these two communities would also have to incorporate information on the unique characteristics of each community.

1.2 UNALASKA AND COLD BAY

1.2.1 Unalaska

The City of Unalaska is located on two separate islands, Unalaska Island and Amaknak Island, both of which are part of the Fox Island group of the Aleutian chain in southwestern Alaska (Figure 1.1). The city is approximately 800 miles from Anchorage. Unalaska has historically been two separate communities, Unalaska Village inhabited largely by Aleuts, and Dutch Harbor, inhabited by Euro-American traders, businessmen, and during World War II, several thousand American military personnel. Both communities lie within the city limits of Unalaska, incorporated as a first class city in 1942. It was not until the construction of a bridge linking the two islands in 1979-80, however, that the two communities began to be seen by residents and nonresidents alike as one.

Throughout its history Unalaska has served as a commercial, transportation, and administrative center for the Aleutian region. Founded on the site of a traditional Aleut village, Unalaska was used first by the Russians and then by the Americans as a center for the fur trade. The proximity to Unimak Pass, connecting the Bering Sea with the North Pacific Ocean, the presence of a natural deep water port, a supply of cheap labor, and the richness of available natural resources, primarily fish and marine mammals, have all been major factors in the growth of Unalaska as a regional center.

In the recent past, Unalaska has experienced dramatic growth in its population and economic structure. The population increased from 342 in 1970 to 1,977 in 1977, and by 1979 the community had become the number one port in the United States in terms of the value of seafood product landed. This growth was primarily the

5

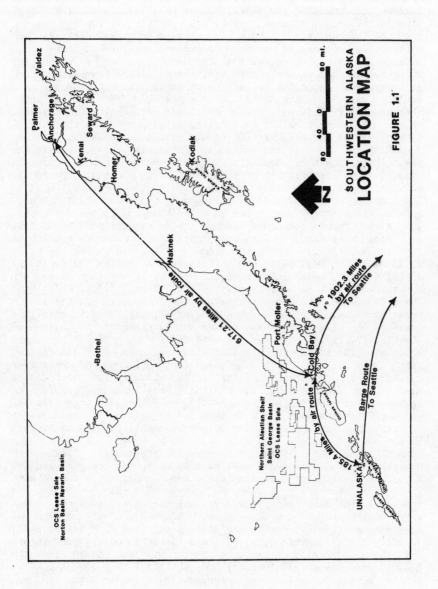

SOUTHWESTERN ALASKA
LOCATION MAP

FIGURE 1.1

result of enormously successful harvests of king crab in the 1970s. However, in the past few years, there has been a significant decline in the amount of crab caught, precipitating widespread concern for the community's future. In response to this decline, two alternative sources of economic growth and development have been considered by local residents: the development of a groundfish industry, and the oil-related activities resulting from exploration and eventual exploitation of resources in the St. George and Navarin Basins and the North Aleutian Shelf. The extent to which the community will be affected by these alternatives, however, depends to a great extent on existing developments and the structure of values and organization of activities in Unalaska.

Much of the existing character of Unalaska, particularly the community's modes of adaptation to environmental change, is the product of a specific set of historical circumstances. Prior to Russian contact, Unalaska was the site of the Aleut village of Iliuliuk, one of several Aleut villages on Unalaska Island. Traditional Aleut society was based on a maritime subsistence economy. The Aleut population subsisted on a wide variety of resources, including sea otter, seal, whale, sea lion, numerous species of fish and waterfowl, shellfish, and wild vegetables and berries. Forms of technology, religious beliefs, socialization and personality, and social interaction were all related in one form or another to this dominant economic activity (cf., Black 1980; Gross and Khera 1980; Hrdlicka 1945; Veniaminov 1840). Social organization in traditional Aleut society was guided by principles of kinship and class. The Aleut kinship system was matrilineal in character (Lantis 1970:227), although the evidence for this is not entirely conclusive (Gross and Khera 1980:60-61). Aleut society was divided into three classes: the chiefs and their children and relatives formed the upper class; the middle class was comprised of ordinary Aleuts and liberated serfs; and the lowest class consisted of slaves (Veniaminov 1840 II:164-165). Political organization, originally acephalous, came to be centered on a chief who ruled by community consent and relations between communities were maintained by kin ties.

Although the natural resources in pre-contact times were usually abundant, resource availability was never constant and the Aleut communities of Unalaska Island were occasionally faced with famine and starvation. With the arrival of Russian explorers and traders in the seventeenth century, the social and economic structures underwent fundamental changes. Disease and warfare with the Russians drastically reduced the Aleut population from an estimated 12,000 in 1741 (Lantis 1970:179) to a low of 1,500 by 1800 (Gross and Khera 1980:47). A system of barter was introduced and the Aleuts were slowly and forcibly brought into a cash economy. Male Aleuts were sent on long and arduous expeditions to hunt for sea otter furs while women and children remained behind as hostages. The pelt trade commercialized Aleut life and disintegrated the networks of intra- and intercommunity ties, breaking up families and aggregating village populations at centralized locations for ease of administration. Many contact villages on Unalaska Island, which numbered about twelve, were abandoned and the population was moved to Unalaska (Tikhmenev 1940:346-395). Orthodox missionaries such as Ivan Veniaminov, the first Russian Orthodox bishop of Alaska, played a critical role in introducing Russian language, culture, and religious beliefs to the Aleuts while indirectly contributing to the gradual disappearance of the indigenous culture (Lantis 1970).

As with the subsistence economy, however, the new economic structure was dependent upon resource availability, and with the decline in the numbers of sea otters harvested in the late nineteenth century, the growth of the economy came to a halt and the community experienced a depression for several years. This state of affairs was interrupted a few times in the twentieth century, usually the result of a minor boom in economic activity associated with the Gold Rush or the harvest of local resources such as herring, salmon and fox furs. The presence of several thousand American troops at Unalaska and Dutch Harbor during World War II also inspired a brief period of growth, resulting the the community's incorporation as a first class city and the construction of housing and utilities which remain in use today. However, this was counterbalanced by the evacuation of the Aleut population to camps in southeastern Alaska and the destruction of much of their property (Kirtland and Coffin 1981; Tutiakoff 1981). After World War II, it was not until the 1960s that the community began to experience any sustained economic and population growth. A crab fishing and processing industry emerged with the arrival of the first shore-based processors in the 1960s and by 1979, seven major processors employed over 1,600 workers on a seasonal basis.

1.2.2 Cold Bay

Cold Bay is located on the North Pacific side of the Alaska Peninsula. In contrast to Unalaska, it is a relatively new community, originating with the establishment of Fort Randall to counter the Japanese invasion of the Aleutians during World War II. Following the war the population dropped rapidly from several thousand to less than 100 by 1950. The enduring facility in Cold Bay is the international class airport, constructed during the war. It is the reason for the community's existence and insures its survival. Control of the airport was transferred from the U.S. Air Force to the Federal Aviation Administration in the late 1950s. The town originated as a military enclave and has remained essentially a community of transients since that time. Population has increased dramatically during the Korean and Vietnam conflicts and has dropped significantly at the conclusion of American military involvement. By the 1960s, Cold Bay had begun to attract a considerable civilian population, but the process of reduced government involvement was aborted by the escalation of military activity during the Vietnam conflict. Since that time, however, the military sector has diminished while the civilian sector has increased.

The history of Cold Bay, therefore, are intimiately connected to the community's dependence on the airport and its centrality as a government and communications nexus for the Alaska Peninsula and Aleutian Islands. The airport has remained under federal and state control, as has the town since it is located on airport property.

The State of Alaska owns virtually all local land, so little is available for private or commercial purchase. Much of the land within the city limits also has been claimed by the Native corporation of the neighboring village of King Cove, making it unavailable for non-Native ownership until 1991, under the terms of the Alaska Native Claims Settlement Act. In 1979 the Department of Natural Resources held a land sale, but the process was dominated by outside speculators and few local residents could afford to purchase lots.

Efforts at establishing a local fish processing industry have thus far met with limited success, despite the presence of the airport. Outside communications, transportation, and government corporations and agencies account for over ninety percent of all employment. These factors have resulted in a high degree of transience and general lack of permanent residents.

In 1982 the community incorporated as a second class city in the belief that incorporation was necessary to acquire funds for the construction of a local clinic. A municipal government was established consisting of a mayor and six councilmen. Since incorporation the city has faced several issues. First has been the definition of official city limits. Second has been the attempt to make some of the land held by the federal and state governments available for private and municipal use. Third has been the process of transfer of control of the major utilities and community facilities (particularly the water and sewage systems, the airport and the dock) from federal and state agencies to the city government. Fourth, the city has been concerned with establishing revenue sources in anticipation of eventual takeover of these facilities and utilities. Finally, the city has attempted to provide adequate medical care through the construction of a modern clinic.

1.3 THE SYSTEMS MODEL OF CHANGE

The strategy for conducting social impact assessments of the two Alaskan communities was guided by four specific methodological requirements. First, some sort of balance between a nomothetic model which could be utilized in a variety of different change contexts and an idiographic model designed to describe and analyze change in the particular historical and socioenvironmental contexts outlined above was viewed as essential to the task at hand. Second, description and analysis of the baseline data and projections under the various forecast scenarios had to include both the etic view of the outsider and the emic view of residents of affected community. Third, the model had to incorporate information on the value system of the affected community and indicate the relationships between the value hierarchy and social and economic behavior. Finally, the methodology had to be capable of integrating quantitative and qualitative data on all aspects of community structure and organization which would be affected by proposed economic development.

In order to meet these requirements, it was decided to use systems analysis and generate a model from the data itself, using a broad systems framework. Systems theory is an intellectual tool for studying the relation between the structure of a system and its functioning. More precisely, systems theory provides a set of rules by which the functions of a system can be associated with a known structure and by which the states of a system as well as its outputs can be correlated with the inputs (Cortes, Przeworski and Sprague 1974:5).

Systems analysis is not intended to be applied in its entirety to the development of forecast methods in social impact studies. Much of its terminology is inappropriate for the desired level of analysis, and much of it is derived from the study of "closed systems" (i.e., models in which all variables are controlled and in which interaction occurs within a limited set of parameters). Social groups, on the other hand, are best seen as "open systems," which implies interaction between a unified set of components or individuals and other independent variables.

1.3.1 Components of Social Systems

In a systems framework a social system consists of more than the sum of individuals residing in a particular community. It also includes the environment with which they interact and their behavior which constitutes a response to that environment. The social system, therefore, consists of three interrelated components: input, structure, and output. The relationship among the three components is illustrated by the following model (Figure 1.2).

Input consists of a series of independent variables which originate outside the social system under investigation and constitute the environment. Since not everything outside the community has relevance for social and economic behavior, only those variables which have an effect on the community or region under investigation comprise the environment. There are three types of environmental input in social systems: ecological, extrasocietal, and intrasocietal. Ecological input consists of such variables as climate, natural resources, local flora and fauna, and geophysical boundaries and limitations. Extrasocietal variables include the presence and influence of exogenous forces such as federal or state government agencies, outside business interests involved in local economic activities, and transportation and communication networks with other parts of the state or nation. The larger sociocultural system, of which the community is a part, and other communities within the region are also sources of extrasocietal input. Usually this takes the form of values, innovations, commodities, and technology imported from other areas of the region, state, or country. Thus, Unalaska and Cold Bay are affected by federal and state agencies; outside commercial interests such as Japanese processors and buyers, air carriers, and oil companies; world market conditions for salmon and groundfish; and urban-oriented values, customs and commodities originating in Anchorage, other parts of Alaska, and the United States as a whole.

The category of intrasocietal variables usually comprises the components of a social system which influence in some fashion a particular system selected for investigation. For example, the

Figure 1.2

Model of a Social System

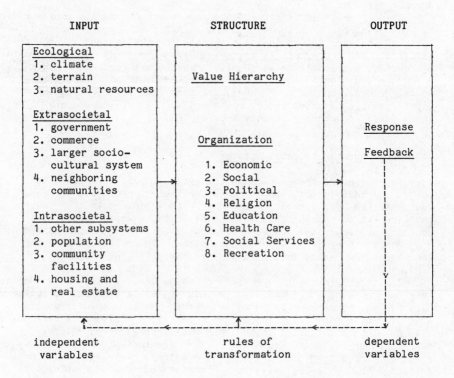

selection of crew members for fishing vessels on the basis of kin relations has certain implications for the distribution of income and labor force participation rates within a community. In this model, three specific components were selected because of their relationship to the subsystems under investigation. They include population, community facilities, and housing and real estate development. While these components may also be regarded as part of the structure of the community, they are placed in this category in order to demonstrate how changes in these components affect the organization of other aspects of the social system.

In addition to the types of input from the environment, it is important to remember that any of these variables can operate within the system in one of two ways. First, they may serve as a set of demands or pressures to which the community must respond. A natural disaster, change in weather patterns, depletion of subsistence resources, increased tax rate, or the removal of local fish processing operation to another part of the state by a multi-national corporation are examples of external variables acting as demands or pressures on a community. In all these cases, the input creates a strain on existing structures to which the community must adapt.

Second, environmental factors may serve as a set of resources or supports. Federal grants or state loans, Native land allotments, modern labor-saving conveniences, and outside employment opportunities are examples of external variables which provide resources or supports for the community. Certain variables, such as the Alaska Native Claims Settlement Act of 1971 or regulations limiting entry to the commercial salmon and halibut fisheries, can serve both as demands and as resources.

The second major component of the social system is its structure. In our application of the social system, structure may be divided into two major categories: (1) values or norms and (2) organization or behavior. Values or norms provide guidelines for behavior; they define not only the goals of social interaction but the means of obtaining these goals. In essence, they constitute a set of rules about how one behaves (Bailey 1969:10). These rules include normative injunctions (how one should behave in a particular circumstance) as well as pragmatic advice (how one must actually behave if he or she is to obtain a culturally-defined goal). These values or norms are arranged in hierarchical fashion. Thus, in a particular community or subregion, family responsibility may be more important than independence, or cooperation may be more highly valued than competition, depending upon the arrangement of these values in a hierarchy. The arrangement of values is not fixed; different values take precedence depending upon the opportunities and constraints in a particular situation.

The value hierarchy, in turn, serves as a set of constraints on social behavior, allowing for its regularity and predictability in the form of social organization. Organization refers to the observed patterns of behavior. These patterns are based on both the structure of the rules which act as constraints on behavior, and the function or purpose the behavior is designed to accommodate. Thus, an act of reciprocity serves to maintain social solidarity, promote family obligations, and maintain egalitarian status, while redistribution can promote the accumulation of wealth, social stratification, and competition.

In a social system, these patterns may be viewed as subsystems. Any collectivity of individuals organizes its behavior for the performance of specific tasks. In the communities of Unalaska and Cold Bay eight specific subsystems have been selected for examination: economic, social, political, religion, education, health care, social services, and recreation. That behavior labelled economic usually involves the tasks of production, distribution, and consumption of material goods and subsistence items. Social organization includes rules for association and interaction of individuals based on kinship, class, residence, or other principles. Kinship is concerned with the organization of individuals into social groups for the purpose of controlling resources through descent, inheritance, or succession and for making alliances through marriage. Political organization is concerned with the allocation of scarce resources and the distribution of power. Religious organization is concerned with the belief in the super- natural as a means of explanation and expression of social solidarity. Educational organization is concerned with sociali- zation and enculturation. Health care organization is directed towards the prevention and treatment of illness and disease. Social services include facilities and personnel which provide counselling, referral and assistance to members of the community experiencing certain social and psychological problems such as alcohol abuse, domestic violence, and mental illness. Recreation includes behavior which is leisure-oriented. That behavior may also have social and economic significance however, especially when it involves social interaction or subsistence activities.

The third major component of a social system is the output. This represents the response of the community to the perceived environmental influences. It is important to keep in mind that it is not the environment *per se* which motivates social behavior, but rather the *interpretation* of the environment by members of the social system. For this reason, an understanding of the value hierarchy becomes all the more important.

The output or response can be deliberate and planned or it may be accidental; it may be direct or indirect. Oftentimes the response is an adaptation to changes in the environment to make the best of existing circumstances. Not all output is productive, however. Increases in morbidity and mortality, crime, and politi- cal conflict can all be potentially disruptive to the community, subregion, or region. System output consists of activities repre- sented by social indices such as population size, income levels, employment levels, crime statistics, morbidity and mortality rates, marriage and divorce rates, and levels of conflict within the community. This output may also feed back onto the structure itself, changing values or forms of social organization which regulate life in the community. For instance, if enough members of the community spend greater amounts of time and energy participa- ting in a commercial or wage-labor activity and less on subsistence activities, the structure of the local economy will be altered accordingly, thus making a cash economy a permanent feature of the structure of the social system. The assessment of impacts on the sociocultural and socioeconomic systems is based on a comparison of projected changes in values and social organization with the existing baseline data.

1.3.2 Relationships Among Components

The relationships between the environment (input), society (structure), and projected change (output) can be analyzed by viewing these components in terms of independent and dependent variables. Variables originating in the environment are usually characterized as being independent. In an open system these variables are difficult to control and are subject to unpredicted changes. The response or output of the system can be likened to a set of dependent variables. The variation in this response is the focus of the forecast methodology. The structure of the social system under investigation is comparable to a set of intervening variables. How a particular input generates a specific response from a community depends upon its structure, the combination of value hierarchy and organized behavior. Thus, the same set of environmental pressures or resources may produce different responses from regions, subregions, communities, or ethnic groups within a single community, all having different structures.

One of the major limits of this analogy, however, lies within the concept of feedback. If a community's response to a certain set of environmental inputs has an impact on the structure of the community's social system, and perhaps even on the environment itself, then the distinction between dependent and independent variables becomes blurred. What is a dependent variable in one context may be an independent variable in another. Relationships of causality are not linear and the systems model takes this into account when examining all three components of the system.

In a forecast model, the relationship between environmental input and socioeconomic output in a social system is expressed in terms of rules or laws of transformation. These laws comprise the structure of the model itself and define the relationship between dependent and independent variables in a quantitative or qualitative manner depending upon the nature of the variables concerned. Rules which establish the relationship between primary and support sector income and employment (economic multiplier) or the relationship between employment availability and willingness to work in particular economic activities (labor force participation rates) define the structure of the system and, as noted above, are based on the existing or projected value hierarchies and organization of behavior.

1.3.3 The Systems Model and Social Change

At the most basic level, one can say that societies are motivated in their behavior by the desire to survive. Social systems are more or less constructed with that goal in mind. If that goal is either facilitated or threatened by changes in the environment, then individuals change their behavior and the social structure undergoes revision. Whether the environment is in a state of flux or is relatively constant, individuals within social systems are motivated to change their behavior for certain positive or negative reasons. A positive motivation for change is the desire to improve the quality of life, e.g., to pursue pleasure. A negative motivation for change is the desire to minimize certain forms of psychosocial and physiological stress and strain, e.g., to avoid pain. Actually, both positive inducements and negative aversions generate certain types of stress to which a community must respond. Not all members will want to respond, nor are all members capable of responding. Innovators, for instance, are usually characterized as members of a community who are able to recombine existing ideas into new ideas, usually under circumstances of ecological stress (Bee 1974:180). They possess both the capability and the motivation to change their behavior, which ultimately leads to changes in the social system.

For heuristic purposes, a social system can be characterized as existing in a state of equilibrium or a state of change. In a state of equilibrium one of two possibilities exists. Either the input, structure, and output all remain constant or the environment may change but the structure is insulated from the change. Under a state of change, one of two possibilities occurs. A change in the input occurs which creates stress on the community's social system. If the community's response does not adequately meet its needs under these new circumstances, the organized behavior may undergo some revision. A new pattern of organization may emerge even though the value hierarchy providing the guidelines or rules of behavior remains relatively intact. This is known as adaptive change. If the stress is so severe that a major modification of patterns of behavior is required, then the values which regulate those patterns may also undergo revision and a new value hierarchy emerges. This scenario is viewed as radical change.

Whether the change is adaptive or radical, it is usually seen as originating in the environmental component of the system (Bailey 1969:190). The impetus to change, however, stems not only from the environment but also from the structure itself. Easton explains that "regardless of the degree of structural differentiation and specialization, no system is endowed with so many channels that it has an infinite capacity to carry demands" (1965:121). Likewise, Bailey speculates that new resources may become available and the value hierarchy or norms may not give sufficient guidance for their use (1969:190). In either case, a community cannot foresee all of the potential changes in the environment and develop guidelines and forms of organized behavior to meet all contingencies. The more the environment changes, the harder it is to be adaptive.

The extent to which environmental input provides an incentive for change can be observed in the systems output, the community's response to environmental demands or supports. This response, as noted above, can take the form of various social indices such as population size, crime rates, morbidity and mortality rates, employment opportunities, or income levels. It can also take the form of conflict between values and between social groups adhering to different sets of values. According to Bailey (1969), the greater the conflict between normative and pragmatic rules, the greater the potential for change in the value hierarchy, the condition for radical change.

1.3.4 Limits of Systems Model in Projecting Social Change

Although this model is able to integrate projections for economic and noneconomic components of the social systems of Unalaska and Cold Bay, it does have certain limitations which should be kept in mind when applying it to these or any other communities. First, while the model works to integrate quantitative and qualitative data, the application of these two perspectives can create certain difficulties. Certain forces of change will be subject to more precise measurement than others. Arbitrary decisions may be required in assigning weights to variables not amenable to quantification or variables for which quantitative data is unavailable.

In addition, it is virtually impossible to predict which changes will occur in the environment, even for a relatively short period of time. Given the complexity of modern society and the rapid rate of social and cultural change, it is extremely difficult to control for all possible changes which may affect the socioeconomic/sociocultural systems under investigation. We are therefore forced to rely on existing trends or changes we know will occur within the projection period and attempt to leave open as many alternatives as possible.

Finally, the systems model is essentially an etic model and reflects the perspective, biases and, interests of the investigator. While this perspective may approximate the study objectives of the manager or government official, it may diverge radically from the perspectives, biases, and interests of the communities under investigation. In other words, unless the investigator can take into account his own culturally constituted set of theoretical and methodological limitations, he can never hope to understand the present patterns of social relations or make projections concerning future changes in the social, cultural, economic, and institutional life of the communities. In order to secure this understanding and make projections with any confidence, an insider's perspective is necessary. This perspective is sought through data outlining options and consequences of change as perceived by residents of the study area.

1.4 FORECAST SCENARIOS

1.4.1 Scenario Standards and Assumptions

The objective of the two social impact studies presented in this book is to provide forecasts of projected levels and directions of socioeconomic and sociocultural change in the communities of Unalaska and Cold Bay. These forecasts are based on the data contained in the ethnographic baseline studies and are predicated on a set of assumptions, provided by the Minerals Management Service, Alaska OCS Region Social and Economic Studies Program, of probable scenarios based on varying levels of development in the groundfish industry and oil-related activity in the region.

The standards and assumptions relate to existing ethnographic parameters of Unalaska and Cold Bay, such as the dependence of the local economy of Unalaska on local resources, primarily fish. They also relate to trends which are projected to exist in the future but are not directly related to either groundfish industry or oil-related development. An example of such an assumption is the projected decline in available state revenues in the next ten to twenty years, the decline of the crab fishery, and a decline in higher order governmental support for the communities.

Our projections for sociocultural change in Unalaska and Cold Bay are based on different scenarios. Two separate scenarios are developed for each community. For the community of Unalaska, the first scenario examines the likely consequences of groundfish development at levels consistent with population and employment projections provided by the Social and Economic Studies Program of the Alaska OCS Region. Included in this scenario is an acknowledgement of an already existing and relatively fixed oil-related development in Unalaska. The second scenario examines the possible consequences of the simultaneous development of a local groundfish industry and oil-related activity in the region. The exogenous factors (i.e., number of oil-related employees in the region, extent to which Unalaska would be involved in oil-development activities) are stipulated by the Minerals Management Service.

The first scenario developed for Cold Bay assumes that there will be no oil-related development in the community or in the surrounding region. It serves as a baseline assessment of sociocultural and economic change based on existing trends and proposed changes in those trends. The second scenario assumes construction of a major oil and gas facility on the south Alaska Peninsula with no direct road link to Cold Bay. The assumptions for such development, as in the case of Unalaska, are stipulated by the Minerals Management Service.

1.4.2 Impact Categories

The impacts of groundfish industry or oil-related development examined in the projection scenarios are intimately related to categories of sociocultural input and structure used in the ethnographic studies of Unalaska and Cold Bay, and are, in fact, based on the findings of these studies. The categories of sociocultural input include population, community facilities, private development, and regional relationships. The categories of sociocultural structure include: the economic, social, political, religious, educational, health, social services, and recreational subsystems and the value system.

1.4.2.1 Categories of Sociocultural Input. Four specific impact categories of sociocultural input--population, community facilities, private development, and regional relationships-- will be subjected to analysis. Many of the changes in these impact categories of sociocultural input are dependent upon projected changes in the economy as well as the exogenous forces (personnel, supplies, infrastructure requirements) associated with groundfish and oil industry development. The effects of these changes on the impact categories of sociocultural structure will be considered within the analysis of each subsystem (e.g., the effect of changes in population or regional relations on social relations, education, health care, and so on).

Projections of population changes throughout the forecast period include consideration of numbers of residents, ethnicity, age and sex distributions, and location of residence. Changes in community facilities include projections of alterations in water and sewerage system, power system, roads and docks, and the airport. Changes in housing and real estate refer to available housing units, patterns of land ownership, and efforts by public and private interests to develop property for commercial or residential purposes. Changes in the existing pattern of relationships with other communities in the region will be examined along economic, social and political dimensions.

1.4.2.2 **Categories of Sociocultural Structure**. In our examination of the impact categories of sociocultural structure, two types of impacts will be distinguished. The type of impact is founded on the notion of the systems model output component. Output represents the community's response to fluctuations in the socioeconomic environment. They represent certain patterns of social and cultural activities which govern community life as well as certain psychological responses to perceived changes in the sociocultural system and its environment. The second type of impact is a specific form of systems output referred to as "feedback." This term refers to changes in the structure itself, changes in the values or the forms of social organization which regulate life in the community.

Under the economic impact category, three major aspects of economic activities or output are examined. Pattern of employment constitutes the first aspect of economic activities examined in the analysis of community response to the proposed changes in groundfish industry and OCS development. An assessment is made of the number of jobs in commercial fisheries, consisting of the harvesting, processing and marketing sectors, projected to exist under the different scenarios. Other commercial employment opportunities examined include service support industries, small retail businesses in each community, transportation, construction, and petroleum production. Non-commercial employment opportunities, largely represented by the government sector or native corporations, and level of subsistence activities, are also discussed.

A second aspect of economic activities examined is the change in income levels among local residents resulting from the projected developments or lack of development in the groundfish industry and/or oil-related activities. Our analysis of this aspect of community economic activities considers both the levels of income as well as the distribution of income among the various segments of each community.

The third aspect of economic activities is the pattern of consumer behavior projected to occur in the various scenarios. This pattern is, of course, intimately tied to both income level and employment opportunity in the community. However, it is also a reflection of consumer choice, consisting of a series of decisions about which items to purchase, when, and in what manner (cash or credit), which in turn are governed by the values held by local residents.

Social activities examined as community responses to assumed developments in the groundfish and oil industries are tied to the extent of social cohesion within each community. This social cohesion can be examined in three separate components. One component is that of social relations among kin groups. This component includes changes in family patterns such as the number and type of family units and marriage and divorce rates. The size and distribution of extended family networks within the community, region, and state, are also examined.

A second component of social cohesion is that of social relations among local residents not linked together by consanguinial or affinal ties. These relations are based on locality (neighbor-hoods), social class, ethnicity, and employment. Each of these bases for non-kin relations in Unalaska are used to determine the quantity and quality of such relations projected to exist under each of the defined scenarios. Such an assessment requires an appreciation of the relative importance of social class status, ethnic ratio of the local population, the character and utility of ethnicity in various social, economic and political contexts, and the extent of friendships and intermarriage among ethnic groups in each community.

Finally, an understanding of the impact of the proposed changes on the cohesivity of community social networks requires an analysis of the community as a whole. This analysis involves a determination of the extent to which local residents adhere to one or more value systems, the levels of social interaction based on identification as a resident of a particular community, and changes in the demographic structure of the local population. With respect to this latter consideration, changes in certain aspects of the population such as the age distribution or sex ratio can have important implications for the character of social cohesion within the entire community.

Political activities in Unalaska and Cold Bay are examined from the perspectives of local administration, levels of political conflict, measures of bureaucratic efficiency, and extent and nature of social control. An analysis of local government includes such facets of administrative activity as participation in commu-nity development from the standpoint of new services demanded, new facilities required, investments shared with other government agen-cies, planning priorities, and projected tax revenues and other funding sources. The extent of local government participation in future community development is determined by a combination of these factors.

The level of political conflict in the community is also important when gauging the possible impacts projected to occur within the defined scenarios. Such conflict involves an under-standing of the issues which are responsible for community fission, the nature of local interest groups, and the activities they engage in to promote their causes. The character of political conflict between permanent residents and transients or between Aleuts and non-Aleuts, for instance, are discussed in relation to the projec-ted impacts under the proposed scenarios.

A third aspect of local political activity examined as a response to proposed developments in the groundfish and oil indus-tries is the measures employed by the community to assess the level of efficiency of local governments. Such measures include admini-strative budgets, deficits, levels of community satisfaction with the structure of local government and expectations of the role of local government in all spheres of community life.

Social control is another aspect of political activity examined in the context of the defined scenarios. Social control is both formal and informal. Formal social control is defined in terms of criminal activity and quality of police protection. Criminal activity is measured by projected crime rates in all major categories (i.e., homicides, assaults, burglaries, petty theft, and traffic violations). Police protection is measured by the projected numbers of available personnel and the quality of services offered by local law enforcement officials. Informal social control is defined by the number and use of moral constraints such as guilt or shame to enforce acceptable norms of community behavior. The proposed changes in the nature of these constraints and their effectiveness in regulating behavior within the community are examined.

Our assessment of changes in community religious activity throughout the forecast period consists largely of projections of levels of participation in established churches. Such levels are measured by size of congregation, numbers of members regularly attending weekly services, holiday services and social gatherings, and extent of member contributions to the church. When possible, an attempt is made to determine the extent of any changes in the belief system of the community as a whole, especially as that belief system influences social behavior in non-religious spheres of community life. For example, we consider the emerging political role of religious groups in Unalaska.

Changes in local educational activities are viewed largely in terms of students, teachers, facility construction, extracurricular activities, and achievement levels. With respect to students, the impact of the assumptions in the defined scenarios on student participation levels are analyzed. Such levels are indicated by measures of student enrollment, dropout rates, and numbers of students who pursue higher education, vocational education, or adult education. The number of teachers and the turnover rate for academic personnel are also taken into consideration when viewing educational activities. Facility construction takes into account both the number of students served by proposed or needed facilities as well as the effect of such facilities on the quality of educational programs throughout the forecast period. The involvement of students and the community in general in extracurricular activities offered by local educational institutions is also subject to analysis. Finally, where possible, an analysis of the effects of increased population and available revenues brought about under the proposed scenarios for groundfish industry and oil-related development on student achievement levels, on student goals, social organization, and so on, is made in the attempt to provide a complete picture of educational impacts throughout the forecast period.

Community impacts on health and social services resulting under the various scenarios are also analyzed as community response to groundfish industry and/or oil-related development. This response is analyzed through rates of illness and mortality and nature and extent of social problems such as alcoholism, psychological disorders, and domestic violence. An analysis of the effects of such illness rates and social and personal problems on existing or proposed facilities and personnel and how this in turn affects the cost and quality of care and service are both discussed in the analysis of health and social service response.

Finally, the impact of the proposed development of local groundfish and/or oil resources on the patterns of recreational activity is also analyzed within each of the assumed scenarios.

How recreational tastes and preferences will be altered with increased or decreased population and revenues, where such activity will take place, and how often, is examined in this analysis.

As noted above, feedback refers to the impact changes in activities have on a community's structure and its environment. It is possible, for instance, that changes in economic activity among Aleut residents of Unalaska will result in certain fundamental changes in their value system and also have an impact on the available natural resources they utilize. It is also conceivable that changes in the activities of the city government of Unalaska could result in an alteration of the relationship between the city government and the Ounalashka Corporation or between Unalaska and other communities in the region. These are examples of how activities could have important reverberations for the community's social structure as well as its environment.

While many of the output categories described above call for quantitative measures, only descriptive summaries are provided in this volume. Our primary objective in utilizing the systems model was to determine the manner in which changes in the environment would be felt among the various subsystems of community life. Precise measurements of these changes were limited by the lack of sufficient data. However, the elaboration of the pathways of change provided by the model is assumed to be a critical first step towards collection of the necessary data for quantitative measures such as these.

1.4.3 Ranking of Impact Categories

Because not all impact categories are equally susceptible to change, our analysis gives greatest emphasis to those categories most likely to change throughout the forecast period under the different scenarios for groundfish industry and OCS development. This requires a determination of those aspects of community life most, and least, susceptible to change. Our method for making such a determination is to rank the impact categories hierarchically. Our procedure for constructing such a hierarchy is based upon the scenario assumptions, the ethnographic baseline data of each community, and the conclusions of cross-cultural studies.

Our ranking system distinguishes between the impact categories of sociocultural imput and the categories of sociocultural structure. The first set of categories, including population, community facilities, private development, and regional relationships, are ranked according to the degree to which existing patterns will be altered by the varying levels of groundfish and oil industry development. The second set of impact categories are placed within three major divisions. The first is that of universal categories. It includes those components of community life most susceptible to change and having the greatest impacts on community life. These categories exhibit the primary effects of environmental change. Within this division we place the impacts of environmental changes on the local economy, social relations, and value system.

The second division is labelled context-specific categories. These are categories which may be of major or minor importance in the analysis of projected impacts depending upon the nature of the environmental input and the importance of the category in the social structure of the community. Change in these categories are usually secondary in nature when compared with changes in the local economy, social relations, and system of values. These categories include the political and religious subsystems.

Within the third division are the minor categories. Changes in these components of the social system comprise tertiary effects of environmental changes; they are more directly influenced by changes in the secondary categories. Health care, social services, and recreation are included within, but not necessarily limited to this category. These impact categories could also conceivably be labelled as context-specific because particular environmental changes may have potentially significant impacts on these categories. In general, however, these categories tend to display the least amount of change.

1.5 VARIATIONS IN MODEL APPLICATION

The following six chapters represent an attempt to apply a similarly constructed systems model to two different communities. While many of the same components of the sociocultural and socioeconomic systems of each community will be examined, it will soon become evident that major variations exist in the way the model is applied in conducting social impact assessments. These variations are due to several factors.

First, the communities themselves are different. As indicated in the above sections, the two communities differ in their history, their size, their economic activities, the composition of their population, and the organization of their subsystems. The sheer size and complexity of the community of Unalaska, in comparison to Cold Bay, demanded a more detailed application of the model in the former case.

Second, the data available on each community differs with respect both to quantity and quality. Relatively little has been written about Cold Bay while a wealth of published material, including ethnographies, historical accounts, population studies, planning studies, and other social impact studies exists for Unalaska. Much of the data on Cold Bay were collected first-hand by Dr. Harris and Dr. Petterson.

Third, the particular interests of the contracting agency (the Minerals Management Service) dictated that different aspects of the sociocultural and socioeconomic systems of each community be emphasized. Hence, regional relationships were accorded greater emphasis in the Unalaska study than they were in the Cold Bay study. In addition, although the Minerals Management Service was concerned with the proposed impacts of oil-related development in either community, it was primarily concerned with examining the likelihood and potential consequences of groundfish industry development in Unalaska. Hence, the scenario based on groundfish industry development was given greater emphasis than the forecast which included the possibility of expanded oil-related activity.

Finally, no model based on a qualitative perspective, such as

the systems model utilized in the two case studies, can remain
entirely free of the biases and perspectives of the person
utilizing the model as well as the community from which the model
is derived. As noted above, sometimes arbitrary decisions are made
with respect to description and analysis which are unique to the
researcher. Similarly, the perspective of the community is itself
influenced by the nature of the social impact assessment and is
subject to change over time. The model strives to bring both a
synchronic and a diachronic perspective to the analysis of social
change, but it is not always successful in doing so. Because of
these limitations, certain variations will always appear in the
application of the model. Nevertheless, the ultimate test of any
model is whether or not it works, in this case by providing a
vision of the future of a community which, within a specified range
of variation, inevitably comes to pass. If this vision can allow
government officials, industry managers, and local residents to
make informed decisions regarding their collective futures, then
the model may be considered to have succeeded.

2
The Physical and Social Environment of Unalaska

2.1 THE PHYSICAL ENVIRONMENT

The City of Unalaska is located on the Bering Sea side of the Fox Islands group of the Aleutian chain in southwestern Alaska (Figure 1.1). It is approximately 790 statute miles from Anchorage, 170 statute miles from Cold Bay, and 1880 nautical miles from Seattle. Unalaska is remote from other major population centers in the state and is accessible from them only by airplane or boat. This isolation has several important social and economic implications, as will be discussed in detail throughout this study. Nevertheless, there are certain factors regarding the community's location which contribute to its importance as a social and economic "center" of the region. Because of its size, location, and relationship with the city of Anchorage, many of the state officials responsible for the entire Aleutian Islands chain are based in Unalaska. Unalaska also has the only developed deep water refuge in the Aleutian chain. It serves as a stopover and refueling point for sea lift operations serving Bering Sea communities, western and northwestern Alaska, and the North Slope. Unalaska is located some seventy miles southwest of Unimak Pass, the first ocean vessel access through the chain west of the Alaska Peninsula connecting the North Pacific Ocean and the Bering Sea. All ship traffic between the southeast, southcentral, western, and northern regions of Alaska travels through Unimak Pass. Unimak Pass is also part of a great circle route in the ocean migration of several species of fish, hence attracting many foreign groundfish processing vessels. Because of this strategic location along a major shipping route, Unalaska receives the benefit of greater frequency in shipping than other areas in the Aleutian chain (Unwin, Scheben, Korynta, and Huettl 1982:2.2).

The community of Unalaska is located on two separate islands. One part of the city, usually referred to as Unalaska proper, is located on the northern edge of Unalaska Island. The other part, known colloquially as Dutch Harbor, is located on Amaknak Island. In the past, Unalaska and Dutch Harbor were regarded as two separate communities. In this study, however, Unalaska refers to the incorporated first class city which includes a part of the island of Unalaska and all of Amaknak Island. Dutch Harbor is a body of water adjacent to Amaknak Island, separated from Iliuliuk Bay by a natural sand spit several thousand feet long. Amaknak Island is separated from Unalaska Island by Iliuliuk Bay to the northeast and Captains Bay to the southeast, both of which are part of the larger Unalaska Bay. A connecting, protected passage between Captains Bay and Iliuliuk Bay is known as Iliuliuk Harbor. The developed portion of the City of Unalaska occupies all of Amaknak Island and a narrow flat area of land along the eastern side of the Bay and a relatively narrow valley extending southward and inland on the main island (Figure 2.1).

The City of Unalaska is located in a mountainous area with hills and flat areas along the coastline. It is bounded by mountain peaks ranging in elevation from 1,500 to 2,200 feet as well as numerous hills with steep slopes such that a considerable portion of the land both within and immediately adjacent to the city limits is unusable for community expansion or development. Elevations within city limits range from sea level to 2,365 feet above sea level. The four highest peaks in the immediate area are Mt. Ballyhoo (elevation 1634 feet) on Amaknak Island and Mt. Newhall (1648 ft.), Pyramid Peak and Mt. Coxcomb on Unalaska Island, in addition to numerous smaller hills which dot the landscape. The downtown area of Unalaska proper is located on a gravel spit which extends outward from Unalaska Island into Iliuliuk Bay, forming the northeastern edge of Iliuliuk Harbor. At the southeastern edge of this spit is Unalaska Lake. The spit is separated from Unalaska Island by the Iliuliuk River which runs from the lake to the harbor.

The climate of Unalaska is characterized by frequent, often cyclonic storms and high winds, countered by dense fog. Weather fronts generally move from west to east, but often climatic conditions on the Pacific side of the chain differ vastly from those on the Bering Sea, thus placing the islands at the center of a continuing weather war. Unalaska, however, with its location on the northern shores of the Aleutians, offers relatively greater shelter from this weather than afforded on the Pacific side of the Chain.

The Aleutian temperature is milder than most parts of Alaska because of the southerly location of the islands and the influence of the relatively warm Pacific Ocean Japanese current. Because it does not vary by more than a few degrees each season, the water temperature warms the air in the summer and cools it in the winter. Consequently, Unalaska experiences less variation in annual air temperature than other parts of Alaska. Mean annual February temperature is about 28 F and mean annual August maximum temperature is about 60 F. The prevailing wind direction in south-southeast and the average wind speed is 17 mph. Winds of up to 100 mph, however, are not uncommon. There is little or no permafrost.

Precipitation in Unalaska is greater than many other areas of the state but still less than the Southeastern region. Mean annual precipitation in 57.7 inches, including 81 inches of snowfall.

The marine resources available locally have traditionally comprised a major source of food for the residents of Unalaska and neighboring villages. These resources can be divided into three categories: marine mammals, fish, and invertebrates.

Traditionally, the major sea mammal resources have been sea otters, whales, sea lions, and seals. "Sea lions have been a major resource of the Aleut people since precontact times" (Veltre and Veltre 1982:59). These animals provided a source of both food and materials which were used extensively by Aleut residents. However, the importance of sea lions as a local food resource has diminished with the decline of these animals in the Unalaska area over the past few decades (Veltre and Veltre 1982:62). The Marine Mammal Protection Act of 1972 limits the hunting of marine mammals to Natives only. An estimated twenty sea lions are killed each year (Veltre and Veltre 1982:62).

Harbor seals have also been a major local resource for the natives of Unalaska. An estimated twenty seals are killed each year by the same individuals who hunt for sea lions. Prior to the passage of the Marine Mammal Protection Act in 1972, seals were taken by non-Aleut residents of Unalaska, though much of the meat was distributed to Aleuts. Since that time, however, they have declined in numbers, although seal meat is still eaten and seal oil used by Aleut residents.

Whale and sea otters were once major resource items available locally which were used by Unalaska Aleuts. These mammals are no longer part of the local food resources of the area. No whaling is done by any of the residents of Unalaska today and sea otters have been protected from hunting since 1911.

The major fish resources used for food in the Unalaska area are the various species of salmon, Dolly Varden trout, halibut and cod. Salmon, according to Veltre and Veltre (1982:87), is the most important local marine resource in Unalaska today and there are few families which do not use salmon. Fish are caught in local streams and from Unalaska Bay with most of the fish coming from the Bay. King salmon are available from February to April while red salmon run to Unalaska Lake from mid-May until the end of June. The largest salmon run in Unalaska, however, are pink salmon which are found in Nateekin Bay, Broad Bay, Captain's Bay, and Humpy Cove in Summer's Bay.

The near shore intertidal zone of the Unalaska area is rich in marine invertebrates. The most important in terms of local resource utilization are: sea urchins (strongylocentrotus sp.), known locally as "sea eggs," shrimp, octopus, limpets (Acamea sp.), mussels (Mytilus edulis), chitons, known locally as "bidarkis," clams, and crabs (Veltre and Veltre 1982:50).

The local vegetation consists largely of Alpine tundra. The windy, cool climate, shallow soil, relatively recent geologic history along with the topography and isolated location of the Aleutian Islands away from larger mainland areas prevents the natural establishment of larger vegetation types, especially trees. There are a few Sitka spruces in the area, the remnants of trees planted by Russian settlers in 1804 and, later, by American troops stationed in the area during World War II.

Plant species found in the vicinity include mosses, grasses, lichens, ferns, herbs, and small shrubs. Edible resources include blueberries, mossberries, crowberries, salmonberries, strawberries, lingenberries, wild celery known as "pootchky," a wild herb called "petrusky" (lingusticum hultenii) and wild rice. While a wide

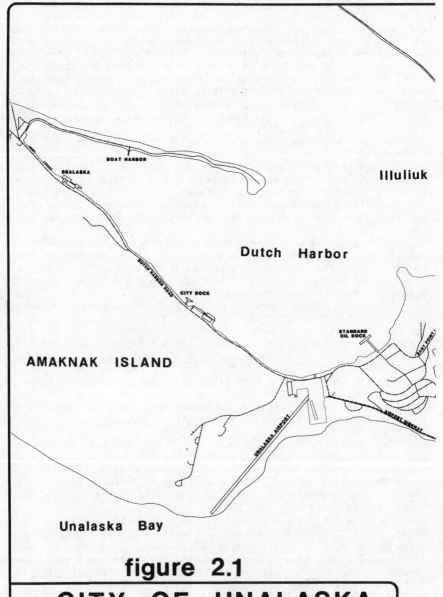

Illuliuk

Dutch Harbor

AMAKNAK ISLAND

Unalaska Bay

figure 2.1

CITY OF UNALASKA
AREA MAP

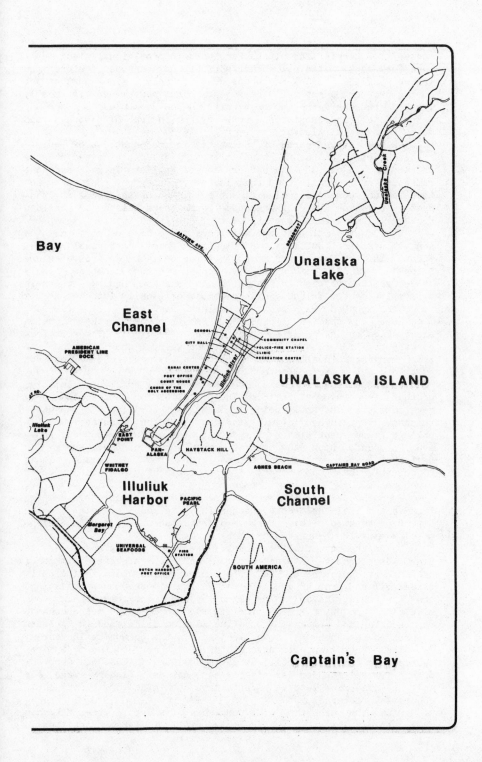

Bay

Unalaska
Lake

East
Channel

AMERICAN
PRESIDENT LINE
DOCK

SCHOOL
CITY HALL

COMMUNITY CHAPEL
POLICE-FIRE STATION
CLINIC
RECREATION CENTER

UNALASKA ISLAND

Iliuliuk
Lake

EAST
POINT

WHITNEY
FIDALGO

PAN-
ALASKA

SAMAI CENTER
POST OFFICE
COURT HOUSE
CHURCH OF THE
HOLY ASCENSION

HAYSTACK HILL

AGNES BEACH

CAPTAINS BAY ROAD

Iliuliuk
Harbor

PACIFIC
PEARL

South
Channel

Margaret
Bay

UNIVERSAL
SEAFOODS

FIRE
STATION

DUTCH HARBOR
POST OFFICE

SOUTH AMERICA

Captain's Bay

variety of berries and plants were used in traditional Aleut culture for food, medicinal, and fabricational purposes (Veltre and
Veltre 1982:98), plant resources comprise only a minor part of the
ecological component of the sociocultural system and is mostly
limited to the gathering of berries in the summer as a form of
recreational and subsistence activity and the use of pootchky and
petrusky by local Aleuts.

Unlike other parts of the state, no major stocks of animal
resources exist in the Aleutian Islands. Sheep are raised at the
Chernofski Ranch on the western end of Unalaska Island and the
remnants of a cattle herd roam in the vicinity of Unalaska but
these do not comprise a significant component of the local environment. Reindeer were introduced on Unalaska Island by Sheldon
Jackson in the late nineteenth century but fared poorly.

The one animal resource which does have some bearing on the
social system of Unalaska, particularly from a historical standpoint, is the fox. Red foxes exist on Unalaska Island which are
trapped by local residents, even though the fur is not as highly
valued as that of the blue fox on other islands. Ground squirrels
also exist on the island, while rabbits, originally imported as fox
food, are found on Hog Island in Unalaska Bay.

Some 183 species of birds have been reported in the Aleutian
archipelago and surrounding areas (Sekora 1973:143). The most frequently utilized resources are ducks and geese; some ptarmigan are
also harvested locally. In addition to the meat, eggs from sea
gulls and ducks are collected and utilized locally.

There are two potential sources of energy available locally,
geothermal and hydroelectric. The potential for geothermal energy
development is currently being explored in the vicinity of Makushin
volcano. Preliminary studies indicate that the resource is available in great quantities. The development of this resource, however, depends upon the current demand for electrical energy in
Unalaska as well as the prospect of future growth in demand. It is
conceivable that the economy of scale is lacking to justify such
development.

Hydroelectric power could also be made available by damming
Pyramid and Unalaska Creeks. According to a local official of the
City Department of Public Works, an estimated one megawatt of elec-
tricity could be generated by these streams.

While the potential for locally developed energy resources is
high, development of those resources will be expensive and most of
the current energy needs are met by imported resources, principally
diesel oil and propane gas. Diesel #2 fuel is used to provide most
the the energy needs in the community, particularly heating and
electrical power. Propane fuel is used in certain neighborhoods
for cooking and heating. Gasoline is also being used in greater
volumes as the number of motor vehicles in the community increases.

The local fisheries have historically provided the major resources for commercial utilization in Unalaska. The contemporary
community was founded largely on the local crab fishery and, as
will be discussed later, efforts have been made to exploit local
groundfish resources.

With the exception of a commercial fishery in the Makushin
area, salmon is not harvested commercially in large quantities in

the Unalaska vicinity and cannot be seen as a local commercial resource. While local salmon are in sufficiently large numbers to sustain subsistence needs, there are not enough fish to sustain a viable commercial fishery. What salmon is processed by local canneries usually comes from the Bristol Bay region and the Alaska Peninsula. Also, only four local fishermen possess temporary Limited Entry permits in Unalaska. Due to the high cost of obtaining such a permit, it is unlikely that salmon will be a important commercial resource for local fishermen in the near future.

Until recently, the major commercial fish resource for the community was crab. Several different species have been available for commercial utilization, the most important ones being king, tanner, and dungeness crab. This resource is available throughout the Aleutian Islands-Bering Sea management area. Much of this resource is processed in Unalaska and for the past ten to fifteen years has served as the major economic impetus behind community growth and development.

Although existing stocks of king and tanner crab have been on the decline for the past three or four years, it. is believed that the resource is a cyclic one. Several different theories exist to account for the recent decline. One theory is tied to the presence of large numbers of fishing vessels and processors in the area, resulting in overfishing of the resource. Another theory attributes the decline in crab stocks to the presence of growing numbers of groundfish, particularly cod, which feed upon crab larvae. A third theory has recently been advanced that a parasitic organism attacks the female crab reproductive system, causing the premature discharge of unfertilized eggs. For whatever reason, however, two definite conclusions can be made as to the availability of crab as a commercial resource for the community of Unalaska. The first conclusion, supported by the numbers of crab caught in the 1980/81 and 1981/82 catches, is that the resource is definitely experiencing a significant decline in availability. The second conclusion is that it is uncertain as to how long this decline will last.

Halibut stocks in the Aleutian region have been on the decline since 1960 with a major factor believed to be an increase in both domestic and foreign trawl fisheries which take halibut as an incidental catch (Alaska Consultants 1981:38). Nevertheless, existing stocks are still believed to be sufficiently large to support an important fishery in the area.

The Bering Sea and Aleutian Islands regions of Alaska contain one of the richest stocks of groundfish in the world. "Current estimates place the optimum sustainable yield for groundfish in the Aleutian Islands-Bering Sea region at around 1.6 million metric tons per year and optimum yields for various groundfish species have also been developed" (Alaska Consultants 1981:39-41). An estimate of the optimum yield of groundfish by each species is provided in Table 2.1. Although these figures refer only to 1981, they appear to be representative of estimated optimum yield for recent years.

Between 1928 and 1942, the stocks of herring available locally were considerable, supporting a moderately sized industry until the outbreak of World War II. Since the war, however, the resource appears to have declined. Although the numbers of herring in local

Table 2.1

Proposed 1981 Groundfish Harvest Levels and Estimated Optimum
Yields, Bering Sea and Aleutian Islands Areas
(metric tons)

Groundfish Species	Initial Domestic Annual Harvest	Initial Total Allowable Level of Foreign Fishing	Estimated Optimum Yield
Pollock	19,550	930,450	1,100,000
Yellowfin Sole	2,050	109,100	117,000
Turbot	1,075	84,425	90,000
Other flatfish	1,300	56,650	61,000
Pacific Cod	24,265	31,500	58,700
Pacific Ocean perch	2,760	7,453	10,750
Other rockfish	1,500	5,677	7,727
Sablefish	1,400	3,100	5,000
Atka mackerel	100	23,460	24,800
Squid	50	9,450	10,000
Other	2,000	68,537	74,249
Total	56,100	1,429,802	1,559,226

a. Bering Sea (statistical areas I, II, and III); Aleutian
Islands (statistical area I)
b. Excludes Pacific halibut.

Source: North Pacific Fishery Management Council. Draft Environmental Impact Statement for the Groundfish of the Bering Sea and Aleutian Islands Area, September 1980.

waters appear to have increased in recent years, it has not yet become an important commercial resource.

Shrimp has on occasion been available locally in quantities sufficient to support a small scale fishery. However, existing stocks appear to have declined in the past few years.

The mineral resources available locally are considered to be negligible. At the turn of the century, some mining for gold was done by prospectors who wintered in Unalaska on their way to the gold fields of Nome, Unga Island, and other parts of Alaska. What gold does exist in the area is in insufficient quantities to support a commercial industry. Sulfur is also available locally, primarily in the vicinity of Makushin Volcano, but it has been seen as too expensive to exploit on a commercial basis. Zinc, iron sulfide and copper also exist on Unalaska island but not in sufficient quantities to be of much commercial value.

There are no known petroleum resources within the immediate vicinity of Unalaska. The community is located close to three major oil lease areas: St. George Basin, Navarin Basin and the North Aleutian Basin, but it is uncertain as to how much oil is actually in these areas. However, judging from recent OCS lease

activity in the St. George Basin, particularly the level of financial commitment of petroleum firms to exploiting certain areas of
this lease area, it appears likely economically viable production
levels will be achieved within ten years.

2.2 EXTRASOCIETAL INFLUENCES

2.2.1 External Government

The federal government has had a consistent influence in the
area through several pieces of legislation and agencies. It has
influenced local fisheries through its establishment of and vacil-
lation concerning the application of the 200 mile limit, through
ANCSA, oil lease area development, and federal agencies such as the
Bureau of Land Management and the Bureau of Indian Affairs.

The establishment of the 200 mile limit is generally seen as a
progressive move by most Unalaskans. However, most residents feel
that the Bering Sea fisheries are subject to manipulation by the
federal government and used to reward countries with whom the U.S.
is on good terms and punish those with whom it is not. Residents
feel these factors influence American fisheries policy more than
local needs and desires.

The establishment of the 200 mile limit itself is believed to
have had major ramifications locally, although the exact effects
of the limit are unclear. Some Unalaska residents feel that the 200
mile limit hurt the local crab fishery by eliminating foreign
harvesting of groundfish, especially cod. This allowed the population to grow and threaten the crab fishery since a prime food for
cod is crab larvae. Others take the view that the foreign fishermen essentially "cleaned out" the crab before they left. In other
words, the 200 mile limit came too late.

The Alaska Native Claims Settlement Act of 1971 has had pervasive impact in Unalaska. The Act resulted in the establishment
of the Ounalashka Corporation which took responsibility for the
determination of the lands to be conveyed to the Aleut residents of
Unalaska. Since 1971 the Corporation has claimed most of the land
in and surrounding the community, and has administered that land in
the name of the shareholders of the Corporation. The Corporation
has also been involved in several local construction projects, and
leases land to several local processors and businesses. We will
discuss these activities in detail in the next chapter. A final
general area in which the federal government has a great deal of
local impact is, of course, in the area of oil development. The
decision by the Department of the Interior to open bidding on
several lease areas adjacent to Unalaska, including the St. George,
Navarin, and North Aleutian Basins in general, has raised the
possiblity of a great deal of oil-related activity in the future.
The initial phases of mapping and exploration have already affected
the community, as we will see when we discuss economic structure,
and if the finds are promising, the future will see an acceleration
of these effects. In all of this the economy of the city is
dependent on the prevailing political climate of Washington, and it

is national priorities and national political currents which will determine much of the future of the community.

There are several federal agencies which have historically played major roles in Unalaska. These include especially the Bureau of Indian Affairs (BIA), which was responsible for management of most of the affairs of the Aleut population until statehood and, later, the passage of ANCSA, and the Bureau of Land Management (BLM) of the Department of the Interior. These two still have a presence in the region, but their role has been much reduced and promises to be reduced even further in the near future. Nowadays, the BIA's major function in the community is to serve as a trustee for property owners of Native allotments and Native Trustee Deeds. The BLM was at one time the trustee for city lands in Unalaska, prior to the enactment of ANCSA. With the passage of ANCSA and the formation of the local native corporation, control of these lands has passed from the BLM to the Ounalashka Corporation.

Another federal presence in town is the Fish and Wildlife Service of the Department of the Interior. They are responsible for the administration of land on "Little South America" on Amaknak Island which is part of the Alaska Marine National Wildlife Refuge. The Ounalashka Corporation currently owns the surface estate to "Little South America" subject to the administration of the Fish and Wildlife Service, which is negotiating with the Aleut Corporation to exchange the subsurface estate for other property in the region.

Unalaska is also under the political influence of the State of Alaska. One area in which state level political decisions have affected Unalaska is the development of alternative energy sources. The geothermal exploration currently under way on Unalaska Island is dependent largely on state funding, which renders it vulnerable to state political forces. These forces have recently begun to cut back on funding for such projects as a result of the decline in oil prices. As the price of oil comes down state revenues decline and political decisions must be made concerning the allocation of funds which are becoming increasingly scarce. In such cases one of the first things to go unfunded is research and exploration for alternative energy forms, since, the reasoning goes, oil is now less expensive than before and there is therefore less need for the development of alternatives.

The state also has a great deal of control over transportation facilities, particularly air transport and harbor facilities, in Unalaska. Recently, airport expansion was approved as a part of the state budget, but the appropriations bill in which it was included was subsequently vetoed by the governor. Nevertheless, the FY84 state budget includes an appropriation of $4.5 million for the Unalaska Airport with authorization to spend up to $45 million in federal funds. The recent construction of a small boat harbor in Unalaska is a state financed project which is part of the state master plan.

The state is also represented in Unalaska through the State of Alaska Department of Health and Social Services, Division of Family and Youth Services which deals with child and adult protection, information and referral, and family and individual counseling. The office in Unalaska includes in its jurisdiction the area from

Anchorage to Atka and north to St. Paul. It is the largest region in the state.

The state court system is represented in Unalaska by a state district court. The court handles misdemeanors and civil suits under ten thousand dollars. The major functionary present is a magistrate who lives in Unalaska.

The state had particular impact in the community through certain legislative programs which it has passed in the last decade. One of the most important of these was the Limited Entry Act which has had major influence throughout the region, though in Unalaska this influence has been diluted by several factors. The Limited Entry Act regulates entry to the state's salmon fisheries. The reason it has had less effect in Unalaska than in other parts of the region is that prior to the introduction of the act there was no significant salmon fishery immediately adjacent to the community due largely to a down cycle in the fishery. As a result relatively few people were involved in commercially exploiting the resource and very few were able to qualify for a permit. The statute, therefore, has precluded the development of a local salmon fishing industry. In fact the area has witnessed the emergence of a salmon fishery in the last decade, but very few people in Unalaska have been able to take advantage of it. There are no permanent permit holders in the community, and only four people have been able to gain temporary permits which must be renewed every year, even though there are a significant number of individuals who have fished every year of their lives that there has been a good salmon run.

Another related area is the halibut fishery. Although the halibut fishery is not technically limited entry, the state has established an overall quota for catches. Once this quota is reached no further fishing is allowed. Effectively this has meant that the "highliners" from Seattle and the west coast rather quickly catch the quota and leave the local fishermen with nothing.

As noted above, the Alaska Native Claims Settlement Act established both local and regional native corporations. The regional corporation relevant to Unalaska is the Aleut Corporation which represents all Aleuts in the islands. The Aleut Corporation owns all subsurface rights to the local corporation lands. Village corporation members are also shareholders in the regional corporation. The regional corporation can gain surface rights in a case where the local corporation has selected land where subsurface rights are not available, as for instance in a federal wildlife preserve. Unalaskan residents, on the other hand, have had a major influence on the overall direction taken by the regional corporation since the city has by far the largest population of Aleuts in the chain, and thus the greatest number of shareholders. The regional corporation has worked in tandem with the local corporation in several projects which we will describe in detail in the next chapter.

For the most part, the non-profit Aleutian/Pribilof Islands Association (APIA) is not as heavily involved in Unalaska as it is in other, smaller communities in the region, largely because the services normally provided by the APIA elsewhere are the responsibility of the City of Unalaska. Nevertheless, this regional non-profit association has been involved in several local projects. One of their subsidiaries is the Aleutian Housing Authority, which was responsible for the construction of HUD (Housing and Urban Development) housing in Unalaska. The association is also involved in procuring reparations money as a result of the relocation of Aleuts during World War Two. They also have provided training for the paralegal now located in town, and are involved with the placement of a regional clinical psychologist in Unalaska.

A political organization which is both state-wide and Native and which has recently opened a branch in Unalaska is the Alaska Native Women's Statewide Organization. Based in Anchorage and formed in 1980, its goals are to preserve culture in the home, to provide shelter for cases of abuse and assault, and to address political issues which it feels are relevant to its membership.

2.2.2 External Commercial Influences

Unalaska and the entire Aleutian chain can be characterized as being dominated by a boom and bust economy. During boom periods the area is dominated by outsiders who come in, make a quick profit, and leave to spend the money elsewhere. When times are lean these outside forces usually leave the area. Even when the city of Unalaska itself hires people for projects these are usually outsiders, although the preference is to avoid outside hire where qualified local residents are available.

Currently the major economic sector subject to outside influence in Unalaska is fisheries. Several outside corporations are represented in the processing industry and most of the fishing fleet is from outside the community as well. As with the economy in general, fisheries-related economic activity in Unalaska is closely tied to the economic health of the rest of the country and world. Prices for fish products can produce prosperity or depression in Unalaska. One example of the influence of external forces on the economy of the city is the recent botulism scare which has plagued the salmon industry. When botulism was discovered in a small sample of canned salmon approximately two years ago it depressed the world market for that product. The result has been the forced switch from canning salmon to producing frozen salmon. The effects of this botulism scare can still be seen in Unalaska where the processors are still producing mostly frozen salmon and only slowly switching back to canned product. By the same token the reverse can also occur. Conditions in Unalaska may constrain economic activity even when outside demand remains high, as in the contraction of the crab industry as a result of a reduction in crab stocks in the Bering Sea.

Several major processing companies which operate throughout coastal Alaska have plants in Unalaska. Universal Seafoods is an important force in the economy of Unalaska. Universal was incorporated in 1974 and has processed crab since 1975. The Unalaska plant is one of several Universal plants throughout Alaska, and the corporation is presently in the process of diversification. Universal also owns the Unisea Mall, the Inn, restaurant, bakery, and bar, Stormy's Restaurant on Unalaska Island, and the restaurant

located at the Unalaska Airport. Universal has also recently
expanded into storage and repackaging operations in Washington
State, which is the destination for the bulk of its product. Universal appears to be attempting a vertical integration of its
operations, thereby eliminating the costs accruing until now as a
result of middlemen.

Pan Alaska was the first major outside processor to come into
town. They arrived in 1962 and established the first shore-based
processor in the city proper. In 1975 they were taken over by
Castle-Cook, a major American processor.

Sea Alaska has been in town for eight years. They are owned
by Consolidated Agriculture which also owns Alaska Packers, the
largest salmon packer in Alaska. Consolidated Agriculture has also
recently taken over many of the holdings of Castle-Cook in Alaska.
Castle-Cook has suffered from the depressed tuna market, as they
own Bumblebee and several other tuna processors.

Like the processing industry, the Unalaskan fishing fleet is
dominated by outsiders. Most fishermen who come into the community, and nearly all of the modern "highliners" capable of harvesting huge amounts of product in a very short time, are from the
west coast of the United States, and in particular Seattle. From
the sixties to the present the growth of the fishing fleet and the
canneries, who employ mostly Seattle workers, has meant a dominant
position for Seattle in the local economy and a flow of capital out
of the community to Washington State. An estimated ninety percent
of the fishing fleet is from Seattle. With the recent downturn in
the economy in general, and in the crab fishery in particular, some
of these Seattle-based fishermen have moved to Unalaska as it costs
about $30,000 to make a round trip to Washington. This outside
control, particularly in the use of transient processor employees
and outside fishermen, has also contributed to the low employment
multiplier in Unalaska's economy (Alaska Consultants 1981:216).

Another fisheries-related development having a major bearing
on Unalaska is the move by Trident to establish a groundfish processing plant in Akutan, just to the east of Unalaska Island.
Begun in 1982, Trident invested over eleven million dollars in the
plant. Many people in Unalaska are anxiously awaiting the results
of this experiment before they decide to invest in the groundfishery. The recent (June, 1983) fire which severely damaged the
existing facility may force Trident to suspend its operations
indefinitely, however. Though there are several pilot groundfish
processors operating in the state, this is the only operation which
has depended solely on private investment and has not used federal
assistance.

Unalaska is also in close contact with several foreign
interests, particularly Japanese. The community is a transshipment
port for many foreign vessels, and foreign interests are also
heavily implicated in the Unalaskan fishing sector, both processing
and fishing per se.

Four foreign shipping agents based in town handle the affairs
of their respective fishing and freighter ships in the area. Many
of their freighters take products directly to Japan. Foreign ships
come into port to pick up loads from the processors. Most of these
are tramp steamers, ranging from about 350 to 5,000 tons. Their

loads vary from two to 500 tons. Because of their high fuel and
labor costs, however, these tramp steamers will eventually give way
to modern containerships.

Foreign fishermen utilizing the waters in the region around
Unalaska include the Japanese, Soviets, Koreans, Taiwanese, Poles,
and Canadians. In the Aleutians the Japanese have concentrated on
the trawl fishery for Pacific Ocean perch and utilize a long line
fishery for sablefish. The Soviets first concentrated on floun-
der, in the sixties, then abandoned that fishery for a Pacific
Ocean perch fishery in the Aleutians which continues today. They
have also exploited a pollock fishery between Unimak Island and
the Pribilofs. Korean ships concentrate on the Aleutian sablefish
fishery, while Taiwan and Poland concentrate on the Bering Sea,
Aleutians, and Gulf of Alaska and catch only relatively small
amounts. In all there is more pollock taken by foreigners in
Alaskan waters than the total catch of all the different American
fisheries combined.

There is also large scale foreign participation, particularly
Japanese, in the processing sector in Unalaska. Universal Seafoods, which operates four local processors, and Dutch Harbor
Seafoods are both 25 percent Japanese owned. Whitney-Fidalgo Seafoods, which until recently operated one processor locally, is 99
percent Japanese owned. Sea Pro, a processor which began operations in 1982, is a joint venture of Americans and Norwegians.
Much of the produce of these processors with foreign involvement in
ownership goes to the countries participating in the venture. In
the case of Sea Pro, for example, much of the cod which is processed is sent to Europe as salt cod.

Another area of increasing foreign involvement in the Unalaska
fishing economy the establishment of direct contractual relations
with individual fishermen. Joint ventures appear to be increasing
as the economy worsens with the decline of the crab fishery simply
because individual fishermen cannot assume the risk alone.

Outside interests are also important in Unalaska in other
sectors of the cash economy, particularly in transportation and
communications. Local consumer patterns are also greatly influenced by this external orientation. Many people, particularly non-
Aleuts, have much or all of their food shipped in from outside,
either from Anchorage or Seattle. By doing so it is possible to
save from thirty to forty percent, and even with the ten percent
shipping cost it is substantially cheaper than purchasing it
locally. It is usually shipped in via the Pan Alaska dock. Pan
Alaska officials, however, have expressed their desire in diverting
all third-party shipments to the municipal general cargo dock.

Transportation and communications are areas of major outside
participation. The Chevron facility in town, the "Standard Oil
Dock", has been there for at least thirty years. Chevron facilities at Dillingham, Naknek, and Bethel are resupplied by barge
through the Unalaska facility. A total of about 75 million gallons
of gasoline and diesel fuel a year goes through the facility. Only
a few Japanese vessels fuel in Unalaska as the dock is not strong
enough to withstand the battering of large vessels. Many tugs and
oil research vessels use the port as well.

Sea Land Shipping is has been in Unalaska since the early

1970s. Most of their shipping is domestic, with about ten percent
going to foreign ports after first going through Seattle. They
ship exclusively fish and fish products out of Unalaska, while
imports include plastic goods, chemicals, and other cannery related
materials. As the competition grows among shipping companies Sea
Land is holding onto a slightly smaller proportion of total shipping than was once the case. They employ varying numbers of people
with a maximum of ten employees during the king crab season.

American President Lines is a major shipping company which
serves Unalaska and is primarily concerned with shipping of fish
products. The company has six permanent employees in Unalaska.
The APL has been working with the Ounalashka Corporation and the
regional Aleut Corporation in the construction and operation of a
dock (the "APL dock") and loading facilities. This is the most
modern and largest capacity dock in town. APL is an international
shipper, and since it is subsidized by the federal government it is
proscribed from undertaking in domestic shipping.

There are also other shipping companies based outside Unalaska
which serve the port. The most important are Foss Alaskan Lines,
which serves the major coastal ports of the state, Western Pioneer
which serves the Aleutians and the southern Alaska coast, and the
BIA North Star. Foss Alaska Lines, however, recently closed its
Unalaska operations due to the loss of the contract for serving the
Adak Naval Air Station to Sea Land.

The community is also a center for air transport in the Aleutians. Reeve Aleutian Airlines provides the bulk of the air carrier service to Unalaska. Air Pac has provided service since the
fall of 1978 and is in competition with Reeve. Reeve flies to the
military bases on Adak, Attu and Shemya Islands, to the Pribilofs
to the north, and to Cold Bay, Anchorage, and Seattle to the east,
while Air Pac flies from Unalaska to Anchorage, and runs a Grumann
Goose amphibious plane from Unalaska to Akutan and the outlying
islands on a charter basis. Air Pac initiated F27 service which
has the capacity to carry thirty-six passengers in late August
1982. Northern Air Cargo flies some charters out of Unalaska and
there are several passenger/freight carriers which have charters,
including Peninsula Airlines which flies weekly to Nikolski from
Cold Bay, stopping in Unalaska as needed.

Potentially the most important outside influence is the intru-
sion of outside petroleum companies into the Unalaskan economy.
Several oil companies are represented in town already. Seventeen
oil companies are operating jointly in a consortium involved in
pre-exploration activities in the Bering Sea, including seismic
studies and the operation of COST wells, and several of these have
already established bases in town, including ARCO and Exxon. ARCO
has offices in town as the overall manager of the consortium
exploring for oil in the Bering Sea.

Although oil-related activity in the community is only in the
pre-exploration phase, there has already been an impact in
Unalaska, with several local merchants making up for the slack in
crab through supplying the seismic and other oil development-
related crews. Oil-related business has been estimated to already
be worth approximately a million dollars a year to one wholesale
outlet alone.

Local private investment by outside firms beyond fisheries and oil-related development has been small scale thus far. Partly this is a result of the difficulties of negotiating for leases with the Ounalashka Corporation, and partly it is a result of the total domination of the local economy by the seafood processors. In addition to Japanese participation in the processing operations of Universal Seafoods, they also have a twenty-five percent share of the retail operations of Unisea. This includes the Unisea Inn, restaurant, and bar, as well as the Unisea Mall.

A geothermal project is currently being carried out with exploratory digs. The project is being financed by the Alaska Power Authority which has given a 4.7 million dollar grant for the work. Republic Geothermal has been contracted to do the geophysical and geochemical analysis. The viability of this resource is also subject to the influence of outside economic forces, in particular the prevailing price of oil.

This section has illustrated the extent to which Unalaska is deeply influenced by outside forces economically. The community is very much subject to outside pressures, both in specific industries and in general.

2.2.3 Larger Sociocultural System

Unalaska is often referred to by local residents as a "suburb of Seattle." This comment reflects not only the social and economic ties between the two communities but also the overwhelming influence of the larger sociocultural system in the value systems, social organizations, and economic and political activities of Unalaska. While Unalaska can be viewed as part of the larger sociocultural system of the United States, components of that system which are external to the community itself can be examined as environmental input. The larger sociocultural system has a particular impact on the community of Unalaska which will become evident throughout this study. For our purposes, however, we will present only a brief summary of those aspects of the larger system which are relevant to the community's sociocultural system.

Perhaps the most pervasive impact of the larger sociocultural system on the community of Unalaska is the introduction of new sets of values. With the influx of non-Native immigrants from other parts of Alaska and the continental United States, Unalaska has become exposed to a set of values that is urban-oriented and places great emphasis on professional and bureaucratic expertise, education, social status based on wealth and occupation, and the latest trends in style and taste. The rapid growth of fundamentalist Christianity is also evidence of the influence of values which originate outside the community.

Local technology is another example of the influence of the larger sociocultural system. Modern conveniences such as hair dryers and washing machines can be found throughout the community. The latest technology in home entertainment systems are very popular and can be found in most homes regardless of household income. Satellite television and telephone connects the community to the outside world. Air transportation links the community to the

mainland and sea transport ties Unalaska to the Far East as well as
to the rest of Alaska and the United States.

The economic structure of Unalaska has been influenced by the
larger sociocultural system in ways more profound than simply the
external commercial forces which affect local markets. The larger
sociocultural system's presence is felt by the wage-labor capital
dependent system of production and distribution, by the instrumental nature of employer-employee relations, the maximization of
profit, and the deemphasis on subsistence activities.

An important element of this pervasive economic influence is
the increasing trend toward modern consumer consumption. The
majority of local residents may be viewed as subscribing to a
Western "disposable" consumer orientation, in contrast to an older,
indigenous orientation that featured conservation and maximization
of resources. These attitudes are often the basis for conflict
between some groups in the community. Conflicts over the short-
and long-term use and development of land can usefully be examined
in this light. Whereas some segments of the community favor rapid
and relatively unrestrained economic growth in .Unalaska, others
advocate slower and more controlled growth with an eye to the long-
term consequences to the community.

One of the major contrasts between traditional and present-day
Unalaska is the growth of instrumental social ties, reflected in
the character of social networks and associations with other residents. Up until the 1960s and the growth of the crab fishery,
Unalaska could be regarded as a small-scale community where residents were linked by numerous "moral" ties. With the influx of
"strangers" social behavior has undergone a transformation. Reciprocity has declined as a means of linking the entire community
together. Informal mechanisms of social control have declined in
favor of a growing system of law enforcement. Even crime has
undergone some changes due to the influence of the larger sociocultural system. The high incidence of drug abuse and the availability of various forms of drugs are evidence of this change.

2.2.4 Neighboring Communities

An important part of the extrasocietal environment of Unalaska
is reflected in the relationships between the community and neighboring communities. The four most important of these communities,
both from a historical as well as contemporary perspective, are St.
Paul and St. George on the Pribilof Islands, and the Aleutian
communities of Akutan and Nikolski. Traditionally, Unalaska was
linked to the Pribilof Island communities through kinship ties and
subsistence networks. Salmon was sent to the Pribilofs in exchange
for seals. Interaction between Unalaska and the Pribilof Islands
was limited throughout much of the early twentieth century by
government restrictions and lack of direct transportation links.
As a result, much of this interaction occurred by way of Anchorage.
Current relations between Unalaska and the Pribilofs are limited to
a few social ties and involvement in the regional Native corporations. This situation is expected to change in the future, but
exactly how it will change will depend upon the efforts of the

Tandagusix Corporation of St. Paul to develop corporation-owned property at Chernofski Harbor on Unalaska Island. The Corporation is interested in developing the harbor for seafood processing and cold storage facilities. Should this development proceed, Chernofski Harbor would have a profound impact on the economy of Unalaska in both a positive and negative sense. Initially, this development would mean increased business for Unalaska commercial interests. Once the Chernofski development begins its own seafood processing activities, however, it could draw business away from Unalaska, adding to the already precipitious decline in the local economy. On the other hand, proposed developments in Unalaska could have a negative impact on the Chernofski development. Adequate facilities in Unalaska could diminish the demand for processing facilities at Chernofski, thus reducing the incentive for development. In any event, economic and political ties between Unalaska and the Pribilof Islands are expected to become more salient a part of Unalaska's extrasocietal environment.

Of the other two communities in the region with whom Unalaska has had considerable contact in the past, only Akutan retains any significance for the socioeconomic and sociocultural systems of the community. There are relatively few cultural, social, or economic ties between Unalaska and Nikolski. Nikolski residents view their ties to the outside world more in terms of Cold Bay and Sand Point, despite significant genealogical ties with Unalaska. Because of the lack of available facilities and employment opportunities, Nikolski is not expected to be a significant factor in the socioeconomic system of Unalaska in the near future.

Akutan, on the other hand, has considerable social and economic ties to Unalaska and development in Akutan could have a significant impact on Unalaska's socioeconomic system. The connections between the two communities have been both historical and contemporary, Aleut and non-Aleut, and social and economic in character. Historically, the two communities have been tied together by kinship links among Aleut residents. However, the network of traditional kin-related ties today is insignificant. Direct kinship ties between two or three families in Akutan with families in Unalaska exist and in the past served as a basis for some seasonal migration for employment purposes and the attendance of some Akutan children at the Unalaska school. With the emergence of a separate processing industry and the construction of a school in Akutan, however, these links have become inactive and do not appear to provide improved access to economic opportunities in the forseeable future.

Recently additional links have been formed between the non-Aleuts in both communities who worked for seafood processors in Unalaska. The managers of both of the shore-based processors in Akutan any many of the administrative personnel are former employees of processors based in Unalaska. Many of the local processors now based in Akutan moved there from Unalaska within the last four years for several reasons, including (1) the inability to obtain discharge permits in Unalaska because of overcrowding, (2) intense competition to purchase a fisherman's catch, (3) a lower fish tax in Akutan, and (4) the greater potential for expansion in Akutan. These factors could have a significant impact on the

socioeconomic system of Unalaska as well as the social and economic
relations between the two communities, particularly in the event of
significant groundfish development in the region.

2.3 INTRASOCIETAL INFLUENCES

2.3.1. Population

The population of Unalaska prior to 1940 was characterized as
relatively stable with a moderate growth rate. With the construction of the military bases and fortifications on Unalaska and
Amaknak Islands, the population grew rapidly. During World War II,
there were an estimated 65,000 military personnel stationed in the
area. Prior to the outbreak of war, the community experienced a
sizeable influx of non-Aleuts who arrived to work in   construction
or to otherwise profit from the military presence. The population
structure was also affected during the war by the .forced evacuation
of the Aleut residents to camps in southeastern Alaska. During the
post-war period, the population of Unalaska declined as economic
opportunities were minimal. It was not until the late 1950s and
early 1960s that the population began to display any noticible
increase. The community experienced another dramatic influx of
outsiders in the early 1970s with the economic boom created by the
crab fishery. The population increased almost fourfold in less
than ten years. With the recent economic downturn, the population
has begun to level off.
Table 2.2 provides an index of the total population in
Unalaska from 1939 to 1981. It can be seen from these figures that
the greatest period of growth occurred between 1973 and 1977 and
that the population has begun to level off in the past few years,
largely as a result of the decline in the crab fishery and concomitant decline in the rate of in-migration.

Table 2.2

Population of Unalaska,
1939-1981

Year	Number of Residents	Data Source
1939	298	Alaska Consultants 1981
1950	173	U.S. Bureau of Census, 1950
1960	218	U.S. Bureau of Census, 1960
1967	254	Unalaska City Council Files
1970	342	U.S. Bureau of Census, 1972
1972	548	Unalaska City Council Census
1973	510	Unalaska City Council Census
1977	1,971	Tryck, Nyman and Hayes, 1977a
1980	1,322	U.S. Bureau of Census, 1981
1981	1,944	Alaska Department of Labor, 1981

Much of the increase in population in the past ten years has been due to the dramatic influx of temporary residents hired by the processors on six month contracts. As Table 2.3 indicates, non-residents represent a significant portion of the population of Unalaska in terms of both population size and proportion of the total population. This figure has begun to level off, however, as the demand for processing workers declines.

Table 2.4 provides a representation of the age and sex distribution of the residents of Unalaska in 1977. In that year, forty-two percent of the resident population was between the ages of 18 and 34. Moreover, the median age decreased during the 1970s, largely due to the influx of young immigrants in their mid-

Table 2.3

Unalaska: Residents and Non-Residents,
1970-1981

Census Year	Residents		Non-Residents		Total	
	N	%	N	%	N	%
1970 (a)	178	52.0	164	48.0	342	100
1972 (b)	430	78.5	118	21.5	548	100
1977 (c)	615	31.2	1256	68.8	1971	100
1981 (d)	1054	54.2	890	45.8	1944	100

Sources: a. U.S. Bureau of Census, 1972.
b. City Council Census, 1972.
c. Tryck, Nyman and Hayes, 1977a.
d. Alaska Department of Labor, 1981.

twenties. Whites represent the bulk of this age group; seventy-two percent of the 25 - 34 age group in 1977 are white while only seventeen percent of the Aleuts in Unalaska are within this age group. Non-residents are also heavily represented in this age group. Thus, the trend in Unalaska has been towards a younger population. The age-gradient for both residents and non-residents may undergo a shift in the next ten years, however, as the rate of immigration slows and the rate of processor personnel turnover begins to stabilize.

The proportion of males in the total population or the ratio of males to females experienced an increase in the 1970s. As Table 2.4 demonstrates, the proportion of resident males increased from 55 percent in 1970 to 59 percent in 1977, altering the ratio of males to females from 1.2:1 to 1.4:1. The consistency of this imbalance is in contrast to a statewide trend towards more equal distribution of the sexes (Tryck, Nyman and Hayes 1977a:16). Moreover, this imbalance in the sex ratio would be even greater if non-resident personnel were included in the estimate; in 1977, 72 percent of the non-resident population of Unalaska was male.

Table 2.4

Age and Sex of Unalaska Residents,
1977

Age	Sex Male	Female	Total	Percent
0 - 4	23	18	41	7
5 - 12	28	40	68	11
13 - 17	28	19	47	8
18 - 24	46	46	92	15
25 - 34	107	56	163	27
35 - 44	42	23	65	11
45 - 54	40	22	62	10
55 - 64	19	14	33	5
65 - 74	4	2	6	1
75 and over	1	-	1	0
Unknown	22	15	37	6
TOTAL	360	255	615	100
Percent				
1977	59	41		100
1970	55	45		100

Source: Tryck, Nyman and Hayes, 1977a.

In the 18 and over category, there were fifty-nine percent more males than females in 1977. This, according to Tryck, Nyman and Hayes (1977a:16), is indicative of the "frontier" nature of Unalaska, especially during the height of the crab fishery boom, when there were greater job opportunities, other than cannery positions, for males than for females.

Although no exact figures are available, it is the perception of local residents that the sex ratio has begun to balance in the past few years, except, perhaps, among short-term, transient workers. This is largely due to the arrival of new male and female residents who are either married or living with someone of the opposite sex.

Table 2.5 provides an idea of the changes in the ethnic or racial balance of the community in the past ten years. In 1970, Unalaska was still principally an Aleut community with Native Alaskans (predominately Aleuts) comprising sixty-three percent of the resident population. By 1977, the ethnic balance between Caucasians and Native Alaskans had almost completely reversed itself. Unalaska has now become a primarily non-Native community.

Another interesting finding is the increase in the number of residents classified as "Other." These consist largely of processor personnel, some of whom have become residents of the community. In 1977, 5.7 percent of the residents and thirty-eight percent of the non-residents in Unalaska were classified as "Other." Most of the non-residents were Filipinos who worked for the processors. In

Table 2.5

Ethnic Composition of Population of Unalaska,
1970-1980

| Ethnic Group | Year | | | | | |
| | 1970 (a) | | 1977 (b) | | 1980 (c) | |
	N	%	N	%	N	%
Caucasian	56	31.0	387	62.9	848	64.1
Black	0	0	7	1.1	19	1.5
Native Alaskan	113	63.4	178	28.9	200	15.1
Aleut	107	60.1	166	27.0	–	–
Eskimo	5	2.8	8	1.3	–	–
Indian	1	0.5	4	0.6	–	–
Other	9	5.6	35	5.7	255	19.3
Unknown	–	–	8	1.3	–	–
TOTAL	178	100.0	615	99.9	1322	100.0

Sources: a. University of Alaska, ISEGR, 1973.
b. Tryck, Nyman and Hayes, 1977a.
c. U.S. Bureau of Census, 1981.

1980, 220 of the 1,322 residents in Unalaska were classified as
Asian and Pacific Islander, reflecting the large percentage of
Vietnamese and Filipinos who worked for the processors. Forty-two
of the non-residents in 1980 were of Mexican descent (U.S. Bureau
of the Census 1981).

In their 1977 survey, Tryck, Nyman and Hayes also examined
length of residence of the population of Unalaska in terms of age,
sex, and race. With respect to race, they found that most of the
recent residents in Unalaska were Caucasian. Eighty-three percent
of the population residing in Unalaska in 1977 for less than one
year were white while eighty-two percent of the population residing
in the community for greater than ten years were Aleut. Moreover,
seventy-four percent of the whites in the community, compared with
fourteen percent of the Aleuts, had lived in Unalaska for less than
four years (Tryck, Nyman and Hayes 1977a:7).

Thus, the major factor behind the recent increase in
Unalaska's population has been the influx of new residents and non-
residents. The majority of these immigrants are non-Aleut, young,
and male. For the past ten years, every fishing season brought
with it newcomers, many of whom decided to live in Unalaska on a
permanent or semi-permanent basis.

There has also been a small but noticible influx of Aleuts who
have ties to Unalaska but have resided elsewhere, often times for
several years. The motives behind this return vary from individual
to individual, but it is noteworthy that this trend is contrary to
the experience of other Native communities throughout Alaska where
migration to larger urban areas such as Anchorage or Fairbanks has
become commonplace. Expanded educational and employment opportuni-

ties, along with a desire to renew family and ethnic ties, appear to be behind much of the Aleut immigration. The improved political and economic position of the Aleuts as a result of the Alaska Native Claims Settlement Act has also contributed to improved living conditions for Aleuts in Unalaska, making the community more attractive than it was in the past.

Until recently, the rate of emigration from Unalaska was negligible, largely because of the increased economic opportunities in the community. There are three exceptions to this rule. First, very few individuals who are not permanent residents choose to spend their older years in Unalaska. With the exception of the Aleut residents, there are only a few permanent or semi-permanent residents in the community age 65 or older. Unalaska is not particularly conducive to retirement unless one has an extensive support network; the climate is harsh and cost of living so high that living on a fixed income is extremely difficult. Semi-permanent residents typically leave the community as they grow older and retire elsewhere.

The second group to leave the community includes semi-permanent residents who come to Unalaska with short-term goals. During the height of the boom in the crab fishery, several individuals came to Unalaska with the object of making enough money to fulfill goals such as pursuing a college education or starting a business elsewhere in Alaska or another state. Others, such as some police officers, come to acquire job experience in order to apply for more attractive positions elsewhere.

The third group to leave the community are the transients or non-residents. These include fishermen and processor personnel. Most processor workers are hired on six month contracts. Air fare to Unalaska is usually paid by the processor and return fare is also provided if the worker stays for a minimum period of time. Although the rate of return appears to be increasing, by some estimates as high as seventy-five percent, the rate of emigration for this segment of the population is roughly equal to the rate of immigration.

The only seasonal migrants in Unalaska are the non-resident processing workers and fishermen. Prior to the recent boom in the crab fishery, most of the males in the community over the age of 18 were seasonal migrants. The usual pattern of migration would be to travel to the Pribilof Islands to work on the seal harvests and, later, to work at a cannery in King Cove. There are a few residents in Unalaska who still travel outside the community to either work or live elsewhere for part of the year, either in Akutan during the fishing season, the Bristol Bay area, Anchorage or Seattle. Some residents own property in other parts of Alaska while others maintain campsites on Unalaska Island, but, for the most part, dual residence is negligible. The only exception to this, other than the non-resident processing workers and fishermen, are some processor management personnel who maintain homes elsewhere, usually in the Pacific Northwest.

The fertility rate for Unalaska is difficult to ascertain due to the lack of centralized records in the community. The clinic does not have birth records for most of the new children in town because virtually all local women leave the community to give birth

in more adequate medical facilities elsewhere. School officials
and the organizers of the new pre-school program, however, have
noted that there is an unusual number of small children in the
community.

The mortality rate in Unalaska is atypical because of the
small proportion of the population age 65 and above. As residents
in the community grow old, they tend to go elsewhere to retire; the
Aleuts are an exception to this. What deaths do occur in the community are usually the result of accident, illness, or violence.

2.3.2 Community Facilities

2.3.2.1 **Electrical Power.** Electricity is supplied in the
community of Unalaska from two primary sources. One is the city
owned electrical utility which supplies power to approximately 142
residential and small commercial consumers located on Unalaska
Island and the other source consists of numerous individual power
generation facilities at each of the individual seafood processors
and other installations on Amaknak Island supplying their own
specific needs (Retherford Associates 1979:27). The Unalaska Electric Utility has recently acquired a small distribution system
owned by the Ounalashka Corporation whuch supplies power to its
rental units and facilities on Amaknak Island. The Unalaska
Electric Utility plans to lease these power production facilities
until a permanent city-owned facility can be constructed.

The sum total of these facilities results in a total installed
generation capacity of 13,530 kW (as of March 1979) with a non-
coincidental kW demand of approximately 7,780 kW. Generation of
electrical power is accomplished in each case through the use of
diesel driven generator sets of 900 kW or less capacity. The city-
owned electric utility has two 300 kW diesel electric generators
and two 600 kW diesel electric generators. The two 300 kW units
have the capability of synchronized operation. At present, only one
of the 600 kW units is in operation and it cannot be operated in
synchronization with the 300 kW units. This does not, however,
create any major difficulty as the current average demand is
between 220-240 kW with a peak system demand of 320kW (Retherford
Associates 1979:27).

The seafood processing industry, however, generates and con-
sumes the vast majority of the power on Unalaska and Amaknak
Islands. In 1978, the processors accounted for 12,250 kW of
installed generation capacity with a peak non-coincidental demand
of 7460 kW (Retherford Associates 1979:28). Each processor indiv-
dually generates electricity to satisfy their own specific load
requirements, which generally consist of the processing plant and
housing facilities. Universal Sea Foods also provides power to the
Unisea Inn and Unisea Mall. Installed capacity of the individual
processors vary in size from 850 kW to 2200 kW; generation units
range in size from 50 kW to 900 kW (Retherford Associates 1979:28).

A 4160/208 volt city owned distribution system is limited to
the Unalaska Island side and is mainly composed of overhead distribution facilities most of which are of World War II vintage, and
approximately three miles of recently installed underground distri-

bution feeders. The overhead distribution facilities service the majority of the consumers and are, unfortunately, in a state of major decay (Retherford Associates 1979:28).

Two additional generation installations are located on Amaknak Island. One supplies power to the Chevron USA docks, Chevron personnel, and airport, while the second, currently being leased by the Unalaska Electric Utility, supplies power to Ounalashka Corporation housing. Each installation consists of two 100 kW generation units.

Amaknak Island currently has no area-wide distribution system. The city has made plans, however, to establish a grid system which would provide power to the entire community, including the processors. Under this plan, the city would normally provide power but if for some reason the power station was unable to supply enough electricity to its customers, the processors would use their generators to provide electricity to the city.

A high distribution (34.5KV) line connecting the boat harbor with the U.S. 310 bridge, energized by a new 2,500kW generator, was scheduled for construction in 1983. This system would serve the existing residential and small commercial load, provide power to various public facilities, and have sufficient power to meet a portion of the industrial load. The city may also assume operation of the Ounalashka Corporation's distribution system if the corporation can solve its current problems with the Alaska Public Utilities Commission.

The current cost of producing energy for Unalaska is 34 cents per kilowatt hour. However, because of a state subsidy on the first 600 kw of electricity for local consumers, the cost is reduced to 22 cents per kilowatt hour to all city customers.

2.3.2.2 Sanitation.

Unalaska's sewage system consists of three principal wastewater collector-outfall lines and numerous individual systems. The sewage lines were built by the Navy during the early 1940s of wood stave pipe. Two lines, one serving a few people along Unalaska Creek Road and one serving the old officer's duplex housing on Amaknak Island, both discharge into Iliuliuk Bay. The third line serves housing and bunkhouses on Amaknak Island. Sewage from this line is treated in a plant operated by one of the seafood processors and then discharged into Captain's Bay. This military sewer system, however, is not owned or operated by the city, which operates only the sewer system serving the HUD housing complex on Unalaska Island. The city, however, has designed a public wastewater collection and treatment system slated for construction in the next two years.

In downtown Unalaska and up Unalaska Creek Valley, treatment and disposal of wastewater is by cesspools and outhouses. Generally, they are effective, although in some instances along Unalaska Creek cesspools have failed. There has also been a problem in Unalaska Valley where broken pipe has resulted in contamination of Unalaska Creek.

Another area of authority for the city is waste disposal. The city is responsible for garbage collection within its corporate limits but currently subcontracts the service to Williwaw Services, Inc. which provides removal service twice-weekly to residents and small businesses. Customers are charged monthly whether or not service is utilized. Most of the fish processors make their own arrangments for waste disposal.

The city also operates a ten acre landfill located on the southeast shore of Iliuliuk Bay. Although the sanitary landfill appears adequate for existing needs, local officials maintain that it will soon become obsolete. The landfill has been plagued with numerous problems in the past, including uncontrolled dumping, open burning and capacity limitations (Alaska Consultants 1981:84-85). The Alaska Department of Environmental Conservation has informed the city that it is unlikely a permit for a landfill operation in the present location will be reissued. Given the shortage of available land, however, an alternative site has not been selected.

2.3.2.3 Water. The city's water needs are met primarily by surface water from Unalaska and Pyramid Creeks. The existing system is believed to be inadequate, however, for several reasons. First, available water supply drops during periods of cold weather because the surface water sources freeze over. During these periods, supply is unable to meet local demands for water (Beyer 1981:1). Second, the existing supply system consists primarily of old wood stave pipe constructed by the military during the Second World War. The distribution lines are badly in need of replacement, wasting an estimated one- to two-thirds of the existing water supply through leakage. Third, existing treatment facilities are inadequate. During periods of heavy usage, chlorine detection time is inadequate, possibly resulting in the survival of pathogenic microorganisms. Additionally, residents who live upstream of the treatment facility on Unalaska Creek must utilize untreated water. Finally, one of the major deficiencies of the existing water supply is the lack of adequate storage facilities. During periods of low stream flow and high demand, little water is available for firefighting purposes. Inadequate storage also contributes to treatment difficulties (Beyer 1981:2).

The City of Unalaska, since assuming control of the existing military water supply system after the Second World War, has since expended funds for operation and maintenance, minor repair, and some capital improvements such as the installation of culverts to replace timber tressles, some replacement piping, reconstruction of the Pyramid Creek diversion dam, and certain other improvements (Beyer 1981:28). Despite the difficulty in obtaining reliable readings, it was estimated in 1981 that the peak demand on the combined Pyramid Creek and Unalaska Creek sub-systems was between 17,200 and 19,200 gallons per minute (GPM) (Beyer 1981:22).

2.3.2.4 Communications. The Interior Telephone Company has provided local telephone service since 1972 from an exchange located in downtown Unalaska. As of September, 1982, the system included 450 separate numbers, not including extensions. Special services include a fire reporting system, 911 emergency service, and a supply of cable to computer terminals. Other services include a key system (business multi-phone lines) and PBX services. The company provides service to all of Unalaska and Amaknak Island, with a few exceptions. Most unmet service needs are on Amaknak Island and the current waiting list is twenty-five.

Long distance telephone communications in Unalaska are provided by Alascom through its earth satellite system. The system

was upgraded by Alascom in 1980 from fifteen to twenty-six channels
(Alaska Consultants 1981:85).

Television first arrived in Unalaska in the early 1970s. At
that time, the school had a broadcast system and programming was
handled by the school board. Satellite programming arrived in
April of 1979. The local Alascom Earth Station was originally
constructed as a "White Alice" facility in the early 1960s and then
taken over by RCA. Alascom eventually assumed control of RCA
facilities in the region, providing satellite communications service throughout the state of Alaska. The Unalaska station was
included in the Alascom system and fully operational by July of
1978. It currently provides two television channels, one educational and one entertainment, to local residents. In addition, the
community has its own television station which provides limited
service on weekday evenings and weekends. Recent efforts have been
made to establish cable television service in Unalaska.

Until November of 1982, Unalaska was served by the Armed
Forces Radio Network which was transmitted to the Alascom Station
and then rebroadcast to the city. Recently, however, local residents arranged to have a Dillingham station, KDLG, provide service
instead. Given that Unalaska and Dillingham belong to the same
state legislative district and share several economic, political
and social ties, it was believed that such a switch would be in the
best interests of the community, providing information and entertainment more relevant to local needs. The switch is on a trial
basis.

The city is served by one biweekly newspaper, the Aleutian
Eagle, written and published in Unalaska. Community bulletin boards
are located throughout the city where notices of meetings and
activities are placed.

2.3.2.5 **Transportation.** Unalaska Airport is the major air
transportation facility of the Aleutian chain. With the exception
of water-borne transport, this airport serves as the major link
between the Aleutians and the outside world. Nevertheless, the
Aleutians is the only geographic area in the state of Alaska without modern jet service (Dames & Moore 1980:2).

The present configuration of the Unalaska airport consists of
a single runway which is approximately 4,000 feet long by 100 feet
wide. Originally certified by the Federal Aviation Administration
with a length of 4,300 feet, it has been reduced in certified
length to 3,900 feet. (Unwin, Scheben, Korynta, and Huettl 1982:2-
5). On the northwest end of the runway a large bluff, 80 to 90
feet high and located approximately 100 to 150 feet from the runway
centerline for the first 1,000 feet of the runway, causes extremely
hazardous wind conditions and is an obstruction within the required
primary surface area. Approximately 3,500 feet of the runway has a
gravel surface. There are no designated taxiways and the one apron
area is divided in half by the runway. An amphibious aircraft ramp
is located to the southeast end of the runway. The runway has no
existing lighting system.

The passenger terminal at Unalaska Airport is a tri-wing
building containing a restaurant, ticket counter, administrative
offices, communications, security check-in and passenger loading
area. In addition to serving as the facilities for Reeve Aleutian

Airlines, it also houses the Reeve Station Manager with some space
for transient lodging of air crews. Recently, the City of Unalaska
issued a notice of award for the construction of a new terminal.

The Naval Air Transport Terminal is used by Air Pac for its
base of operations. This building is similar in size to the adjacent RAA terminal. In addition, Air Pac and Peninsula Airways
share the east half of a large World War II hanger as a maintenance
facility, with the west half of the hanger in a state of disrepair.

There are currently two access routes linking the airport with
the community, the Airport Highway and the Dutch Harbor Road. Both
roads are currently gravel surfaced and the former is designated as
U.S. Highway 310.

Instrument and visual approaches to the airport runway are
limited by the runway location and alignment in relationship to the
surrounding terrain. In particular, Mt. Ballyhoo with a height of
1,634 feet located approximately 1/2 mile northeast of the runway,
with cliffs almost abutting on the airstrip itself. Straight-in
approaches are constrained by Mt. Newhall and Mt. Coxcomb to the
southeast and Hog Island to the northwest. Because of the navigation hazards in the immediate vicinity of the airport, the restricted length of the runway, and the lack of modern equipment,
all landings must be made by VFR. Visibility of at least three
miles is essential.

At present, there are two regularly scheduled air carriers
which provide service to Unalaska. Reeve Aleutian Airlines has been
the principal air carrier to Unalaska for many years. Although
current activity varies seasonally, normal flights consist of one
passenger flight daily except Sunday from Anchorage by way of Cold
Bay and one air cargo flight weekly from Anchorage by way of Port
Heiden. Most flights are combination passenger and cargo. During
the peak season, RAA increases its passenger flights to two daily
as well as charters on demand. Air cargo increases as need
dictates.

The principal aircraft serving Unalaska is the Japanese Nihon
YS-11, a high performance twin engine turbo-prop aircraft capable
of carrying six tons of cargo and/or up to sixty passengers.
Occasionally, Reeve operates a Lockheed L-188 Electra to Unalaska.
The Electra is capable of carrying nearly thirteen tons of cargo
and seventy-four to ninety passengers. However, given the limited
runway of the Unalaska airport, these flights are limited and when
they do occur, are not filled to capacity, thus making it unprofit-
able to fly such an aircraft (Unwin, Scheben, Korynta, and Huettl
1982:2-17).

The other scheduled air carrier providing service to Unalaska
is Air Pac. It recently increased its flight to two daily non-stop
between Unalaska and Anchorage utilizing a Cessna Conquest (nine
passengers) and a Merlin Metroliner (eighteen passengers - limited
to twelve by fueling requirements). Air Pac also utilizes a Grum-
man Goose Amphibious aircraft for local flights to surrounding
islands. Recently, however, Air Pac has begun to serve the community with the F 27, a larger turboprop that seats forty passengers.

In addition to the two regularly scheduled carriers, Unalaska
is served by Peninsula Airways, a small charter service which flys
from Cold Bay to Nikolski but may be flagged to Unalaska, or from

Unalaska to Akutan, False Pass or Cold Bay.

General aviation at Unalaska is quite minimal due to its remote location and extremely hazardous flying conditions. Somewhere between three and five general aviation aircraft are based, at least part-time, in Unalaska. Military aircraft occasionally use the Unalaska airport and are usually associated with search and rescue or medical evacuation activities.

At present, the airport is incapable of handling modern jet aircraft such as the Boeing 737s which service other regions of the state. This limitation has the effect of making air travel to Unalaska an expensive proposition. According to a City report (1982:2), "compared to 737 service, the YS-11 (the turboprop aircraft flown by Reeves) costs nearly three times as much per passenger mile." Travel time between Unalaska and Anchorage is also increased by as much as 2.5 times using the YS-11. A jet needs 6,000 feet of paved runway and greater airspace clearance. In order for the existing airport to accommodate such aircraft, the runway would need to be extended over 2,000 feet and an estimated 1.5 million cubic yards of the adjacent bluff carved away to provide greater clearance (City of Unalaska 1982:4). The runway would also need to be raised thirty feet to protect against high waves.

Until recently, the principal land owner at the Airport and within the surrounding areas has been the Ounalashka Corporation. The conveyance of the properties at the Airport to the State of Alaska, after the Native Land Claims Settlement Act of 1971, was with the stipulation that management of the Airport buildings would be retained by the Corporation. However, in the past few months the existing air terminal and Air Pac building, as well as other airport property, have been acquired by the City of Unalaska. The Ounalashka corporation retains ownership of the hanger building and is expected to make leasehold applications for an expansion of sites of either side of the new terminal buildings.

City officials and local residents almost unanimously agree that the suggested improvements to the airport are vital if the community is to grow and prosper. In the last local election, the community acknowledged this need by voting in favor of a bond measure that would enable the city council to take out $3 million in loans for a new airport terminal. The Alaska Municipal Bond Bank was only able to buy $2,015,000 of this, however, because of existing debt limits. In the last state legislature, the $11 million dollars needed to expand the runway, build an additional apron and remove the bluff from adjacent Mt. Ballyhoo was eliminated from the state budget. Part of this funding was restored by the Sheffield Administration and included in the FY84 budget awaiting signature. As part of the supplemental FY83 budget there was an appropriation of $700,000 to the city for construction of a new airport terminal.

The existing system of roads in Unalaska was constructed by the military during the Second World War. The system is forty-two miles long and the city maintains all but six miles of it (the overland route to Summer's Bay is not maintained by the city). There is one state highway which runs from the airport to the bridge connecting Unalaska and Amaknak Islands at Iliuliuk Harbor. None of the roads are paved. The city has placed road construction as a high priority but has also encountered resistance from some residents who feel that existing roads are adequate to meet current needs.

The bridge connecting Unalaska with Amaknak Island was constructed in 1979 and is known simply as "the bridge to the other side." Prior to its construction, the primary means of transport between Unalaska and Amaknak Islands was by skiff. In inclement weather, this was inconvenient and often hazardous. The construction of the bridge, however, has has a tremendous social and economic impact on the community. Small businesses on both sides of the city have prospered with the increased number of available customers and the social interaction between residents of Unalaska and Amaknak Islands has been affected in both frequency as well as quality according to local residents. Perhaps more than any other form of local development in the area in the past forty years, the bridge has united the two population centers of Dutch Harbor and Unalaska into one integrated community. The opening of the bridge serves as a common chronological reference for local residents. The bridge is the responsibility of the Alaska Department of Transportation and Public Facilities and is part of the Federal Aid Secondary Highway System (designated as U.S. Highway 310, "the Trans-Aleutian Highway").

Within the vicinity of Unalaska are several docks. The docks in the inner harbor are owned by the canneries and the Ounalashka and Aleut Corporation. The city purchased a dock in Dutch Harbor from Sea Land in 1981 and recently award a contract for the construction of a 5,000 square foot warehouse. Funding for the project has come from state and federal agencies. The dock is used by the transfer companies who operate in the region and available for use by anyone. A new boat harbor has recently been constructed at the head of Dutch Harbor with state funds. In combination with the new ship repair and supply facility, it is hoped that such a complex will encourage more outside fishermen to utilize local facilities and perhaps even reside here for longer periods of time. Local fishermen and businessmen, however, are not optimistic because the facility is incapable of handling all but small vessels and has suffered significant damage from heavy winds during construction.

There are also two large docks on Captains Bay. One is owned by Crowley Marine and the other is used by Pan Alaska as a pot dock. A new dock and storage facility has recently been completed in Captains Bay, built by Off-Shore Systems, Inc at a projected cost of $3 million. There is also a small, privately-owned dock complex on Agnes Beach in Captains Bay.

2.3.3 Housing and Real Estate Development

There are three major groups represented in the private sector of community development in Unalaska. The largest group, by virtue of its membership and ownership of the majority of land in the area is the Ounalashka Corporation. The second group consists of the local commercial interests in the community, a variety of businesses ranging from the seafood processors to small businesses. The third group consists of small landowners who have been involved in developing their properties for residential and commercial purposes. Each of these three groups is involved in three separate development activities: real estate, housing, and commerce. This section will examine the private real estate and housing development in Unalaska.

A 1977 survey of local housing conducted by the firm of Tryck, Nyman and Hayes found 213 conventional housing units in Unalaska with a vacancy rate of 1.9 percent (1977b:116). Alaska Consultants reported 393 conventional housing units with a nine percent vacancy rate in 1980. However, their report also stated:

> ...City officials indicate that there are essentially no vacant units in town, a contention supported by August 1980 field observations of Alaska Consultants, Inc. At that time, City, school, and health officials were unable to locate housing for anticipated new employees, and officials and local residents alike were unanimous in identifying the shortage of housing as the most serious problem facing the community (1981:56).

Of the housing available in Unalaska in 1977, at least half were reportedly in need of some repair and fourteen percent of the units had major structural deficiencies. The high proportion of substandard housing was attributable to the lack of local construction prior to the recent economic boom, the high cost of building materials, and the difficulty of obtaining loans for construction or repairs.

Since that time, new housing has been made available, particularly in the form of duplexes, new homes, and apartments. Nevertheless, there is still a shortage of available housing in the community. At the time of the field data collection, local residents reiterated that the lack of adequate housing was one of the major constraints to development in Unalaska.

The number of residents per unit varies widely in Unalaska. Virtually all of the permanent residents live in single homes, while virtually all of the transients live in group quarters owned by the various seafood companies. With the exception of Pan Alaska, these group quarters are located adjacent to the processors themselves and are effectively isolated from the rest of the community. Extreme examples of this isolation are the quarters of Sea Alaska at the northern most end of Dutch Harbor itself, and Sea Pro, located on Captains Bay more than two miles from downtown Unalaska.

The quality of housing in Unalaska can be divided into three distinct grades: The highest grade includes new, modern wood frame homes. The second grade consists primarily of renovated World War II buildings converted into duplexes or single family homes. The third grade consists of older homes or shacks which were hastily constructed and lack essential services or utilities.

The majority of houses in Unalaska are from the World War II era (the few remaining from the 1930s and earlier have been renovated), and there are several distinct residential areas with different styles of housing. The houses in the downtown Unalaska area are typically wood frame buildings built during the war years. Many are converted "cabanas" which were originally designed to house four soldiers during the war, without plumbing or cooking facilities. Several houses are composed of two or more cabanas attached together. There are a few pre-war era buildings that have survived, some of which are private homes. Additionally, there are individuals living in house trailers in this area, and Pan Alaska owns several trailers that house some employees in the downtown area and across the river from the main downtown area. In 1981 the Aleutian Housing Authority provided twenty "HUD homes" to some of the low income Aleut families, five of which are scattered in the downtown area and the remainder clustered in an adjacent neighborhood. These wood frame homes were prefabricated and shipped to Unalaska by barge.

Unalaska valley, running east of the downtown area and Unalaska Lake, is the site of the first major new construction housing development since the war years. Scattered throughout the valley are military buildings that have been converted for use as homes. There are also three privately owned small apartment buildings, and two city-owned duplexes. On the south side of the valley, not far from the lake, is a new neighborhood, comprised of ten homes built recently, the majority of them in the past year. As the first major private housing construction since the war, it as seen as a milestone in the growth of the community. The homes are of various woodframe designs, and are relatively expensive. The shortage of available land for housing is underscored by the fact that though the countryside around the development is open, these expensive new homes are tightly clustered together, and every lot in the development is sold and being built on.

Haystack Hill, located across the Iliuliuk river south of the downtown area, is the site of several recently built homes, some of which are quite expensive. The ownership of the land on Haystack is currently in dispute. The area has been the site of homesteading attempts, some of which have featured homes of quite poor construction.

In Unalaska all of the seafood companies have group housing for their employees. The employees at the various companies are housed in bunkhouses, trailers, and aboard ships. Management personnel for some of the companies on Amaknak Island are provided with company owned homes or rental units on Standard Oil Hill. Few individuals choose to live in other than company housing because it is provided free of charge or at a nominal rate.

Until the mid 1970s there were only a handful of families living on Amaknak Island, and these families lived in company-provided housing at the airport, near the Standard Oil dock, and near the one operating processor. With the fisheries boom-related population increase the number of residents on Amaknak Island increased at an even faster rate than on the Unalaska side.

Standard Oil Hill on Amaknak Island is the site of the rental duplexes owned by the Ounalashka Corporation. These duplexes are converted World War II era military duplexes which were unoccupied until the Corporation began to renovate them in 1979. There are now forty-seven units and all but a few of them are occupied with an estimated ten percent turnover rate per month. These duplexes effectively form a neighborhood of their own, and are located contiguously on a hill overlooking Dutch Harbor.

There are no individually owned private plots of land on Amaknak Island. Most of Amaknak Island is owned by the Ounalashka Corporation, with the exception of some parcels owned by Universal Seafoods, Sea Alaska Seafoods, and East Point Seafoods, located adjacent to the respective processing operations, and the State of Alaska, which owns the airstrip. City property interests on Amaknak Island include three small upland lease parcels at the boat harbor, the general cargo dock site, a two-acre waterfront tract near the Unalaska Airport, a ten foot reserve strip around a lake which is a water supply source for the Ounalashka Corporation's private water supply system serving its Standard Oil Hill housing, and a site for the proposed wastewater treatment plant near the Universal Seafood Complex.

Strawberry Hill is a small neighborhood composed of renovated World War II era buildings, located adjacent to the East Point Seafood processing facility on the point that separates Iliuliuk Harbor from Iliuliuk Bay. The buildings have been purchased from the Ounalashka Corporation, and the land that they are on is rented to the occupants on a month to month basis.

Universal Seafoods owns a parcel of land, obtained as the other private land not owned by the Ounalashka Corporation on Amaknak Island, through a Government Services Administration land sale prior to the passage of ANCSA. On this land is located the Unisea Inn building, the Unisea Mall, an apartment building for Univeral employees, group quarters for processing workers, homes for Universal management personnel, and some processing-related buildings. All of the buildings in this area are relatively new, having been built since 1978. The Unisea Inn is a forty-eight room inn for short-term transients. The apartment building was originally intended to be a rental building, but the demand was such that it is now used exclusively by Universal employees. A second apartment building is in the construction phase, which is designed to be rented to the public. On the hill behind the Unisea Mall are homes of the upper level Universal Seafoods management.

One of the major complaints of individuals who have moved to the community in recent years is the shortage of available housing of a style that they wish to rent or own. Rental rates are high when units are available: the the units in the duplexes on Standard Oil Hill rent for close to $1,000 per month. All of these units are occupied, and there is a waiting list to get in. As of the summer of 1982, the average wait was approximately four months. There is an acute need for reasonably priced housing for individuals not employed by the processors, but it is expected that this will change as the decline of the economy continues and the demand drops. Even now, the Ounalashka Corporation is beginning to experience a positive vacancy rate for their duplexes on Standard Oil Hill. The housing market is far enough behind the demand however that most individuals feel that this will take a while.

There is a wide range of private investment in Unalaska. The seafood companies of Sea Pro, Pan Alaska, Pacific Pearl, Universal, Whitney Fidalgo, East Point, and Sea Alaska, have all invested to some extent in the community, though Universal has made investments removed from the seafood operation far in excess of the others. Universal owns the Unisea complex, which includes the Unisea Inn

and Unisea Mall. Less conspicuous but equally important in terms
of private investment are the small businesses in the community,
including markets, hardware stores, cab companies, engineering
firms, bars and restaurants, and service industries. Shipping
lines also represent a source of local private development.

Only 1,896 acres or 11.6 percent of the acreage within the
city limits is available for development, either because of the
topographic limitations or because of the need to preserve the
local water supply (Tryck, Nyman and Hayes 1977b:84-85). Of the
land that is available for development, there are three major
groups of property owners. The group owning the largest amount of
land, both within city limits and surrounding environs, is the
Ounalashka Corporation. "Under the terms of Section 12(a) of the
Alaska Native Claims Settlement Act, the Corporation's enrollment
of 266 persons entitled it to select five townships or 115,200
acres of land in the Unalaska area" (Alaska Consultants 1981:53).
The land currently owned by the Corporation includes 9,400 acres
within the city limits (about ninety percent of the city's total
land area), most of Amaknak Island, and contiguous coastal lands on
Unalaska Bay, Beaver Inlet and Makushin Bay.

The city is the second largest landholder in Unalaska. It is
responsible for 1,280 acres scattered throughout the community,
most of which is currently used for public services and facilities
or intended for such use. Included in this property are the city
hall and Public Safety offices, the Standard Oil Hill reservoir and
surrounding land, city shop, city dock and surrounding land, land
designated for a city park, town cemetary, school, town landfill,
land designated for a proposed sewage treatment plant, and Unalaska
Creek watershed land.

Private landowners constitute the third group possessing property in Unalaska and surrounding areas. There is an estimated 400
acres of private property in the area, most of which was formerly
owned by the federal government. This land was sold by the General
Services Administration in the 1960s to private individuals.
Included in this sale were 109 acres of waterfront property in
Iliuliuk and Dutch Harbors and Captains Bay and 200 acres in
Unalaska Valley. Most of the waterfront property is currently being
used by the seafood processors and other commercial industries
while some privately owned property has been sold for residential
development.

At this time there is no land available for purchase in
Unalaska. Industrial, commercial and residential property can be
had, at a price, if the buyer is persistent. However, few private
individuals or corporations own tracts of land of any appreciable
size that are not currently being used, other than the Ounalashka
Corporation. The Corporation has no plans to make this land available for sale in the near future.

The Ounalashka Corporation owns most of the land on the
Unalaska side, and there are long range plans to subdivide and sell
a portion of this land for private housing. These plans have been
pushed further into the future however by the rising costs of
surveying and developing the land. Some of the land around Captains Bay is privately owned, the land having been granted to Aleut
families through a Native Allotment program run by the Bureau of

Land Management. There is a strong possiblity that some of this land will be leased for development in the near future to some of the oil companies or oil support companies interested in doing business in the area.

Construction has grown in the past several years after an almost thirty year slack period. After World War II, no new homes were built in Unalaska until the early 1970s. The summer of 1982 saw construction of new homes on Nirvana Hill, a new apartment building near the valley road, and the growth of a new neighborhood in Unalaska valley.

Although the community has experienced an impressive rate of growth in the past few years, the downturn in the local economy combined with the increase in interest rates for housing loans from 8.75 percent to 10 percent in September of 1982 is expected to result in fewer new housing starts in the coming years.

Commercial construction continues, but has slowed after several years of impressive growth. During the summer of 1982, the ship repair facility on Amaknak Island was built out of an old military building, but an apartment building being built by the Universal Seafoods Corporation was halted during the construction phase. The Ounalashka Corporation during the summer was in the process of building a new gasoline service station on Amaknak Island. Since the Unisea Inn was built there has been remodelling done every year, but no new buildings went up in that complex this past year. Duplex conversions are complete on Standard Oil Hill. Airport terminal construction is planned for the near future.

3
The Community Structure
of Unalaska

Our discussion of the structure of Unalaska will distinguish between the value system which organizes the socioeconomic system and the various subsystems of organization which precede from these values. The subsystems to be examined include the economy, political organization, social organization, religion, health care, social services, education, and recreation.

3.1 VALUE SYSTEM

The value system of Unalaska today may be characterized as being in a state of flux, resulting from several factors. Of particular importance are: (1) the rapid economic growth in the 1970s, (2) the large influx of outsiders attracted by this growth, and (3) the increased exposure to the wider sociocultural system. This flux is particularly evident in the increasing social heterogeneity of the community as well as the conflicts associated with opposing value systems.

There are currently three major value systems in Unalaska: traditional, "frontier," and modern. The traditional value system is largely associated with the Aleut population but is also possessed in varying degrees by the older non-Aleut, permanent residents of Unalaska. Included within this value system is a rural orientation, pattern of reciprocity based on kinship and locality, a respect for age and authority, emphasis on self-reliance in work but concern for the welfare of the community, and a preoccupation with subsistence activities.

Historically, Unalaska has been regarded by non-Natives as a frontier community because of its relative isolation from urban centers and its economic dependence on the exploitation of primary resources. Although the city today possesses the accoutrements of modern urban living, to many from other parts of the United States, the community still retains a frontier image. The value system characterized as "frontier," includes elements which can be characterized as traditional and elements characterized as modern. It is rural-oriented and gives emphasis to individual initiative, acquisition, enterprise, and effort. It is also male-dominated and very competitive. Within this value system, the rules pertaining to

social relations in a "civilized" context are relaxed somewhat and
the environment is viewed as providing a wealth of resources to be
exploited.

The modern value system is that of the larger sociocultural
system. It is largely urban-oriented and gives great emphasis to
both individual initiative and "community spirit," relationships
based on contract rather than status, economic success, and occupational expertise. Education, income, occupation, and community
involvement are used as criteria for the assessment of social
status. Aesthetic tastes are influenced by the latest styles in
other parts of the United States. Conceptions of the "quality of
life" are based on the attitudes and opinions residents bring with
them from other areas of the U.S.

To varying degrees, it can be said that certain elements of
each of these value systems are shared by all segments of the
community, although these segments in themselves are identified and
distinguished by their commitment to a particular value system.
Nevertheless, there is in general a certain progression in the
community as a whole from a traditional to a modern value system.
This is reflected is the behavior, attitudes, and opinions of all
residents, regardless of age, sex, or ethnic identity.

This progression does not occur without some difficulty, however. The influence of more than one value system within individuals, families, and the community as a whole has resulted in
numerous forms of social and psychological conflict. These conflicts are not unique to Unalaska and are inevitable when an individual or a community must choose between two or more values.
These value conflicts are evident in the formation of distinct
social groups, each representing their own interests in social,
political and economic activities. They are evident in generational conflicts which lead to alienation of youth and domestic
violence. Finally, they lead to psychological disorder, especially
in the forms of identity crises, lack of self-esteem, depression,
and alcoholism.

The extent to which this transition is occurring and the
conflicts associated with this process will be evident throughout
this chapter. In this section, however, we are particularly
interested in the components of the value systems. These components are grouped into the categories of status, beliefs, world
view, ethnicity, and reciprocity.

Social status in Unalaska is determined on the basis of
several different criteria from the traditional, frontier and
modern value systems. Among the permanent residents of Unalaska,
especially among the Aleuts, family status is important in determining the status of the individual, although it is less true today
than it was in the past. Some of the older residents, for instance,
have expectations for children of the younger generations based on
past achievements of the children's families. If these expectations
are not realized disappointment results and the children are chas-
tized.

There has been a renewed interest in family history with the
positive renewal of an Aleut identity in recent years, and accom-
panying this interest, there is for many a sense of pride where the
family can be traced to a person significant in the history of

Unalaska.   Relationships to historical figures are not viewed with
equal importance by all Aleuts, however. Naturally individuals able
to trace such a relationship invest more importance in it than
those who cannot, and such considerations seem of little importance
to younger children, though it is possible this interest will
increase as they grow older.

Recently, status among Aleuts has been measured more along the
lines of Western culture than was the case in the past.   With this
shift has come a regard for commercially successful individuals.
Wealth is associated with prestige and functional independence and
this prestige has carried over to children of economically successful parents.

Among the non-Aleuts of the community, there are few families
with more than one generation in Unalaska. Among these few, family
status is also important for determining the status of the individual, and for a number of reasons having to do with the past
activities of the family.   These families have often had important
roles in the economic, political, and social life of the community.
The business and investments controlled by these families have come
to be passed down within the family, thus several considerations
are implicated in the determination of status.

The role of wealth in determining social status in Unalaska is
changing.   Before the boom in the fisheries there were, generally
speaking, two economic classes of individuals in Unalaska: the
haves and the have-nots. Within these two categories there appears
to have been little differentiation.   The distinctions which were
made and are made today are more subtle than is the case in other
parts of the United States.   Little attempt was made to maintain
any distinction on the basis of dress, housing, or material possessions, for example.   In the case of housing and other material
possessions, however, class distinctions are becoming more
explicit.

Of greater importance to the determination of social status
than the amount of wealth accumulated were the factors of when and
how the wealth was achieved. If the individual was percieved of as
having gotten wealthy at the expense of others in the community,
the person's status and prestige were gauged accordingly.   Among
the economically successful Aleuts in the community, the same
behaviors that were accepted if performed by a non-Aleut were seen
as unacceptable if performed by an Aleut, and unfortunately for
them, they were seen as exploiting their own people by other
Aleuts.

With the recent infusion of money gained from the crab fishery
into the community, perspectives on wealth changed.   Expectations
were raised, effecting perceptions of employment opportunities.
Wages viewed as acceptable a few years ago are no longer so.   Outside fishermen were flush with money in the good years, though
their involvement with the community was minimal. A few local
families have made a good deal of money off of the fishery but most
families either were unable to or chose not to do so for one reason
or another.

Associated with the value placed upon wealth in the assessment
of social status is a value placed on consumer consumption. In the
days when economic opportunities in Unalaska were few, little

income was available for luxury items such as stereos, automobiles, vacations to Hawaii, and dining out. Nowadays, however, these items and activities have become commonplace. Even among local residents who are still unable to afford these items, consumer commodities play an important role in the determination of levels of status, prosperity, success and even happiness. This new set of values has important ramifications for the "have nots" in the community as being unable to afford these items sometimes results in a lack of self esteem, depression, or alcoholism.

Another of the criteria used in determining social status in Unalaska by permanent residents of the community is stability over time, assessed in terms of length of residence both within the community itself and within a particular location in the community. Individuals who have left the community and then moved back in subsequent years have most often had to start over in terms of finding a place in the social structure. Many local residents, particularly Aleuts, hold the belief that if the individual has left the community once, a certain period of time should elapse before social bonds are renewed.

Emotional stability is also a criterion for the assessment of social status. Those residents given to periods of personal instability, regardless of wealth, family status or length of residence, have a lowered social status as a result. Individuals suffering from periodic bouts of alcohol abuse are taken less seriously because of it.

Status differentiation based upon occupation also occurs in Unalaska. This is perhaps more common among semi-permanent residents and long-term transients than among either permanent residents or short-term transients. Among the first two groups, occupations are often accorded a status similar to that held in urban areas elsewhere. The occupations in Unalaska viewed as most prestigious by these groups include professionals, businessmen, processor managers, fishing vessel owners, and skilled technical personnel. The least prestigious occupations are fishing crewmen, processing line workers, and unskilled laborers.

Political acumen also is the basis for status assignment in the community. Individuals are especially highly rewarded socially if they are successful in making gains for the community or a special interest group in dealings with the outside world, especially the government.

There are significant differences in belief systems among the different population groups represented in Unalaska. Virtually all of the Aleuts of the community are at least nominally members of the Russian Orthodox church. Although the congregation is typically small on any given Sunday, the system of ethics and morality prescribed by the Russian Orthodox faith is quite pervasive among the Aleut community. In addition to the Russian Orthodox belief system there is another system of beliefs held by many of the Aleut residents, particularly the older generations. A system of folk medicine is shared by a few of the older persons in the community, though the implementation of folk cures is becoming less common as time goes on. There is also a shared belief system that features supernatural beings known as "outside men," who are marginal beings in stature, time and place of appearance, and dress. These beings present a danger to living individuals in that they take people away to an unknown fate. As is typical with so-called "animistic" belief systems, the presence of the outside man is used to account for otherwise unexplained phenomena, such as the disappearance of food or treasured possessions and the unnatural deaths and disappearances of local residents. Belief in the existence of "outside man" is fading as reported contacts are becoming less frequent, though the belief is retained by many.

Among non-Aleuts there is a diversity of belief systems. There is a strong religious component to life for many in Unalaska, as the "frontier" attitude and the isolation of the community seems to foster religious growth. In the absence of other social networks for a transient population the church fills a important need for many. The strongest and most visible "non-Aleut" church in the community, the Unalaska Christian Fellowship, features the most social activity for it's members and makes the most aggressive attempts to contact a broad spectrum of the population and draw them into the church. The other churches play similar roles in the lives of their members.

The system of values discussed thus far provides the foundation for the world view of Unalaska residents. A people's world view, according to Geertz (1973:127), "is their picture of the way things in sheer actuality are, their concept of nature, of self, of society. It contains their most comprehensive ideas of order". There are divergent world views represented in the population of Unalaska. For most of the long- and short-term transient members of the population, Unalaska is an environment to be exploited in service of other life goals. These people tend to be instrumental in their relations with other community residents and bring with them the world view dominant in their respective cultures. For most of the community's permanent residents and some of the semi-permanent residents, there is a conflict between their world view and those of the more transient members of the population. Many of these people moved to the community, among other reasons, because it was an isolated and relatively pristine environment. They see the relative newcomers as wishing to shape Unalaska to their life-style, rather than adapting to current conditions and maintaining the community's small town flavor. In the words of one resident, "if they want it to be like the place they came from, why didn't they just stay there?"

Many of the permanent residents perceive the instrumental attitude of the newcomers as exploitative, and react accordingly. Thus, when some permanent residents feel that when they have the upper hand in business dealings with transients, often they will attempt to exploit their advantage to the maximum extent possible. In a world where there are exploiters and the exploited, they are determined not to be the exploited again. Many local businessmen feel this attitude has made the Ounalashka Corporation difficult to deal with at times. As a group, Corporation representatives have seen themselves as having been exploited so many times that they are unwilling to take the chance of this happening again, resulting in a difficult atmosphere for conducting business.

Perception of history, both recent and relatively distant, is thus important in the community to the extent that it patterns life in the community today and affects the formation of an individual and shared world view. For many Aleut residents, the events of the war and the conditions following the war still have a strong bearing on the direction of their life. For those born after the war, the events of that era nevertheless have made their impression. The reactions of their parents and their own growth and development during the period of economic depression have inevitably shaped the way the world is understood. There are definite differences in attitude or world view on the part of permanent residents of the community based on their age, and the corresponding relationship of the age that they were at the time significant and formative events took place in the community.

In their perceptions of the future, once again residents hold diverging beliefs and opinions. For the non-Aleut residents, assessment of the future is governed by the economic circumstances of the present. Some view the future as a bleak period and have made plans to leave the community. Others place a good deal of faith, either upon themselves or the economic system, and believe that the community will continue to grow and the quality of life will continue to improve. Semi-permanent residents tend to be highly ambivalent about the future. On the one hand, they are the most vocal in expressing their belief in continued economic growth. However, they are also most prepared to leave the community if such growth does not materialize. Permanent residents tend to be slightly less optimistic about the prospects of growth, perhaps because of their experience with growth (or the lack of it) in Unalaska in the past. Nevertheless, they are more committed to residing in the community than transients and semi-permanent residents and this commitment is reflected in their world view.

Among the Aleut population in Unalaska, perceptions on the future also differ. Older residents see the future as a continuation of the present, both viewed in pessimistic terms. Younger residents see their future tied to certain political and economic opportunities resulting from the Alaska Native Claims Settlement Act. Their commitment to the community is influenced, in large part, by the degree to which the local native organizations are able to represent the interests of Aleut residents, securing for them a stable economic base in the form of land and a greater voice in community affairs.

As Hallowell (1955) and Redfield (1952) note, an important element of world view is a sense of self. Self identity has both an individual and a social component. In Unalaska, the major form of social identity is ethnicity. Relations between the different ethnic groups present in Unalaska have varied considerably across time, and are of course highly variable with respect to particular individuals. The two ethnic groups having had the longest contact are the Aleuts and the Euro-Americans. On an individual level, there are some Aleuts in Unalaska who profess to hate "whites." There are also some non-Aleuts who are quite hostile, at least in private, towards Aleuts. At the same time there are inter-ethnic marriages between the two groups, which are generally accepted by most of the people in the community and a large number of friendship ties across ethnic lines. For a significant number of individuals, ethnicity is of little importance in their interpersonal dealings. For many of the transient members of the community, interethnic relations is not the subject of much thought or concern.

The assignment of an ethnic identity is not a clear issue, and individuals have varying degrees of concern with their own ethnic identity. An Aleut ethnic identity was widely seen several years ago as something that was not a source of pride, and something that many people sought to hide or deny if possible (Jones 1969). For several decades, Aleuts possessed an ethnic identity negatively defined by their experience of discrimination in the context of the larger sociocultural system. Even today, a few older Aleuts still refer to themselves in derogatory terms, an artifact of an educational system which devalued their beliefs, language, customs, eating habits, and modes of dress. With the passage of ANCSA there were tangible rewards for the declaration and instrumental use of an Aleut identity, and there were individuals in the community who for the first time in many years declared themselves to be Aleut, much to the chagrin of others who had maintained an Aleut identity all along. Along with the rewards offered by ANCSA, an attitude change in the country as a whole in the late 1960's and early 1970's placed a renewed intangible value and pride on a Native American identity.

The criteria for the assignment of an Aleut identity is unclear for many individuals, however. Traditionally, Aleut identity was associated with residence and place of origin. A few of the older Aleut residents still express pride in having come from one of the now extinct villages on Unalaska Island such as Makushin or Chernofski, but for the most part, residence is no longer an important element of Aleut identity. Moreover, the system of understandings that comprised traditional Aleut culture is now gone. According to one man: "Young parents have trouble today. Their children ask them what it means to be an Aleut, and they don't know what to tell them, because they don't know themselves." Current Aleut "cultural preservation" or enrichment attempts focus mainly on material aspects of traditional Aleut life: traditional crafts, tools, and arts. Additionally there is an emphasis placed on pursuing activities related to subsistence fishing and gathering, and pride is taken in preparing traditional foods obtained by subsistence methods. Interest in learning the Aleut language is lacking among younger residents, however. The lack of motivation, combined with other factors, is seen as contributing to the small success of the local Aleut language program.

Voluntary groups and some recreational activities within the community tend to be divided along ethnic lines. Employment patterns also vary by ethnicity, particularly with respect to place of employment and position in the business hierarchy. Political movements along ethnic lines, and political actions based upon ethnicity are not uncommon.

As noted in the discussion on demographic structure, ethnic groups represented within the short-term transient population are varied. Typically, these individuals have little direct contact with the community outside their respective places of employment, and usually the employers hire large numbers of only one ethnic group. In the past, where there have been large numbers of more than one ethnic group working for a single processor, strained relations between the groups have been common.

Within traditional Aleut culture there were formalized systems of reciprocity and redistribution. While this system has disappeared, similar institutionalized relationships exist in Unalaska, though less formal than in the past and more highly variable by individual case. The "atcha" relationship, described below, is a relationship that features reciprocity as one of its attributes. The "kroosna" relationship is similar in this respect, though often more formal. Within memory of the older generations there was a redistribution of foodstuffs at Christmas time, although this has also faded. This practice involved the collection of food and clothing from local families to give to needy families or individuals.

The only formalized redistribution system now operating in the community is government assistance, in the form of AFDC payments and the federal foodstamp program. In the summer of 1982 there were approximately twenty families receiving foodstamps and ten receiving AFDC payments. These numbers vary seasonally and were were nearly double this in the winter of 1981-1982. The largest informal redistribution system in the community is the network that encompasses the core of the congregation of the Unalaska Christian Fellowship. Informal assistance is given in finding of jobs for new residents, and many social functions include the sharing of food. Shelter is also provided for those in need. Among some the Aleuts of the community, and a few non-Aleuts, there is an informal network of redistribution of subsistence goods to older residents unable to support themselves. There is also some redistribution of goods between friends within many networks at such social functions as holiday parties, going away parties, and other celebrations of various sorts. Community-wide redistribution occurs at holiday celebrations which often feature potluck dinners.

3.2 ORGANIZATION

3.2.1 Economic Organization

The economic subsystem of Unalaska is comprised of the cash economy and the subsistence economy. The cash economy of Unalaska includes the harvesting and processing sectors of the commercial fisheries, small- and large-scale entrepreneurial activity, alternative employment, including federal, state, city government, and external commerical agencies. Subsistence activities to be discussed include fishing, hunting, and trapping.

Unalaska's economy derives from its geographical location as a gateway to the Bering Sea region and its position as the only developed deep water port in western Alaska. The port facility in Unalaska serves as a stopover and refueling base for ships serving the Bering Sea and Arctic ports. It also serves as a customs clearing port for foreign vessels entering and departing the Bristol Bay fishery. Unalaska is favorably situated with respect to several major fisheries, and commercial fishing has come to occupy the central place in the Unalaska economy. Fisheries exploited include salmon (of several varieties), crab, and, to a lesser extent, herring, halibut, and groundfish. Unalaska's favorable location has led, in the past two decades, to the growth of a large processing industry as outside processors have located their vessels in Iliuliuk Bay and Harbor ("Inner Harbor"), Captain's Bay, and Dutch Harbor.

3.2.1.1 **Cash Economy**. The cash economy of Unalaska is dominated by fisheries and fisheries-related activities. Most of the non-fisheries activity is designed as support for the fishing industry. This includes shipping companies, local retail and support businesses, and other transportation activities.

Iliuliuk Harbor is the most developed commercial section of Unalaska today and includes the plants of Whitney-Fidalgo Seafoods, East Point Seafoods, Universal Seafoods (and their associated commercial complex), Pan Alaska, Pac Pearl, and Panama Marine. To the south, in Captain's Bay, are the Pan Alaska dock and Crowley Maritime. To the north, in Iliuliuk Bay, is the APL Dock, and further north, in Dutch Harbor, are the Sea Alaska dock and processor, the Exxon Dock, the City Dock (municipally owned), the Standard Oil Dock (operated by Chevron U.S.A.), and the boat harbor.

The backbone of the cash-based economy of Unalaska is the commercial fishing industry. This industry consists of two segments, the fishing fleet and the processors. The processors are divided into shore-based operations and floating processors. This industry is largely responsible for the increase in population during the past ten years and much of the projected growth of the community is tied to its continued prosperity. However, for several reasons, this industry is unlikely to grow to any degree in the next five to seven years, despite the projected increase in bottomfishing.

Table 3.1

Aleutian/Bering Sea Seafood Catch, 1970-1982
(million pounds)

Year	King Crab	Tanner Crab	Total Crab	Salmon	Herring	Foreign-Caught Bottomfish
1970-74 (av.)	42.6	1.6	44.2	58.7	0	N/A
1975	66.1	7.1	73.2	46.7	0	3750
1976	68.4	22.9	91.3	N/A	0	3376
1977	79.7	53.2	132.9	0	0	2782
1978	81.4	70.7	152.1	0	0	3016
1979	107.3	76.0	183.3	5.3	0	2824
1980	132.3	77.1	209.4	11.8	0	2870
1981	164.0	83.1	247.1	N/A	1.4	2798
1982	55.5	N/A	N/A	N/A	6.4	N/A

Source: City of Unalaska 1982:17.

Although a major herring fishery existed in Unalaska during the 1930s, for most of its subsequent history commercial fishing was of minor importance to the local economy. The major source of income was seasonal employment in the Pribilofs during the fur seal harvest. In the 1960s, however, processors began to move into the area to harvest king crab. This shellfish was the foundation of a boom in the commercial fishing industry in the 1970s and most of the local vessels were purchased and equipped with revenues from this harvest.

In addition to crab, other species of fish have been harvested in the Bering Sea or North Pacific and processed in Unalaska, as indicated in Table 3.1.

It is clear the town depends heavily on the crab harvest. Salmon is relatively unimportant and the community is unusual for this region of Alaska in that Limited Entry, which regulates the salmon fisheries, has had little effect. The community as it exists today is essentially the result of a crab boom in the mid-seventies which brought sudden and massive growth, followed by a decline in the crab fishery which has forced adaptation and diversification on the part of those exploiting the resource. Today the community is characterized by flexibility in economic activities as it has become obvious that crab alone will not be a sufficient economic base for either the individual or the community in the future.

Unalaska, despite the fact that it is the location of the largest Aleut population in the Aleutians, did not benefit from Limited Entry, which was designed, in part at least, to guarantee Alaska Native peoples a portion of the salmon fishery. This is because there was no real fishery in the area at the time of and immediately prior to the introduction of Limited Entry as a result of poor salmon runs for several years. These years of bad runs are just those selected by the state as the qualifying years for a Limited Entry Permit. As a result, no one in Unalaska, even though they had long fished when the runs were good, was able to get a permanent permit. The only permits held by locals are temporary and must be renewed each year. This is a risky process and entails an investment each year of up to thirty or forty thousand dollars based only on the hope that the Department of Fish and Game will grant the extension. Four local residents have temporary permits. kind.

The crab boom peaked in 1979-80 and has since undergone a disastrous contraction. As noted in the last chapter, there are several reasons given for the decline in the crab population. The total amount of king crab processed in Unalaska two years ago was 164 million pounds. Last year the total was only 55 million pounds, and processors and fishermen alike say this year they will be lucky to get 30 million pounds.

The decline in catches and revenues from the crab fishery has resulted in some difficulties for, and adaptations among, local fishermen. Many feel one solution to the decline in the crab fishery is to convert to the groundfishery. However, there are problems with this, not the least of which is the cost of conversion. The owner of a local boat told us that a three million dollar crab boat would require an investment of between $600,000 and $800,000 to convert it to midwater or groundfishing; others put the cost at a million dollars or more. There are several joint ventures now and one plant processing significant quantities of groundfish. However, these are exceptions.

During these relatively difficult economic times the investment for conversion to groundfish is simply too large for most. The fishery has yet to be proven lucrative, and most have less capital now than they had a few years ago. Nonetheless, to the extent that it is possible most local fishermen are diversifying. Where a few years ago one could make a substantial income from the crab fishery alone in two months; now it is necessary to exploit as many resources over as much of the year as possible. This is felt more acutely by the smaller, local, fishermen than for the highliners. Several of the highliners actually preadapted for the crab crash. Spurred by tax incentives they added groundfish capability to their vessels in the "good years". They are now quite successful at exploiting diverse species; the disparity between the highliners and the rest of the fleet is remaining steady, and probably growing, during a depressed period for the industry as a whole.

One means of adaptation is to spread the risk among several partners. Several local individuals have entered into joint ventures with foreign companies in the last few years. One locally-based highliner has been successfully involved in joint groundfish ventures for three years, first with the Poles and later with the Koreans. Several others are also negotiating such agreements, and the future promises more of the same.

There are some still able to make a living by concentrating on crab, but there is insufficient quantities of the resource for everyone to do so. Those who are able to get enough crab, however, have been receiving handsome prices for the product. The scarcity has led to rises in the price paid by the processors as they bid it up in competition for limited catches. Last year (1981) the price went from $0.86 per pound to $1.70 per pound. Crab was selling for $4.00 a pound during the 1982 season. Thus, those who can get crab still do well, but decreasing numbers of fishermen are able to do so. This year, according to local fishermen, there is no fixed price for crab. The fishermen did not desire one, as they expect the shortage of the resource to result in a dramatic bidding up of the price on the part of the processors.

In addition to novel structural and business arrangements, fishermen have also diversified into other fishery resources. One fishery which has harvested more in the last few years is halibut. However, the fishery is dominated by outsiders at the expense of local fishermen. This is because the halibut fishery is run on a total quota system in which open fishing is allowed until the quota is filled. It is first come, first served, and it has resulted in a near monopoly of the fishery by the Seattle highliners who catch most of the quota so rapidly the local fisherman has little chance. A number of local people fish for halibut in skiffs for sport or subsistence, but few so far fish commercially.

Another possible strategy which has re-emerged is exploitation of the herring fishery, which has been historically important in Unalaska but moribund since before World War Two. This has so far consisted of only a few runs at the local processors. Questions must be resolved concerning whether the fishery around Unalaska is actually a separate fishery or part of a more encompassing Bering Sea fishery. If the latter is the case it may be dangerous to heavily exploit the fishery as it would result in a decline in stocks in already established fisheries. On the other hand, if the Unalaska fishery is a discrete one, then exploitation could proceed without adversely affecting other areas.

Another fishery receiving increased attention is the salmon fishery. Most of the processors in Unalaska have packed salmon in the last few years and are in the process of increasing their salmon output as they try to eliminate down-time and cut wasted overhead. Unalaska is well situated with respect to runs of, particularly, reds and pinks and this is becoming an increasingly important sector of the fisheries economy. However, the lack of local permits means that most of the salmon processed in Unalaska is caught in the Bristol Bay area. If that fishery declines Unalaska plants would probably suffer more, and sooner, than Bristol Bay plants.

The out-of-state fishermen and processing workers who dominate the industries in Unalaska come predominantly from the northwest U.S. and the west coast as a whole. Fishermen come up from Seattle and other west coast ports yearly for the salmon and crab runs, and they generally have vastly superior ships, equipment, and capitalization. These "highliners" are able to exploit huge amounts of the resource, and leave local fishermen far behind in terms of volume and income generated. As a group locals, and Aleuts in particular, are very underrepresented in the harvesting of marine products. Altogether probably less than a dozen boats are owned by local fishermen. Crews on these boats consist either of family members or close friends. While the preference seems to be members of one's family, fishing expertise is considered the most important factor.

Not only is the number of locally owned and operated boats small, they are also as a group smaller boats than the highliners from Seattle and thus have much less capacity. The processors take almost all of their product from the highliners, and relatively little from the the smaller boats. In fact, many of the processors refuse to go to the trouble of offloading product from the smaller boats. The highliners either deliver to the most convenient processor paying the highest price or enter into contractual agreements with a processor to deliver their product. The processors frequently broadcast the current price over the citizens band radio system, and the highliners are free to evaluate where to deliver their catch.

The downturn in the crab fishery has resulted in the financial overextension of many fishermen. The manager of the local bank estimates that as much as fifty percent of the fishing fleet may be in financial trouble, and notes that most are being forced to go into other areas than crab. He says that several fishermen have either begun to "feed" large catcher-processors who are themselves having difficulty catching their capacities, or have converted their own ships into small combination catcher-processors.

The processing industry is the dominant sector of the local economy. There are seven large processors in town capable of processing a total of more than 3 million pounds of product per day.

Table 3.2

Unalaska Shore-Based Processors, 1982

Company	Species Run (major)	Capability (lbs/day)	No. of Employees	Major Ethnic Group
Pan Alaska	Crab, Salmon	1,000,000	500	Filipino/ Caucasian
Universal	Crab, Salmon	1,000,000	500	Vietnamese/ Caucasian
Sea Alaska	Crab, Herring, Salmon, Cod	500,000	350	Filipino/ Mexican
Pac Pearl	Crab, Salmon	250,000	200	Vietnamese
East Point	Crab	250,000	90-150	Korean/ Mexican/ Caucasian
Whitney	Crab, Shrimp	250,000	35	Caucasian/ Filipino
Sea Pro	Cod, Salmon	80,000	60-70	Caucasian/ Vietnamese

The figures in Table 3.2 represent production and employment when the plants are operating at capacity. As we will note below, the slowdown in crab catches has resulted in cutbacks in both employment and output.

The major product is king crab, although the diversification forced by the decline of the crab fishery has seen the processors moving into salmon, other varieties of crab, shrimp, herring, halibut, and groundfish.

The processing sector burgeoned during the crab boom. From two small processors in the sixties it has become a massive industry. Today there are seven major processors in town. Universal Seafoods and Pan Alaska are the largest. Universal began with the processor the Unisea, and later (in 1977) acquired the Vita. They now have two separate processing lines in each facility. During the peak king crab season Universal is capable of processing one million pounds of product per day. When operating at full capacity during king crab season the processor usually employs around 500, and has employed as many as 600. However, with the current downturn in the crab industry Universal is only employing between a quarter and a third of that. In the summer of 1982 Universal hired only 200 people in the processing sector, thirty to forty percent of whom were Vietnamese with the rest Caucasian. Employees are hired on a six month contract. Universal has concentrated almost exclusively on king crab in the past, but has now diversified into salmon, and has even attempted to process cod. The cod experiment involved two runs of salt cod, but lost money and has not been repeated. They have found that at this time and with the present methods they are unable to compete with foreign groundfish processors.

Universal's response to the decline in the crab fishery has been to diversify. One strategy has been to devote most of the resources of Dutch Harbor Seafoods, a wholly owned subsidiary of Universal, to processing salmon rather than crab. Dutch Harbor Seafoods operates two processors, the Galaxy and the Viceroy. Both of these have recently been sent out of Unalaska to follow the salmon fleet at close range to guarantee access to product.

Universal has also diversified operations in its other two processors, the Unisea and the Vita. These two were originally little more than empty hulks which were towed up from Seattle. Their will never be able to leave their berths. They have been the major local processor of halibut, and in the summer of 1982 they experimented with herring.

Pan Alaska is the only processor in town which can equal the output of Universal Seafoods. The Pan Alaska plant consists of a shore plant and several barges, one of which can act as a small processor. They are located on Iliuliuk Harbor. The plant is capable of processing a million pounds of crab a day. The processor has run primarily crab, but since 1979 has run salmon as well. Running salmon puts the plant to use in the crab off-season.

Pan Alaska runs three lines currently, up from one in 1980. Salmon processing runs from May to August. Pan-Alaska normally employs approximately 500 people when king crab is running at high levels, but with the downturn they, too, have been employing far fewer. Current employment, for the salmon runs, is about 120. Of these about half are Filipino and most of the rest are Caucasian. The employees work on a six month contract. Pan Alaska also received a grant to run a batch of pollock on an experimental basis, but the results were not encouraging. Recently, Pan Alaska announced plans to suspend their operations in Unalaska in September for an indefinite period.

Sea Alaska is the third largest processor in town. Sea Alaska has also diversified its operations, and now processes crab, herring, salmon, and cod. Cod is done as frozen fillets. The company is moving toward more cod and pollock, but is still developing the expertise and technology and has not begun to process groundfish on any large scale. The company operates two floating processors out of Unalaska, the Sea Alaska and the Sea Producer, and during salmon season the floater Resoff, usually tied up in Unalaska, goes out to follow the fishing fleet.

Sea Alaska has a capacity to process approximately 500,000 pounds of salmon or king crab per day. The capacity for tanner, brown, and opilio crab is about 300,000 pounds per day. Cod is just being tried, and so far has been running at about 10,000 pounds per day. They also process herring occasionally, but it is very cyclic and is run mostly for bait. Reportedly, there isn't much of a market for it as food at this time.

Sea Alaska employs about 350 people during the peak of the king crab run. When salmon is being run employment is slightly less, usually around 300. Tanner crab requires only 200 employees, and cod only 150. However, all these figures have dropped somewhat with the deterioration of the economic climate. In 1982 the ethnicity of the workers was approximately fifty-five percent Filipino, twenty-five percent Mexican, fifteen percent Caucasian, and five percent Vietnamese. Workers are on a six month contract.

In addition, there are four smaller processors in town. Three of these, Pacific Pearl, East Point, and Whitney-Fidalgo, are capable of processing up to 250,000 pounds per day, and the fourth, Sea Pro, is capable of 80,000 pounds per day.

Pacific Pearl usually employs around 200 people. However, as with most of the other processors, this season (1982) they are employing far fewer, probably around eighty-five. The dominant ethnic group is Vietnamese. The processor runs primarily tanner and king crab. They have also, in the past, run red and pink salmon, some halibut, some cod for bait, and herring.

Pac Pearl has one processing line which can be adapted for two shifts of sixty-five to seventy people or be geared down to one shift of only fifteen people, which increases efficiency. Pacific Pearl has recently suspended its operations in Unalaska, however, and sold it's Captain's Bay Plant to Crowley Maritime.

Another smaller processor in town is Whitney-Fidalgo, which is ninety-nine percent owned by Kioko Ltd., a Japanese company. Whitney has been in town since 1976 and has run primarily crab and shrimp. They also freeze bait cod and anticipate running salmon in the future. The cannery, though not large, is versatile and capable of running any of several products.

Whitney employs, on the average, around fifty people on a six month contract. Most employees are relatively young, in their early twenties, and many are return employees, coming back for three to five years. The major ethnic groups are Caucasian and Korean.

Whitney is capable of running 250,000 pounds of crab per day. In the past they have run between 1.5 and two million pounds of shrimp per year as well. In 1981 they ran 1.75 million pounds of shrimp. This year (1982) has been very disappointing and in the first month of the shrimp run virtually none was processed. The plant is diversifying this year into dungeness crab, whereas previously they had run king crab exclusively. Whitney has two floaters, the Mokohama and the Yardarm Knot, as well as a shore plant (which is actually a permanently moored floater). As with Pan Alaska and Pacific Pearl, however, the recent downturn in the crab fishery has forced Whitney to suspend its operations in Unalaska for an indefinite period.

The third medium-sized processor is East Point. East Point processes mainly crab and, like Whitney and Pac Pearl has a capacity of about 250,000 pounds per day. East Point employs approximately equal numbers of Koreans, Mexicans, and Caucasians. During full scale operations during the king crab season East Point employs over 150 people, however the downturn in crab has resulted in employment being cut back to between eighty and ninety.

A relatively new entrant to the Unalaska processing sector is Sea Pro which began operations in 1982 and is a joint venture with a Norwegian company, Johanson. Sea Pro is the only processor in Unalaska which regularly runs cod. It operates partially on land owned by Pac Pearl and Crowley Marine, and for this reason has a "no crab" contract which states that Sea Pro cannot compete with Pac Pearl by processing crab. At times, however, Sea Pro does run salmon. One reason the company is unique is that it can make a profit running cod because the parent Norwegian company has direct access to the major European markets.

The operation consists of five boats fishing for cod and the shore-based processor. They employ a total of about seventy people. Because Sea Pro does not depend on crab, but is the only processor in Unalaska to do primarily groundfish, employment has actually risen in the last year from about sixty to seventy-two (as of the summer of 1982). The goal of the company is to keep volume down and quality up in order to compete with the Japanese, Poles, and Koreans. Occasionally the plant runs salmon also, but the primary product has consistently been salt cod. They have been operating at a rate of approximately 300,000 to 400,000 pounds of product per week.

Though groundfish processing is seen by many in town as a potentially major industry, currently only Sea Pro is processing cod in any quantity. People in town are carefully watching this operation to see whether it succeeds and with the recent suspension of operations by the processor for an indefinite period, the question remains an open one. One additional problem with establishment of a groundfish industry is the lack of a cold storage facility. According to local opinion, if such a facility were built it would be of great service to the fishing industry, and would allow much more efficient use of the shipping which comes into town. Groundfish, as well as other marine resources, could be both processed and transshipped through Unalaska. Unalaska's location on main shipping lines could then be exploited to the fullest.

The decline in crab stocks has not only forced diversification on the part of both the fishermen and processors, but has changed the nature of the processors' work forces as well. We have already noted the contraction in work force which has affected all the processors with the exception of Sea Pro. With the resulting scarcity of positions, all processors agreed there had been a change in the recent past in the rate of worker return. During the height of the crab boom, which coincided with a favorable economic climate in the rest of the United States, the rate of return was usually around twenty five percent, that is only one out of four workers would actually return to work the next year. However, with increasingly difficult conditions in the lower forty-eight and the increasing difficulty in getting a job at the processors the employment market has stabilized since a job is much less readily given up now. As a result rates of worker return are now reported at between fifty and ninety percent. Nonetheless, workers are still overwhelmingly outsiders. As has been clear throughout this discussion, locals are greatly underrepresented in the processing sector. Almost none of the processing workers are local hire. Regardless of ethnic group, almost all the processing workers come from the west coast of the United States, in particular from the Seattle area.

Another recent trend which has affected the processing sector of the Unalaska economy is the movement of several processors from Unalaska to Akutan. There were about thirteen processors in Akutan in 1981, most of which chose that location over Unalaska, and many of which moved from Unalaska to Akutan. This is of concern to local businessmen and politicians alike.

Akutan does not have readily available land suitable for shore-based operations to the extent that Unalaska has and lacks the capacity for transportation of processed seafood products. However, Akutan has been selected by the Army Corps of Engineers as one of four locations in the Aleutians suitable for harbor and channel improvements designed to encourage development of a ground-fish industry.

The control by the Ounalashka Corporation of most of the land in the community has meant that a few of the processors have had to lease land from the Corporation in order to operate. One of the reasons Unisea has been able to maintain a large presence and high profit level in Unalaska is that it actually owns the property on which it is located. They were able to acquire three General Services Administration parcels purchased prior to the passage of ANCSA which total twenty-nine acres, and in this respect are favorably situated compared to most other processors in town. East Point, Pac Pearl, and Sea Alaska also own some land in town, and have been able to survive without a great deal of interaction with the Corporation.

A final trend of great importance in the last few years has been the unionization of the processing and transportation-related workers. Most of the processors in town now run union shops. Sea Alaska and the Royal Sea and Royal Venture of Pan Alaska have been in the International Longshoreman and Warehousemen's Union for some time. In March of 1981 the current organization, the Inland Boatmen's Union, came into being with the elections at American President Lines (the IBU is essentially the marine division of the ILWU). The Union is also at Crowley Maritime, and a majority of the employees at Sea Land are members.

The long range goal of the union is to organize all the processing workers in town, and any of the workers who have to do with transportation and processing. The people who work on the oil support ships are also a target. Right now they get $65 a day for very dangerous work. Under the IBU they would get $132 a day as a deckhand and earn five hours vacation time for every eight hours worked. Wages in Unalaska have increased markedly already as a result of unionization. For example, APL used to pay $7.50 an hour before it was unionized. Now the pay is $18.60 plus medical, dental, optical, retirement, vacation, and holiday pay.

Local entrepreneurial activity in Unalaska can be divided into small scale and large scale enterprises. The explosive growth of the town in the last decade has meant that population has rapidly outstripped services and support facilities. Such facilities are only now beginning to catch up with this rapid population growth. There has therefore been a proliferation of small-scale enterprises in the last few years. Large-scale enterprises have been in town in some cases for considerably longer than the last decade, but even they have been greatly expanded and have adopted new and more modern business practices and techniques in an attempt to cope with rapid growth.

Small-scale entrepreneurial activity is beginning to grow as the need for support industries has grown. The period of the crab boom, and the time since, has seen a major expansion of small local

businesses, including a garage, laundromat and drycleaning establishment, a branch of the Alaska State Bank, cab companies,
several construction companies, marine supply companies, and so on.
In general the town has come firmly into the modern consumer/credit
economy, and people now have checkbooks, credit cards, and all the
accoutrements of that society.

The growth in population has meant a need for new building,
and several contracting companies have emerged in the last few
years. Marine Construction and Engineering Company was started
three years ago, and is primarily in the contracting business.
This was the first professional contractor in town. The company
now employs a total of sixteen workers and is also involved in sale
of gravel, concrete aggregate, and road topping. They also do some
transfer of material, move some cargo, and handle and stack crab
pots. As in many other areas of the economy of Unalaska, it is
difficult to survive as a specialist and diversification is the
rule of the day.

Three other licensed contractors have recently set up business, and among them they employ a total of approximately fifteen
workers. There are also several unlicensed individuals who do
general contracting and related work. The major construction project at this time is the renovation and conversion of the sub dock
to a drydock for small and medium sized ships. In the past some of
the major projects have been housing and apartment construction,
dock facilities (such as the American President Lines dock), and
the Ounalashka Corporation is now completing plans for the construction of a full service gas station and garage. All of the
construction companies in town look forward to the possibility of
oil development in the region and express the belief that it will
mean a good deal of business for them.

Northwest Marine Instruments was established in 1979 and is
involved in electronics repair and supply. The company employs
between three and four people. It is based in Unalaska for nine
months of the year and in the Bristol Bay area for three months.
Dutch Harbor Divers is another small-scale business which is
basically support for the fishing and processing industry. Their
major business is underwater construction and vessel repair. A
related business is Aleutian Explosive Services. One of the major
marine service and repair businesses in town is Magone Marine.
They are heavily involved in the construction of the drydock going
in on the site of the World War Two sub dock. Another support
activity is the Aleutian Marine Pilots Association which brings
ships in and out of the port of Unalaska.

Several smaller support businesses were begun by fishermen who
found themselves earning too much money during the crab boom and
who needed another business for tax purposes. This was the case
with the two individuals who began the Alpha Cab Company, one of
two now operating in town (the maximum allowed by the city council). This company was established two years ago and has three
cabs.

The Ounalashka Corporation has also embarked on some small-
scale enterprises. They have formed Unmaknak, a company which
rents trucks and equipment, and own a laundromat on Standard Oil
Hill. They have also recently received exclusive dealership rights

for a Chevron service station.

Large scale local entrepreneurial efforts are spearheaded by the major local retailers. These include Carl's Commercial, Alaskan Commercial, Aleutian Mercantile, and the Unisea complex. Carl's consists of a store and motel complex located on the Unalaska side. The motel has thirteen units. Carls has dry goods, groceries, liquor and general merchandise. They also are the major supplier of fuel oil to the community and sell between 300,000 and 400,000 gallons per year. That figure has declined some in the last few years, probably in response to the decline in the crab fishery. A large proportion of Carl's business is in supplying fishing vessels and summer oil research vessels. Oil development has already had a dramatic effect in terms of supplies needed by the seismic and exploration crews working in the Bering Sea. Carl's has received several rush orders for thousands of dollars worth of groceries and supplies from oil-related businesses in the last few years. However, local retail business provides the day to day income. The manager of Carl's estimates that oil business is now worth approximately a million dollars a year for his store alone.

With the growth of the community and its businesses has come increasing efficiency and professionalism in business practices. For example, until recently Carl's had a large backlog of accounts due, and there was little coherence to the bookkeeping and financial management. However, this has been rectified in the last couple of years. Much of this can be traced to the present manager who increased business by twenty-five percent in the first quarter of his tenure. This was achieved through more efficient management of inventory. Carl's has also eliminated personal credit in the belief that the town is now cosmopolitan enough that there are credit cards, a bank, and checking accounts available, making personal credit arrangements unnecessary.

This transition to a consumer society is by no means total, however. Though it is true there is now a bank in town it is still not a full service facility. All loans in the Unalaska branch must be handled through Anchorage, resulting in long delays. It is hard to do business, even though things have improved, because there is no resident inspector or surveyor, yet all building must still comply with all state and federal regulations. The bank did finance much of the Standard Oil Hill housing rehabilitation project of the Ounalashka Corporation as well as some other small housing developments but its role in the overall development of the community appears to have been minor.

Alaska Commercial (AC) is another major retailer in town. It is located in the Unisea Mall on Amaknak Island. It was opened just a few years ago and has done well, though their gross is not as large as Carl's. The presence of the AC is generally welcomed by the consumers in town because it means there is more competition and prices don't fluctuate as widely as they seemed to in the past.

The Aleutian Mercantile (AM) is a third major retailer. AM has in the past acted as a caretaker for the community by extending long-term credit to permanent community members. Most of these customers are Aleut as the store is in downtown Unalaska, and at present the store is carrying between seventy and eighty thousand dollars in credit on its books. The owner has written off thou-

sands of dollars which he feels is uncollectable.
Most of the major retailers in town bring in their own goods
rather than rely on Sea Land or American President Lines. As in
much of Alaska, the stores register their own ships as "fisheries"
to avoid tariffs. Most of them bring their cargo in at the APL
dock.

Another major commercial enterprise in town is owned and
operated by Universal Seafoods. In addition to their processing
operations, Universal also run several retail and commercial outlets in town. Unisea owns the Unisea Inn which was built in 1978
and has been expanded several times since. Part of the building is
devoted to a bar, and part to a restaurant. The Unisea tends to
cater to the fishermen and processing employees and has been very
successful. Even during the off-season occupancy rates have been
over ninety percent, and it is difficult to find a room without a
reservation during fishing season.

The Unisea Mall was completed in March of 1980 and has been
completely leased to businesses. Paradoxically, the inn and mall
were originally conceived as support structures for the processors.
However, with the downturn in crab in the last few years the mall
and inn have eclipsed the processors as the main income generators.

The Ounalashka Corporation is involved in a project which will
give Unalaska the capability to repair boats in drydock for the
first time. This involves refitting the World War Two sub-dock to
act as a drydock for small boats. The facility will be operated by
Panama Marine, Ltd., a subsidiary of the Aleut Corporation. Even
so, most boats will probably continue to go to Seattle for major
work and resupply because things are cheaper and more readily
available there.

In addition to the private sector, employment opportunities
are available in the public sector of Unalaska. In recent years,
with the crab boom and attendant growth, there has been an explosive growth in city government, particularly in the police department. Whereas the city had only one police officer in the late
1960s, today there are sixteen. Other city departments have also
grown in size, making public sector employment an attractive alternative for professionals and skilled blue collar workers. The
major salaried official is the city manager. Elected officials,
including the major, receive no compensation for their services.

Unalaska's economy and economic structure is strongly linked
with the external economic structure of the region, state, nation,
and world. Products, particularly fishery related, go out of the
town bound for the west coast, the Orient, and other points even
further removed. Most of the income which is earned in the community is not spent in the town itself but is destined for other
locales around the country and world. This has been a major complaint of locals for some time. Very little of the money earned in
the community actually redounds to the town's benefit. This is
known locally as the "rape and run" syndrome, and is particularly
characteristic of the fishing and processing community.

Very few of the needs of the people of Unalaska are supplied
from products produced within the community. Almost all food, dry
goods, household goods, business needs, and so on are imported.
Thus, the community is closely linked to the outside economic

world, but the link is an expensive one. People pay very high prices for the necessities of life. Though there is a fair amount of subsistence activity, most daily needs are filled by imports. Thus far the local business sector has been more oriented to support for the fishing industry rather than to local production of necessities per se. Since 1980, however, there has been a discernible trend for the fishing industry to rely upon the local economy for goods and services rather than to continue being self-supplied.

The major shipping lines handle by far the majority of imports, although some is brought in by the air carriers as well. The local retailers stock themselves almost totally from outside, and the time and distance involved has resulted in necessarily inefficient warehousing and inventory maintenance strategies, which has led to even higher prices for the local consumer. This is the major distribution problem to be confronted by the city in the future.

One recent change in the community which has had a major influence on distribution and consumption patterns is the construction of the bridge from Amaknak Island to Unalaska. Residents of Unalaska now frequent stores on the Amaknak Island side much more often than before, and competition for the consumer has increased between the two sides.

3.2.1.2 <u>Subsistence</u>. Subsistence in Alaska refers to local resources which are harvested by local people for personal use. Traditionally, Aleuts have relied on marine resources for subsistence. Salmon provided the bulk of the Aleut diet, followed by seals and sea lions, mussels, clams and sea urchins. Gull eggs were gathered, ducks and geese were hunted, fox were trapped, and various forms of vegetation, including berries and wild celery, were gathered and consumed.

There were two periods of change in subsistence patterns among the residents of Unalaska. Following World War Two, during the period of Unalaska's depression, patterns changed to greater dependence on subsistence items, in particular salmon. People in Unalaska harvested salmon and exchanged it with people in the Pribilofs for seal. This pattern lasted until the 1960s when the fisheries began to play an important part in the Unalaska economy. As the fisheries developed, and particularly during the crab boom of the seventies, dependence on subsistence items, and utilization of them, began to decline.

Today subsistence activities continue, though in altered form. In the 1950s and 1960s people still prepared sea lion stomachs for storage, and manufactured some needed articles out of seal gut. No one does this any more. Clams are harvested, but are disappearing. Sea eggs (urchins) and bidarkis (chitons) are eaten. Crabs are gathered when they are near to shore and the tide is low. Salmon and halibut are popular, as is cod, which is available year round. Blueberries, mossberries and salmonberries are gathered. Seal and sea lions are used occasionally. Other than berries, plants are not much used. Medicinal plants reportedly were used quite frequently until the late 60s, though their use is infrequent now. <u>Pootchky</u> (wild celery) is eaten, mostly by children, and <u>petruskies</u> (a type of herb) are widely used for seasoning. They

are boiled with fish, dried, frozen, and put in peru (fish pie).
Bird hunting is still done, mostly for ducks and geese.

In the last five years a problem of increasing incidents of
illegal subsistence activity has developed in Unalaska. The major
problems include people who "snag" salmon (hooking them illegally
through their bodies using rod and reel and outsized hooks with no
bait) and take fish with unmarked gill nets. Contributing to the
increase in illegally taken fish is the recent reduction in the
number of subsistence fish allowed by the state. Prior to 1982 an
individual could get subsistence salmon permits for 250 fish. This
was reduced to seventy-five fish in 1982. The reaction has been
heated in many cases. Additional subsistence permits are issued,
however, to permanent residents who are clearly in need of the
resource. The permits have been abused in the past, primarily, it
appears, by processing workers. These individuals would catch
their limit of 250 fish and have them sent to the lower forty-eight
where they sold them. However, according to the regulations the
fish caught are supposed to be for personal use. Overfishing of
major subsistence areas has been a problem as well, and contributed
to the reduction in the number of subsistence salmon allowed.

Aleuts in Unalaska maintain that subsistence continues today,
but for different reasons than in the past. With the "Anglici-
zation" of the community the Aleuts became, for the first time, a
minority. This was a threatening situation, and one of the
responses has been to reaffirm the Aleut identity and the traditional value system on which that identity is based whenever
possible. Subsistence activities are an important part of this
reaffirmation. Several of the Aleuts said it made them "feel good"
to eat "Aleut food" or engage in Aleut crafts. Different people
use different subsistence activities for the same end. Thus
sealing or duck hunting or even fishing may be done not so much out
of a need for the resource as out of a need for the activity
itself.

Subsistence activity among Aleuts in Unalaska is also representative of competing value systems in the community and the role
of the Aleut in the non-Native economy. As noted above, subsistence activities were an inextricable part of the traditional value
system. While certain aspects of subsistence activities, notably
the social exchange of subsistence items among Aleuts and the
affirmation of Aleut identity, continue to reinforce the traditional value system, these activities also constitute a set of
social boundaries distinguishing ethnic groups within the community. The continued use on subsistence items for food and the
affirmation of ethnic identity by Aleuts in Unalaska is indicative
of their limited involvement in the non-Native, cash-based economy,
although, as noted earlier, there are few if any Aleuts who are not
involved in this economy in one form or another, usually as consumers. While this limited economic activity may reinforce the
overall socioeconomic position of the Aleuts vis-a-vis the non-
Native population of Unalaska, it also represents a mode of adaptation to the fluctuations and relative insecurity which has characterized the Unalaska cash-based economy in the past. The increase
in illegal subsistence activities also represents a type of reaction to certain aspects of the modern value system, particularly

the importance of rules and regulations which are perceived as restricting the adaptive value of these activities. Thus, while not a conscious attempt to violate the law, illegal subsistence may be as much a form of "reference group alientation" (Berreman, 1964) as it is a response to certain economic needs.

Hunting is not a major activity on Unalaska Island as there are no large terrestrial species which could serve as a source of food. Trapping, however, does occur. The island has a fairly large population of fox, mostly red fox, as a result of attempts in the early part of the century to establish a trapping industry, noted earlier. There are still substantial numbers of fox present and trapping seems to be making a modest comeback.

3.2.1.3 <u>Non-Labor Force</u>. Unalaska has a relatively small non-labor force. The nature of the community as isolated and dominated by processing and fishing means that few people come to town without previous arrangement, and it is equally difficult for someone to stay in town without gainful employment of some kind. This is somewhat less true for the Aleut population than for the outsiders, but even here unemployment appears to be as much a matter of choice as of necessity.

3.2.1.4 <u>Oil-Related Development</u>. Mineral development has already had an effect on the community of Unalaska. To one degree or another almost every major decision facing Unalaska today involves consideration of this projected development. While groundfishery projections have until very recently been seen as the likely source of future support for the Unalaska economy, given the short-term demise and dim prospects of the crab fishery, oil development is now coming to be seen as a significant future support for the community, at least in the short-term.

The City of Unalaska, after having enjoyed several years of boom crab fishery returns, resulting in a very high tax base (relative to population), and associated rapid population growth, is now in the process of retrenchment. The pressing economic issue has become: "How can we make the most out of a declining economic resource base?" This involves careful consideration and scrutinization of the relatively high administrative overhead and the priorities of the community. Part of the argument used to support current levels of administration and services involves the anticipated effect of projected oil-related development in Unalaska. However, fiscal effects of the recent crab decline on city revenues should not be overemphasized. The fiscal year 1984 budget of $14.6 million includes $3,693,962 in the General Fund portion which is derived primarily from fish revenue. While revenue in this fund is only $150,000 less than was budgeted for FY1983, the long-term consequences on indirect taxes from processing facilities may be very significant if processors elect to depart from the community or to resist increases in their tax rates.

While the city's position is that fixed sources of revenue (i.e., local property tax, federal revenue sharing, etc.) will allow for continued slow growth in the community for the next three to five years, this flexibility could conceivably be restricted by several factors. First, most local leaders take for granted several more years of minimal crab harvests which will dramatically reduce income from the city's share of the State of Alaska's fish tax. These harvests may be even smaller than currently forecast. Second, we can foresee some difficulty in the city collecting property taxes from the processors. Their taxes have increased markedly in the last two years as a result of an increase in assessed value of the processor-owned property. While these firms are not expected to default, we have noted in similar lean circumstances in other communities a tendency for processors to postpone, negotiate, and, in other ways, attempt to avoid timely payment of taxes. Third, the generally restricted capital markets, and the current economic position of the State of Alaska, along with other factors, combine to make it difficult to float bond issues or in other ways generate capital for local projects. With the tenuous nature of funding sources for projected budgets of Unalaska, administrative and service cutbacks are expected to be required within the next year or two.

It is within this fiscal context that the leadership of Unalaska has begun to consider both detrimental and beneficial aspects of projected OCS development. Those in decision-making positions or with commercial interests, not the average fishermen, processor employee or short-term resident, will be most concerned with the financial ramifications of oil development at these early stages. Almost invariably, it is only after actual effects of development felt to be detrimental are evident that significant numbers of average citizens will take a position; but by then, of course, it is too late to avoid these effects. In general, individuals cannot be meaningfully brought into a decision-making process when they (1) do not understand what is being considered, (2) do not see any immediate relevance to the discussion, and/or (3) do not feel their input can possibly affect the process. There is a nearly universal feeling in Unalaska among those who are at least mildly concerned with trying to control development and growth in the community that the whole process of oil-development is predetermined, fixed, and cannot in any way be altered by "the people."

Individual's opinions on the subject also vary according to their structural position in the community. Leaders and entrepreneurs are likely to view development in positive or necessary terms while Aleut residents, many long-term Euro-American residents, and recent immigrants are likely to be opposed to such activity. It is clear that those individuals who can see no direct benefits arising from oil development will not be favorably inclined toward, or may, in fact, be opposed to such development.

If there is a position that is considered universal in Unalaska it is that oil development cannot be considered as a long-term solution to the problems of the community and hence to be viewed with caution. Groundfishery development, on the other hand, is seen as a long-term solution. Nevertheless, the absence of significant local development in this area and the generally ambivalent attitude of local processors toward the likelihood of imminent development of this fishery has tended to enhance positive attitudes toward oil. Many now agree that given the marked decline in the crab fishery and the seeming failure to progress in the groundfishery, if community expectations regarding local development associated with OCS activity and expectations of new monies generated by oil development are not met, then the city will be "in a bad way" economically.

The current economy of Unalaska is in a transitional period. Over the last decade, it has been dominated by the crab fishery. It was crab that made Unalaska the number one port in the United States in terms of value of product landed in 1979. The crab industry generated the capital, the employment, and the industry that spurred a 400 percent population increase in less than a decade. During the last three years, the physical resource on which this growth was based has virtually collapsed, affecting every commercial, governmental, and private entity in the area. During this same period the community experienced the incipient growth of activities related to oil exploration and development. These activities included leasing land, establishing contractual relations with local suppliers of fuel, the purchase of equipment and supplies, the letting of transport contracts, and so on. During this period there was also the beginning of various public relations activities such as community presentations on the benefits of oil development, attendance of oil representatives at all appropriate community discussions, and a generally concerted effort to assure that exploration company personnel have a minimal contact with the local population, thus avoiding any negative social effects or impressions which might affect their future activities.

The effects of recent oil exploration activities and incipient oil development-related activities on Unalaska can be broken down into direct and indirect consequences. The direct consequences are predominately economic, while indirect effects include political and social effects, as well as indirect economic consequences. Among the direct economic effects are local purchase of supplies and equipment, docking and lighterage fees, vehicle rentals, fuel costs, and other expenditures which directly buoy the local economy. These have been significant though remarkedly unnoticed.

Local services currently utilized include a contracting company which hauls materials for ARCO, the purchase of oxygen and other gases, the purchase of fuel, the use of local hotels when the rigs come into town, a few groceries for most vessels and contractual total resupply and logistical support for a few, and periodic use of the airport. The outside seismic vessels and crews also make use of similar services when they are in port on a relatively modest scale. ARCO has contracted with local fishing boats to be used as standby for possible evacuations, other emergencies, or when they are short of transport. Three fishing vessels have been under contract in the past. ARCO has also used Sea Land and American Presidents Line for trucking and barging of supplies on a periodic basis. Future service contracts are expected to be made during the oil production phase, should it come, when turbines, generator repair and other types of support activities will increase.

Indirect economic effects occur mostly as a result of advance preparation on the part of planners and established enterprises and speculation on the part of investors or potential entrepreneurs. Both amount to taking calculated risks in order to be in a more advantageous position in the future economic environment. For city planners this means formulating budgets which attempt to anticipate development needs. The purchase or leasing of land, letting of

construction contracts for local utilities, and many other requirements must be met long in advance to take full advantage of the
economic opportunities offered. Unfortunately, the boom in the
crab fishery which created the perceived demand for services ended
as abruptly as it had begun, leaving the community overextended.
The size and cost of the police force and city administration have
been the first targets of public concern and complaint, but other
expenditures are likely to face reduction as well. In a sense, oil
development is seen by many community leaders as a "stop-gap"
solution to the more long-term problems of the economy.

For commercial enterprises that must anticipate long in
advance the needs of petroleum development, hopes for oil-related
development are second only to the hopes for rapid groundfishery
development combined with at least a partial return of the crab
fishery as a support for the local commercial economy. Were all
three to fail to materialize, the viability of these enterprises
would be in question.

Though there was considerable activity in 1976 as a result of
test drilling in the St. George Basin, current oil-related activity
in Unalaska can be said to have begun in 1981. In that year, nine
seismic vessels en route to locations in the Bering Sea passed
through Unalaska. These vessels typically carry crews of twenty-
five to thirty-five and remain in Unalaska only long enough to
refuel, load equipment or make necessary repairs. Delays for parts
or equipment which must be flown in from Seattle or Texas, however,
are frequent, lasting an average of three to five days.

ARCO established a facility in Captains Bay to supply vessels
tending the COST (Continental Offshore Stratigraphic Test) wells
operating in the Bering Sea. These wells operate with between
eighty-three and ninety-three crewmembers. The rig now active is
located about 220 miles from Unalaska or about sixteen hours by
boat. The ARCO operation began in March of 1982 and has grown
rapidly. The site contains three large and well-equipped trailers
originally designed to support a much larger crew than in now
present. The land is leased from Crowley Maritime. The total crew
present at this time is five plus a crane operator.

Two rig tenders (the Biehl Trader and the Biehl Traveller) are
the only oil support vessels that can claim to be stationed in
Unalaska. These two vessels are part of the ARCO-operated COST
well development and are used to supply and support the drilling
currently underway. They carry a crew of eleven each and one
vessel is always located at the well itself for evacuation or other
immediate support activities.

The dominant concern of community relations have been with
holding the lowest possible profile in the community. This
approach has come from very high levels of authority and is a
product of good understanding of what the most likely impediments
to oil development will be: the consequences of the presence of
large numbers of oil-related employees in the social environment of
small communities. For example, local employees are "given to
understand" that they should not visit local bars at all, should
not participate in local social functions, and should not even
spend leisure time in the city.

Another example of how efforts to maintain a low profile are

effected is the periodic movement of crews to and from the COST
rigs. The old crew arrives via a chartered helicopter, the new
crew gets on and takes off while the old crew gets on another
waiting chopper and departs. They have little interest in remaining in Unalaska for long periods of time and, thus, have literally
no social effect on the community.

The attitude of these outside agents, and the effects of this
attitude, must also be taken into consideration. The transient
seismic and exploratory crews that have visited Unalaska are, on
the average, about five years older than their fishermen counter-
parts. They are predominately well educated and highly skilled
workers. They are full-time employees with lengthy employment
histories and strong oil-related career objectives. The fishermen
who come to Unalaska are younger, less educated, primarily concerned with temporary high paid positions and would willingly shift
to another occupation if it paid as well. Fishermen enter the
community after several weeks at sea with large amounts of cash and
with the objective of "having a good time" before they must leave
again. The outside crews of the seismic vessels have much of their
pay withheld or sent directly to their families, and are not as
interested in the local bars, entertainment or "hobnobbing" with
the "locals." If they do seek local entertainment, they usually go
to the Unisea Restaurant and Bar located on Amaknak Island. It is
for this reason that very few people on the Unalaska side are at
all familiar with these transient oil workers.

Local employees of ARCO at Captains Bay are in a slightly
different position, having to live for longer periods near the
community. During the early period of their residency they noted
more curiosity than concern on the part of Unalaska residents.
While no formal instructions have been given, these workers are
given to understand that the less interaction with local residents
the better. The ARCO facility is located outside of town and the
only transportation available is the company vehicle, effectively
limiting travel to town.

A larger, more transient oil-related population are the crewmen associated with the seismic research now actively examining the
bottom of the Bering Sea for indicators of potential oil and gas
deposits. Seismic research activity increased significantly in
1982. At least fifty-three research vessels docked in Unalaska by
October of 1982. The nearly 1,500 crewmen of these vessels have
actually had less direct social effects on Unalaska than one might
expect. There are rarely more than two vessels in port at any one
time. More importantly, however, there has been a concerted effort
to allay community concerns over the effects of the presence of
these workers. Each member of every crew has been formally and
informally given to understand that there should be minimal contact
with local residents and facilities. This effort has been quite
successful. There have been no arrests, reported barroom incidents, accidents or reports of inappropriate behavior on the part
of any of these employees. As a result, many local residents are
unaware of the presence of the crews of the COST rigs, seismic
vessels, and rig tenders.

3.2.2 Social Organization

While several social categories exist throughout the community, the two most relevant distinctions appear to be that between
resident and transient and between Aleut and non-Aleut. The first
distinction became particularly salient during the last ten years
when the population grew at an enormous rate. Much of the transient population is involved with the seafood industry, either as
fishermen based elsewhere or as processing employees divided into
supervisors who usually remain in the community for a few years and
line workers who typically renew their six month contracts less
frequently than do the supervisiors. Line workers also tend to
represent non-white ethnic groups, particularly Filipino and Vietnamese.

3.2.2.1 Residential Groups.

Among the resident population,
distinctions are often made between the population residing in the
community before the decade of rapid growth in the 1970s (permanent
residents) and those who arrived during or after that period (semi-
permanent residents). The second group is much larger than the
first.

The following are the residence categories of Unalaska and
their composition:

Transients are those individuals who are in the community for
six months to a year. The goals of the individuals in this group
are often to take advantage of the opportunities offered by the
six-month employment contracts common in Unalaska, and then to move
out of the community as soon as some relatively short-term financial goals are accomplished. This group is primarily composed of
people who work at the processors in town. Ethnically this group
is quite diverse, with the dominant group being Southeast Asians.
Most often these individuals do not become actively involved with
the community, but rather live, work, and interact socially with
the other transients at the processors. These individuals do not
often seek to gain other employment outside of the work that they
are involved with currently, that is, they do not compete with
others in different segments of the employment market.

Long-Term Transients are those individuals who are in the
community for a specific period of time longer than one year. The
normative length of stay is approximately two to five years. These
individuals have some stake in the affairs of the community and
often participate in community activities. Their perceptions of
the city are influenced, however, by the knowledge that Unalaska is
not their permanent residence. Often these individuals are in town
to save enough money to make some ambitious financial goal a reality. The ethnic composition of this group is predominantly Euro-
American.

Semi-Permanent Residents are those individuals who have settled in the community since the development of the crab industry,
yet consider Unalaska their permanent place of residence. Some of
these individuals may in fact be in town no longer than some of the
long-term transients, but they are differentiated from this group
by their perceptions of their role in, and their commitment to, the
community. Only a small minority of these individuals, however,
plan to spend their retirement years in Unalaska. Their decision

to move to the community was informed by the conditions in Unalaska
at the time of their move, and those economic, social, and cultural
conditions differed significantly from the conditions which existed
prior to the development of the crab fishery. As a result these
individuals often have different value orientations and expectations than those who were settled in the community prior to the
economic boom. Like the long-term transients, the ethnic composition of this category predominantly Euro-American, though in this
case it is almost exclusively so. There are some Aleut individuals
and families who have moved to the community since the coming of
the crab industry; however most of these individuals or their
parents have ties to the community that pre-date the crab fishery
and have lived in the community previously.

Within this group, there is a further distinction between the
"pioneers" and "newcomers." While both groups share similar social
characteristics, they are distinguished by their time of arrival
into the community. Those who arrived before 1978 (the height of
the crab boom) are referred to as pioneers while those arriving
afterwards are considered newcomers.

Permanent Residents are those individuals who have been living
in the community since before the development of the crab fishery.
These individuals are often influenced by a different set of values
and goals than the other groups. They are a minority in the community today, and in terms of ethnicity they are predominantly Aleut.

Until recently, the interaction between the resident and transient populations was characterized as inconsequential. Outside
fishermen were regarded as troublemakers who would come to the
community to get drunk and get into fights. Despite the fact that
these fishermen would patronize local businesses, many local residents resented the fact that the bulk of earnings from the fishing
industry would not remain in the community and outside fishermen
became a convenient target for their ire. With respect to the
processing workers, interaction has traditionally been minimal.
Most of these transients were housed on the Amaknak Island in
facilities provided by the processors. Until the construction of
the bridge linking Unalaska to Amaknak Island in 1979, residents
would rarely see transient processing personnel, other than those
from the Pan Alaska plant. The inability to speak English of many
processing employees who were Vietnamese or Filipino also added to
the perceived social distance between residents and transients.

While there appears to be some animosity toward outside
fishermen, relations between resident and transient members of the
community have improved in the past few years. This is largely due
to two factors. One has been the trend toward longer stays of
transients in Unalaska. The extended fishing season due to declining crab stocks has created an incentive for fishermen to move to
Unalaska with their families. The processing crews have also
become more stable, partly because of the poor economic conditions
in the continental U.S. and partly because of the incentives provided by the processors through stock options and bonuses.

A second factor promoting improved relations between resident
and transient segments of the population is the increased frequency
of contact. With the construction of the bridge between Unalaska
and Amaknak islands, interaction between the residents of the two

areas has increased. Processing workers are now able to utilize
the stores, restaurants, and businesses on the Unalaska side.
Interaction between the two groups also occurs in the form of
recreational activities such as basketball and softball.

Interaction between permanent and semi-permanent residents
appears to be more tenuous. Within the last ten years, "strangers"
has become an important social category and many of the old-time
residents lament the diminished utility of traditional networks of
association and interaction.

3.2.2.2. **Ethnic Groups.** The second major distinction found
in the sociocultural organization of the community is that between
Aleut and non-Aleut. Although Unalaska has not been regarded as a
"Native community" for a number of years, until recently, Aleuts
represented the majority of the local population. A tradition of
racial discrimination and forced evacuation of Aleuts from the area
during World War II created the potential for hostile relations
between Aleuts and non-Aleuts. Additionally, ethnicity has become
a major issue within the last ten years, as a result of two particular developments. The first was the passage of the Alaska Native
Claims Settlement Act in 1971. The impact of this act on the reaffirmation of traditional Aleut ethnic identity has already been
discussed in the examination of value systems in Unalaska. We can
note here, however, that with this reaffirmation, ethnicity has
become polarized in the community, creating at times rigid boundaries between Aleut and non-Aleut where none may have existed
before. It would be unfair to characterize all Aleut-non-Aleut
relations as being affected by this one piece of legislation, but
both segments of the population readily acknowledge the tension
generated by this legislation and its political and economic ramifications.

The second development has been the rapid increase of the non-
Aleut segment of the local population. Since the time of the
Russian explorers and traders, Aleuts have been dominated politically and economically by non-Aleuts even though they constituted
the large majority of the population in the region. Although the
passage of ANCSA helped rectify this situation, the recent influx
of non-Aleut residents to Unalaska has resulted in increased pressure on Aleuts to reassert their traditional ethnic identity. Many
feel their traditional language and culture are rapidly disappearing and attribute high levels of alcoholism and depression to
the rapid encroachment of the larger sociocultural system. This
encroachment is most visibly represented in the large number of
non-Aleut immigrants. The effect of this encroachment has been
widespread. It is estimated that there are somewhere between
eleven and fifteen individuals left in the community who can speak
Aleut. A generation gap exists between older adults desiring to
retain traditional beliefs and values, younger adults who wish to
maintain an Aleut identity for political reasons among others, and
the youngest generation which is most exposed to the values and
beliefs of the larger sociocultural system, especially through
participation in the local school system.

As a result of these developments there is some voluntary
segregation, even among younger-age school children. Non-Aleuts
express resentment at control of local land by the Native corpora-

tion, claiming that the corporation has acted as a barrier to growth and development. Aleuts, on the other hand, express resentment at the perceived continuation of non-Aleut domination of community affairs. Many older residents prefer to associate only with members of their own ethnic group. Interethnic relationships are common and occur in the form of friendships, marriages and workplace relationships. Most of the local Aleut population is self-employed, work in blue collar positions, or are employed by the Ounalashka Corporation. Non-Aleut employers report that they are often reluctant to hire Aleuts because of lack of adequate skills and a history of poor work attendence.

3.2.2.3 Kin-Based Relations.

In addition to the two major dimensions of length of residence and ethnicity, several other features of the sociocultural dimension are used to divide the population into segments of association and interaction. Social interaction and association are based on a series of primary and secondary networks.

Unalaska is an unusual community with respect to the transient nature of much of it's population. As a result, kinship ties are much stronger among some parts of the population than others. There are a large number of individuals who have no kin in the community or no kin relationships outside of spouse and children. The largest kinship networks are found among the permanent residents of the community, the majority of whom are Aleut. Historically, there has been a good deal of intermarriage between Aleut families, both within Unalaska and between Unalaska and neighboring Aleut villages. Consequently, there is an extensive network of relationships. These relationships are important in determining behavior and serve as a focus for interaction across a broad range of contexts from political and economic to highly personal ones. The Aleut population of Unalaska should not be thought of as a historically contiguous, homogenous one however. Because of economic and ecological conditions before World War II, wartime relocation to southeastern Alaska, and subsequent resettlement after the war, a significant number of Aleut individuals and families originally from other villages on Unalaska Island and residents from other villages in the region settled in Unalaska.

Traditional Aleut society was based on a matrilineal descent system with the preferred form of marriage being between cross-cousins. In Unalaska today, descent could be better characterized as bilateral or unilineal, although for older residents, one of the vestiges of the matrilineal system was the special relationship between mother's brother and sister's son. Boys were often sent to live with their maternal uncles for brief periods of time. The uncles were responsible for instructing them in certain traditional subsistence activities and, in general, seeing to their welfare. This practice does not appear to be common among younger Aleuts today, however.

Among Aleuts there are four fictive kin relationships still quite strong in their ability to influence behavior: the two most important were atcha and kroosna relations. Atcha is a reciprocal relationship between individuals of any age and is assigned in a number of ways. The primary obligation of the relationship is to protect each other's interests and reputation: to see that the

other person gets a fair deal in exchanges and to defend his or her
honor in the atcha partner's absence. Atchas are sometimes assigned
at birth based on physical resemblance or personality characteristics. If a child bears a resemblance to another, for instance,
they are assigned by elder kin members as atchas. Two adults who
share a bond of friendship can agree to become atchas, and at times
two individuals are assigned to be each other's atchas by a third
person who sees either a similarity between the two or a good
reason the two should enter into the relationship.

Atcha relationships were not merely dyads. If one person was
an atcha of a second person, who in turn was an atcha of a third
person, the first and third person would also be considered atchas.
In this manner, a network of fictive kin relations encompassed the
entire Aleut community.

The kroosna relationship is a godparent relationship under the
auspices of the Russian Orthodox Church. Historically, godparents
had a much larger role in the raising of children than they do
today, and reportedly were the objects of both respect and fear.
It was their reponsibility to see that the child was brought up in
the ways of the church, and with this responsibility came the
authority to act contrary to the wishes of the parents, should the
need arise. Even today, kroosnas are the objects of special attention and consideration on special occasions.

Two other traditional Aleut relationships were chusa and
ungtassee. Chusa relations were very informal and were held by
individuals who possessed the same first name but were not directly
related. These individuals usually came from different communities
in the Aleutian Islands and relations were established when one
individual visited the community of another possessing the same
name. Chusa usually provided the basis for friendship, and sometimes food and shelter. Ungtassee were business associates or
partners. The term originally was used to describe the close,
mutually dependent association between hunting partners who owned
one baidarka. It is still used by a few local Aleuts to describe
business associates between whom a strong bond of friendship
exists.

Among the non-Aleut permanent residents of the community generational depth is lacking. While there are some extended families,
there are no families where the original generation that moved to
Unalaska is not represented by at least one surviving individual.

Among semi-permanent residents and even long-term transients
there are a small but significant number of consanguineal (blood)
kin relations. As a "frontier town" there have been a number of
father-son and brother-brother dyads that have come to the community to work together. With the isolated nature of the community,
business relations with kin has proven to be an adaptive response
to a situation where good help is reportedly hard to find, and the
undertaking of an economic investment is a potentially high risk
situation where the reliability of a partner is a great asset. In
other cases, two adult generations of a family have come into the
community, one at the recommendation of the other. Although the
two generations may participate in different economic activities,
they spend a good deal of time together in social interactions.

Patterns of family structure within Unalaska must be viewed in

terms of Aleut and non-Aleut families. Aleut families were traditionally extended networks with affinal ties to other communities
in the region maintained through well-established patterns of
intermarriage. Although many of these networks remain, extended
kinship has declined in importance in Unalaska. The focus of
family relations has shifted to the nuclear family and although
extended kin still constitute the major network for social interaction, this network has begun to diminish in importance in recent
years under pressure from the larger sociocultural system.
Traditional patterns of reciprocity and redistribution have been
seriously weakened as values and attitudes have assumed more of an
individualistic and less of a collective orientation.

Parent-child relations within the Aleut nuclear family are
characterized by a particular fondness for and extreme tolerance of
infants. However, there is an increasing indifference on the part
of parents as children grow older, reportedly resulting in an
increasing incidence of child abuse. Involvement in the education
of children has also diminished over the years as this task is now
almost exclusively handled by the local school system.

One of the major problems confronting the Aleut family is the
generation gap. The incidence of alcoholism and spouse and child
abuse in Aleut families have become the objects of considerable
local concern. These problems weaken family structure and have
contributed to a high number of single parent households among the
Aleuts in Unalaska. Although several factors contribute to this
state of affairs, the willingness of younger family members to
adopt the values and beliefs of the larger sociocultural system to
the disdain of their parents plays a crucial part. Parents complain of a lack of respect from their children, both for their own
authority and for traditional values and beliefs. Children, on the
other hand, complain that their parents are too "old fashioned" and
are unwilling to make the necessary adjustments to survive in the
changing sociocultural environment. The problem of alcoholism
within families is a result in part of the loss of traditional
status and the inability to adjust to the new environment. The
problem, through socialization, has also become intergenerational
(i.e., transferred from parents to children through imitative
behavior.)

Relations among non-Aleut families tend to be exclusively
centered on the nuclear family. The non-Aleut permanent resident
families are involved with several different enterprizes, and account for a disproportionately large segment of the economic
activity in the community. One of the families owns the majority
of the privately held land in the community and a retail business,
another owns a fishing boat and is involved in several other ventures. Others are or have been involved in various investments
from ranching to transportation services. Few non-Aleut adult
permanent residents have spent the entirety of their childhood in
Unalaska.

Among the non-Aleut population, the number of single parent
households is also increasing in conformance with national trends.
The major family structure among semi-permanent residents, however,
is a young married couple without children. Of those recent immigrants and those projected to immigrate to the community within the

next few years, unattached young adults and young married couples will comprise the overwhelming majority.

3.2.2.4 **Neighborhood Relations.** In the past, there was little sense of neighborhood relations in Unalaska independent of other relationships. Until very recently there was only one neighborhood in all of Unalaska, though as construction and growth have taken place, the geosocial map of the community has changed dramatically. The large majority of new housing is located away from the city center in new neighborhoods or in relatively isolated locations. With this growth, neighborhood identification, if not interaction, is growing in importance.

Until the recent population boom, the vast majority of the individuals in Unalaska lived in what is now the Unalaska side downtown area. Prior to World War II, most of these residents were Aleut. After the war, a new area of housing was added, forming a sub-neighborhood adjacent to the existing housing. This was composed of two rows of cabanas, located perpendicular to the Iliuliuk River across from the community center. Housing primarily individuals from the other villages on the island that resettled in Unalaska, the area was known as "new town". The individuals who moved from the other villages were distinguished as outsider Aleuts. As time has passed, much of the distinction has faded, though it has not disappeared completely.

With recent development, the Aleuts come into daily contact with the rest of the community. This area is the center of the city's commercial and recreational activities and thus draws a considerable amount of traffic. This traffic serves to weaken the sense of neighborhood for Aleuts living in the area by placing them in constant contact with "strangers" as well as exposing them to intoxicated patrons of nearby bars.

Adjacent to the downtown area, though physically separated, is another housing area composed primarily of HUD housing discussed earlier. These fifteen homes, occupied exclusively by Aleuts (or Aleuts and their non-Aleut spouses or kin) effectively form a new neighborhood. Ethnically homogenous, the development is removed from the traffic of the downtown area. Though this might be classed a "low income" neighborhood, there appears to be no stigma attached to living in the development, which may in part be due to a lack of class differentiation based on wealth in the community and in part due to the fact that the new housing is superior in construction and appearance to much of the existing housing.

Nirvana Hill forms a neighborhood of sorts. The bulk of the property on the hill was purchased by a group of friends who originally came to the area to fish and have since sold portions of the property to individuals whom they know. Most of the social ties are based on friendship, and no longer run along occupational lines. A minimal number of kinship ties exist.

The new housing development in Unalaska Valley forms another new neighborhood. The individuals who have built the recently constructed homes that form the neighborhood are mostly professional level individuals. Interaction due to the proximity of housing is reportedly minimal; however, some of these individuals interact in other contexts. Due to the economic status of most residents and the relatively expensive homes, the area is sometimes sarcastically refered to as "snob hill". It is perhaps the first example of a concentrated area of geosocial differentiation based on wealth in Unalaska.

The Ski Bowl area is another area of relatively concentrated housing. At one point, when the cabanas were first being reoccupied, many of the individuals worked for the Department of Public Works, and therefore had cross-cutting occupational and residential ties. As time has passed, these employees have scattered to housing elsewhere, and the individuals living on Ski Bowl now work at a variety of jobs and belong to a variety of social networks.

On Amaknak Island, outside of the processors, there are two clusters of housing that could be considered neighborhoods: Standard Oil Hill and Strawberry Hill. Standard Oil Hill is composed of rental duplexes, and the tenants that live there are a broad spectrum of individuals with respect to occupation, background, and social interests. As an area of heavy population concentration there are a number of social ties that exist within the neighborhood that are based on relationships other than residential proximity. There are peer group relationships between some of the children in the area, and some differentiation of living arrangements by occupation. The area is quite transient due to the high rent and the transient nature of a major portion of the population of Unalaska. It is the only large concentration of rental housing, and the high turn-over rates effect the growth of neighborhood-based social ties.

Strawberry Hill is another area of concentrated housing forming a neighborhood. It has been described as the only area with a "true feeling of neighborhood" outside of the downtown Unalaska area. Some residents have lived in the same place over a number of years, and a core group of individuals form a relatively stable housing cluster with social ties between the neighbors that apparently were originally based on residential proximity.

3.2.2.5 **Voluntary Associations**. Voluntary social organizations form the basis for significant social interactions primarily for semi-permanent residents and long-term transients. There are several organizations sponsored by the city of Unalaska. These include the Unalaska Volunteer Fire Department, and the Volunteer Emergency Medical Service. These organizations serve as the focus of interaction for some individuals in the community, though a large percentage of their ranks are made up of professional public safety officers volunteering their time.

Recreational organizations draw a good level of participation from many segments of the community. One of the most popular is the recreational softball league. This past summer the league was composed of twelve teams sponsored by a number of the small businesses in town, one of the churches, and several of the seafood processors. The softball league is reportedly one of the only activities that brings a wide range of individuals in the community into contact with one another outside of the usual social networks. The city basketball league is a wintertime version of the softball league, performing the same social function. One of the higher visibility recreational groups in Unalaska is the square dance group, whose members perform at quite a few of the civic functions.

The only formal service clubs in Unalaska at this time are the recently organized Lions Club, with fifty-one male charter members, and an all women's Chamber of Commerce (formed in part as an counterpart to the Lion's Club). The Unalaska Aleut Development Corporation performs several social service club style functions, and draws participation from beyond it's staff and shareholders.

One of the most recently formed voluntary associations in Unalaska is the local chapter of the Alaska Native Women's Statewide Organization. Membership is open to all women in the community and currently numbers seventy-five Unalaska. The objectives of the organization include: (1) administering to the health, educational and cultural needs of native women; (2) improvement of home, family, and community life; (3) provide events that promote cross-cultural communication; (4) work towards preventing domestic violence among local families; and (5) promoting ethnic pride and preserving cultural tradition. The organization is based on a network of women in the community, many of whom are also linked by extended kin ties, who represent an increasingly powerful political voice in Unalaska. It is highly likely that the organization also will become the functional equivalent of the now defunct Sisterhood of the Russian Orthodox church, which was an organization that performed many social services for Aleut families, along with serving as an important social group for the women involved.

The churches of the community form the basis for many of the most active social networks. Although the Russian Orthodox church does not perform this function as explicitly as it did in the past, members of the congregation have many cross-cutting ties that facilitate their interaction as a social network. The most explicit of the network forming churches is the Unalaska Christian Fellowship which seeks to incorporate new and old members of the community into it's ranks and also brings in individuals from outside of the community to Unalaska to perform community service work and help build the congregation. The Fellowship provides numerous opportunities for social interaction, in addition to religious activities, including picnics, pot-luck dinners and sporting events. Much of this network is based on extended family relationships but includes newcomers, members of the local Catholic mission, and processing personnel as well. It also appears that the network has been used by some of the recent immigrants to find employment.

3.2.2.6 **Workplace Relations.** Relations between crew members on the fishing boats that work the area are highly variable by vessel. On vessels owned by permanent residents of the community, the crew tends to be drawn from among family members where possible, and then along extended kinship and friendship lines as needed, though ability as a fisherman is always a major consideration irrespective of ties of kinship or friendship. Relaxation of standards of course applies where young sons are being trained in the business.

On vessels owned by semi-permanent residents there are two distinct hiring patterns. Some of the skippers hire locally, employing interested and available kin in addition to using friendship networks to locate available and competent crew. Others hire their crew exclusively out of Seattle. The cited advantage of hiring crew from outside of the community is to keep the crew relations on a more formal basis, allowing more freedom of action when it comes to hiring and firing decisions.

The vast majority of the fishing vessels in the fleet in the waters around Unalaska are not locally owned or operated. The bulk of the fleet is based in Seattle and most of the crew members are hired there, though they come from a diversity of backgrounds and from a variety of places around the country and the world. Most of the crew members are young, especially those in the crab fleet. Crab fishing is considered a young man's occupation because of the agility and quickness required under adverse fishing conditions. Fishing vessels are also treated by some as an avenue of escape from financial, personal, or legal responsibilities elsewhere.

The rate of turnover of fishing crews is also highly variable by vessel and appears to depend upon the personality of the skipper, profitability of the vessel, and the crew share percentages offered. Social factors that come into play are the operating dynamics of the crew and the goals of individual crew members. Life aboard the relatively small boats in cramped quarters with fatigue common can be a very trying experience for many people. If the crew members are unable to get along with one another the situation can quickly become intolerable. The lifestyle forced by the nature of the fishing industry is hard on the family life of many of the crew members, and many leave the fishery, at least for a period of time, because of personal relationship difficulties. Some of the crew members have very specific goals which, once attained, means their departure from the fishery. At times vessels are left short-handed after such departures, and even boats that usually do not hire out of Unalaska take on temporary crew from the community. Most vessels spend little time in the community, though this is changing as the result of current economic conditions.

Workplace, or occupational relations vary in importance by social group in Unalaska. Among permanent residents, many of whom are entrepreneurs or have held a wide variety of jobs in the community over the years, workplace relations do not form a central focus for social networks. Social relationships among these people are multi-dimensional with cross-cutting ties, though less so than in the past. Typically, length of residence in the community is inversely related to the significance placed upon occupational social networks as primary social arenas. Exceptions to this rule are certain occupational groups which have formed strong social bonds for a number of reasons. These include teachers and public safety officers among others.

For the long-term transients, workplace relations are the prime focus of social life. As mentioned above, long-term transients usually have a specific goal, external to the community. This being the case, a great deal of time and effort is directed toward achieving this goal and the individuals could easily be seen as "workaholics". Such behavior is understood in Unalaska however and not considered unusual, though it at times places strain on family relationships.

For transient workers, the only extensive contact with the community is usually through employment. Working long hours and long weeks during the fishing seasons and living in company group housing, the workers by fatigue and often by choice are effectively isolated from the community. Another important factor in this isolation is ethnicity. Different ethnic groups dominate the work-force at the different processors, and a significant portion of the workers at each of the processors speak little or no English, which effectively reinforces the isolation from the community. Largely independent social networks are formed at the different processing companies, which overlap only slightly with other social networks. Most of the processors employ a large number of individuals only from any one ethnic group. In the recent past there have been disturbances with the disputing groups drawn along ethnic lines and management feels it prudent to try and avoid these situations. One force tying the various workplace networks together is the move toward unionization that is gaining momentum. The International Longshoremen's and Warehousemen's Union has successfully organized. The group is providing a measure of overlap between the various workplaces, though at the individual level social contacts have not increased significantly in many cases.

3.2.2.7 **External Social Networks.** Many people of Unalaska have important social ties to other areas of the state. For some of the Aleuts of the community there are important kinship ties to the other villages in the region, notably Nikolski and Akutan on neighboring Aleutian islands, and the villages of St. Paul and St. George in the Pribilof Islands. Several spouses of Unalaska Aleuts are from these villages. For a few Aleut families in Unalaska, these ties have been maintained by reciprocol exchanges of subsis-tence items such that seal meat and oil is sent from the Pribilof Islands communities to Unalaska and salmon is sent to the Pribilofs in return. Additionally, several families have relatives in Anchorage. Visits to the other villages are not uncommon, particu-larly for marriages and funerals. These ties appear to have dimi-nished in intensity in the past decade, however, and while certain kinship links still exist, patterns of reciprocity and social interaction are much less evident.

In the past, ties with other communities in the region were also created by employment opportunities. Before the recent crab boom, many Unalaska Aleuts would journey each year to the Pribilof Islands to work in the seal harvests and, later, to King Cove to work at a cannery during the salmon fishing season. During the early 1970s, a few residents from Akutan and the Pribilof Islands would come to Unalaska to work on the processors, but this is no longer the case. The development of educational facilities and economic opportunities in other communities in the region have reduced the need for travel to Unalaska by residents of these communities.

With the coming of the ANCSA corporations there has been an increased awareness of the region as a social unit. Corporation business of both the Aleut Corporation and the Aleutian/Priblof Islands Association often necessitates contact between villages in the region, at least on the part of the management of the corpora-tions, which has fostered new regional social networks.

For some non-Aleut residents of Unalaska involved in the fishing industry there are social ties to individuals in the fishing industry in the region, most notably Akutan. The superin-tendents of both of the shore-based processors in Akutan and many of the upper level workers were formerly employed in Unalaska. Individuals who fish some seasons in different parts of the state develop social ties in those areas. Other non-Aleut residents have social ties to Anchorage and a few have ties to other communities in the state, though typically the individuals moving to Unalaska come directly from out of state. City administration officials have social ties to Juneau and Anchorage as a result of the need to work with individuals in those cities.

Most of the individuals involved with the fishery have social ties to the Pacific Northwest, especially the city of Seattle. Most the the processing companies and the vessels of the fishing fleet are based there, and the individuals hired by these companies were hired out of this region. Processing employees are literally from around the world with strong and important ties still existing for some in such places as the Philippines and Southeast Asia.

3.2.3 Political Organization

3.2.3.1 Local Affairs. Local political affairs are dominated by two institutions. The first is the city government, consisting of the city manager, various city officials, the city council and mayor, and associated agencies and offices. These positions are almost totally dominated by non-Aleuts. The second important institution from a political standpoint in the community is the local Aleut profit corporation, the Ounalashka Corporation. Although the corporation is not a political institution per se, in its attempt to meet the proprietary economic needs of its shareholders, it has occasionally come into conflict with the city administration over specific development issues.

The current political structure is a reflection of historical circumstances as well as current sociocultural conditions. Since the establishment of Unalaska as a trading center by the Russians in the late eighteeenth century, and the consolidation of residents of other villages on Unalaska Island at the site of the Aleut village of Iliuliuk, there has always been two distinct but co-existing forms of government, one dominated by the Natives and the other by the non-Natives. Although the village council held authority over the Aleut population of Unalaska, the real power lay in the hands of non-Native institutions. This state of affairs underwent a significant change in 1971 with the enactment of the Alaska Native Claims Settlement Act and the eventual formation of the Ounalashka Corporation. Although responsible for the management of land reconveyed to the Aleut population, the Ounalashka Corporation has been called upon to take an increasingly political role as it seeks to protect the interests of its shareholders.

A second factor contributing to this division of power is the fact that even though there are more Aleuts in Unalaska than in any other town in the Aleutian chain, they are nonetheless a minority of the total population. This is a unique situation for the Aleutians, and one result has been a tendency for the Aleut population to withdraw, both socially and politically. Unalaska Aleuts are often characterized, usually by non-Aleuts, as politically apathetic, but much of this is certainly a result of the suddenness with which the population became a minority of the total city population during the days of the crab boom, and of the vigor and assurance with which outside non-Aleuts assumed positions of power. Only with the economic, and resulting political, clout conferred by ANCSA did the Aleut population begin to regain some of its self-confidence.

The structure of leadership in Unalaska is organized along certain well-defined lines. The municipal government is dominated by recently arrived outside professionals. These are usually people who have been in Unalaska for only a few years and who, in all probability, will remain in town for only five years or so. This group is not committed to permanent residence in Unalaska (with certain individual exceptions) but is using the experience gained in Unalaska as a stepping stone to positions in other urban areas in the United States. They are development-oriented and appear, whether consciously or not, to be the spokesmen of the commercial interests in town, despite the often sharp conflict between the city administration and local industry on short-term development issues. On the other hand, the Aleut community is in a state of transition with respect to leadership. With the formation of the Native corporation, Aleut leaders have concentrated on that structure and abdicated most positions in the municipal institutions. The Aleut leadership cadre is currently in transition from the traditional leaders to more militant younger leaders.

This division between the city government and the Ounalashka Corporation is usually centered on specific issues regarding community development. The corporation, though they own most of the land in Unalaska, cannot afford to subsidize a new subdivision. One reason for this, as perceived by the corporation, is that with increasing bureaucratization and regulation the city has enacted legal restrictions requiring an investment of between twelve and twenty thousand dollars in a lot before selling it. Restrictions include surveying work, assurance that the property meets all the requirements for which it is zoned, and so on. The corporation has had difficulty obtaining funds for subdividing their property from a bank because they cannot meet all the regulatory restrictions. Thus, the Ounalashka Corporation perceives the city as standing in the way of its development enterprises. For its part, the city argues that it has a statutory obligation to regulate such activities. The perception of the city on this issue is that the Ounalashka Corporation seems to feel that the public at large has the responsibility of improving corporation-owned land for the corporation's benefit.

While disputes such as this are often exaggerated by the rhetoric of the opposing institutions, it should be kept in mind that the source of this conflict is disagreement over the costs and benefits of future development, not over the future of Unalaska which is assumed as a given. Far from detracting efforts at community development, most participants seem to regard such conflict as the essance of community development and consider that there is no risk that delay associated with such conflict might retard the developmental process. This is consistent with the underlying attitude that the determinants of economic development are external in nature and not under the control of any local group or coalition of groups.

There also are other potential political forces in the community besides the municipal government and the Native corporation. The processors are a potentially powerful political force, but as of yet they appear to lack integration and common purpose. There are signs this is beginning to change, however, as they are forced by economic necessity to coordinate their production activities. A second potential political faction is centered on the Unalaska Christian Fellowship. This group, along with other non-Aleuts in Unalaska, has been the motive force behind the creation of the Citizens for Responsive Government, a citizens' watchdog committee concerned with what it perceives as the inordinate growth of city government, particularly law enforcement, in the last decade. Women in the community are also a potential political force. Women administrators and managers are a visible representation of this. The Alaska Native Women's Statewide Organization is becoming a focus of this political power.

3.2.3.2 **Native Corporations/Associations.** The Native Corporation was established with the passage of the Alaska Native Claims Settlement Act (ANCSA) of 1971. Under the conditions of the Act, local and regional Native corporations were organized to manage the property claims of all Native residents of Alaska. The regional organization which includes Unalaska is the Aleut Corporation and the local organization is the Ounalashka Corporation. There are also two non-profit Native associations represented in Unalaska. They are the regional Aleutian/ Pribilof Islands Association and the local Unalaska Aleut Development Corporation.

The Aleut Corporation owns all subsurface rights to lands held by the local corporation. If such land is unavailable, the regional corporation may claim surface estates (as when the local corporation claims land in a federal preserve). Village corporation shareholders are also shareholders in the regional corporation. The Ounalashka Corporation was founded in 1973 and has 265 shareholders, 150 of whom live in Unalaska. It employs about fifteen people year-round, though the number varies slightly seasonally, and oversees about ninety-six percent of the available land in the area.

The major source of income for the Ounalashka Corporation is derived from long-term leasing of land to commercial interests and local residents. Its chief goal is economic efficiency and land investment is seen as the key to the future of the Aleut segment of the community. The Ounalashka Corporation has also acted to remodel over forty World War II vintage housing units on Standard Oil Hill but, given the high rents ($1000. or more per month) that must be charged in order to realize a profit, it has not been regarded as a worthwhile investment, even though rentals provide the major source of income for the corporation at present. The corporation also rents lots on Strawberry Hill and Ski Bowl for $150 per month and individuals must provide their own housing. The corporation appears to be unwilling to invest in the commercial fishing and processing industry because it is seen as too great a risk. Land is regarded as being the only real asset because it provides a steady income, involves little or no additional investment, and the person leasing the property usually improves it. The corporation has negotiated with Chevron U.S.A. to operate a gas station in the community.

The Unalaska Aleut Development Corporation is the local non-profit Native corporation in the community. It currently administers four government grants to fund: 1) a project to restore the Russian Orthodox Church in Unalaska, 2) the restoration of the Bishop's House, 3) Aleut education programs, and 4) operating expenses for the corporation itself. The UADC's major problem is that it possesses no revenues of its own and must rely on external funding or the generosity of the Ounalashka Corporation for its existence. This has led to some friction between the OC and the UADC, particularly since the building in which the UADC is housed is rented from the OC. The two groups also have different perspectives on the best way to improve the quality of life for the Aleut community. While the OC places its emphasis on economic efficiency, with the long range goal of financial returns for stockholders, and pragmatic education of Aleut shareholders with respect to their stock before 1991 when shares may be sold, the UADC is concerned with improving the quality of life through cultural enrichment and Aleut-oriented educational programs.

According to the provisions of ANCSA, the shareholders will have the right to sell shares publically in 1991. One of the fears of many Aleuts is that the corporation will not be successful in organizing its affairs enough to turn a large profit by then. If by that time the Corporation is not making money for its shareholders the danger is that the shareholders will be tempted to sell to outside interests rather than hold on to seemingly worthless stock. Many fear the Japanese interests who they feel are waiting in the wings for the shares to become available to the public. Oil companies are also the subject of similar rumors, and many feel they will also attempt to buy up shares when they become publically available.

The Ounalashka Corporation and the Aleut Corporation have joined together in a development project called Dutch Harbor Development. The American Presidents Line docking facility was constructed by the two Native corporations, with the OC owning fifty-one percent and the Aleut Corporation owning forty-nine percent. The facility is leased to APL for $30 million. Panama Marine, a subsidiary of the Aleut Corporation, has renovated the World War II sub dock, leased from the Ounalashka Corporation, on Amaknak Island and operates it as a marine repair facility.

3.2.3.3 **Municipal Government.** The other community-wide political organizations in Unalaska are associated with the municipal government. Unalaska was incorporated as a first class city in 1942. It is run by a city council and city manager. The city council members are elected for three year terms. There are six members. The mayor is elected separately from the council. Although he attends city council meetings, the mayor is a nonvoting member except in the case of a tie. His position is generally regarded as a figurehead office.

The city government is broken down into Administration, Public Safety, Public Works, Planning, and Parks, Culture and Recreation. The total number of city employees varies seasonally, but the average is between forty-five and fifty. Revenues are currently generated through a property tax, use tax (including a one percent sales and use tax), shared state revenues, state grants, and fees and permits. The FY82 budget was $4.1 million in the General Fund alone.

The City Council has established a set of priorities for the future development of the community. These priorities reflect the interests of the commercial, and basically non-Aleut, sector of the community. Priorities for FY84 capital project requests to the State Legislature were: 1) Unalaska airport expansion (on-shore improvements), 2) Phase II Water System improvements, 3) vocational education facility, 4) boat harbor expansion/relocation, 5) multi-purpose community recreation facility, and 6) public safety facility.

The Planning Commission is seen as sympathic to the commercial interests in the community. One of the priorities of the city council strongly supported by the Planning Commission is the expansion of the airport. This expansion was included in one of the DOT/PF draft capital programs and an appropriation of $4.5 million in State funds and authorization for expenditure of up to $45 million in federal funds has been included in the FY84 budget. The local electorate also approved the taking out of a general obligation bond for the construction of a new terminal.

Despite these planned improvements, there is resistence to airport expansion by a significant portion of the population, especially those who are not involved in processing or fishing activities. They are particularly concerned that the expansion is primarily for the benefit of fishing and processing interests, but that these interests are mostly outsiders. Many local residents feel they are being asked to pay for improvements which they do not really need and which will benefit people who are assuming none of the financial burden. City officials argue, however, that the facility could be self-supporting if well-managed.

Another local political issue concerns the size of the city government itself. According to a former mayor of Unalaska, the city administration has become too top-heavy. Much of this is ascribed to ill-advised expansion during the period of the crab boom. Now that the boom period has passed the city possesses a large bureaucratic and administrative apparatus which may not be necessary for existing needs. At the same time there is no question that the city will likely continue to grow, and if oil or groundfish industry development occurs what appears to be a top-heavy structure may turn out to be a brilliant case of pre-adaptation.

Another source of controversy has been the recent efforts of the Citizens for Responsive Government to call attention to the supposedly extravagant salaries of certain city officials. At the heart of this controversy was a proposal to convert the department heads from the classified service to contract employees. A significant provision in the agreements was a termination for convenience clause (the current policy requires cause). The proposed agreements were rejected by the council in February, 1982 and one incumbant has since resigned. The remainder continue in the classified service.

3.2.3.4 **Social Control and Crime.** The Department of Public Safety is responsible for the protection of property and lives in the community. The DPS consists of three administrative divisions: police, volunteer fire department, and Emergency Medical Services. Full time personnel include the chief, seven police officers, a police division commander, a fire department division commander, an EMS director, four corrections officers, and a clerk typist (City of Unalaska 1981:2). The fire department consists of two companies, one based on Amaknak Island and one on Unalaska Island, each with thirteen volunteers. There is also an Emergency Dive team. The DPS assumes a sizeable proportion of the City budget with $613,491 allocated for police protection in 1981, $102,999 for fire protection, and $25,608 for EMS (City of Unalaska 1981:17). The 1982 budget for the entire Department of Public Safety in the General Fund was $751,788. The revised FY83 budget was $960,832 and the approved FY84 budget is $937,998.

The police powers of the city actually extend only to the city limits, although the DPS is often involved in emergency medical action or search and rescue for a much larger area. In addition to the DPS, law enforcement services are provided by an Alaska State trooper, stationed in Unalaska since late 1981. There are also two State Fish and Wildlife Protection Officers in Unalaska who possess certain police powers, although they are generally concerned only with fish and game violations.

The police department is located in the center of Unalaska. The station consists of a waiting room, a squad room, office, and a small kitchen. The Unalaska jail, located in the same building, contains three cells designed to separate women and juveniles from male prisoners. However, the facility has, in the past, been overcrowded during the king and tanner crab seasons. The facility also is used to house prisoners being transported from other Aleutian jurisdictions to Anchorage pending completion of travel arrangements.

Police equipment includes eight late-model patrol vehicles with portable FM radios with telephone capability, a 17-foot Boston whaler for search and rescue operations, and a 1980 modular ambulance (Alaska Consultants 1981:61).

Criminal activity in Unalaska adheres to a pattern which is typical both of a frontier environment and a "boom town." Much of this activity is related to the use and abuse of alcoholic beverages. According to the local magistrate, the nature of criminal activity in Unalaska has changed somewhat in the last few years. When the crab boom began there was considerable public violence, especially alcohol-related assaults and fights. The next stage was an increase in rapes and robberies. Finally, families began to move in as the boom became institutionalized, and with them came a demand for greater police protection. This was the phase which led to the rapid growth of the police department from one to sixteen officers. Professional people began to move in and demand further protection. Once the boom began to wane there was a decrease in assaults and theft and an increase in civil suits.

Nonetheless, the level of criminal activity in Unalaska is remarkably high for a community its size. In 1981, the police department responded to over 13,200 calls for assistance. The most

Table 3.3

Criminal Cases by Year, 1979-81,
City of Unalaska

Category	Year 1979	Year 1980	Year 1981
Total Cases	224	655	756
Homicides	2	0	2
Burglary	13	31	31
Assaults	66	87	72
Theft	28	78	86
Sex Crimes	1	4	9

Source: City of Unalaska 1981:3.

serious crimes are assaults, rapes, burglaries, and thefts. As
indicated by Table 3.3, all have undergone significant increases in
the past three years, and almost all, particularly rapes and
assaults, are alcohol-related.

According to the Department of Public Safety Report of 1981:

> 1981 saw a stabilization of prisoners incarcerated in the
> Unalaska safekeeping facility. Prisoner count for 1979 was
> 233, 1980 being 329 and 1981 counted 322. However, it should
> be noted that the actual time served by these prisoners has
> seen a steady increase from 376 in 1979 to 533 in 1980 and a
> record 655 days served in 1981. That is an average of two
> people per day in 1981. Better support from the Court and
> well investigated cases are reflected by these statistics
> (City of Unalaska 1981:4).

The same report notes that in 1981 custody cases included thirty-
four felonies, 302 misdemeanors, and many agency assists. Unalaska
Public Safety Officers also assisted in the arrest of two felons
wanted by U.S. Marshals.

It should be noted that these figures do not seem to support
the contentions of the magistrate reported earlier that assault and
related crimes are declining. However, it should be remembered
that the recent expansion of the Department of Public Safety has
probably resulted in a greater response ability on the part of the
police, with the result that the statistics may have been an artifact of the increased availability of the police to respond to more
calls.

Traffic-related incidents are also on the rise. The DPS
Report for 1981 notes that:

> In 1980 a total of 28 traffic accidents were reported with no
> fatalities. 1981 records show 58 traffic accidents with two
> fatalities. Both fatalities were alcohol-related accidents.

Driving while intoxicated charges in 1980 were 55 with 32
convictions. This year had 38 individuals charged with D.W.I.
and 27 convictions with 4 cases still pending. Regular court
calendars, professional investigation practices and increased
traffic enforcement have resulted in 84% convictions of criminal cases filed. The officers wrote 190 traffic citations and
64 warnings in 1981. This was an increase over the 1980
totals of 127 citations and 34 warnings (City of Unalaska
1981:6).

The department is the focus of a good deal of local controversy. As recently as 1974 there was only one policeman in town
and there were three or four public works employees who occasionally doubled as policemen. Now there are sixteen Public Safety
Officers, trained in law enforcement, firefighting, and emergency
medical care. Some are also trained as search and rescue scuba
divers. Few residents seem neutral, but rather most are either
strongly in favor of the expansion which has occurred or strongly
opposed. Many feel that the department over-expanded during the
period of the crab boom, and now is too large for the city in the
aftermath of that boom.

Faced with several problems the DPS has increased its emphasis
on public relations in the last few years. To combat the problems
of high turnover and the lack of supervisory experience, personnel
have been involved in various training programs. The role of the
department in providing emergency medical services also promotes
goodwill in the community. Much of the hostility against the
police force comes from members of the Aleut community who fear
them because of past experiences with police brutality. In the
past, harassment of Aleut residents by law enforcement officials,
both military and civilian, was common and while there is no indication that such harassment occurs today, many bitter memories
remain. The current administration of the department appears to be
sensitive to these issues and has made progress in allaying these
traditional fears.

The second administrative division of the Department of Public
Safety is the volunteer fire department. The Unalaska Volunteer
Fire Department is housed in two separate stations. The oldest, a
wood frame structure with two bays, is located in Unalaska adjacent
to the Unalaska Creek bridge, while the second, containing a single
bay, is housed in the Unisea Mall complex on Amaknak Island. Fire
protection is provided throughout the road-connected area within
the City's corporate limits, including fish processing vessels tied
to docks along the waterfront.

Firefighting equipment consists of five vehicles: A 1978 quick
response vehicle, a 1946 Dodge truck with a 750 gallons per minute
pumping capacity stationed on Unalaska Island and a second quick
response vehicle, a 1,000 gallon tanker, and a new Crash-Fire-
Rescue truck with a 1,000 gallon water capacity stationed on Amaknak Island. The department also has two portable pumps and a 1,000
gallon holding tank used for pumping and storing water from surface
sources in areas without hydrants (Alaska Consultants 1981:62-63).

Fire calls declined from fifty-two in 1980 to forty-eight in
1981. There was a corresponding drop in dollar loss from $1.2

million in 1979 to $130,000 in 1980 to $94,000 in 1981, largely the result of increased training and equipment and the development of a fire prevention plan. Despite this improved safety record, however, firefighting efforts in Unalaska continue to be plagued by its inadequate hydrant system, particularly on Amaknak Island. This is especially acute during the winter months when water levels are very low. High winds also pose a problem, "particularly in the Unalaska townsite where many buildings are old and close together and where a wind-swept fire could spread rapidly from one unit to another" (Alaska Consultants 1981:63-64).

The court system is represented in Unalaska by a state district court which handles primarily misdemeanors and civil suits under ten thousand dollars. The court hears approximately 300 to 350 misdemeanor cases per year and about forty to fifty felonies. However, since the crab boom has subsided these figures have dropped somewhat, and the court today probably handles two-thirds as many cases as it did a few years ago. The most frequent kinds of case involve assault and theft, and usually these are alcohol-related.

The magistrate handles the day-to-day proceedings of the court, but as yet Unalaska does not have a resident public defender nor is there a district attorney in town. More serious cases must await the judges who come into town on a six week or two month rotation, during which time local residents also have access to public defenders and a district attorney. There is no professional legal service available in town, although there is one paralegal aide. Because of the inadequacies of the legal system, there is a high risk of legal errors resulting in case dismissals.

In addition to formal institutions there are informal social sanctions for the maintenance of social control, particularly on a day-to-day and face-to-face basis. Among the Aleut portion of the community social control appears to be very much an individual affair. There is little social censure for fighting or alcohol abuse. Although there is evidence to suggest that alcoholism on the part of Aleut leaders is the cause of some loss of prestige for these individuals, alcohol abuse and alcohol-related assaults and other criminal behavior do not meet with social censure as a rule. This is not to suggest that the Aleut population is uninterested in the social actions of its members. The fact that Aleut residents are well known to one another and interact with each other frequently over periods of many years means that there is a strong support network available for the individual. It is simply less accepted among this segment of the community that public censure of an individual is justified. Nonetheless, when an individual does become intoxicated or runs into difficulty, there are almost always people ready to take care of him/her and insure that they are safe. Social controls do operate, but they are not aired as publically as would be expected by an outsider.

The Aleut population is more integrated and cohesive than individuals on Amaknak Island which is made up primarily of people from outside the community. There, dependence is much heavier on formal means of social control, largely because of the lack of an integrated social network which would allow for the efficacy of informal controls. Thus, the police and formal agencies are used

with less compunction by this group than is the case with the
Aleuts. The Aleuts generally avoid interaction with the police,
and prefer to settle their difficulties among themselves if possible. The non-Aleut group, however, is very quick to call on
these formal agencies.

3.2.4 Religious Organization

The religious system of Unlaska, in contrast to several other
communities in Alaska, plays a significant role in the tone and
direction of social life for all residents, directly or indirectly.
For the members of the Russian Orthodox Church and the other
denominations, religion is an important locus of social identity
and provides important networks of social interaction. Religion
also plays a role in the provision of certain social services such
as counselling, and is increasingly becoming a factor in the political arena as community residents with similar religious preferences work together to influence the course of community development and affect community policy on various issues.

The great influence of religion on the social system of
Unalaska is largely a product of two different factors. The first
is the community's historic importance as a regional center for the
Russian Orthodox Church. The local church is regarded as one of
the most impressive in Alaska and was the seat of a Russian
Orthodox bishop who administered church activities throughout the
Aleutian and Pribilof Islands. The Russian Orthodox church was a
major institution of the Aleut community and remains a direct link
between the traditional Aleut villages of Unalaska and the present-
day Aleut population of Unalaska. Second, religion is viewed by
many community members as playing a role in the future of the
community. With the increase in social and psychological problems
resulting from the period of rapid economic and population growth,
religion has relevance to local residents as a possible stabilizing
factor. This opinion is not shared by all local residents, however, resulting in the creation of rigid social boundaries.

There are three major components of the religious structure of
Unalaska, each identified with a segment of the local population.
The first component, associated with the traditional Aleut community, is the Russian Orthodox faith and church. The second component, associated with many of the recent non-Aleut immigrants to
the community, is Christianity, most visibly represented in
Unalaska in the Unalaska Christian Fellowship. The third major
component, also associated with a large segment of the non-Aleut
population of Unalaska, is actually nonreligious or secular. This
component is more a state of mind and attitude than it is a set of
institutions and behavior. Each of these three components will be
examined in this section.

3.2.4.1 Russian Orthodox Church. The oldest church in Unalaska
is the Russian Orthodox Church of the Holy Ascension. Since its
original construction in 1820, it has served the religious needs of
the community as well as provided the focus for the identity and
social organization of the Aleut population. Although introduced by
the Russians in the late eighteenth century, it has come to be

regarded as an Aleut institution, with Aleut clergy and Aleut members. Throughout its history, membership in the church was synonomous with residence in the community.

Throughout the years, the role of the church has undergone several different revisions. With the initial conversions to the Russian Orthodox faith, the church in Unalaska served as an intermediary between the Aleut community and the Russian authorities. As noted above, the first Russian Orthodox priest to have visited the community travelled back to Russia in the late eighteenth century to petition the government for better treatment of the Aleuts (Gross and Khera 1980:85). Under the leadership of Ivan Veniaminov, the church became the focal point for an effort to preserve traditional Aleut culture in the face of growing encroachment by Russian traders and the values, attitudes and behavior of the West. At the same time, membership in the church was a badge of 'civilization,' entitling the Aleut members to a measure of respect, or at least a measure of tolerance, from the Russians. The educational system which was an important part of the early church enabled the Aleuts to learn the language and culture of the Russians so that they could improve their own position in terms of dealing with the traders and local authorities. In the American period, the Russian Orthodox church was the focus of Aleut community life. Even during the postwar period, the village council and church council were one and the same and with the decline of Aleut leadership after the community became incorporated as a first-class city, the church became even more important because it was the one institution in which the Aleuts were able to achieve some measure of control over their own lives. The village chief was also the warden of the church and while his political role diminished with the influx of non-Aleuts, his leadership role in the church continued well into the post-war period.

Nowadays, the church plays a somewhat reduced role as the focus for the social organization of the Aleut community. The power and prestige of the church in community affairs has been weakened by the influence of the larger sociocultural system and the growth of the non-Aleut segment of the population in Unalaska on the one hand and increasing secularization among the Aleuts on the other. Nevertheless, the church continues to play an important role as a focus for ethnic identity, particularly in the sense of tying the present community to its past by virtue of the church's status as a national historical landmark, and in the sense of providing them with a set of beliefs, customs, and networks of interaction which distinguish the Aleuts from the non-Aleut residents of Unalaska.

The current church membership is estimated by the Russian Orthodox priest to be somewhere between 175 and 200 people and consists almost exclusively of Aleuts or non-Aleut spouses of Aleut residents. Attendance at weekly services, however, is much smaller, usually ranging in size between twenty and forty members. Those who attend church services on a regular basis are for the most part either older community members or church leaders and their families. The weekly attendance appears to be overrepresented by the old members and the very young. During the holidays, however, particular Christmas and Easter, participation in church activities increases.

Despite the small weekly attendance, belief in the Russian Orthodox faith continues to be strong. Religious icons and crosses, for instance, can still be found in the homes of most of the Aleut residents of Unalaska. Many of the value conflicts affecting the Aleut community are due to the continuing influence of the traditional religious belief system.

There are two types of leaders in the church: religious and secular. The religious leadership is vested in the office of the priest. The local priest has a great deal of influence over the direction in the church in the community and plays a visible role in certain secular aspects of community life as well. In the recent past, the priest has served on the city council and continues to be active in many aspects of community life such as teaching courses in Aleut language and culture.

The priest and his wife are supported by a small salary but both supplement their income by working in other positions as well. It is for this reason that the two are working as teacher's aides in the local school and run the Aleut language and culture program.

Lay leaders are also important to the performance of church services and social activities and are usually individuals who hold leadership positions outside the church. There are two formal offices held by lay leaders in the church. The warden is the caretaker of the church building. It is his responsibility to make certain that the church is open and well-maintained. He is also in charge of hiring new priests when necessary. The president is in charge of church finances. He manages the funds which are obtained from the congregation and sees to it that bills are paid and funds are made available for special purposes such as church festivals and special events. These lay leaders are assisted by a church committee. In recent years, however, the duties of the warden and the church committee have declined and even the current membership of the board is unclear.

In the past, the church also supported a social infrastructure in the form of religious brotherhoods and sisterhoods. Principally fraternal and sororal institutions, these groups usually saw to the welfare of the church itself as well as the entire community. In times of economic hardship or famine, these groups would bring food or provide assistance to needy community members. In the early twentieth century the Unalaska Russian Orthodox Church supported two brotherhoods and one sisterhood. One of the brotherhoods disbanded prior to World War II and the other disappeared shortly after the war. The sisterhood remained in existence until the early 1970s, largely due to the strong leadership of one of the older female Aleuts until her death.

2.2.4.2 **Unalaska Christian Fellowship**. There are different Christian institutions in Unalaska. Historically, a Methodist mission played a major role in the community, operating a local school, small clinic, and the Jesse Lee Home for orphans from 1890 to 1925. The mission was run by the Women's Home Missionary Society of the Methodist Episcopal Church.

The major Christian religious institution in Unalaska today is the Unalaska Christian Fellowship. The Fellowship was an Assembly of God mission for several years. It has been independent from the

Assembly of God denomination for the past two years and currently
maintains a non-denominational status.
   The congregation of the church is an active one, believed to
be somewhere between seventy-five and eighty individuals. It consists of three major components: a group of recent immigrants who
have come to Unalaska to perform community service through the
auspices of the Fellowship, a group of "permanent" non-Aleut residents who have lived in the community for a number of years, and
processing workers and management personnel. Participation in
church activities is very high. The majority of members attend the
Sunday services and social activities also draw large numbers of
members and visitors.
   The Fellowship is also very active in its efforts to recruit
new members. These efforts have enjoyed some success among two
particular segments of the community. One segment is the transient
processing population. The Fellowship is the only religious institution in Unalaska to actively pursue members from the processors,
largely by inviting them to attend various social functions and
providing transportation for those interested in attending
religious services. The other segment of the community which has
been subject to missionary activity is the young. Unalaska may be
viewed as a community ripe for missionary activity because of the
social and psychological problems associated with recent growth.
Given the high percentage of broken families and the increasing
problems of alcohol and substance abuse, the Fellowship makes a
special effort to minister to young members of the community.
   One segment of the population of Unalaska which has thus far
resisted for the most part the Fellowship's efforts to recruit them
is the Aleut community. The Fellowship does include a few Aleuts
within its congregation, but these are primarily fishermen or
individuals who have a marginal status in the Aleut community of
Unalaska, either because of their income or because they are from
other communities.
   The present minister of the Fellowship came to Unalaska in
1981. A former schoolteacher, the minister has worked to enlarge
his role by participating in several different community
activities. He usually directs the organization of social events,
Fellowship activities such as the renovation of the Jesse Lee Home,
and church ministry policy. The minister also provides counselling
for church members, assisting them in dealing with various social
and psychological problems.
   The Fellowship provides a full weekly schedule of religious
and social activities for its members. On Saturday evenings,
communion services are held at the community church for Roman
Catholics in Unalaska. Protestant worship services are held on
Sunday mornings. A Cooperative Woman's Ministry meets on Monday
evenings and a Men's prayer meeting is held on Friday evenings. A
Church Bible School for children is also held on Monday evenings.
On Wednesdays, there is a Bible Study for young adults and a Home
Fellowship for adults which are held at the same time. After
Sunday services, a luncheon or picnic is held with recreational
activities such as softball being held afterwards. There is also a
pot-luck dinner on Wednesday evenings before the Home Fellowship.
These social activities provide the major opportunity for church

members to interact with each other as well as with visitors from other segments of the community.

In contrast to the Russian Orthodox Church, the Unalaska Christian Fellowship is very social in its orientation. Whereas the Russian Orthodox church was one institution in a cluster of of social groups which comprised Aleut social life, the Christian Fellowship has become an institution of greater relevance to the social life of its members. It is the center of a well-defined group of Unalaska residents, the Christian community. Fellowship members share an explicit set of beliefs and interact principally with each other in both social and religious contexts. In contrast, while there are activities in the community that predominately involve Aleut residents, it is ethnicity and not church membership which is the critical factor in determining networks of participation and interaction. Membership in the Russian Orthodox Church is exclusive, whereas membership in the Christian Fellowship is inclusive. This is to say, the latter institution is used by members to isolate themselves from other segments of the community while members of the Christian Fellowship use the church as a basis for including other segments of the community in their sphere of social life and religious practice. The Fellowship places a higher priority on recruitment than the Russian Orthodox church.

The role of the Unalaska Christian Fellowship in the community is a strong one. It is the church with the highest attendence and it can be argued that this church has greater political clout in the community than the Russian Orthodox Church. In recent political debates over the extension of hours that bars may serve liquor several of the prominent members of the Fellowship's congregation spoke on the moral aspects of the issue, appealing to religious values in the attempt to influence a political issue.

The Unalaska Christian Fellowship is also coming to be used by the community at large in their efforts to deal with some of the social problems currently plaguing Unalaska. The minister has been approached by local residents for counselling and the city government has approached the Fellowship to provide a facility to temporarily shelter victims of parent or spouse abuse. The Jesse Lee Home has recently been used for this purpose although no established procedures have been developed to handle cases of this nature.

3.2.4.3 Other Religious Groups. Other organized religious groups in Unalaska include Roman Catholics and Mormons. The Roman Catholic Church is represented in Unalaska in the form of St. Christophers by the Sea Mission. There is no priest in Unalaska and the responsibility for the mission is currently assumed by a Catholic nun. The congregation is a small one and usually gathers together for a communion service held in the facilities of the Unalaska Christian Fellowship. These services are also attended by members of the Fellowship; the Catholics, in turn, frequently attend the religious services of the Fellowship. There is a good deal of overlap in the social networks of the two congregations and in some contexts, particularly in contrast to the Russian Orthodox Church, they can viewed a one social group.

There also is a small Mormon congregation in Unalaska. Members gather for Sunday worship at the high school. The congre-

gation recently attempted to seek funding from the Church of the
Latter Day Saints to construct a church of their own but were
unsuccessful because they could not sustain the required minimum
weekly attendance at their services.

Unalaska also has a small Baha'i fellowship which began as a
mission in 1957 and reached its peak in the 1960s. The fellowship
experienced a decline in the 1970s, but recently, there has been
some resurgence of activity. Members get together twice a week for
"Fireside Meetings."

3.2.4.4 **Secular Organizations.** For a large segment of
Unalaska's population, religion plays little or no role in social
organization. Religious beliefs are replaced with "secular
beliefs" and participation in religious organizations and attendance of religious services is minimal if it occurs at all. There
are, however, no "secular" organizations in Unalaska which replace
the role of the church.

While secularism has been on the rise throughout rural Alaska,
in Unalaska it takes a peculiar form. The growth and influence of
the Unalaska Christian Fellowship has, to a certain degree, served
to polarize the religious and non-religious segments of the community. Among many non-religious individuals in the community, there
is resentment over what is perceived to be the "righteous attitudes" of the Christians and a concern over their increasing
political power. For those attracted to Unalaska because of its
"frontier spirit," the thought of the possibility of the legislation of morality is particularly distasteful. If the Unalaska
Christian Fellowship does indeed become a politically powerful
voice in the community, it may result in a unification of the
disparate secular elements of the population and the coalescence of
distinct non-religious, perhaps even "anti-religious" opinions and
attitudes.

3.2.5 Education

Formal education has been available in Unalaska since the
first school was established by Veniaminov in the early nineteenth
century. Nevertheless, much of the existing educational system is
relatively recent, having come into existence with the economic
boom of the 1970s. Furthermore, community attitudes toward education have undergone some revision with the recent economic decline.
As the crab fishery continues to be depressed, staying in school
for longer periods of time seems a likely possibility. As the
community becomes increasingly involved in the larger sociocultural
system, whether through fishing or oil development, the role of
education in the community becomes all the more important for local
residents. As more outsiders move into the community, the diversity of interests and needs increases accordingly, placing additional demands on the existing educational structure. This has
already been evident in the growth of adult education classes and
the pre-school in recent years. For many residents, these classes
are seen as improving the quality of life in Unalaska.

The educational subsystem of Unalaska can be divided into pre-
school, primary, secondary, and adult. Educational opportunities

exist for virtually all members of the community. However, not all segments of the community make equal use of the educational system.

3.2.5.1 **Pre-school.** The Unalaska-Dutch Harbor Cooperative Preschool is a relatively recent institution in the community. It began during the 1981-82 school year as a pilot program and met with such success that it has opened on a full-scale basis for the 1982-83 school year. Classes are held for three and four year olds each week day at the Unalaska Community Center. Funds for running the activities have thus far come from parents whose children participate in the program. Community response to this program has been very favorable with virtually all of the parents of pre-school age children electing to enroll their children.

3.2.5.2 **Primary and Secondary School.** Because of its status as an incorporated first-class city, the educational needs of the community of Unalaska are met by an independent school district rather than the Rural Education Attendence Area which serves other communities in the Aleutians. The Unalaska City School District provides educational services for students from Kindergarten through high school. These services are provided at the Unalaska School which includes both primary and secondary grades. The School, however, is not accredited although it is scheduled for an accreditation review by the State Board of Education during the winter of 1982-83.

The Unalaska School is organized into two basic units, elementary and secondary, both of which are located in the same complex on a 5.5 acre site on the Unalaska side of the city. Within the school complex, however, the elementary and secondary grades are physically and administratively separated. The secondary school component is located in the main building, constructed in 1973. The elementary school component is housed in a new wing at the northwest end of the main building. Existing facilities include twenty general classrooms, two special education rooms (one for elementary and the other for high school students), two shop areas, a band room, a library, a full gymnasium, a kitchen, two lounges, a nurse's office, adinistrative offices and several storage and work rooms (Alaska Consultants 1981:67).

Outdoor school recreation facilities include a playground with a variety of play equipment and a general sports area. The community pool is also located near the school plant and is often used for school activities. The school also has a small fish hatchery on the Iliuliuk River within walking distance of the school. During non-school hours both the library and gym are available for public use.

With few exceptions, the Unalaska School serves the entire school-age population of Unalaska. Occasionally, students from Unalaska have been sent to other school districts in the region on a temporary basis to bolster attendance figures in the communities of relatives for funding purposes. The fact that the existing school in Unalaska is not accredited has been responsible for the loss of some of the long-term transient and semi-permanent resident families for the community who would like their children to be more adequately prepared for post-secondary education.

In the past, the school provided services for students from the communities of Nikolski and Akutan as well, but since the construction of facilities in these two communities, the school, with few exceptions, serves children and adolescents from Unalaska only. Several students are children from processor families and spend no longer than one or two years in the local schools. Of the students who attended school in the past year, forty percent were estimated by the principal to have been new to the community. Bus service for Amaknak Island and those living in the more remote areas of Unalaska Island is provided by a private contractor (Alaska Consultants 1981:67).

Enrollment figures for the past ten years are included in Table 3.4. From 1976 through 1981 the school population grew at a rate of 12.5 percent. The junior-senior high school grades grew at a rate of 15.5 percent during the same period. The enrollment showed a decline in the past two years, however, indicating that the school-age population has begun to level off with the decline in the seafood processing industry (Haeg Bettis Associates 1982:20-21). In fact, because the second grade only has five pupils, it will be combined with the third grade and taught by one instructor.

School district personnel include a superintendent and one principal for grades Kindergarten through Twelve. There are nine certified elementary school teachers and nine certified high school teachers, a part-time librarian, two half-time bilingual (Aleut) education teachers, and nine classified personnel.

Table 3.4

Total Unalaska School Population (K-12),
1972-1983

| School Year | Grade Level | | |
	K-6	7-12	Total
1972-73	64	49	113
1973-74	52	51	103
1974-75	53	64	117
1975-76	56	66	122
1976-77	61	58	119
1977-78	70	63	133
1978-79	77	63	140
1979-80	87	73	160
1980-81	106	93	199
1981-82	81	84	165
1982-83 (projected)	72	88	160

Sources: Haeg Bettis Associates 1982:20
Alaska Consultants 1981:69.

The teacher rate of return is viewed as generally stable. Traditionally, the turnover rate for qualified teachers in Unalaska, as has been the case throughout Alaska, has been high. In the past decade, this rate has levelled off and begun to decline somewhat. In the past few years, the average turnover rate has been somewhere between ten and fifteen percent per year. In the past year, however, only one teacher elected not to return. Due to a projected decline in enrollments and the combination of second and third grades into a single class for the 1982-83 school year, it was decided not to replace the teacher. There appears to be a higher turnover among school administrators.

The Russian Orthodox priest of Unalaska and his wife serve in part-time capacities as bilingual/bicultural education instructors. They teach courses in Aleut language and cultural traditions which are attended mostly by Aleut students. Another teacher serves as a vocational counsellor although there is no officially designated counselling position at the school.

The Unalaska City School District is governed by a five person, city-wide, elected school board. This board is responsible for the selection of school administrators and ultimately responsible for course selection and curriculum. The chief administrative officer is the superintendent and the chief academic official is the school principal. The school administration is responsible for the hiring of teachers and maintenance of the school plant, while the city is responsible for the construction of new school facilities, as required by state law (Alaska Consultants 1981:67).

Funding for the school comes from a variety of sources. The 1982-83 school budget was $1,970,726. A significant amount of the funding for the school comes from the city. In the 1980-81 school year, the city's share of the budget was $140,000. By 1982, this figure had jumped to $210,000. Other funding sources include the state and federal governments. Funding for the Aleut education programs come from three sources: Indian Education Act funds, Johnson-O'Malley funds which filter to the school by way of the Bureau of Indian Affairs and the Unalaska Aleut Development Corporation, and the State Department of Education.

The primary objective of the Unalaska school is to provide a basic education comparable to that of any school system in Alaska. Besides regular academic courses, a number of special programs are available to Unalaska students. Title I and Title IV federal funds provide individualized instruction in mathematics, reading and language, and specialized instruction is also available for students with learning disabilities, including hearing problems (Alaska Consultants 1981:68). In addition, the school operates a Graduate Equivalent Degree (GED) program, a fish hatchery program for high school students, and the Aleut language and culture program. The "Cuttlefish" program, for which academic credit is given to high school students, produces a published history of the Aleutian Islands each year.

Both the level of achievement and motivation appear to be quite high for a rural school district. Recent test scores placed local students at a slightly higher level than the state average. The dropout rate is very low with only three high school students leaving out of a population of eighty-five in the past year. Despite the transience of many of the non-Aleut students, the motivation to learn appears to be high. A significant number of Aleuts are oftentimes under pressure from their families to pursue other activities or receive little encouragement for academic achievement in the home (Kleinfeld 1981). Some of these students are also encouraged to abandon attempts to pursue further studies outside the community at a college or university and motivation suffers accordingly. The number of students who intend to go on to college is quite high. Of a recent senior class of fourteen students, four were planning to attend a four year college and four were planning to attend a junior college or technical school. In the previous senior class of seventeen students, eleven attended a four year college, junior college, or technical school.

Despite the high levels of achievement and numbers of students who leave the community to attend college, the number of local students who actually graduate from college is quite small. This is perhaps due to the sense of isolation in urban communities and homesickness. Aleut students have a particularly difficult time because often they are under a good deal of pressure from their families not to leave the community. Unlike students from other rural communities, Unalaska students also often lack the financial incentive to pursue a higher education. As they witness fishermen earning more money in a single season than their teachers do in several years, these students often decide that the pursuit of excellence in school is not as rewarding as the pursuit of wealth in the commercial fisheries.

There is a widespread belief that more vocational counselling and training is needed. Until recently, the objective of the local educational system has been to encourage and prepare students for higher education outside the community. However, this has been revised in light of the local need for trained workers and the high dropout rate of local students in colleges and universities. An effort has been made by the special education teacher to secure jobs in the community for students but the school administration appears to be less enthusiastic about this venture than local employers. Vocational programs do exist in business and office machines, woodshop, welding and metalshop, and home economics, but these are seen as being low priority.

Providing leadership skills is another major concern among local educators. This is particularly important within the Aleut population as local leaders are increasingly called upon to assume additional responsibilities requiring greater expertise. With the passage of the Alaska Native Claims Settlement Act and the formation of the Native corporations came a need for a number of Aleuts with business and management skills beyond those currently available. It is a concern among those in power in Native organizations now that their children acquire these skills, although the sentiment is not often shared by the children themselves.

In addition to formal classwork, the Unalaska school provides numerous opportunities for extracurricular activities. The most popular form of extracurricular activity in the schools is basketball. Interest in varsity and intermural competition as well as informal games in quite high. Other athletic events such as wrestling, cross country and track have met with only limited success. The student newspaper is also popular. Recently, the school has been under pressure from parents to increase the number of extracurricular activities available for students.

Formal parental involvement in the educational program is

116

fairly minimal. Two notable exceptions are the parents committee
for the Indian Education Program and a bilingual/bicultural committee. There is no local parent-teachers association at the moment,
although in the past, such an organization attempted to wield great
power and influence in matters of school policy. Informal participation by parents varies widely by individual and by population
segment.

2.2.6.3 **Adult Education and Extension Classes**. In addition
to the Unalaska School District, there are two other programs which
provide educational services for local residents. One is the
Unalaska Rural Education Center of the University of Alaska. Established in 1978, the Center maintains an office in the city-owned
Parks, Culture and Recreation Building. The program is managed by
a part-time director and instructors come from all segments of the
community. Occasionally, guest lecturers are brought into the community for short-term courses. A wide variety of courses on such
topics as art, literature, typing, vocational skills, and EMT are
offered. In the past year, the most popular courses were: Aleutian
history, Watercolor Painting, Drawing, and Microcomputers. In the
1981-82 school year, twenty-nine classes were taught and over 187
students were enrolled. Eighty-four percent of these students were
Caucasian, seven percent were Aleut, and the remainder were Asian
and Hispanic processing workers (Unalaska Rural Education Center
1982:10). An estimated seventy-five percent of the students are
permanent residents. Tuition is $25 a credit for all courses except
the EMT classes, which are free.

The second program is the Adult Basic Education Program. The
program is funded by the State of Alaska and the Aleutian/Pribilof
Islands Association and employs two half-time teachers. It has
been in Unalaska for one full year and is aimed at people with math
and reading skills at or below the eighth grade level. The program
also offers GED programs for local residents and English language
classes for processing workers. Community response to the program
has thus far been light. Of those who have attended classes, about
fifty percent are Aleut and all are young adults.

2.2.6 Health Care

Health services in Unalaska are provided by the Iliuliuk
Family and Health Services Clinic. The clinic was constructed in
1976 and a major addition was completed in 1980. The facility has
two overnight holding areas capable of accommodating three patients
at a time, an emergency room, an X-ray room, a well stocked pharmacy, a laboratory room, four examining rooms, a dental area, a
kitchen, four offices, bathrooms and, waiting room (Alaska Consultants 1981:65).

The current facility provides outpatient services, radiology,
general ambulatory medicine and acute care to local residents,
including the fish processing industry, the domestic fishing fleet,
crew members from foreign vessels, and residents of Nikolski
(Alaska Consultants 1981:64-65). In addition, the Clinic's radiology facilities are sometimes used by Cold Bay residents.
Emergency transportation services are provided by a Department of

Public Safety ambulance manned by a volunteer EMT-trained crew.
Surgery performed at the clinic is usually limited to hernias,
appendectomies, sterilizations, and D&Cs. Bad accidents that occur
on fishing boats in the area are usually brought to the clinic for
treatment. Serious cases are taken by medivac flights to Anchorage
but that usually takes about six hours depending on the weather,
whether or not a suitable aircraft is in town, and the time of day
(as the local airport cannot accommodate night landings). The
facility serves roughly 8,500 outpatients per year with patient
loads being heaviest during the king and tanner crab seasons,
sometimes reaching as high as eighty patients a day (Alaska Consultants 1981:66).

In addition to the clinic, emergency medical services are
provided by the Department of Public Safety. Every member of the
department is an EMT I with some completing Level II and Level III
training as well (DPS Report 1981:11). In addition, the EMS branch
is responsible for providing EMT training to other members of the
community.

Health care is also provided by a few different clinics which
operate on a periodic basis. A private dentist from Anchorage
provides services to Unalaska residents on a fee-for-service basis
during periodic visits and the APIA sponsors an ophthalmologist who
visits the community four times a year. A veterinarian also makes
periodic visits to the community at which time he makes use of the
clinic facilities.

There are two policy-making organizations which are responsible for the health care needs of the community. The first in the
Health and Human Services of the City of Unalaska. Members are
appointed by the City Council and advise on such matters as rat
control, pollution and sanitation, and other health issues not
directly related to clinical care.

The clinic operates under the auspices of Iliuliuk Family and
Health Services, Inc., a non-profit corporation, and is administered by an eleven member Board of Directors. The board receives
no compensation and serves as a policy-making body. It is ultimately responsible for determining health care and staffing needs.

The clinic's staff includes a full-time physician who came to
Unalaska in the summer of 1982. Prior to 1982, a physician from
Kodiak was hired by one of the processors to provide service on a
seasonal basis. Other staff members include a student physician's
assistant, a lab/x-ray technician, bookkeeper/acting director, and
several clerical personnel. As noted above, a dentist visits the
community once every two months and an ophthalmologist visits on a
quarterly basis.

In addition to the clinic, local health care is provided by a
team of EMS technicians and some of the processors. The EMS team,
consisting of volunteers and employees of the Department of Public
Safety, handle mostly accident trauma cases. The Pan-Alaska processing facility has a full-time RN while the other processors have
untrained personnel who perform tuberculosis screenings and basic
checkups for transient workers. The APIA funds a community health
representative who visits the elderly and conducts blood pressure
checks.

Some of the funding for the health clinic has been provided by the Alaska Native Health Center and from the fishermen who visit Unalaska. The city provides some of the operating revenues for the clinic but most of the funding comes from fees charged to patients. The Ounalashka Corporation donates $6,600 a year in land rental for the facility and has donated the property for two trailer homes for the medical staff. Despite this funding, however, the clinic loses money each year. Only a few individuals in the community (4 or 5) are qualified to receive Medicare benefits.

The major problems of local health care are perceived in terms of a lack of qualified personnel and health care costs. The clinic recently lost its funding for a physician's assistant and the physician is now assisted by only one student physician's assistant. The wide range of the area served by the facility demands additional personnel. According to the resident physician, the clinic could use the services of two RNs, an LPN, and another technician. Because of the isolation of the region and the uncertainty of future funding, however, obtaining qualified personnel is expected to be difficult.

The high cost of existing health care is another major problem. Currently, the cost of medivac flights range between $3,000 and $6,000. In 1981 alone, there were 111 such flights to Anchorage from the Aleutian/ Pribilofs Region (D.E. Raven Associates 1982:18). Despite the reliance on outside hospitals, however, there are no immediate plans to build a hospital in Unalaska. In April of 1982, D.E. Raven Associates and Providence Hospital published a report on the possibility of constructing a hospital in Unalaska. Despite the high morbidity and mortality rates of the region, it was concluded that such a project would not be feasible because of the lack of community support. Patients in need of medical care would continue to travel outside the community to Seattle or Anchorage for treatment and existing economic conditions could not guarantee that such a facility would be adequately funded (D.E. Raven Associates 1982:35). Nevertheless, the present facility will undergo some expansion in the near future. The city has allocated funds to construct a 20' x 30' addition to the facility and expand the laboratory. There are also plans to establish a blood bank and provide a facility for water quality testing.

Health care is a major concern in Unalaska for a number of reasons. Historically, contact with the West has created several health risks for the Aleut population, particularly in the area of infectious diseases. The rapid economic growth of the region has also resulted in a dramatic increase in stress-related disorders. This increase is reflected in high rates of mortality and morbidity.

Death rates in the Aleutian Islands appear to be higher than for the state of Alaska as a whole. In 1974, the crude death rate for Alaska was 418 deaths per 100,000 residents. The non-Native death rate in the South-Central Health Service Area (which incompasses the Aleutians and Pribilof Islands in 1974 was 350.4 per 100,000 while the Aleut death rate for 1970-1977 was 739.2 per 100,000 (Aleutians/Pribilof Islands Association 1978:36).

Accidents constitute the highest single cause of death in the Aleutians followed by heart disease and cancer (D.E. Raven Associates 1982:11). The accident death rate in the Aleutians for the years 1970-1979 was 102.8 per 1,000 population compared to a rate of 47.9 for the U.S. (1979) as a whole (D.E. Raven Associates 1982:12). Drownings account for a large portion of the accidental deaths in Unalaska and many of these are alcohol-related. A typical scenario is a crew member trying to return to his vessel after an evening of drinking at a local bar and falling between the boats tied to the dock. Due to the low water temperature and the diminished resistence to cold caused by alcohol, drownings occur quickly, greatly reducing the odds of self-rescue or rescue by others.

The morbidity rate among Unalaska residents appears to be higher than average, although no statistics are available. The major health problems among local residents are accidental injuries, alcoholism, poor dental health, gastrointestinal and skin diseases, mental health, and heart disease. Aleuts appear to have higher morbidity rates relative to their proportion of the population. In 1981, thirty-seven percent of the individuals treated for major illnesses at the Unalaska clinic were Aleuts (D.E. Raven Associates 1982:15). One must use caution in interpreting this figure however. Aleuts are less likely to avoid the clinic than non-Aleuts because of costs of service, for example, as free health care is relatively easy to obtain for Aleuts. (As health care has traditionally been provided largely free of charge to Aleut residents in Unalaska, there is little likelihood that attempting to continue receiving free health care, at a time when clinic fees are beginning to be charged to all persons who use the services, will be strongly negatively sanctioned behavior.) In addition, non-Aleuts are more likely than Aleuts to seek health care for major crises or disorders outside of the community.

Processing workers display numerous stress-related disorders as well as back and bone injuries. Among transients in the community, youth, dormitory-style living conditions, long working hours, inhospitable climate, and easy access to drugs and alcohol contribute to a high incidence of accidents and trauma. Venereal disease is a problem and, with a recent influx of processing workers from Southeast Asia, there is an increased potential for local outbreaks of hepatitis and typhoid fever (Alaska Consultants 1981:66).

Among all segments of the local population, the major health-related problem resulting in hospitalization is accidental injury. This high rate is attributable in large part to the working conditions in the fisheries and the number of hours that people in the industry work per day. As the fisheries have become more competitive with the value of the product increasing, the fleet fishes in much worse weather conditions than it had in the past. Fishing under adverse conditions makes the work more dangerous as individual boats try to fish as quickly as possible to maximize their catch before the fleet quota is met. Under such constraints, there is little opportunity for the crew to sleep during the short seasons. The resulting fatigue is clearly a contributing factor to many of the accidents that occur.

Injuries at the processing plants also increase during the busy seasons, both because of the increased number of workers at the plant and the extended hours worked by each employee. As with the crew on the vessels, fatigue is a contributing factor to many

accidents. Both on land and on sea, alcohol is seen as a contributing factor to many injuries as well.

While only ten residents of the Aleutian/Pribilof region were
hospitalized for psychiatric illnesses in 1980, local officials,
residents and health care personnel maintain that psychiatric illness is a major problem. Neuroses appear to be common among both
Aleuts and non-Aleuts. Major psychoses usually appear among the
Aleuts, perhaps because of the reluctance to seek outside assistance until the problem becomes acute or the fact that most non-
Aleuts coming into the community go through a job screening process
before arriving in Unalaska, which would catch some of the more
acute disorders. The Aleut population is more representative of a
random population sample. Depression is viewed as a common disorder in both Aleut and non-Aleut segments of the community, as is
alcoholism.

Perhaps the most common as well as serious medical problem in
Unalaska is alcoholism. It is not only related to certain psychiatric disorders as depression, but is also a contributory factor in
such diseases as cirrhosis and infections, as well as accidents and
homicides. Aside from the health hazards for those who abuse alcohol, excessive drinking is seen as affecting the quality of life in
the community for non-excessive drinkers. In the recent debates
before the City Council regarding the motion to increase the hours
of operation of the local bars, several comments were made by
residents concerning the unacceptable nature of drinking in
Unalaska.

There appears to be three primary drinking patterns in the
community among abusers of alcohol. First, there is the individual
who is a steady drinker but is able to hold a job or otherwise earn
a living. These individuals drink during the times when they are
not working or engaging in responsible domestic activities. Second,
there are those individuals who abuse alcohol sporadically.
Although they do not drink regularly, they nonetheless create
problems for themselves and others. These individuals are usually
the ones who become violent when intoxicated though they are able
to hold a job and maintain a relatively normal way of life when not
drinking. Third, there are those who go on binges, during which
time they are incapable of functioning in normal social situations
or performing required duties at their jobs.

Alcohol is by no means the only drug that is abused, particularly among the transient and very short-term residents, with
regularity in Unalaska. Marijuana use is common and when money is
available in great quantities, especially during the end of the
fishing season, cocaine is also quite common. The city has been
characterized by local citizens and police officials alike as the
"cocaine capital of Alaska" and the drug is especially common among
fishermen. There are several stories in the community of enormous
amounts of money spent on 'coke' and how the drug has ruined businesses and fishing ventures. The general impression is that, in the
recent past when money was plentiful, a large percentage of fishing
crew incomes were spent on drugs. Boredom, isolation from family
and friends, work-related stress, and sizeable incomes earned in
relatively short periods of time are frequently cited as contributing factors to this abuse. Fishermen, however, are by no means

the only abusers of drugs. Drug abuse is also typically found among adolescents and young adults in Unalaska. Reasons for drug abuse among the stable resident population differ somewhat from that of fishermen and include lack of self-esteem, perceived lack of alternatives, and peer pressure.

Infectious diseases are also a problem in Unalaska. Infections appear to be common to the region and, given the local climate, do not heal rapidly. Among children, upper respiratory infections are the most common complaint. Among adults, venereal disease is regarded as a problem but has diminished in intensity in the past decade. A common industrial ailment, particularly among processing line workers, was "crab asthma," an allergic reaction to shellfish. With pre-screenings conducted by the local processors in the past few years, however, this problem has decreased.

3.2.7 Social Services

Social services in the form of counselling, referral, and aid to the needy have been an important part of Unalaska society since pre-contact times. In its modern, westernized form, such services can trace their origins in Unalaska with the founding of the United Methodist Women's Home Missionary Society which operated a health clinic and operated the Jesse Lee Home from 1890 until 1925 (Jones 1969). The existing structure of social services in Unalaska was a direct result of the formation of the Unalaska Health Board in 1970 and the activities of Alaska Children's Services to implement a child and family welfare service in Unalaska. These activities led to the formation of Iliuliuk Family and Health Services.

3.2.7.1 Legal Services. Social services in Unalaska today can be broken into two separate components: legal services and counselling and family services. The major responsibility for legal services in the community is assumed by a local representative of Alaska Legal Services, Inc. a private, non-profit corporation providing legal assistance to low income families. The paralegal advisor works as a part-time public defender in criminal cases which appear before the local magistrate's court and is employed full-time in civil case paralegal work. One of her chief tasks is to assist local residents with legal forms such as the drawing of wills. Although the advisor is not qualified to handle cases on her own, she is the only form of legal counsel available in the community, other than the local magistrate. In addition, her office is a regional one, stretching from Nelson Lagoon to Atka.

There is also a fee agent, with the Public Assistence Division of the State Department of Health and Social Services, in the community who assists individuals with government documents, especially food stamps and AFDC applications, and income tax preparation.

3.2.7.2 Counselling and Family Services. The major responsibility for counselling and family services is handled by the regional representative for state Department of Health and Social Services, Division of Family and Youth Services and by the clinical psychologist hired by the Aleutian/Pribilof Islands Association. The representative of the State Department of Health and Social

Services is responsible for the entire Aleutian Islands chain and the Pribilof Islands. Her primary duties include individual and family counselling and referral, particularly in cases of spouse and child abuse, crisis intervention, and referral.

The Aleutian/Pribilof Islands Association has contracted with a clinical psychologist to provide services including counselling and therapy. Although the psychologist is responsible for the entire region, he is based in Unalaska and thus devotes the bulk of his time to providing services to local residents.

Another source of social services in Unalaska is the minister of the Unalaska Christian Fellowship. The minister is frequently called upon to provide counselling and advice, but for the most part services are limited to church members. Recently, the minister was approached by city officials to provide crisis intervention services to victims of spouse and child abuse.

The APIA Community Health Representative may also be viewed as providing social services. This individual is particularly involved with providing services to the elderly in Unalaska and conducts an informal "outreach referral" program.

With the exception of the psychologist, all of the existing social service personnel in Unalaska could be classified as paraprofessional. None has had formal training the social work or law and their expertise in the field is based on experience. Nonetheless, these individuals are viewed as essential components of the community, given the degree and nature of many of the social and personal problems present.

In addition to these individuals who are acknowledged by the community to be responsible for providing social services, there exist several individuals who provide such services in a voluntary capacity. These include members of the Department of Public Safety, representatives of the Unalaska Aleut Development Corporation, the local representatives of the Alaska Native Women's Statewide Organization, and the local crisis intervention team organized by the state social worker to deal with problems in her absence.

There is also a local Alcoholics Anonymous program in Unalaska. Currently, there are ten residents participating in the program who meet three times a week during the winter and spring and once a week during the remainder of the year. Although the number of residents attending the program is small compared with the number of alcoholics in Unalaska, the program is generally regarded to be very successful.

3.2.7.3 Social Issues. The social issues requiring professional involvement in intervention and treatment are numerous and varied. One of the major social problems in the community is that of domestic violence. This violence can be attributable to several factors, including the conflict between traditional and modern value systems, the increase in single-parent households, and alcohol abuse. Domestic violence is usually manifested in such forms as wife abuse, child neglect and abuse, incest, and abandonment. As noted above, it was community concern over the high level of domestic violence which led to the organization of the existing structure of health and social services.

Most of the social problems in Unalaska are related in one form or another to the problem of alcohol abuse. Alcohol abuse in

Unalaska is as serious a social problem as it is a medical problem for it affects the very fabric of the entire community. It affects virtually all segments of the community, young and old, Aleut and non-Aleut, permanent resident and transient alike. It is usually involved in local criminal activity, particularly assaults, rapes, burglaries, and acts of vandalism. It is often associated with the stress that comes with unemployment and poverty. It is behind much of the domestic violence among families in the community. Finally, alcohol abuse is usually associated with other psychological difficulties, particularly depression and schizophrenia.

Equally of concern to local residents is the problem of drug abuse. This is of particular concern among fishermen and adolescents. Most of the drugs available in the community are introduced by transients, usually fishermen or processing workers.

Another serious problem in Unalaska addressed by the social service system is the level of misinformation. This problem is particularly acute among adolescents who know little of birth control or the hazards of alcohol and drugs. The chief aim in dealing with problems such as these is to educate the local population.

All of these problems are tied to the phenomena of social and personal disintegration among the residents of Unalaska. They are not unique to Unalaska and are usually associated with rural areas which undergo rapid social change. The issue of social disintegration is not a uniform one and affects each major segment of the community in different ways. In terms of the transient population, there has never been a high level of social integration on any but a temporary basis. This problem is particularly acute among ethnic minorities who work for the processors and are unable to speak English. They are culturally isolated and have difficulty communicating their needs to the larger community.

For many transients, Unalaska is perceived to create strains on marriage and family ties, an atmosphere that has been blamed for more than one divorce. The expectation of most transients is that the community is undesirable as a permanent residence. Many, therefore, explicitly come to Unalaska looking for an atomistic social environment, either because of their experience in other parts of the United States or the type of personality they possess. Whatever the incentive to work in Unalaska for brief periods of time, these individuals are regarded as 'loners' and prefer not to include themselves in community activities or social networks.

Among permanent residents in Unalaska, there is a different set of social problems. Many such residents reported that the community has experienced considerable fragmentation and disintegration over the past few decades. Present-day Unalaska is seen as being less cohesive and integrated a community than Unalaska prior to the crab boom, and much less so than before World War II. With the economic growth and the large-scale influx of outsiders new social networks have emerged and expanded at the expense of the traditional networks. This is seen on the community level with the decline in importance of the church and village structure and on the family level with the breakup of the traditional family structure.

At the heart of this social disintegration is the previously discussed conflict between traditional and modern values. This conflict is represented in distinctions between Aleut and non-Aleut segments of the population and between permanent and transient residents. In the family, this conflict is manifested in generational differences which often lead to family violence and alienation of children.

Concomitant with the high level of social disintegration is the phenomena of personal disintegration. Most visible in the form of alcoholism, the roots of this disintegration are varied. For the Aleuts in the community, personal disintegration stems from identity conflicts and a lack of self-esteem. Although the Alaska Native Claims Settlement Act has had a significant positive effect on the ethnic identity and self-esteem of local Aleuts, recent political and economic gains have only begun to address the psychological problems associated with decades of discrimination, poverty, and feelings of inferiority.

For new residents, personal disintegration may result from a lack of preparedness to the community. For those used to the amenities commonly found in urban areas in other parts of the United States, the lack of certain goods and services, forms of entertainment, and so on, can be disheartening. This contributes to a feeling of isolation and despair which eventually manifests itself in depression, anxiety neuroses, and alcoholism.

Finally, a potential source of personal disintegration is unemployment and economic decline. As a chief incentive for moving to Unalaska for most of the non-Aleut residents was the recent crab fishery boom, the prospect of a decline in the local economy and a scarcity of jobs is a potential source of stress. For those who do not move out of the community or who are unable to adapt to the changing economic opportunities, the economic situation may contribute to the level of personal disintegration.

2.2.8 Recreation

The recreational subsystem of Unalaska is comprised of numerous activities which may be classified along several different dimensions. One such dimension is based on the distinction between traditional and modern forms of recreation; another dimension distinguishes between those activities which require a cash income and those which do not; a third distinguishes between urban and rural-oriented activities; and a fourth is based on the location of such activities. While there is a considerable amount of overlap between each of these dimensions, there are nonetheless certain activities which may usefully be classified differently along each dimension. For instance, use of a motorcycle in Unalaska may be considered an activity that is rural-oriented, internal (as opposed to taking place outside the area), and cash-based.

The major recreational activities in Unalaska are similar to those found in other small communities in Alaska. These activities can be divided into those involving the use of vehicles, home entertainment, outdoor activities including hunting and fishing, athletics, social events, and vacations. In addition, given its size and resources, Unalaska provides recreational opportunities not found in smaller communities. These activities include restaurants and bars, adult extension classes, and special events such as festivals and musical concerts.

3.2.8.1 **Activities Involving Vehicles.** In many rural Alaskan communities, flying is a common form of recreation. Privately-owned planes enable their owners to visit other communities or travel to remote areas for hunting, fishing and camping. Recreational flying is not a particularly popular form of recreation in Unalaska even among those in a position to afford it, due in large part to the poor flying conditions in the area. At the time of the field data collection there were two aircraft owned by local residents that were used, although not exclusively, for recreational purposes.

Perhaps the most common vehicle in use for recreational purposes in Unalaska is the small boat or skiff. In addition to the commercial vessels in Unalaska, there are a number of small boats that are used for subsistence and sport fishing. Some of these small craft are used on occasion for purely recreational purposes, and even when used for subsistence fishing there is often an element of recreation that is considered to be an indispensible component of the activity. There are at least two sailing craft that are used for recreational purposes in Unalaska, despite air and water temperatures that make this sport less attractive than it is in other climes. With the coming of the bridge between the two sides of the community, the prestige associated with owning a fast skiff has lessened considerably, though it has not disappeared. Besides fishing, skiffs are used recreationally for the transport of individuals to places that are difficult if not impractical to reach by land for day outings, camping, hiking, and picnics.

Trucks are also a popular recreational vehicles used for driving to the back country of Unalaska Island. Usual destinations include Summers Bay, Morris and Humpy Coves, and Captains Bay. In addition, four wheel drive cars are popular for back country excursions. The purposes of such trips are camping, fishing, hiking, picnicing, or just enjoying the ride.

3.2.8.2 **Home Entertainment.** One of the most popular recent forms of home entertainment in Alaska today is the home video system. There has been a marked growth in the number of videotape and videodisc machines in the community over the past several years. Even some low income families own video machines, as this is a high priority recreational item. Video machines are the focal point of many social gatherings, and it is a popular pastime, especially among younger people, to watch movies into the late evening. Individuals purchase tapes or rent them from commercial outlets in town. Exchanging tapes with other machine owners is also commonly practiced.

Another form of home entertainment which has become very popular in Unalaska in the past ten years has been television. Television has been available to local residents since the early 1970s. The local school had a broadcast system and programming was handled by the school board. Satellite programming via Alascom arrived in April of 1979. The local Alascom Earth Station provides two television channels, one featuring educational programming and the other being entertainment oriented. These are the same two channels that are available throughout rural Alaska.

In addition to satellite programming, there is a local television station that broadcasts features such as area news and events of local interest along with entertainment selections on tape. Unalaska community television operates during the evening hours on weekdays from 4:30 p.m. until midnight and has a full day of programming on Saturdays and Sundays.

Television, beyond it's particular programming content, has affected life in Unalaska in two major ways. First, it has brought the community, particularly the Aleut segment, into closer contact with the outside world. Of course, this effects different individuals in different ways. For those that have moved into the community from the outside, such contact is often a pleasant reminder of the outside world. For those that were raised in a relatively isolated social environment, such programming provides instant perceptual access to varying lifestyles, expectations and value systems. For example, one of the regular features on the network is local news taken from a southern California television station. One may watch the freeway traffic jams in Los Angeles while sitting in a cabana in Unalaska.

Second, television has had a significant influence on the patterns of social interaction of those having access to it. Prior to the arrival of television in Unalaska, a popular form of entertainment was attending movies shown at the processors. Visiting family and friends was also a popular form of entertainment. Although both forms of entertainment still exist, it is now not unusual for evenings to be spent in front of the television set. Though there is not adequate baseline data to make a valid comparative analysis of socializing patterns before and after the advent of television, many people agree that there has been a significant change.

3.2.8.3 Outdoor Activities. In addition to the recreational activities which are associated with an income (vehicles, home video systems), and those associated with the larger sociocultural system (television, radio), outdoor, rural-oriented activities are very popular among all segments of Unalaska society. Camping and hiking are especially popular but the most common forms of outdoor, rural-oriented, and traditional activities are subsistence-related. Given the scarcity of land mammals, such activity is usually limited to fishing for salmon and Dolly Varden, hunting for ducks and geese, collecting marine invertebrates, and gathering berries. As mentioned above, the recreational component of subsistence activities is widely acknowledged. Some subsistence activities, such as berry-picking are often the focus for social interaction. In addition to the collecting of the resources themselves, the sharing of subsistence resources also provides a focus for social interaction. For example, jams are often made from the berries, and then shared at a later date over coffee, and so on.

As noted earlier, there is a great deal of affect associated with subsistence activities that goes far beyond the nutritional needs that subsistence resources provide. For the Aleuts of the community, subsistence pursuits are often taken as markers of an Aleut identity. For non-Aleuts, subsistence pursuits are often thought of as an essential aspect of the Alaskan experience, a part of the adventure or lifestyle for which many came to Alaska. In these and other ways, engagment in subsistence pursuits provides emotional gratification, making such activity truly recreational in addition to pragmatic.

3.2.8.4 **Local Bars and Restaurants.** A popular form of entertainment generally unavailable in smaller communities of Alaska is the frequenting of local bars and restaurants. Bars are particularly popular. Unalaska has three bars, with the possibility of a fourth opening in the near future. The present bars are: the Unisea bar on the Amaknak side, and the Elbow Room and Stormy's on the Unalaska side. In addition, alcoholic beverages may be ordered in the Unisea restaurant. There is presently an application for a license to dispense alcoholic beverages at the airport restaurant, which is owned by Universal Seafoods, the owner of the Unisea complex.

3.2.8.5 **Visiting and Vacations.** Visiting and vacationing are also popular forms of entertainment and may usefully be divided into intracommunity and intercommunity activities. For many of the older permanent residents intracommunity visiting makes up the bulk of their social world. There is an informal information network among many of the older residents. For the more transient members of the community, visiting takes a lesser role to such activities as going out of the homes to bars or the restaurants. For a large portion of the short-term transients visiting is effectively restricted to the companies by which they are employed.

Visits to other communities in the region are not frequent for most of the people living in Unalaska. Among the Aleuts, however, there is a greater degree of visiting, either on Native corporation business or just to visit relatives and friends in the neighboring villages. Events that commonly draw intraregional visits are weddings and funerals. For the population at large, there is some visiting in connection with sporting events between high schools in the region and sports competition involving players from the recreational leagues.

By far the most common intrastate travel destination for individuals from Unalaska is Anchorage. Anchorage is seen as the closest "outside" destination, and for individuals that do not have a lot of time to spend but want to get outside, Anchorage is the destination of choice. Many individuals do a good deal of shopping there and take advantage of the entertainment opportunities available. Most people who have enough time and money do not end their vacation in Anchorage, but continue on to an out-of-state destination.

The most common out-of-state destination from Unalaska appears to be Seattle. The vast majority of the vessels in the fishing fleet that frequent the waters around Unalaska are from the Seattle area, and most of the crew members for the boats and the processors for the seafood plants are hired out of the Seattle area. As a result many of the transient workers return to Seattle for their vacations, and a good number of the semi-permanent residents do also as they often are originally from that area. Another popular destination for vacations is Hawaii. Many people prefer to go to warm-weather destinations for their vacations, and do so when they are able to afford it.

3.2.8.6 **Community Activities.** Unalaska also provides numerous recreational opportunities in the form of community activities. Such activities largely take place in the churches, schools, and community center. Church recreational activities vary widely by denomination. The Unalaska Christian Fellowship has by far the most recreational activities for its members. The Fellowship sponsors picnics or lunches after church services that often include recreational activities. In addition, there are Wednesday evening dinners at the Jesse Lee Home that also include sporting activities, and the church informally sponsors hikes, picnics, softball games, evenings at the pool, and boat trips, along with fielding a softball team in the recreational league.

The most popular school recreational activity, basketball, draws large numbers of participants and spectators. It is by far the most popular extracurricular activity among students and local games are well-attended by Unalaska residents. The city basketball league, of which the school was a part, has enjoyed greater popularity in the past few years than it does today, though it appears to be making a recovery. In 1982 there were seven teams and games usually drew an average of fifty spectators per game.

The new pool at the school is quite popular with many residents, though participation levels are not what the school administration had hoped. After an initial period of heavy use after the pool first opened in October of 1981, swimming attendence has dropped off to a low but steady level.

The City Department of Parks, Culture, and Recreation sponsors a wide range of activities at the community recreation center. These include open recreation hours, classes, movies, and special events for holidays. In addition, the center is utilized by other groups. For example, the Unalaska Aleut Development Corporation hosts a weekly evening bingo game in the center. Different activities attract different segments of the population. For example, the percentage of participation of Aleuts is much higher for open recreation, as opposed to low Aleut participation levels for city sponsored classes. Bingo is one of the few public secular activities that is predominantly Aleut.

As noted above, the University of Alaska, in cooperation with the City Department of Parks, Culture, and Recreation sponsors a number of classes in Unalaska through an extension office located in the community center. The classes cover a wide range of subjects from first aid to fine arts. In addition to the educational value of these classes, they also provide recreational opportunities.

The Aleutian Slow Pitch Softball Association is widely popular in the community. During the summer of 1982, there were twelve teams sponsored by several of the seafood processors, some of the smaller businesses, the Ounalashka Corporation, and the Unalaska Christian Fellowship. The softball league is one of the few steady activities that draws from a wide population range. Several people have indicated that this is a positive thing in the community, one of the few activities that draws people from different backgrounds together, which helps to create a sense of community.

The Aleutian Allemanders is a social square dance group that enjoys some popularity. The group, consisting largely of married couples, entertains at the major community functions and hosts pot-luck dinners.

4
Forecast Scenarios
for Unalaska

4.1 INTRODUCTION

In this chapter we present an analysis of projected levels and
directions of socioeconomic and sociocultural change in Unalaska.
This analysis is based on the data contained in the last two chapters and is predicated on a set of assumptions provided by the
Minerals Management Service, OCS Social and Economic Studies
Program of probable scenarios based on varying levels of development in the groundfish industry and oil-related industry.

The standards and assumptions relate to existing ethnographic
parameters of Unalaska, such as the dependence of the local economy
on local resources, primarily fish. They also relate to trends
which are projected to exist in the future but are not directly
related to either groundfish industry or oil-related development.
An example of such an assumption is the projected decline in
available state revenues in the next ten to twenty years, the
decline in the crab fishery, and a decline in higher order governmental support for Unalaska.

Our projections for sociocultural change in Unalaska are based
on two scenarios. In the first scenario we examine the likely
consequences of groundfish development at levels consistent with
population and employment projection provided by the Alaska OCS
Region Social and Economic Studies Program. Included in this
scenario is an acknowledgement of already existing and relatively
fixed levels of oil related-development in Unalaska.

The second scenario is based on our experience with and data
on existing trends and patterns of change in the community. This
scenario examines the prospect of the co-occurrence of groundfish
industry and oil-related development at levels already projected by
the Alaska OCS Region Social and Economic Studies Program. This
scenario pays special attention to the community's perception of
these differential forces, described in the last chapter, and how
this perception in turn will affect local decisionmaking processes
which will determine the magnitude and direction of change in
Unalaska.

4.2 FIRST SCENARIO

4.2.1 Assumptions

The population basis for the first scenario of social change in Unalaska throughout the forecast period is provided in Table 4.1. This table contains an estimate of potential changes in residence and employment in the Bering Sea/Aleutians Region which are based on projected groundfish harvest levels. The estimates of employment and residence are based on a set of assumptions derived

Table 4.1

Projected U.S. Groundfish Harvest and Related Employment
Bering Sea/Aleutians Region

	Total U.S. Catch, Including Joint (Foreign/U.S.) Ventures (in 1000's of metric tons)			Number of U.S. Groundfish Workers By Residence Status In Aleutian Islands Census Division				
Year	(1)	(2)	(3)	(4)	(5)	(6)	(7)	(8)
1981	87.3	78.5	0.4	8.4	212	3	25	240
1982	111.4	100.0	0.5	10.9	269	4	31	304
1983	174.7	160.0	0.7	14.0	406	5	47	458
1984	259.1	240.0	1.0	18.1	588	7	69	664
1985	344.8	320.0	1.4	23.4	775	10	91	876
1986	432.1	400.0	1.9	30.2	969	13	115	1097
1987	521.7	480.0	2.6	39.1	1172	18	140	1330
1988	614.1	560.0	3.6	50.5	1384	24	168	1576
1989	670.1	600.0	4.9	65.2	1530	32	191	1753
1990	690.9	600.0	6.7	84.2	1611	43	200	1854
1991	718.0	600.0	9.2	108.8	1711	57	232	2000
1992	753.2	600.0	12.6	140.6	1835	77	263	2175
1993	798.9	600.0	17.3	181.6	1987	103	305	2395
1994	858.4	600.0	23.7	234.7	2175	139	361	2675
1995	935.6	600.0	32.4	303.2	2405	185	436	3026
1996	1036.1	600.0	44.4	391.7	2685	248	537	3470
1997	1166.9	600.0	60.8	506.1	3027	331	673	4031
1998	1337.0	600.0	83.2	653.8	3441	442	857	4740
1999	1558.6	600.0	113.9	844.7	3942	590	1107	5639
2000	1559.0	311.8	155.9	1091.3	3968	787	1382	6137

(1) Total U.S. Catch
(2) Harvested by U.S. Trawlers for Joint Ventures (foreign/U.S.)
(3) Harvested by U.S. Trawlers for Onshore Processing
(4) Harvested by U.S. Catcher Processors
(5) Non-Resident Workers on Vessels
(6) Non-Resident Onshore Processing Employees
(7) Resident Workers on Vessels or Onshore
(8) Grand Totals: All Workers in Region

from two previous OCS studies and modified to correspond to actual levels of development and updated population estimates: OCS Technical Report Number 51: Western Alaska and Bering-Norton Petroleum Development Scenarios, Commercial Fishing Industry Analysis, August 1980, prepared by the Alaska Sea Grant Program, University of Alaska; and OCS Technical Report Number 60: St. George Basin and North Aleutian Shelf Commercial Fishing Analysis, prepared by Earl Combs, Inc (1981).

Also implied within this scenario is an existing and stable level of OCS development in the region. The nature of that development and its current impact on the community of Unalaska are detailed in the last chapter.

In utilizing the figures provided by the OCS Region, several caveats are in order. First, we do not believe that the number of non-resident processing employees in the shellfish industry will remain constant, as these figures seem to imply. Given the already drastic reductions in the annual harvests of crab for the past two years and the withdrawal or announced plans for withdrawal of processors from the area, it is more realistic to assume that for the next few years at least, and more likely until the 1990s, there will be a continual reduction (at least major fluctuation) in the number of employees in the crab processing sector. Many of those formerly employed on the crab processing lines will be hired to process groundfish but, for reasons to be outlined below, this will not occur immediately.

Second, we anticipate that growth in the groundfish industry will be relatively slow in the 1980s and then pick up considerably in the next decade. This assessment is based on several factors. As the market for groundfish and groundfish products is currently organized, there is no guarantee that the projected increases in the annual harvest of groundfish by American fishermen will be profitable, economically feasible, or even processed in Alaska. In a recent study, R&M Consultants (1981) concluded that the high relative cost of Alaska harvesting and processing compared with prevailing world market prices was a major impediment to groundfish expansion in Alaska. The R&M report cited several examples of recent groundfish processing experiments in Kodiak (New England Fish Company), Petersburg (Icicle Seafoods), and the Aleutian Islands (Icicle Seafoods) which terminated after short periods of operation despite sizeable subsidies to underwrite losses.

Third, as Rogers (1979:8-9) noted in his critique of Arthur D. Little's analysis of the prospects for growth in the U.S. groundfish industry, any projection of increased catch, processing and employment is dependent upon interrelated costs which are external to the industry itself. Such costs include local community expenditures for improvement of harbors, docks, storage facilities, transportation, and so on. To date, it does not appear that these factors have been taken into consideration in evaluations of the impact of groundfish industry development on Unalaska in particular. Such considerations are especially important in the assessment of Unalaska's potential as a center of groundfish processing because of existing limitations in utilities and infrastructure. Such limitations were outlined in the 1979 study of the Alaska Department of Community and Regional Affairs, "Community Planning

and Development for the Bottomfish Industry." These limitations
include: inadequate community water distribution, electrical, and
sewage systems, lack of land suitable for plant expansion and
worker housing. Local officials also point to the existing limitations of the Unalaska Airport as an impediment to the development
of the commercial economic sector.

These concerns were also voiced in a recent study conducted by
the U.S. Army Corps of Engineers (1982), which found that, while
Unalaska is a more attractive locale for groundfish processing
facilities than many other communities in Alaska, it is still faced
with several limitations. They state, for example, that:

> This reconnaissance investigation analyzed harbor sites for
> Akutan for an annual capacity of 200,000 metric tons, but it
> is possible that the already crowded port at Unalaska/Dutch
> Harbor, which is one of the Nation's top fishing harbors, may
> be unable to handle its projected bottomfish yield without
> substantial additional development there. Some of that pro-
> jected yield may in fact be displaced to Akutan or go unreal-
> ized. The State of Alaska, concerned about the prospects of
> demand exceeding capacity at Unalaska/Dutch Harbor, is active-
> ly pursuing community and port development plans at Chernof-
> ski, further west along the island of Unalaska (1982:69).

On the other hand, the decline of crab was not anticipated and may
well have provided sufficient capacity for processing in Unalaska
during the initial stages of groundfish industry development.

Fourth, the current trend for American involvement in the
groundfish industry is in the form of joint ventures. "The processors guarantee markets and prices and the fishermen guarantee
catch—all within guidelines established by the North Pacific
Fisheries Management Council (NPFMC), which allocates fisheries
resources among domestic and foreign producers and monitors their
performance" (Nebesky, Langdon and Hull 1983:III-114). As was noted
in the Bristol Bay Cooperative Management Plan report of 1983,
because of the limited number of vessels in Alaska currently available for such joint ventures, any expansion of the form of groundfish industry activity will probably involve fishermen from outside
Alaska. Moreover, in the event that most of the groundfish harvest
is undertaken by American fishermen in joint U.S./foreign ventures,
processing will be handled by foreign floating processor vessels
and there will be little community-level development or effort.

Fifth, there is currently a movement to explore the possibility of limiting entry to the halibut fishery in Alaskan waters.
Should legislation be enacted for this purpose, the result could
well be to favor outside fishermen at the expense of local fishermen. A similar consequence is associated with the enactment of
limited entry legislation in the salmon fishery (Petterson 1982).
If this were to occur in the halibut fishery, it could serve to act
as a restraint on the number of fishermen expected to reside in
Unalaska throughout the forecast period.

Finally, and perhaps most importantly, groundfish industry
development hinges upon local perceptions, and while most Unalaska
businessmen and residents see such development as both desirable

and vital to the community's future, many are unwilling to commit themselves to it. Some of the local fishermen have begun to convert their vessels for groundfish but most are uncertain whether the conversion is worth the cost or the effort because of the expense in refitting vessels, the degree of foreign dominance in the market, and the uncertainty of success. Many of the existing processors in Unalaska have examined the possibility of conversion to groundfish processing and all but one or two have determined that the effort is not warranted at present. Even with the recognition that groundfish industry development is important to the community's future, it may be some time before processors and local fishermen alike are willing to commit the time, energy, and financial resources necessary to make such development anything but experimental.

4.2.2 Summary of Effects

Changes in the socioeconomic system of Unalaska depend on a variety of factors. The two most important are anticipated population growth and the ability of the local infrastructure, especially housing, transportation facilities, and public utilities, to meet the demands of both economic and population growth. In turn, economic growth will be the primary factor in determining the character of growth in population and community infrastructure. The three features of the community which are expected to change the most, and have the greatest effect on the character of change in other features or subsystems, are the local economy, the value system and social networks. Economic growth, population size and development of community facilities are interrelated such that changes in one affect the course of change in other subsystems. The local political administration will also experience some change, but these changes in turn will be dependent upon projected changes in the local economy, value system, and social networks. Other features of the socioeconomic system of Unalaska, such as the subsystems of education, health care, and social services, are dependent, in turn, on the state of the economy and local government as well as population size. The local religious and recreational subsystems are dependent upon projected changes in population size, values and social networks. Intraregional relationships will be dependent upon the degree of economic growth in each of the communities within the region.

In general, we expect that the sociocultural system of Unalaska will experience some consolidation during the 1980s. What changes do occur will result from an expected leveling off and slight reduction in the rate of growth in the local economy, even though groundfish industry development is expected to occur during this period. Significant change in all facets of the sociocultural subsystem is expected to occur during the 1990s when levels of groundfish industry activity and population growth is expected to increase dramatically. While Unalaska will retain much of its "frontier" or "boom town" character during the latter part of the forecast period, it will slowly acquire the permanent features of a growing community which is more closely integrated with the outside world. Intraregional relationships will be characterized by an increased level of economic competition between the communities of Unalaska, Akutan, and the Pribilof Islands, especially as these communities develop their own facilities for groundfish processing. The use of Unalaska's port facilities for transshipment of processed seafood products, however, will involve a certain degree of economic cooperation between communities as well as a possible expansion in Unalaska's role as hub of regional air transport.

4.2.3 Regional Relationships

During the forecast period, Unalaska's ties with other communities in the region will undergo substantial changes in some areas and remain unchanged in others. These include economic, social, and political ties. Other dimensions, specifically health care and education, which have served to link Unalaska with surrounding communities in the past, are expected to decline in importance.

4.2.3.1 Economic Relations. The key to change in all of the links between Unalaska and other communities in the region is the effect of groundfish industry development in these communities. Of the other communities in the region which currently have some relationship to Unalaska, all but Nikolski are expected to benefit to one degree or another from groundfish industry development in the region. Such development is expected to occur in Akutan, the Pribilof Island communities of St. Paul and St. George, and Chernofski Harbor. If this development occurs along the lines of scenarios developed in other studies (c.f., Dames & Moore 1982a, 1982b; U.S. Army Corps of Engineers 1982), there will be three major consequences in regional relationships involving Unalaska.

The first and most immediate consequence of groundfish industry development throughout the region will be increased economic competition between Unalaska and other communities in the region. Such competition is already becoming evident between Unalaska and Akutan. The development of harbor facilities in Akutan, as projected in the Army Corps of Engineers (1982) scenario, could attract groundfish processors who might otherwise locate in Unalaska. Such development would also mean that vessels which currently must travel to Unalaska for supplies, making an average of fifteen trips per year (U.S. Army Corps of Engineers 1982:38), would not have to do so. This would have an effect on wholesale suppliers, retail establishments, and marine engineering firms in Unalaska.

Despite this projection, however, it is uncertain as to how extensive groundfish industry development will be in Akutan. The location of several processors in Akutan in the late 1970s and the growth of the Trident Seafood groundfish processing complex in the community led to several estimates of rapid economic growth. However, in the past few years, the number of processors in Akutan has declined from eleven in 1981 to five in 1983. Moreover, Trident has been unable to sell their product and appears to be in some financial difficulty. Given these indications, the optimistic projections of economic growth in Akutan may have to be revised.

Economic competition could also result if the Tanadgusix Corporation of St. Paul proceeds with their plans to develop facilities at Chernofski Harbor for groundfish processors. The location of this site and the potential for development (Dames & Moore 1982b) could potentially have greater consequences for Unalaska than the occurrence of groundfish industry development in Akutan. Such development could draw both existing and potential processors and support services from Unalaska. Initially, however, processors which do locate in Unalaska will have to rely on Unalaska's existing commercial infrastructure for supplies and support services. In the short run, therefore, Unalaska could benefit from such development at Chernofski Harbor, although in the long-run such development could be detrimental to the Unalaska economy. However, while this competition may be to the disadvantage of the Unalaska economy, by the time groundfish processing at Chernofski Harbor becomes fully operational, the Unalaska economy should be sufficiently strong to effectively mitigate the potential negative consequences of economic competition.

Second, assuming that significant improvements are made on the airport by the early 1990s, Unalaska's role as a transportation hub will increase. Cold Bay, because of its existing facilities, will remain the major center for air transportation in the region. Unalaska will be linked to Cold Bay, Akutan, and Nikolski by air and, with the addition to jet service, may be linked with the Pribilof Islands as well. These links will be especially important to the community of Akutan which will require expanded air service if the local population and economy continue to grow.

Perhaps even more important than the airport, however, will be Unalaska's role as a containership port. As the groundfish industry to expected to develop throughout the region, a cost-effective means of transporting processed seafood products will become essential. One likely possibility is the use of Unalaska, because of its existing or planned port facilities, as a center for cold storage and shipment of processed products. This port would be especially useful to processors located in Akutan or Chernofski Harbor and would allow for the shipment of seafood products by containerships, reducing transportation and overhead costs.

Third, with the revenue derived from taxes on fish landed and processed, the other Aleutian communities will be able to construct or improve facilities of their own rather than rely on those of Unalaska. The use of the Iliuliuk Health Clinic by residents of Akutan and the Pribilof Islands, for instance, will decline as clinics in these communities are developed. The one exception to this trend will be the community of Chernofski Harbor. Because of the lack of existing facilities, the projected community of groundfish processor and sheep ranch employees may initially have to rely on Unalaska for educational and health care facilities and services. This dependence will probably remain until the end of the forecast period when Chernofski Harbor is large enough to develop facilities of its own.

4.2.3.2 **Political Relations.** Political relations involving Unalaska and other communities in the region are not expected to change significantly in the short term. Currently, Unalaska is used by other communities in the region as a negative example of uncontrolled growth. Officials of other communities, in their efforts to plan for and manage the projected growth associated with groundfish industry development, are seeking to avoid the problems experienced in Unalaska.

Once economic competition between the communities in the region increases to the point that one or more communities is negatively affected, as when processors are drawn to other communities, then some effort at political cooperation between communities may be initiated. Growth throughout the region will eventually necessitate the establishment of management policies for regional development adhered to by all the communities in the region. Because of its location, Unalaska would be likely to benefit from the development of any regional forms of government responsible for managing such growth.

4.2.3.3 Social Relations. Kin-based social relations between residents of Unalaska and the communities of Nikolski, St. Paul and St. George should be minimal through the forecast period. It is possible that ties between Unalaska and the communities of Akutan and Chernofski Harbor may develop, because of the proximity of these communities to Unalaska, their dependence on Unalaska for transportation, and increasing economic ties.

4.2.4 Population

Based on the levels of growth projected by the Minerals Management Service for the entire Aleutian Islands region, contained in Table 4.1, and keeping in mind the caveats to these projections outlined above, the population of Unalaska for the next seventeen years is described the following tables. Table 4.2 provides a comparison of the rate of growth in the number of residents and non-residents in Unalaska and the entire Aleutians region. As this table indicates, Unalaska will represent an increasing proportion of residents in the Aleutians region through the forecast period, rising from 25 percent in 1981 to 51.2 percent by the year 2000. At the same time, the proportion of non-residents in the region working in Unalaska will decline from 37.5 percent in 1981 to 20.2 percent in the year 2000. This is largely due to the assumed increase in the number of residents in the groundfish industry.

The annual rate of growth in total population (residents and non-residents) throughout the forecast period is expected to be 10.2 percent. Most of this growth will come after 1990, when the groundfish industry is expected to increase its rate of growth by 14.2 percent. The number of non-residents will decline through the 1980s, even as the groundfish industry develops, because of the continued decline in the crab fishery. This segment will begin to grow again in the 1990s, but not as high a rate as occurred during the expansion of the crab fishery in the 1970s.

These forecasts are based on five sets of assumptions. First, of the population increases projected for the entire region, outlined in Table 4.1, only a certain proportion will reside in Unalaska. This proportion, however, will grow at a constant rate of 1.3 percent per year such that, by the year 2000, almost two-thirds of all residents in the Aleutian Islands Census Division will be in Unalaska. Almost all of this growth can be attributed

Table 4.2

Projected Population of Unalaska:
First Scenario, 1981-2000

Year	Residents		Non-Residents		Total	
	Number	% of Region	Number	% of Region	Number	% of Region
1981	1054	25.0	890	37.5	1944	29.5
1985	1272	26.0	985	31.8	2257	28.3
1990	1530	28.0	916	24.0	2446	26.4
1995	2129	33.9	1007	21.2	3136	28.4
2000	4521	51.2	1397	20.2	5918	37.6

to migration from outside the region.

Second, despite the projections of the Minerals Management Service, we anticipate a reduction in the non-resident workforce involved in the traditional processing sector. Most of the new employees in the groundfish industry will fill positions which were lost with the decline in the crab fishery. This situation will continue until 1990 when the crab fishery can be expected to display signs of growth.

Third, by the early 1990s, a severe strain will be placed on available housing and certain community facilities and utilities. These strains could act as constraints to further growth unless prompt action is taken to alleviate these problems.

Fourth, fertility and mortality rates should remain constant throughout the period, with minor fluctuations. A possible increase in mortality in the 1980s will be offset by a possible increase in the birth rate in the 1990s. These fluctuations are tied to the increase in accidents and stress-related diseases associated with limited economic growth in the 1980s and the subsequent increase, in the 1990s, in young couples among the semi-permanent resident segment of the population, contributing to an increase in the number of births.

Finally, patterns of migration are expected to change somewhat as the rate of immigration declines and the rate of emigration increases over the next few years. Toward the end of the decade, however, this pattern will reverse itself and immigration will exceed emigration throughout the remainder of the forecast period.

Table 4.3 outlines the projected changes in the proportion of residents and non-residents in Unalaska. The resident category includes permanent and semi-permanent residents and long-term transients. As this table illustrates, the percentage of non-residents will decline throughout the forecast period to 23.6 percent by the year 2000.

Several different assumptions are implied in this forecast. For a while at least, processors will continue to hire employees on a six month basis. This will discourage any significant increase

Table 4.3

Unalaska Resident and Non-Resident Population Projections:
First Scenario,
1981-2000

Year	Residents		Non-Residents		Total	
	N	%	N	%	N	%
1981	1054	54.2	890	45.8	1944	100
1985	1272	56.4	985	43.6	2257	100
1990	1530	62.5	916	37.5	2446	100
1995	2129	67.9	1007	32.1	3136	100
2000	4521	76.4	1397	23.6	5918	100

in processor employees wishing to reside in Unalaska on a permanent basis. Therefore, the rate of growth of the resident population attributable to former non-resident processing employees will be minimal throughout the 1980s. When twelve month contracts do become the rule, as is expected by 1990, the rate of growth of residents will increase significantly. The turnover rate of long-term transients not involved in the processing sector (e.g., government employees) will remain high and possibly increase slightly in the short term. This turnover rate is expected to decline in the 1990s, however, as opportunities for long-term transients (who may be considered residents) increase. The differential rates of growth of residents and non-residents is also based on age, sex, and household size differences. The dependency multiplier for non-residents is smaller than for residents.

No major changes in the age and sex distribution among Unalaska residents is expected for the next seven years. In the early 1990s, there may be an increase in males aged 25-34, but by the latter part of that decade more balanced age and sex distributions will emerge as more residents with families replace non-residents in the seafood processing industry. These projections assume that, for the next few years, at least, newcomers to Unalaska will be primarily young, unmarried males or young couples. This is because of the frontier environment of Unalaska and the nature of the renewable resource economy. Even so, families will continue to grow throughout the forecast period, especially toward the end of the period as the processing workforce experiences a shift from non-resident transients to semi-permanent residents.

Among the non-resident population of processor employees, the existing trend toward older employees who are returnees and toward a larger proportion of males is expected to continue throughout the forecast period.

Finally, the proportional contribution of the various ethnic groups in Unalaska is expected to undergo some change throughout the forecast period, as indicated in Table 4.4. These estimates are based on several different assumptions. First, the estimates for the Aleut population are based on an average annual 5.4 percent rate of growth. This figure is derived from the average of the annual growth rates for 1970-1980 (7.6%) and 1977-1980 (4.1) (see Table 2.5). Second, the estimates for the Black population are derived from an extrapolation of the proportional representation of Blacks to the total population for 1977-1980. This would give Blacks a 2.0 percent share of the population in 1985, 2.5 in 1990, 3.0 in 1995, and 3.5 in the year 2000. Third, the estimates for the "Other" category, including Filipinos, Vietnamese and Mexicans, are derived by taking the current percentage of processor employees belonging to this category (60%) and assuming this proportion will remain constant throughout the forecast period. Because members of this category employed in the processing sector will retain their non-resident status until the enactment of twelve month contracts in the late 1980s, the dependency ratio is assumed to be lower than that of the population at large, but increasing during the forecast period to the same level as other ethnic groups in the community. The dependency ratio for members of the "Other" category will increase from 1.2:1 (1.2 dependents for every worker) in 1985 to 1.4 in 1990, and 1.6 from 1995 to the year 2,000. .

Table 4.4

Projected Ethnic Composition of the Population of Unalaska:
First Scenario,
1985-2000

Ethnic Group	1985		1990		1995		2000	
	N	%	N	%	N	%	N	%
Caucasian	1314	58.3	1297	53.0	1475	47.0	2949	49.8
Black	45	2.0	61	2.5	94	3.0	207	3.5
Aleut	254	11.2	322	13.2	409	13.1	519	8.8
Other	644	28.5	766	31.3	1158	36.9	2243	37.9
Total	2257	100.0	2446	100.0	3136	100.0	5918	100.0

From these figures, three major trends are evident. First, the absolute numbers of each ethnic group will increase in a linear fashion through the forecast period, with the exception of Caucasians who are expected to exhibit a slight decline between 1985 and 1990. This might possibly be accounted for by out-migration due to delays in groundfish industry development. Second, the proportion of Filipinos, Mexican and Vietnamese residents and non-residents will increase such that, by 1995, the "Other" category will comprise over one-third of the total population of Unalaska. Third, if the Aleut population continues to grow at a 5.4 percent annual rate through the forecast period, their share of the total population will remain relatively constant, perhaps even increasing slightly, until the last five years of the forecast period when it will begin to drop off.

One must keep in mind, however, that these figures reflect total population, including residents and non-residents. Among the resident population, Caucasians and Aleuts will comprise a slightly larger proportion of the population than reflected by the figures in Table 4.4, while Blacks, Mexicans, Vietnamese, and Filipinos will comprise a slightly smaller proportion.

4.2.5 Community Facilities

In the next five to seven years, with or without groundfish development, some improvement will be made on existing facilities, including electricity, water distribution, and sewage. There will also be improvements in the docks and in the Unalaska Airport. It is not expected, however, that these improvements will be suffi-cient to accommodate the anticipated groundfish industry develop-ment for three reasons. First, the improvement of these facili-ties depends largely upon the availability of revenue. Such revenue can come from three potential sources, local taxation, state or federal funds, or municipal bonds. The amount of revenue available from local taxation is not expected to increase in the near future and may decline as processors reduce activity or leave because of the decline in the crab fishery. State and federal funds, as noted earlier in this report, will also not increase as local development is increasingly delegated to local authorities and state revenues diminish with the anticipated decline in oil revenue. Bonds may become a possibility in the next few years but run the risk of local resistence to community debt and to develop-ment in general.

A second factor limiting expansion of community facilities and utilities is existing environmental limitations to renovation. As noted in the baseline ethnographic description of the community, facilities and utilities in Unalaska are faced with problems of soil erosion, difficulty of access, and the age of existing struc-tures. The airport in particular is confronted by limitations on runway expansion and improvements with respect to both length and width. While these limitations will not prevent improvements from being made, they do serve as obstacles which make the task of renovation a difficult one at best.

Third, a distinction should be made between increased ground-fish development and increased population in Unalaska. It is expected that most of the improvements in community infrastructure planned for the next few years will help to promote growth in the groundfish industry but will not meet the demands associated with increased numbers of residents in the 1990s. Even with the planned improvements, community facilities and utilities will be under great strain with increased levels of demand. The improved systems of water distribution, sewage, and landfill, in particular, may not be able to serve the projected levels of industrial and population growth anticipated for the 1990s.

The first community utility slated for significant improvement is the electrical power system. With the improvements in the distribution system and the centralization of power generation in the hands of the City Department of Public Works, a uniform and updated electrical power system should be in operation by 1988. The proposed system of power exchange between the city and the processors will contribute to a greater level of efficiency and a uniform distribution system will provide electrical power to all neighborhoods by this time. Declining crab processing activity projected during the next five to seven years will tend to free power for use in groundfish industry development. Standard Oil Hill, an area owned by the Ounalashka Corporation, has only recently (1983) been integrated into the area served by the Unalaska Electric Utility.

Improvements in the city's sewerage and water distribution systems may be delayed because of projected decreases in city revenues available for public facilities. Planned improvements will probably be completed in the next four or five years. By the 1990s, however, neither of these systems will be able to accommodate the increased demand caused by greater numbers of residents in the community. Likewise, while existing landfill is sufficient to meet current needs, there are already indications that this is about to become a pressing problem, particularly in the face of additional development.

Significant improvements in local systems of communication are not expected until the mid 1990s. The local telephone system will make some improvements in equipment and gradually expand in areas serviced through the 1980s, and the existing system should meet local needs for the next seven years. Other forms of communication, including television, radio and the local newspaper, may experience some growth in the 1990s, but this will be largely dependent upon external factors beyond the purview of this report.

The Unalaska Airport has been perceived by local officials as the key to economic growth during the forecast period. Without significant improvements, the airport could act to limit future development because of an inability to accommodate jet aircraft. The high fares (eighty-eight percent greater than comparable routes using the B-737 elsewhere in Alaska) and tariffs (estimated to be fifty-six percent higher) required by operating costs for existing aircraft serving the airport restrict the flow of people, goods and communications to and from the community.

Because of the recent bond measure approved by the community in the last election, funds will be available to make some improvements in the Unalaska Airport terminal building (indeed, as of August, 1983, the new terminal building was under construction), though no funds have been authorized for hangar improvements. There will probably be a delay in the planned runway improvements because of problems in obtaining funds from the state for this purpose, although the project has been included in the state's FY84 budget. Because of these delays, the Unalaska airport will continue to be a liability for the community and a potential impediment to the expected levels of groundfish industry and oil-related development in Unalaska in the 1990s.

Improvement in the harbor and docks in the area will continue throughout the forecast period. The recently constructed small boat harbor will probably undergo some renovation in the early 1990s to accommodate increased usage and larger vessels. The city and the Department of Transportation are currently assessing the feasibility of relocating a portion of the boat harbor facility to Expedition Bay near the Unisea Inn and Universal/Pac Pearl plant sites. Construction of docks is seen as essential to the projected levels of growth both in oil-related activity and the local groundfish industry. In the case of the latter activity, construction of one or more cold storage facilities will also occur in the next few years.

4.2.6 Housing and Real Estate

At the proposed levels of groundfish industry development, perhaps the most dramatic shift in economic activities will be the increase in housing and real estate indices. With the decline in the traditional seafood processing industry, the vacancy rate in Unalaska is beginning to rise. Improvements in local utilities such as electricity, water and sewerage, could help to ease the average residential density, reducing housing costs and expanding the supply of available housing. This, in turn, would help to attract more outside fishermen to live in the community as semi-permanent residents and more long-term transients and semi-permanent residents working for groundfish processors. As more processing employees move into permanent housing throughout the community, the use of processor bunkhouses for employees will diminish.

Construction and development of land is expected to remain at current levels of growth for the next ten years and then increase significantly in the 1990s. However, one of the major limitations to such development is the lack of available land. Both because of the local terrain and market conditions, relatively little land within the city limits of Unalaska is usable or available. The value of existing property, both commercial and residential, will increase significantly. This will have the result of increasing the total assets of existing residents, particularly the Aleut segment of the local population, at the expense of newcomers. In fact, the shortage of available land for development may work to encourage greater reliance on floating processors and dormitory arrangements for transient and semi-permanent processor employees.

In the next ten years, land speculation is expected to increase, both because of the possibility (if not the actuality) of increased OCS activity in the region which may affect Unalaska directly, and because of projected increases in groundfish industry development. Most of the land available for speculation is in the hands of the Ounalashka Corporation. The value of the small amount of land available for housing will rise to levels out of the range of most incoming residents. If fishermen do move to Unalaska, they will be among the few newcomers capable of purchasing the developed lots in Unalaska Valley.

4.2.7 Value System

Because of the nature of the value system of any social group, output and feedback are one and the same. Each response to external resources or demands necessitates either a validation of the existing set of values or changes in the hierarchy of values which range from subtle shifts in preference to radical changes which alter the fundamental character of the community itself.

In the last chapter the value system of Unalaska was characterized as being in a state of flux due to the rapid economic growth of the 1970s, the large influx of outsiders attracted by this growth, and the increased exposure to the wider sociocultural system. Of these three factors, only the third is expected to be of any real significance through the 1980s. Advances in telecommunications and transportation will help to reduce the perceived isolation of Unalaska from the rest of the state, nation and world. The "traditional" value system, held primarily by the older generations of the Aleut population, will continue to decline despite the renewed emphasis on traditional ethnic identity. A reflection of this decline may be the almost complete absence of Aleut speakers in the community by the year 2000.

The expected increase in the social heterogeneity of the population of Unalaska should maintain the opposition between the "frontier" and "modern" value systems. The intensity of this opposition, however, depends on the context. In the short run, for instance, as the increasing social heterogeneity of the community's population is expected to level off, a stable value system will begin to emerge. This value system will comprise a synthesis of "frontier" and "modern" values, giving great emphasis to individual initiative, acquisition, enterprise, and effort. At the same time, a greater concern for "community spirit" will develop as local residents acknowledge the need for combined efforts if the community is to weather the transition between the traditional crab fishery and the development of a local groundfish industry.

By the 1990s, however, it is possible that the opposition between "frontier" and "modern" values could again become more distinct as the number of new residents and long-term transients increase. Those intending to settle permanently in the community will expect a frontier environment; associated with these expectations will be a value system emphasizing individual initiative, a rural orientation, male domination, and competition. Long-term transients, and perhaps the remaining permanent residents, will be oriented to an urban environment, economic success, occupational skill, and relationships based on contract rather than status.

Nevertheless, the current trend toward the adoption of a "modern" value system should continue in the long run, fueled by the economic growth associated with the groundfish industry and the expectations associated with oil-related development. The conflicts associated with this progression will continue in the form of generational conflicts, stress and alcohol abuse.

A reflection of this shift to a modern value system will be evident in the community's assessment of social status. Membership in particular kin groups will remain an important criterion for determining social status through the 1980s but will diminish

144

significantly in the 1990s as the proportion of local residents not associated with large kin-related groups increases. In its place, wealth and occupation will be the dominant criteria. How money is earned and how it is spent are already coming to play a large role in the stratification of Unalaskan society and these factors will continue to be of importance, replacing some of the more traditional indices of status. Consumption of goods exported from outside the community will continue to grow in importance as a means of assessing status, particularly among the long-term transients. Status differentiation based on occupation will increase in Unalaska as the number of new semi-permanent residents and long-term and seasonal transients increase. Those occupying the highest levels of this system will be the professionals, managers, fishing vessel owners, and skilled technical personnel.

Length of residence will decline as an index of status, except for the few remaining permanent and semi-permanent residents. Political acumen may also increase in importance as skill in negotiation and administration will assume greater importance, both with the projected stabilization or downturn of the economy in the 1980s and the dramatic rise of the groundfish industry and other local developments in the 1990s.

Despite the renewed and possibly continued emphasis on traditional cultural patterns and beliefs among the Aleut segment of the population, it is expected that the traditional Aleut belief system will decline in importance throughout the forecast period. This is largely due to the increased exposure of younger generations of Aleuts to the beliefs and world view of the modern sociocultural system. The system of ethics and morality associated with the Russian Orthodox faith will continue to be an important part of the belief system of Aleut residents, but for an ever-decreasing segment of that population. The other system of beliefs held by Aleut residents, including folk medicine and beliefs in "outside men," will perhaps decline at a more rapid rate, especially as the older Aleuts begin to die or move out of Unalaska.

For the non-Aleuts, religion will continue to inform a major portion of the belief systems of local residents. In addition, many new residents will maintain a wider variety of religious belief systems, especially the Vietnamese, Filipinos and Mexicans. Beliefs associated with Roman Catholicism and Buddhism will exist alongside the fundamentalist Protestant belief system held by many current residents.

The world view of Unalaska residents will be influenced by the projected shift towards a "modern" value system and the anticipated shifts in the economy throughout the forecast period. The conflict between those who view the community as an environment to be exploited and those seeking to improve the quality of life in the community will remain as long as a large segment of the population continues to be seasonal transients. With the projected increase in the number of semi-permanent residents and long-term transients, however, this conflict could change as a larger proportion of the population shares a greater sense of commitment to the community. Some conflict will remain between those who wish to make Unalaska a modern city and those wishing to preserve its "frontier" flavor.

As was noted in the last chapter, current perceptions of past, present and future differ among specific segments of the local population. The divergence in these perceptions may continue as the community becomes socially more heterogeneous in the long-run. In the next five to seven years, however, there will be a trend towards convergence of perception, largely because of the common experience of economic stabilization or decline. As long as initial groundfish industry remains limited in size and scope, expectations will be revised to accommodate reduced capabilities and a possible air of pessimism may be shared by greater numbers of local residents. In the 1990s, however, the anticipated levels of growth in the local groundfish industry will generate new expectations and contribute to a renewed sense of optimism throughout the community.

The one component of world view which will continue to be important is ethnic identity. This will be particularly true for the Aleuts throughout the forecast period and the expected numbers of Vietnamese, Filipino, and Mexican residents in the 1990s. Although Aleut ethnic identity is expected to become less of a political issue in the 1990s, it will remain a crucial aspect of self-identity for the Aleut residents. Economic success and political expertise will be an important source of ethnic pride and will contribute to existing efforts to affirm a traditional ethnic identity through education. For the growing numbers of ethnic groups in the 1990s, ethnic identity will remain important even as members of these groups seek to integrate themselves into the larger community. Ethnic identity provides a measure of security and certainty in a novel environment. While successive generations of these ethnic groups will gradually become part of the mainstream of American/Alaskan society, the adaptive use of ethnicity will be important throughout the forecast period.

Reciprocity and redistribution will slowly become more formalized and a function of both church and state in Unalaska. Government involvement in redistribution will occur in the form of welfare and Social Security payments, particularly in the next five to seven years. With the predicted downturn in the economy, churches will also become more active in providing assistance for needy local residents. While this assistance currently takes the form of job referral and food sharing, it may also take the form of fundraising activities for direct contributions to local residents.

In the 1990s, non-government redistribution networks may develop and expand as a way of cementing social relations in a new environment. These networks will become important to different segments of the community for different reasons. Among long-term transients and semi-permanent residents, reciprocity and redistribution will acquire importance as a means of establishing social networks and adapting to the new "frontier" environment. Among older residents, these networks will be crucial to maintaining existing social networks, preserving "traditional" values, and identifying themselves as a separate segment of the community.

4.2.8 Economic Subsystem

4.2.8.1 Output

4.2.8.1.1 Employment.

With the increase in employment oppor-
tunities at levels stipulated by the projected groundfish harvest
in the Bering Sea/Aleutians Region, the local economy will represent the most significant level of change in output activity in
Unalaska. The bulk of this change, however, will come in the
1990s, particularly after 1995. For the immediate future, given
the current decline in the crab fishery, the projected increase in
groundfish industry activity would, at best, only fill the vacuum.

Certain limitations must be kept in mind when viewing the
projected levels of employment in the groundfish industry in
Unalaska. First, not all of the anticipated employment positions
will be available in Unalaska. Akutan is emerging as a major port
for processing vessels and a clear trend exists for groundfish
processing to be handled by large vessels rather than shore-based
plants. Second, most employment opportunities will be seasonal and
not provide sufficient incentive for permanent residence. Even
though groundfish processing will occur on a year-round basis, non-
resident employees will more than likely continue to be hired on
six-month contracts for a number of reasons. One is the fact that
the labor pool from which non-resident workers are drawn may not be
available year-round because of participation in other economic
activities in other parts of the United States (e.g., Filipino or
Mexican workers who are employed in the agricultural activities in
California or Washington). Also, with relatively low wages as an
incentive, and the fact that groundfish processing has a lower
profit margin than crab or salmon processing, processors may find
it financially desirable to continue the current contract system.
This conclusion was also reached by the Alaska Department of Community and Regional Affairs study in 1979. According to this report, "unless current hiring practices by processors change, the
advent of bottomfishing may lengthen the period of sustained plant
operations but will not contribute to the establishment of a permanent resident work force" (1979:11).

Thus, while the employment opportunities in the fishing industry are expected to replace job opportunities lost in the declining
crab fishery, it is not expected that these opportunities will
attract a significant increase in permanent residents in Unalaska
in the near future. From 1990 onward, however, the assumed growth
in the groundfish industry may provide enough jobs to result in a
significant rate of growth in this segment of the population.
Combined with a possible resurgence in the crab fishery in the next
decade, the seafood processing sector in Unalaska will become a
major factor in the course and direction of sociocultural change in
the community.

On the basis of this information, it is assumed that under
this scenario, non-residents will comprise a decreasing proportion
of the total work force in the commercial harvesting and processing
sectors of the Unalaska economy, declining at a rate indicated in
Table 4.5.

Table 4.5

Proportion of Residents and Non-Residents in Commercial
Harvesting and Processing Sectors, Unalaska: First Scenario,
1980-2000

Year	Residents %	Non-Residents %
1980	1	99
1985	5	95
1990	15	85
1995	30	70
2000	50	50

    Table 4.6 provides a representation of the employment opportu-
nities by economic sector in Unalaska throughout the forecast
period. The number of jobs available and the rate of growth in
each sector is based on three specific sets of assumptions. First,
population projections assuming groundfish development provided by
the OCS Region were used to establish a baseline rate of growth in
the commercial harvesting and processing sectors of the Unalaska
economy. Second, assumptions regarding the changes in the employment multiplier used by Alaska Consultants in their groundfish
forecasts (1981:223) were incorporated. The employment multiplier
is estimated to increase from a 1980 level of 1.1 (meaning that for
every ten jobs in the primary sector, there is an additional job
created in the secondary sector), to 1.2 in 1985, 1.3 in 1990, and
1.4 from 1995 to the year 2000. Third, the percentage of the total
increase in new secondary employment in each economic sector is
also taken from assumptions provided by Alaska Consultants
(1981:227). Specifically, thirty percent of new secondary employment is allocated to the government sector, twenty-four percent to
trade, sixteen percent to services, fifteen percent to construction, ten percent to transportation, communications, and public
utilities, and the remaining five percent to finance, insurance and
real estate.
    Under the assumptions of this scenario, total employment in
Unalaska is projected to grow from the 1980 estimate of 1,600 jobs
(Alaska Consultants 1981:216) to an estimated 3,855 jobs in the
year 2000 (see Table 4.6). This represents a total increase of
140.9 percent within a twenty year period or an average annual
increase of seven percent. It should be noted, however, that the
significant growth in all sectors of the commercial sector of the
local economy will come after 1995.
    Table 4.7 provides an estimate of the contribution of the
projected development of the groundfish industry to the Unalaska
economy in terms of basic employment. Included in these estimates
are assumptions regarding growth in basic employment taken from
Alaska Consultants (1981:219). This table notes the number of jobs
in three specific sectors to be directly affected by such develop-

148

ment: commercial fishing; contract construction; and manufacturing. From this table, it is evident that the developing groundfish industry in Unalaska will gradually supplant the traditional crab processing industry, but not until the end of this decade.

Table 4.6

Estimated Total Employment,
City of Unalaska:
First Scenario,
1980-2000

Employment Sector	1980.[a] (actual)	1985	Year 1990	1995	2000
Commercial Fishing	150	141	165	232	456
Mining	2	2	2	3	3
Contract Construction	12	54	71	100	162
Manufacturing	1,166	895	912	1,206	2,337
Transportation, Communications and Public Utilities	57	45	49	70	150
Trade	60	72	84	127	260
Finance, Insurance and Real Estate	27	21	20	28	54
Services	44	52	59	89	184
Government	82	65	81	127	259
Total Employment	1,600	1,347	1,442	1,982	3,855

a. Source: Alaska Consultants 1981:217.

In 1980, only twelve local residents were involved in the harvesting sector of the commercial fishing industry. A few of the local fishermen have already begun to harvest groundfish, particularly halibut, and others have made plans to convert their crab fishing vessels for groundfish harvesting. With the projected declines in the crab fishery, it is doubtful that more of the existing Unalaska residents or new residents will become involved in harvesting crab, shrimp or salmon for the next five to seven years. If the number of resident fishermen does increase, it will be those involved in the harvesting of groundfish. Because this fishery is active throughout the year, it is possible that some of those fishermen from outside the region who participate in the Bering Sea and Aleutian Islands groundfishery will relocate in Unalaska and reside there as long-term transient of semi-permanent residents. Initially, this number will be small, as the expected amount of fish processed by local businesses will be small. In the 1990s, however, as existing processors expand their capacity for processing groundfish and new processors move into the community,

Table 4.7

Estimated Basic Employment in Selected Sectors,
City of Unalaska:
First Scenario,
1980-2000

Employment Sector	1980 (actual) [a]	1985	1990	1995	2000
			Year		
Commercial Fishing	150	141	165	232	456
Traditional	(150)	(80)	(50)	(46)	(78)
Groundfish	(0)	(61)	(115)	(186)	(378)
Contract Construction	5	24	32	38	40
Traditional	(5)	(3)	(2)	(2)	(3)
Groundfish	(0)	(21)	(30)	(36)	(37)
Manufacturing	1,166	895	912	1,206	2,337
Traditional	(1,166)	(620)	(388)	(361)	(612)
Groundfish	(0)	(275)	(524)	(845)	(1,725)

a. Source: Alaska Consultants 1981:219.

more fishermen will reside in Unalaska. With a potential resurgence of the crab fishery in the 1990s, this segment of the local economy will be proportionately larger than it is today.

The number of workers in the seafood processing sector depends on the number of processors, their interest in and capacity for processing groundfish economically, and the improvement of local facilities and community infrastructure which would encourage other processors to locate in Unalaska. For the next few years, the overall number of jobs in this sector is expected to decline, perhaps by as much as ten to fifteen percent of existing jobs. This is a result of the expected closures of some of the smaller processors in Unalaska, such as Pacific Pearl, Whitney-Fidalgo, and Sea Pro. The growth of jobs that does occur with expansion of groundfish processing will offset the anticipated reductions in workforce and planned sale or closure of some facilities because of the decline in the crab fishery. In the 1990s, however, the number of jobs is expected to rise significantly. The seafood processing sector will continue to be the largest source of employment in Unalaska throughout the forecast period.

The transportation sector is expected to provide fewer employment opportunities in the short term. While certain employment opportunities will be created with the initial expansion of the groundfish industry in Unalaska, this may be offset by both the decline in the crab fishery and the withdrawal of Foss Shipping Lines from the area. In the 1990s, however, this sector will experience a rate of growth commensurate to the anticipated growth in the seafood processing sector.

The number of employment opportunities associated with construction is expected to remain at constant levels for the next five years at least. This is for two reasons. First, assuming new processors do move to Unalaska as part of the projected developments in the groundfish industry, these companies will probably occupy facilities vacated by processors currently confined to the traditional seafood industry (i.e., crab and salmon). This is indicated by an already growing increase in the vacancy rate in Unalaska associated with the declining crab fishery. The anticipated increased number of non-resident workers will be housed in existing facilities or in a few additionally constructed dormitories. Second, the current number of construction workers in Unalaska appear to be capable of meeting both existing demand and the projected demand for new housing in the near future. While constuction of new docks or facilities may increase slightly in the next few years or remain constant, the number of construction workers will remain constant or will increase by drawing from other employment sectors.

In the 1990s, the number of construction workers in Unalaska is expected to increase significantly, both as a result of changeovers from other employment sectors of existing residents and the immigration of new residents for construction purposes.

Government employment is not expected to increase until the 1990s and may, in fact, decrease slightly due to attrition. With a projected decline in municipal revenues and a corresponding decline in the number of individuals hired from outside the community, the overall number of positions held by this group will diminish as current employees leave the community to pursue opportunities elsewhere. The number of employees who are hired locally and occupy a position for extended periods, mostly clerks and public works employees, will remain constant or decrease slightly over the next five to seven years.

By the 1990s, the government sector should begin to exhibit a rise in the number of available employment positions, particularly as government revenues are expected to increase as well as local demand for individuals with bureaucratic and managerial expertise. As Table 4.6 indicates, the number of positions will have increased by 298.5 percent in the year 2000. Most of this increase will come from outside hires with a smaller increase coming from local hires, and much of it will be a result of the increase in the number of teachers as the school expands or new schools are constructed.

Throughout the forecast period, one of the greatest increases in employment opportunities will occur in the support services and retail sales sectors. This growth will occur with the increase in the number of fishermen in the region and current levels of OCS development. Retail sales to non-resident fishermen and crews of seismic vessels will increase as will the demand for boat repairs and engineering services.

4.2.8.1.2 **Income**. In the next ten years, income levels will increase throughout the community, but the rate of increase will not be as great as in the past ten years. There will also be a noticible discrepancy between in the rate of growth in different income groups. For those local residents involved in support businesses and industries such as transportation, wholesale sales and ship repair, income levels will rise most dramatically. A second rate of increase will affect those directly involved in the seafood processing industry (i.e., processor managers, local fishermen). A third rate of increase will affect the small retail businessmen and individuals providing particular services (i.e., bars, cab companies, etc.). Those not directly involved in the fishing industry (i.e., those receiving public assistance, certain non-employed or marginally-employed segments of the local population) will experience the smallest rate of growth in income.

4.2.8.1.3 **Consumer Behavior.** Consumer activity in the short-term is expected to reflect reduced spending on certain luxury items such as new automobiles, vacations, home entertainment systems, and dining out. The market for used automobiles and motorcycles will develop during this period. With the projected downturn in the economy in the next few years, greater reliance upon credit for consumer purchases may become evident. Given the expectations of the different social groups in Unalaska and their resources for adapting to this downturn, consumer behavior may become more homogeneous for a few years.

Once the economy begins to grow with expanded levels of groundfish industry development, however, differences in consumer activity will begin to emerge as those residents making more money purchase more luxury items and those making less money rely more extensively on subsistence activities. The types of items purchased will conform to the dominant influences of an urban-oriented, "modern" value system. Such behavior will magnify existing differences in socioeconomic status of local residents to a greater degree than at present.

4.2.8.2 Feedback

4.2.8.2.1 **Cash Economy.** The economic organization of Unalaska is expected to undergo changes immediately. The number of local residents involved in the commercial fishing industry is expected to increase, slowly at first and then dramatically during the 1990s as the twelve month groundfish harvesting season requires fishermen and processing employees to be in the area for most or all of the year. The anticipated rate of increase in the proportion of local residents in the harvesting and processing sectors of the commercial fishing industry is indicated in Table 4.5 above.

The commercial fishing industry will continue to exploit the crab fishery, but this will begin to diminish as greater effort is placed into groundfish industry development. This effort will include refitting of existing fishing vessels, changes in equipment on the processing lines, and allocation of personnel for specific tasks. As noted above, however, a shift from crab fishing to year-round groundfishing will be an extremely difficult one for many fishermen to make.

With respect to the modernization of vessels, it is believed that significant changes in the existing local fishing fleet will not occur until the 1990s. Improvements are tied to income which, in turn, is tied to markets, resource availability, and operating

costs. Because of the decline in the crab fishery, income necessary to upgrade or change equipment will be in short supply, and
there will be less willingness to commit oneself to long-term debt
for such modernization. Moreover, because of the competition with
foreign processors for existing markets, the price for groundfish
will be low while the initial startup and changeover costs will be
high, further discouraging vessel modernization.

Changes in the processing sector will occur in one of two
ways; either changeovers in processing lines and equipment will be
made by existing processors in Unalaska or those processors which
currently handle mostly crab will close down and sell their facilities to new companies specializing in groundfish processing.
Current indications are that both of these changes are occurring.
Some of the existing processors are already leaving or have
announced their intention to leave the community. The Pan Alaska,
Pac Pearl, and Sea Pro plants are for sale and Pac Pearl and Sea
Pro have already discontinued operations. Whitney-Fidalgo has
announced plans to close down for a minimum of two years.

Attempts have already been made to experiment with groundfish
processing but with results too inconclusive to warrant full-scale
operations. The processing sector, therefore, will probably be
assumed by companies which make a greater commitment to groundfish
than do existing processors and which are large enough to handle
the initially high overhead costs for processing groundfish. Sea
Alaska and Universal, currently in Unalaska, appear to meet both of
these requirements. Johanson, the Norwegian firm which had contracted with Sea Pro to process cod, is looking for another processor.
Of those companies remaining in Unalaska, most will begin conversion to groundfish processing in the 1980s while retaining the
capacity for processing crab on a reduced scale. Sea Alaska
already has begun to process fresh frozen cod fillets for the
domestic market and Universal has one of their floating processors
processing groundfish. The processing of other species of such as
salmon or herring will help to fill the gap between declining
stocks of crab and the emerging groundfish industry. Nevertheless,
the proportion of these species processed will also decline as the
effort devoted to groundfish processing increases.

By 1990, there should also be a change in the contract period
used by Unalaska processors to hire employees from a six-month to a
twelve-month contract. It is also likely that the wage scale will
increase, particularly as the competition for labor throughout the
state will increase if the industry does grow at the anticipated
rate. Raising the wage level will also attract more long-term
transients, changing the population structure of Unalaska as well
as affecting the growth rate of other commercial businesses in the
community. The processor workforce will continue to be mostly
Filipino, Mexican, and Vietnamese with perhaps a small increase in
the number of current local residents. The rate of worker return
among seasonal transients throughout the forecast period will continue to increase, but actual levels will be tied to two major
factors: economic conditions of the "lower forty-eight" and wages
paid by the processors in Unalaska.

Large scale enterprise will continue to flourish through the
forecast period, even as the overall level of economic growth in

the community is expected to level off and remain constant for the next five years. Existing size and current or potential contracts with oil companies or local processors are factors underlying this assessment.

In contrast to the optimistic forecast for large-scale businesses, smaller businesses in Unalaska may not fare so well in the short run. The 1980s will be difficult for certain small businesses, particularly those relying on permanent or semi-permanent residents for customers. A few of the smaller operations may even go out of business; the major exception to this assessment will be businesses such as marine engineering or ship repair which will benefit from the growing number of outside fishermen in the area. Moreover, unlike the larger operations which currently have contracts with some of the oil companies in the region, the small-scale businesses are less capable of handling the demand from oil-related activity and hence will not be able to compensate as well for the loss of processor-related business.

Hotels, bars and restaurants currently operating in Unalaska will remain at least for the next five to seven years and, more than likely, throughout the entire forecast period. A few of the less prosperous businesses may change ownership, particularly in the next few years, if the local economy does experience a downturn.

One major business concern which will play a key role in the forecast period is the Ounalashka Corporation. The ability of the corporation to survive a possible takeover by larger, non-Aleut corporations after 1991 will largely depend on its ability to formulate clear policy objectives, ability to compromise with the city and with non-Aleut corporations, and the economic success of its existing financial ventures. Some current investments such as the ship repair facility, gas station, and truck rental company will grow moderately during the 1980s and then at accelerated levels in the 1990s. Other investments such as the laundromat and the duplex rentals on Standard Oil Hill may lose money in the 1980s as the rate of population growth drops and vacancy rates begin to climb, and the Corporation is faced with the choice of either lowering rents or accepting a larger percentage of vacant units for extended periods of time. The corporation will also be faced with decisions regarding the value of its property and determining the criteria on which that value is to be placed. If exorbitant prices are charged for corporation property, the Ounalashka Corporation faces a greater possibility of takeover by non-Aleut interests.

In short, all forms of entrepreneurial activity are expected to grow significantly during the 1990s under the assumptions contained in this scenario. There are certain factors acting as limits to growth in this sector of the cash-based economy which may continue to be implicit throughout the forecast period, particularly in the next few years. These include the lack of both adequate transportation and motivated help. Nevertheless, by 1991 the factors promoting growth of local business should outweigh the disincentives. Among these factors are the development of a uniform electrical power system for the entire community and an anticipated reduction in the level of conflict between local entrepreneurs and the Ounalashka Corporation. The use of local businesses (primarily large-scale commercial firms) for the supply of certain goods and services to oil companies in the area will also contribute to growth in this sector, even assuming that oil-related activity remains at current levels. With the anticipated increase in population during this period, there will be new entrepreneurs as well as new customers in Unalaska. This increase will also be promoted by the increase in income levels associated with groundfish industry activity and the potential sale of some of the property currently held by the Ounalashka Corporation. Large-scale businesses will be forced into increasing levels of competition with one another as demand increases. This competition, in turn, could help to promote better service and lower prices for local consumers. It is also expected that a few new businesses designed to cater to the needs of long-term Filipino, Vietnamese or Mexican transients will emerge in Unalaska during this period.

In the 1990's the service sector of the economy will emerge as a significant portion of the entire economy. This sector will grow with an increase in the number of trained professionals who will provide services on a fee basis. These professionals will include lawyers, accountants, and health care providers.

The trend toward dichotomization of employment as professional or non-professional will continue. Salaries designed to attract qualified professional administrators from outside the community will continue to increase at levels greater than those for non-professional employees. This will lead to an increasing disparity in income throughout the forecast period. Despite this increase in professional salaries, however, it is likely, given the prospect of limited economic growth in the next few years, that the vacancy rate among qualified administrative personnel will increase throughout the 1980s and then begin to level off and decline in the early 1990s.

Among external commercial agencies, the two major areas of growth will be the oil companies, which plan to use Unalaska as a base for certain activities, and outside construction companies. ARCO's presence in the community will increase slightly with the completion of the new dock in Captains Bay providing the foundation for a support base in Unalaska for ARCO's offshore operations. Chevron has announced plans for expansion of its activities in the community, probably in the late 1980s or early 1990s. Exxon will also increase its level of activity in Unalaska to match that of ARCO. While these operations assume only current levels of oil-related activity, they will increase over current levels and make greater use of the local support and service sector. The real question will be the extent of their interaction with the rest of the community. By attempting to maintain a relatively low level of visibility in the community so as not to attract public concern, oil company employees will have less effect on the social fabric of Unalaska than will the seafood processors. The use of outside contracting firms for construction projects in Unalaska will also increase, particularly during the 1990s. While an effort will be made to employ local workers in these projects, the number of transient construction workers is expected to increase in the 1990s.

Other external businesses are expected to maintain their current level of organization with some potential for reorganization in the next five years, to accommodate to the reduced levels of growth, and probable expansion of organization in the 1990s to handle increased demand for services. The existing structure of air transportation services will remain essentially the same in the short run, with a possible reduction in the number of flights as the demand for service diminishes slightly. Growth in the 1990s will be induced by the projected increases in population, economic activity, and the completion of certain essential airport improvements.

Some change is expected in the organization of shipping and container companies which provide service to Unalaska. Each of the shipping and container companies will expand operations in the 1990s as the demand associated with groundfish industry activity increases. Even if much of the groundfish processing were to be done elsewhere in the region, the economics of containership operation providing the most efficient means of transport of seafood products outside the region would suggest the use of Unalaska's facilities as a transshipment center. The construction and use of cold storage facilities in Unalaska will also have an impact on the organization of these companies and the way items are exported from the community, allowing for larger shipments of processed products at reduced costs.

The economy of Unalaska will continue to rely primarily on external markets, both for distribution of local seafood products and as a source of necessary goods and services for the community itself. In the 1990s, however, a trend toward the development of local markets will emerge. This will help stabilize the local economy and reduce its dependency on cyclic variations in the national or international value of local resources and consequent economic effects. The increasing reliance of oil companies and groundfish processors on local businesses for goods and services and the increase in population will be largely responsible for this trend. Small businesses may come to rely upon one another, helping to integrate and expand the local market for their goods and services, but they will still rely heavily on external markets for goods, services and labor supply.

4.2.8.2.2 Subsistence. The subsistence sector of Unalaska's economic organization is expected to remain unchanged with one important exception. A distinction will emerge between Aleut and non-Aleut subsistence strategies beyond merely the quantity of items harvested. For some Aleut residents, subsistence will continue to be based on economic need. It is possible that with the projected downturn in the economy in the next few years, the limits for subsistence-caught salmon will increase or there will be an increase in the number of salmon caught illegally. While some items or activities will diminish in frequency because of the level of effort involved or possible reductions in the resource, they will continue at reduced levels because of their importance in retaining a sense of Aleut ethnic identity (Veltre and Veltre 1982). In general, however, subsistence activities among Aleuts will increase in the 1980s, then level off or decline in the 1990s. The increased pressure on local resources resulting from projected growth of the non-Aleut population may result in the enactment of

156

regulations limiting the number of resources harvested. Illegal subsistence activities may increase and competition for existing resources with non-Aleuts may lead to some conflict between Aleuts and non-Aleuts.

Non-Aleut subsistence organization is expected to remain constant throughout the forecast period. Subsistence activities among this segment of the community are more recreational than economically necessary. Salmon fishing, duck hunting, and berry picking are expected to remain important aspects of subsistence activity for this group.

Fur trapping on Unalaska Island is expected to retain its current organization. It will involve relatively few individuals and experience the traditional fluctuating levels of activity dominated by external market demand.

4.2.8.2.3 **Non-labor Force**. The organization of unemployment in Unalaska is expected to remain the same throughout the forecast period, with the possible exception of the next few years when limited economic growth may increase the importance of unemployment benefits and public welfare for local residents. With the anticipated growth in the economy in the 1990s, however, the community could well return to the current organization of the non-labor force, with unemployment often being a condition of choice and not one of necessity.

4.2.9 Social Subsystem

3.2.9.1 **Output**. As with the economy, the component of the sociocultural system of Unalaska expected to undergo significant changes during the forecast period is the subsystem of social relations. The degree to which this susbsystem does change will largely be determined by the level of population growth and economic activity. Changes in the structure of social relations, in turn, will have implications for the output and structure of other subsystems in the community, including political organization, religion, and values.

Projected increases in population, employment, and income, and existing trends towards fragmentation of traditional extended kinship networks are expected to combine to further weaken traditional patterns of social cohesion among the indigenous population based on kinship. This trend will extend to the level of the nuclear family as the influx of values and attitudes associated with outsiders who move into or work in the community on a seasonal basis generate further conflicts within Unalaska families. Marriage rates are expected to remain stable, but the number of single heads of households will increase as the rates of divorce and separation increase. These changes will occur in any event, but increased economic activity in the form of groundfish industry or OCS development will accelerate and exacerbate the process.

Inter-familial patterns and inter-community ties are expected to weaken, while inter-regional ties may be strengthened. With the projected economic activities, there will be less need, as well as less desire, for inter-familial ties. Inter-community ties will also weaken as social class differences become more pronounced.

Inter-regional ties may increase as more residents search for
marriage partners outside the region or spend increasing amounts of
time in other parts of the state, particularly Anchorage. If there
is any change in the intensity of intra-regional ties, it will
occur primarily between residents of Unalaska and Akutan. No
change in the pattern of social relations between residents of
Unalaska and those of Nikolski or the Pribilof Island communities
of St. Paul and St. George is expected during the forecast period.

Non-kin behaviorial patterns will also change with increasing
levels of groundfish industry development. The major change is
likely to be the formation of social class distinctions based on
income. Social class will cross-cut traditional social networks
based on ethnicity or length of residence. Social relations will
emerge increasingly among members of the same social class,
although relations among ethnic group or residential category members are expected to remain strong throughout the forecast period.
This trend is due to the growth of income disparities and the
projected increase in seafood processing employees and residents
from outside the region. While the income disparity will promote
the formation of social classes and the emergence of a network of
social relations based on social class status, the presence of a
large number of processor workers and non-Aleut residents will
crystalize existing networks based on ethnic group and residential
status.

Inter-ethnic relations are expected to increase most noticibly
in the field of economic activities, but levels of inter-ethnic
social activities will vary along the lines of socioeconomic class.
Members of different ethnic groups belonging to the upper levels of
the socioeconomic status hierarchy will interact socially with each
other more frequently than will members of different ethnic groups
belonging to the lower levels of this status hierarchy. Among the
latter, inter-ethnic social relations are expected to remain at
current levels.

After 1991, ethnic identity itself will be challenged by the
potential alienation of property rights for Aleut residents.
Should local Aleuts divest themselves of their property interests
once the current restrictions regarding property transfer are removed, the economic power which helped to renew a sense of pride in
Aleut ethnic identity will be compromised.

As almost all of the projected newcomers to the community are
expected to be non-Aleut, the ethnic ratio in Unalaska will conti-
nually change at the expense of the Aleut segment of the population. In the next seven years, however, this ratio will remain
relatively constant due to an assumed annual growth rate of five
percent and the relatively small number of non-Aleut immigrants
residing in the community. In the 1990s the ethnic ratio will be
affected by the potential increase in new residents involved in the
groundfish industry. A large percentage of these immigrants will
represent Filipino, Vietnamese, and Mexican ethnic groups.

The ethnic ratio, in turn, will have noticible effects on the
quality of social relations between Aleut and non-Aleut segments of
the community. Factors which could increase friction between the
two groups include: the desire among Aleuts to articulate, at the
encouragement of local Aleut leaders, a traditional ethnic

identity; the strong economic base Aleuts gained through land ownership and investment in commercial ventures (assuming that property is not alienated by 1991); increased economic competition between the two groups, particularly among lower-class Aleuts, Filipinos, and Vietnamese not involved in the processing sector for the same jobs; and increased political competition as the Ounalashka Corporation struggles to maintain some political control over the Aleuts in Unalaska while promoting their interests in the context of the larger community.

With the projected decline in the proportion of Aleuts in Unalaska, however, social relations between Aleuts and non-Aleuts could conceivably improve in the long run. As the proportion of Aleuts in the community declines, their economic position will be less of an issue in the eyes of the non-Aleut population. Those Aleuts who do become financially successful could adopt the residential pattern found in other communities, namely seasonal migration between Unalaska and Anchorage or Seattle. The economically successful members of the Aleut population would be more assimilated into non-Aleut social networks than unsuccessful Aleuts.

Ethnicity will continue to be an important factor for the Aleut community for several reasons. A group ethnic identity in Unalaska is coming to be tied to economic, if not political, power. To retain control over land resources as well as consolidate existing and projected business investments, the Ounalashka Corporation will continue to utilize ethnicity as a means of mobilizing its constitutents, particularly in the face of the 1991 changes in property transfer restrictions. When these changes do occur, ethnic identity will be challenged and perhaps even weakened, especially when social relations throughout the community based on socioeconomic status begin to supplant relations based on ethnic group membership. While differences in ethnic identity may appear between upper-class and lower-class Aleut residents in Unalaska in the 1990s, among both groups, this identity is not expected to revert to its pre-ANCSA character (Berreman 1956; 1964).

As more individuals move into the community, the population will become more diverse and heterogeneous with respect to social class, ethnic group membership, and values and world view. This will result in an alteration of social interaction levels. Social groups will become smaller.

4.2.9.2 Feedback. The structure of social relations based on length of residence in Unalaska is expected to remain constant throughout the forecast period. The social divisions outlined earlier will remain pretty much the same. The major difference will lie in the proportion of individuals belonging to each group. It is expected that in the next five to seven years, the proportions will remain constant with a slight decline in the number of semi-permanent residents, long-term transients, and non-resident transients. In the 1990s, however, these three groups will experience the greatest increases and come to represent significant social networks. In the last ten years of the forecast period, the proportion of the local population comprised of long-term, permanent residents (i.e., those residents who have resided in Unalaska since 1970) will diminish considerably, both as a result of natural population decline (through death or emigration) and in relation to the projected increases in other social groups. By the mid 1990s, the proportion of seasonal transients will decline as more processor workers come to reside in Unalaska on a 12 month basis.

With the predicted decline in permanent residents and transients by the end of the century, it is possible that length of residence will play less a role in the demarcation of social boundaries among various segments of the population of Unalaska than is currently the case. Residents who currently belong to the semi-permanent category (both the "newcomers" and the "pioneers") will ultimately come to be regarded as permanent residents. Interactions between permanent and semi-permanent residents will increase, reducing the distinctions between the two groups. Similarly, there will be less distinction between long-term and seasonal transients than there is at present, especially as many of the long-term transients will also be involved in the processing sector and belong to the same ethnic groups as seasonal transients. Therefore, while today there are four residential categories, by the year 2000 they will have merged into two, resident and transient, and even then length of residence will be of little importance in distinguishing the two groups.

Although socioeconomic status is expected to cross-cut ethnic group boundaries, ethnicity will continue to remain important as a basis for social organization in Unalaska, but for different reasons than currently. For the Aleut segment of the population, ethnicity will remain important as long as family networks remain intact and as it is useful for economic or political purposes. With the sale of some Aleut-owned land in the 1990s and the projected rise in income of some Aleut residents, however, ethnic identity will begin to have different meaning for upper- and lower-class Aleuts. Among lower-class Aleuts, ethnic identity will remained linked to subsistence (Veltre and Veltre 1982) and "reference group alienation" vis-a-vis the non-Aleut community (Berreman 1964). For upper-class Aleuts, ethnic identity will remain a key to economic power and will also be important in a psychological sense of maintaining continuity with the past.

It is possible, however, that ethnicity will become relevant in another context. As the expanding groundfish industry attracts a greater number of long-term transients, many of these new residents will represent different ethnic groups, largely Vietnamese, Filipino and Mexican. As has been the case throughout United States history, immigration of any minority group in a relatively short period of time results in the formation of fairly rigid social boundaries between ethnic groups. Occasionally, these boundaries are marked by incidents of violence and other forms of hostility. No projections for ethnic conflict between white residents and non-white immigrants are being made for Unalaska. There is no doubt, however, that as these segments of the population increase, ethnicity will be a factor in the formation of social networks, choice of residence, job opportunities, and patronage of local businesses.

In place of social distinctions based on length of residence and ethnicity, socioeconomic status and neighborhood will emerge during the forecast period as criteria for membership and activity in social networks. As noted above, socioeconomic status will cross-cut ethnic group boundaries in the early to mid-1990s. As will be detailed below, social distinctions based on neighborhood of residence are already becoming prominant in Unalaska. Given the nature of housing and current pattern of community development, neighborhoods will become distinguished by the socioeconomic status of their residents.

Neighborhood identification is already growing in importance as local residents identify themselves as living on Haystack, Nirvana Hill, Skibowl, or Strawberry Hill. This identification will increase as neighborhoods tend to comprise residents belonging to the same socioeconomic classes, ethnic groups, length of residence categories, and economic sectors. Neighborhoods will serve as boundaries, establishing certain social networks for neighborhood residents while excluding non-residents. As the number of Filipino, Vietnamese and Mexicans working in the groundfish industry increases, some of these neighborhoods may even take on the appearance of ethnic enclaves.

Kinship ties will remain important throughout the forecast period, largely because of the community's size, but they will not be dominant in social relations as in the past. This is due to three specific factors. First, there is a clear trend throughout Alaska, as well as in the community of Unalaska, toward small nuclear families in contrast to large extended kin networks. This appears to be the case even among the indigenous residents. Second, the largest proportion of new residents in the next seventeen years will be either young, single males or young couples without children. The large majority of the population, therefore, will not be in large extended kin networks. Third, as was noted in the last chapter, family stability in Unalaska is threatened by value conflicts which serve to polarize the generations. While this has been particularly evident among indigenous families, resulting in alcohol abuse and domestic violence, it is likely some newly formed families will be similarly affected as the conflict between "frontier" and "modern" values contributes toward a generation gap.

What kin networks do exist will more than likely be the result of extensions of existing families in Unalaska, particularly those families which are either financially prosperous or hold positions of prestige and authority.

With the projected changes in kin relations in Unalaska, the structure of social relations will be based more on secondary social networks. These networks include the church congregations currently in existence, particularly the Unalaska Christian Fellowship, workplace relations, and formal social organizations such as the Lions Club, Volunteer Fire Department, and Volunteer Emergency Medical Service.

Recreational activities will continue to be an important focus for social interaction. Interest in community softball and basketball leagues appears to be firmly rooted as a means of social interaction and are expected to grow in size throughout the forecast period. Classes offered by the City Department of Arts, Culture and Recreation and the University of Alaska Extension Office will also remain focal points for social gatherings, although, in the short run, participation in these activities may

161

decline as funding for the programs decreases. In the 1990s, however, these programs will be important means of social inter- action for two reasons. One is the recreational nature of these activities, which is particularly important in the relatively harsh environment of Unalaska. The second reason is that these activi- ties are successful in integrating the diverse elements of the community, if only for brief periods of time. This in turn functions to reduce social tension and promote community cohesiveness.

Other secondary social networks also help integrate the diverse elements of the community. This is especially true of church congregations. Some organizations such as the Volunteer Fire Department and the Lions Club may involve specific segments of the community; their membership will probably not be broad-based. The Lions Club, for instance, while including Aleuts and non-Aleuts in its membership, does not include women. Workplace relations will remain an especially important focus for social interaction among new residents and long-term transients, particularly if the processors become unionized.

External networks are expected to remain the same throughout the forecast period. The major external social ties which involve residents of Unalaska will occur primarily with urban centers such as Anchorage and Seattle. Because of the projected increase in outside fishermen, Unalaska will remain "a suburb of Seattle," conducting much of its trade and commerce and deriving many of its residents and transient workers from there.

4.2.10 Political Subsystem

4.2.10.1 Output. The response of Unalaska's political subsys- tem to the projected increases in groundfish industry will be evident in four specific areas of activity: administration of community development, levels of conflict, measures of efficiency, and social control. Each of these activities will be discussed in turn.

The administration of community development will become the major activity of the Unalaska city government throughout the forecast period. This administration will be necessitated both by increasing expectations of the current population and by increasing pressure on existing community facilities and services exerted by the projected number of transient and permanent residents. This increased pressure will come in two forms. One will be the needs of groundfish industry processors which are expected to move into the community, particularly in the 1990s. These processors will require improvements in local utilities, transportation facilities, cold storage facilities, housing for employees, and a favorable tax structure. The second form of pressure will be exerted by the increased number of residents and employees in the community. As noted earlier, in the 1990s the local population is expected to increase significantly in response to expanded opportunities in the groundfish industry and the potential resurgence of the crab fishing industry. Those individuals wishing to become permanent residents or long-term transients will require adequate housing and community services. Pressure, therefore, will be placed on the local government structure to provide adequate housing, utilities, health and social services, police and fire protection, education, and recreational activities.

The success of city government in meeting these demands depends largely on the revenues it is able to obtain through local taxation. As most of the land is owned by the Ounalashka Corporation, property revenues will be minimal until 1991. Even after that point, property administered by the Ounalashka Corporation may continue to be exempt from taxes by transfer of title to the non-profit Unalaska Aleut Development Corporation which can avoid taxes if the property is used for certain privileged purposes. City officials estimate that property taxation will not support major expansions of public utilities until the City achieves a permanent population of about 5,000 people. Federal and state sources of revenue-sharing funds are expected to decline throughout the forecast period so the city must depend on the municipal sales and use tax which includes the fish tax. Because of the decline in the crab fishery, the amount of revenue generated by this tax has also declined in the past two years, although much of this loss has been compensated for by revenues acquired from taxes on petroleum products. This situation is expected to continue with a possible stabilization resulting from expansion of the local groundfish industry. If processors demand a more favorable tax structure as a prerequisite for relocation or expansion in Unalaska, however, this stabilization may not occur until 1989 or 1990. The decline in revenues may necessitate a few years of "austerity budgets." With the projected increases in tax revenues, both from property taxes and sales and use taxes, in the 1990s, however, the city will undoubtedly move further, and with greater speed, into improvement of existing, and the development of new, facilities and services.

Levels of political conflict are expected to increase in the next ten years. This conflict will occur in three specific forms. One will be among the various segments of the community interested in securing control of the city council. The objective of this control will be to influence the direction of the city's role in economic development, provision of services and management of growth in the private sector.

The second form of conflict may occur between the Ounalashka Corporation and the city council. This conflict is expected to occur as a result of the city's interest in managing local development and meeting the anticipated levels of demand noted above. It is the Ounalashka Corporation, however, which will have the greatest capacity, at least in the short term, for implementing many of these development schemes because of its control of property and its expansion of private investment in the commercial sector of Unalaska's economy. Although some form of compromise must inevitably be reached if both agencies are to meet their stated objectives, such compromise may not be reached without a certain amount of competition and disagreement in the next few years. Nonetheless, this should not be overemphasized. The City and the Corporation have already demonstrated the ability to work cooperatively, as, for example, in the case of the current draft land use plan which was developed by the City in consultation with the Ounalashka Corporation.

Third, political conflict, as has emerged in other communities in the region, may occur between the profit-oriented Ounalashka Corporation and the non-profit Unalaska Aleut Development Corporation. As noted in the last chapter, the two corporations currently differ on how to best serve the interests of the Aleut population of Unalaska. However, there has already been some discussion of possible transfer of some responsibilities from the Ounalashka Corporation to the Unalaska Aleut Development Corporation as a means of protecting certain investments and interests from divestiture in 1991. Such a transfer in itself could engender further conflict between the two organizations, because of differences in philosophy and objectives and because of the increase in political power of the UADC with its increasing economic power. However, in the long run, the two organizations will also have to achieve some measure of compromise if either is to operate effectively. As the utility of each corporation becomes apparent in competition with other social groups, a measure of cooperation and concerted action between the two could emerge.

The measures used by local residents to assess the efficiency of the city government will also change, particularly in the next ten years. This change will result from new expectations on the part of local residents, particularly the expectations of recent newcomers who will bring with them the measures used to evaluate the efficiency of local government in other parts of the United States. In the next ten years, community debt is expected to increase as the tax base declines, and revenue-sharing funds available from state and federal sources diminish. The city government will have to accommodate increasing numbers of residents who possess higher expectations of city government performance with decreasing revenues. This condition alone will fuel political conflicts among various segments of the community. In the short run, community satisfaction with local government will decline. However, if the local groundfish industry begins to replace the revenues lost with the decline of the crab fishery, the city may be able to improve its level of efficiency, reducing the level of local dissatisfaction with services and facilities.

If the population of Unalaska increases at levels projected with the development of the regional groundfish industry, one of the most dramatic consequences will be a rise in the crime rate. As social differentiation based on income becomes more prominent in the next ten years, those at the lower end of the socioeconomic scale will be increasingly subject to the temptation to burglarize and rob. In addition, as population increases while levels of police protection remain constant, increases in violent crime and traffic violations will occur.

In the next five to seven years, the increase in crime will consist largely of a rise in the number of misdemeanors, especially traffic violations, alcohol-related offenses, and crimes against property. With the projected increase in population in the 1990s, felony offenses will also begin to rise.

4.2.10.2 **Feedback.** While the levels of certain political activities are expected to increase throughout the forecast period, the political organization of Unalaska is expected to remain relatively constant, at least for the next ten years. A slight reduction in the number of city employees is expected in the next five to seven years, but in the 1990s the city government will expand in both size and scope. In the meantime, however, a gradual shift will occur in city administration from the current pattern of long-term transients who assume certain responsibilities such as planning and administration, to semi-permanent residents. There will be a greater reliance on advisory boards in the next few years to obtain feedback from local residents and to assist in the decision-making process, particularly as population grows and these boards essentially compensate for a lower level of informal contact among community members. However, any growth in local government will be dependent upon its financial resources, which are not expected to increase in the short run.

In the long run, the structure of the city government is expected to expand to accommodate the increased demand for services. The greatest increases will come in the area of public works, with perhaps somewhat smaller increases in planning and development, and financial administration.

In contrast to the short-term stagnation in the growth of the city government, the Ounalashka Corporation may experience some growth and alteration in structure as it becomes more involved in management of commercial investments. The one factor militating against such growth, however, is the relative absence of a pool of qualified leaders in the Aleut community. Existing leaders will be confronted with increasing demands, while younger, qualified Aleuts may continue to be reluctant to assume leadership positions.

In the 1990s, the Ounalashka Corporation may begin to undergo further changes in its structure. These changes will be necessitated by two factors. First, in 1991, the Corporation will lose much of its control over the property of its shareholders. Although they will retain the right of first refusal, they will have to compete with other bidders for the property of individual corporation members. To retain control over the property, and to continue policies of economic development and financial investments, some changes in the organization will be required. In this endeavor, it is possible that many of the responsibilities currently undertaken by the Ounalashka Corporation will be transferred to the local non-profit corporation, the Unalaska Aleut Development Corporation, both for tax purposes and in the interest of preventing the wholesale transfer of land held by the Ounalashka Corporation to non-Aleut businesses or individuals. Another possibility is reorganization of the Ounalashka Corporation under the Indian Reorganization Act to institute trust status on Aleut-owned lands.

Second, by the end of the decade, some compromise between the Ounalashka Corporation and the city government will have to be achieved if both organizations are to meet their goals. This compromise may eventuate in a closer working relationship between the city and the Ounalashka Corporation. Certain changes in the objectives or the structure of the Ounalashka Corporation, however, may result from the compromise made to achieve this relationship.

The structure of social control will continue in the direction of greater emphasis on formal mechanisms of control, while informal mechanisms, such as gossip and traditional sanctions, become inef-

fective. The range of criminal activity associated with a frontier
environment (e.g., public drunkenness, assaults) will remain constant or decline throughout the 1980s while overall crime rates
increase. Law enforcement will also remain relatively constant,
handled almost exclusively by the Unalaska Department of Public
Safety. The demand for police protection will first decline then,
about 1990, begin to increase again. However, the number of police
officers is expected to remain at relatively constant levels,
possibly declining by one or two officers, with a fairly high
turnover rate. It is possible that as population increases in the
1990s and the community experiences a period of rapid economic
growth, increased demand for services and increased revenues will
result in more personnel.

4.2.11 Religion

4.2.11.1 Output. Religious activities in Unalaska will
remain essentially unchanged for the next seven to eight years.
The belief system will continue to be characterized by the dicho-
tomy between religious and secular beliefs. Religious beliefs will
continue to have great influence among Unalaska residents. The
Russian Orthodox faith will continue to meet the spiritual and
psychological needs of Aleut residents, especially since that
belief system is tied to ethnic identity and concern for that
identity will increase as the ratio of Aleut population to non-
Native population continues to decline.

Similarly, levels of participation are expected to remain
constant. The Unalaska Christian Fellowship, because of its vigo-
rous efforts at recruitment of transient processor employees for
weekly services and its focus as a voluntary organization for
social interaction, will see a gradual rise in weekly attendance of
religious services and perhaps an even greater rise in attendance
of church-sponsored social events.

4.2.11.2 Feedback. The religious subsystem is not expected
to change much over the next eight to ten years. It is possible
that distinct congregations of Baha'i and Mormon faiths will eventually disappear due to their small size and lack of separate
facilities or sources of support. Similarly, the Russian Orthodox
church will remain relatively constant in terms of its role in the
community, the size of its congregation, and its leadership.

The Unalaska Christian Fellowship will continue to play an
expanded role in the community, especially as its leadership becomes a permanent part of the community. It will serve as a potential political force as well as a voluntary social organization.
The schedule of activities will remain constant, but some fragmentation of social events is bound to occur as the congregation
becomes more heterogeneous in membership. It is also possible that
one or more splits may occur within the congregation, either on the
basis of differences in religious belief or because of increasing
socioeconomic differentiation. If such fission does occur, small
groups may break away to form their own fellowship groups, meeting
informally in each other's homes or renting community facilities
for purposes of worship. One or two of these splinter groups may

even become strong enough to establish their own churches, more than likely of a fundamentalist variety. Such fission, however, is not expected to generate any serious conflict within the religious community of Unalaska and, given the current strength of the Unalaska Christian Fellowship, would not seriously weaken the original church within the forecast period.

In the next ten years, the small Catholic mission in Unalaska may experience some growth, largely through its association with the Unalaska Christian Fellowship, and its potential for attracting Mexican and Filipino processor employees for religious services.

In the 1990s, the religious organization of Unalaska will begin to experience considerable change. With the projected increases in population due to both groundfish industry and oil-related development, some of the existing religious institutions will experience growth in membership while a few new institutions, perhaps missions of one or more Protestant denominations, will emerge in the community. Particularly likely is the emergence and growth of another fundamentalist congregation. These groups appear to be on the increase with respect to missionary activity and are flexible enough to adapt to a frontier environment. Also, as noted above, the most likely source for such a congregation would be the fundamentalist members of the Unalaska Christian Fellowship.

The Catholic Mission, because of the anticipated growth in transient processor employees, may develop into a full-fledged church with a facility of its own and a resident priest. This growth, however, will ultimately depend on the efforts of a small group of semi-permanent residents to seek out a priest to reside in the community on a long-term basis and acquire the funds necessary to construct a church. The Unalaska Christian Fellowship, because of its current policies of recruitment, will also benefit from the growth in population.

The Russian Orthodox Church of the Holy Ascension may also experience some growth in the 1990s, largely as a result of the projected increase in the number of Aleut residents. It is not expected, however, that the Russian Orthodox congregation will grow to the same degree that the non-Native congregations do. There has already been some involvement of Aleut residents in the Unalaska Christian Fellowship and this may continue in the future as the UCF becomes a focus for the social activities of permanent residents, Aleut and non-Aleut alike.

As has been implied in the above discussion, one aspect characterizing each of the major religious institutions in Unalaska is their association with a specific ethnic group. The Russian Orthodox Church will remain an Aleut ethnic church while the Catholic church will serve the spiritual needs of Filipinos and Mexican-Americans. The Unalaska Christian Fellowship will include members from all ethnic groups but the bulk of its congregation will continue to be Caucasian. Other churches or missions associated with various fundamentalist Protestant groups may also assume the character of ethnic churches.

4.2.12 Education

4.2.12.1 **Output.** Projections of educational activities
through the next twenty years are tied to: 1) the number of school
age children likely to be in the community, 2) the amount of
revenue available for school programs and facilities, particularly
municipal revenues, 3) the importance of education for different
segments of the community, and 4) the rate of teacher turnover.

The number of school-age children likely to be in the
community through the forecast period is related to the population
of permanent residents. In the 1981-82 school year, the total
Unalaska School population (165 students) comprised 15.6 percent of
the total population of residents in Unalaska. Assuming that this
percentage remains constant through the forecast period, the estimated enrollment levels in Unalaska will increase by an average
annual rate of 16.4 percent. Table 4.8 provides an estimate of this
enrollment by five year periods.

Despite this projection, however, it should be noted that
school enrollments have been declining for the past few years and
may continue to do so for the next few years. The basis for this
projection is as follows: First, the groundfish industry will not
develop rapidly enough to completely replace the losses suffered
with the decline in the crab fishery. Because of this, families
of processor managers will not be as numerous, reducing the school-
age population. Second, the proportion of professional families
residing in Unalaska experience a relatively high rate of turnover,
averaging five years residency in the community. We expect this
pattern to continue, at least in the short-term. The expected
immigration of professionals with families, therefore, will not
necessarily mean an increase in the number of school-age children.
Third, most of the new residents in the community will be single
males or young couples without children and will not contribute to
an immediate increase in school-age residents.

The dropout rate at the primary and secondary school level is
expected to decline slightly or remain constant throughout the
forecast period. Participation in the educational system is tied
to both employment opportunities and the value placed upon education in the wider sociocultural system. With the limited number of
employment opportunities available in the short-term, education

Table 4.8

Unalaska School Enrollment Forecast:
First Scenario,
1985-2000

Year	Enrollment
1985	198
1990	238
1995	332
2000	705

will be perceived as essential to obtaining a well-paying job. This perception will be reinforced by the value placed on education in the wider sociocultural system. Consequently, there will be increased pressure within families to keep children in school. This will occur, even among Aleut families which have been more ambivalent about sending children to school in the past.

Participation rates in adult education and vocational education are expected to experience slight to moderate growth in the next seven to ten years. Adult education is a mechanism for social interaction as well as recreational activity, particularly among the permanent residents of the community. Adult basic education will largely serve Aleut residents who have not been able to benefit from the regular educational program of the Unalaska schools and transient processor employees wishing to learn English or acquire a basic education. The need for vocational programs offered through the Unalaska High School will increase as the demand for skilled local labor increases with projected construction associated with the anticipated levels of groundfish industry and oil-related development. Such programs, however, will depend upon the availability of funding and are likely to decline dramatically if a source of city revenue is not available.

In the 1990s, adult and vocational educational programs will experience a period of rapid growth as funds become available for the expansion of existing programs. Participation levels will increase as the projected new residents seek adult education as a form of social and recreational activity and as existing residents seek vocational training in order to utilize new employment opportunities.

Higher education throughout the forecast period is expected to increase gradually. Several factors contribute to this assessment. The decision of an Unalaska student to attend college or university outside the community is tied to: 1) the degree of willingness of the student's family to allow him or her to leave the community 2) the attractiveness of local economic opportunities, and 3) the ability of local schools to prepare students for higher education. In all three respects, circumstances exist which could encourage more students to leave the community to attend college or university elsewhere. With the expected continuation of the pattern of short-term residence of professionals and processor managers, the lack of a long-term commitment to the community would encourage students to seek educational opportunities elsewhere. As economic opportunities remain at constant levels or decline slightly over the next seven to ten years, there will be little financial incentive to remain in Unalaska, unlike other fishing communities where high school students have been known to earn over $50,000 a year in the salmon fishery. Lacking such an incentive to remain, higher education will become a more attractive option.

The local school system also appears to be improving in quality, as indicated by a comparison of recent achievement test scores with the statewide average. If this trend toward provision of quality education continues, and we expect it to, the students who do graduate from the Unalaska High School will be better prepared to handle the experience of attending college or university outside the community.

The rate of teacher return is expected to decline slightly over the next seven to ten years because of the projected state of the local economy. However, in the 1990s, the rate of return will be at levels which are comparable to the existing high rate. As the overall quality of life in the community improves, teachers will remain in Unalaska for longer periods of time.

Extracurricular activities are expected to remain at current levels throughout the forecast period. Participation levels in extracurricular activities will remain high because of their social and recreational importance. As the school-age population increases, more students will be involved in these activities but the overall level of participation will remain the same as other opportunities for social and recreational activity will emerge. The same can be said of overall community participation in these extracurricular activities.

4.2.12.2 **Feedback**. For the next ten years, the organization of the educational system of Unalaska will remain essentially unchanged. Educational opportunities will continue to be available for all segments of the population. A pre-school will remain in one form or another with the possible development of a second pre-school in the late 1980s. This assessment is based on two factors: one, the anticipated increase in residents and transient processor workers with children during this period; and two, an increasing dependence upon such a facility as a form of day-care while parents are working.

Primary and secondary education will be handled by the Unalaska School District. The Unalaska School will remain the sole source of primary and secondary education in Unalaska well into the 1990s. Given the projected increase in school enrollment as outlined in Table 4.8, additional schools may be constructed. One likely scenario would be the exclusive use of the existing Unalaska school as a secondary school while two primary schools, one on Unalaska Island and one on Amaknak Island are constructed. A school on Amaknak Island is particularly likely because this is where most of the new residents will be located, although the cost-effectiveness of a multiple campus system will have to be carefully evaluated. The catchment area of the Unalaska School District is expected to remain the same throughout the forecast period.

The number of teaching personnel may diminish by one or two in the next few years but will then increase by as much as 100 percent from current levels by the year 2000. This projected growth is based on potential increases in numbers of students as well as available revenues resulting from projected groundfish development and property taxes.

Educational objectives will begin to change in the next few years. There will be a greater emphasis on vocational education; programs which offer on-the-job experience for local students. Efforts will also be made to improve achievement levels of Aleut students who currently lag behind other students in Unalaska. Such efforts will be directed at involving Aleut parents in the formulation of educational objectives and the direction of extracurricular activities.

The structure of the Adult Education and Extension programs will remain intact for the next five to seven years, though there will be changes in the funding available, the number of instructors, and the administration of such programs. These programs are expected to suffer from a lack of adequate funding in the short-term, resulting in fewer courses offered and a reduction in salaried positions. In the long run, however, the programs are expected to expand, especially since they provide a basis for social and recreational activities for those segments of the community expected to experience the greatest growth in the 1990s.

4.2.13 Health Care

4.2.13.1 **Output.** Health care needs are expected to increase through the forecast period. A major portion of the increase will be due to stress-related disorders, primarily alcohol abuse, alcohol-related accidents, and hypertension. In the short term, these disorders will be related to the levelling off of economic growth and the disparity between a stable or declining economy and increasing expectations resulting from the past increase in the crab fishery and the anticipation of growth in the groundfish or oil industries. As this disparity between capabilities and expectations increases, so will the perception of deprivation which is related to the occurrence of stress-related disorders. Thus, in the short term, a greater number of illnesses will occur among a slightly smaller number of residents.

In the 1990s, the number of disorders will continue to increase, but be exacerbated by both the increased number of residents and the stress associated with boom-town conditions. While the projected increases in employment opportunities and per capita income will help to relieve certain economic tensions, the strain on existing community facilities and services will result in forms of stress similar to those experienced in the 1970s and early 1980s.

The morbidity rate is expected to increase accordingly. Mortality will increase slightly as a by-product of the projected increase in alcohol-related illnesses and accidents. Mortality due to other causes, however, will remain constant, as elderly residents move out of the community to live in retirement elsewhere.

While the demand for health care will continue to increase, the level of service provided in the community is expected to remain constant for the next few years. The quality of medical care provided by the Iliuliuk Health Clinic, measured in terms of number of personnel and facilities, will remain constant until the late 1980s. Funding for the clinic provided by the city is not expected to increase until more revenue becomes available through taxation or external sources.

Those increases which do occur in the provision of services will take the form of emergency medical technicians and emergency transport to facilities outside the community. Emergency medical technicians now comprise the major part of the medical care offered in Unalaska and, given both the types of health problems expected to occur in the near future and community interest in EMT training, the number of residents trained as emergency medical technicians and the kinds of service provided by these individuals is expected

to increase.
4.2.13.2 **Feedback**. According to the study conducted by D.E.
Raven Associates (1982), the structure of health care in Unalaska
will remain unchanged through the 1980s. This assessment was based
on the perceived lack of community interest in expanded facilities,
conflicts between the city administration and the Ounalashka Corporation (although these are unspecified and, according to others
in the community, may be less than implied) and preference for
health care outside the community. In the 1990s, it is possible
health care will undergo major changes in Unalaska. As the number
of cases increases and as the cost of emergency medical transport
becomes prohibitive, there will be considerable pressure to expand
the facilities and range of services provided by the Iliuliuk
Health and Family Services Clinic. Such expansion could take the
form of additional personnel, perhaps one or two additional
physicians, a dentist, and two or more nurses or physician's
assistants. The clinic itself will probably undergo some renovation and expansion, with the possible addition of rooms for treatment and short-term stay, an additional operating room, and a
dental clinic.
Toward the end of the forecast period, the population of
Unalaska will have become sufficiently large to support a small
hospital in the community itself. The construction of such a
facility, however, will depend on the availability of funds, the
relative cost of health care outside the community, and a change in
local preferences for outside medical care.
The cost of health care for Unalaska residents is expected to
increase during the 1980s. Much of this cost is attributable to
high transportation costs for medical emergencies and hospitalization outside the community. If Unalaska is serviced by jet aircraft once necessary airport improvements are made, this cost could
decline. Relative costs for care received at the Iliuliuk clinic
will also increase during the next few years because of the projected downturn in the economy, even though absolute costs remain
constant.

4.2.14 Social Services

4.2.14.1 **Output**. As is the case with health problems, the
frequency of social problems requiring professional assistance is
expected to increase throughout the forecast period. Alcoholism,
generational conflicts and family violence are expected to remain
issues within the community. While much of this problem will be
handled by the existing infrastructure, it is likely that the
demand for services will exceed supply. This situation will per-
sist throughout the forecast period, particularly since social
services are largely funded by external agencies such as the
Aleutian/Pribilof Islands Association or the Alaska Department of
Health and Social Services. As the state is expected to have less
revenues derived from oil in the 1990s, social services could be
adversely affected and perhaps will increasingly become the responsibility of the city. Because Unalaska is the major population and
economic center of the region, it could benefit from an expansion

of APIA social service programs, although such programs will be
primarily intended for smaller communities.

4.2.14.2 **Feedback**. With the recent addition of a clinical
psychologist to the community, the range of services provided will
expand. However, because of the increased demand, it is possible
that the quality of service may suffer. By the 1990s, the demand
will have increased enough to produce several changes in the structure of social services. The psycholgist may be supplemented by
one or more trained social workers with specialization in individual and family therapy. An alcohol rehabilitation program will
become crucial as alcoholism comes to be seen by local residents as
more of a serious problem.

4.2.15 **Recreation**

4.2.15.1 **Output**. The extent to which Unalaska residents
participate in recreational activities is expected to remain relatively constant, though some variation in the choice of activities
will occur as a result of changes in the local economy. In the
next five to seven years there will be a greater increase in
subsistence-related forms of recreation and a decline in outside
vacations as the economy experiences a downturn and then stabi-
lizes. With less income available for recreational activities,
more time and energy will be spent of forms of recreation which are
local and relatively inexpensive. In the 1990s, however, the
community will return to levels of recreational activity which
roughly correspond to existing patterns. Outside vacations, dining
out, and activities requiring motor vehicles will increase.

Because these patterns are tied to income levels, the projected changes will not affect all segments of the population
uniformly. Subsistence-related forms of recreation among the Aleut
population, regardless of income level, are expected to remain at
constant levels, at least until 1995 when the overall population of
the community is expected to increase markedly. This assessment is
based on the fact that these activities serve important social and
psychological functions for local Aleuts. Among the non-Native
segment, participation in these activities will be based on income
level and value system. Those who reside in or are expected to
move to Unalaska and wish to enjoy the "frontier" character of the
community will undoubtedly spend more time on these activities than
long-term transients or semi-permanent residents wishing to enjoy
activities associated with a modern, urban environment. This
latter group, particularly those with the incomes to do so, will
spend greater amounts of time on vacations, home entertainment
systems, and dining and drinking in public places.

By the end of the forecast period, if the population does
increase to levels assumed in the scenario, per capita subsistence
activities may decrease because of the pressure exerted on local
resources by the overall increase in demand. While the level of
subsistence activity of non-Aleut residents in the community is
expected to be less than that of Aleut residents, the overall
numbers of non-Aleuts participating in subsistence activities may
pose a threat to available supply of local resources, resulting in

increased regulation and the imposition of further limits on the amount of resources harvested. This could lead to conflict within the community, especially given the importance of these activities to the Aleut segment of the population, and perhaps result in an increase in illegal subsistence activities.

4.2.15.2 **Feedback**. While the degree to which local residents engage in different types of recreational activities Unalaska may undergo some change throughout the forecast period, the range of these activities will remain the same. In the 1990s, it is conceivable that a few more bars and restaurants may open in the community, providing more opportunities for dining and drinking outside the home. Already, the restaurant at the airport has applied for a liquor license, providing an additional location for entertainment of this nature in the community. The number of community-sponsored recreational activities may also expand as municipal revenues begin to increase during this period. For the most part, however, even with expanded levels of groundfish development and current levels of OCS-related activity in the region, the dimensions which distinguish recreational activities in Unalaska (traditional vs modern activities, urban and rural-oriented activities, requirements of a cash income, and location of activity) will remain. In the 1990s, the structure of this subsystem will experience a shift in the direction of modern, urban-oriented, cash-based activities and vacations outside the community but there will always be a significant part of the population participating in more traditional forms of activity as well. As the population becomes less transient, the use of modern forms of transportation, particularly skiffs and motorcycles, for recreational activities will increase. Towards the end of the forecast period, there may also be an increase in the number of trucks and airplanes owned by local residents and used for recreational purposes.

4.3 SECOND SCENARIO

4.3.1 Assumptions

The following discussion of an alternative scenario will examine only those features of the sociocultural and socioeconomic systems of Unalaska that are expected to show major variation from the first scenario. It is not intended to be as comprehensive but rather provide alternative sequences and levels of development supported by information currently available.

This scenario comprises our assessment of the effects of groundfish development (at levels provided by the MMS and modified in the first scenario) occurring in conjunction with projected levels of development related to outer continental shelf oil activity. The level of oil-related population growth has been stipulated by the Social and Economic Studies Program of the OCS Alaska Region. For the purposes of this analysis, the figures, contained in Table 4.9 below, are accepted at face value. It is assumed under this scenario that most OCS activity in the region

174

will occur in areas which are remote to Unalaska. The community
will continue to be a staging area for shipment of supplies and
personnel to project sites, largely because of its existing
transportation facilities and service sector. Onsite oil-related
workers are projected in this scenario to begin residing in
Unalaska in 1985 and reach a maximum of 222 workers by 1995.

Table 4.9

Projected Population Growth of Unalaska due to
Groundfish Industry and OCS-Related Development

Year	Permanent Residents	Transient Fishermen/ Processing Workers	New Perm/Res	Onsite OCS Commuters	Total
1981	1054	890	0	0	1944
1982	1076	890	0	0	1966
1983	1144	940	0	0	2084
1984	1214	969	0	0	2183
1985	1272	985	220	120	2597
1986	1329	973	32	38	2372
1987	1372	946	95	80	2493
1988	1416	902	112	89	2519
1989	1477	908	223	139	2747
1990	1530	916	169	106	2721
1991	1597	924	220	98	2839
1992	1684	937	347	118	3086
1993	1792	955	562	164	3473
1994	1939	978	745	209	3871
1995	2129	1007	812	222	4170
1996	2381	1049	821	222	4473
1997	2724	1102	841	222	4889
1998	3182	1174	848	222	5426
1999	3811	1270	860	222	6163
2000	4521	1397	877	222	7017

4.3.2 Summary of Effects

This scenario is one extreme in a continuum from no change to
major externally-induced change. The most severe forms of negative
consequence occur under this scenario. Population grows at a rate
which is higher than the physical, social, and political
infrastructure of Unalaska can support. Even if we assume that
OCS-related construction activities are relatively isolated and
internally maintained, virtually all community facilities and support services now in place are inadequate to accommodate the projected growth in population.

Community facilities, depending on how abrupt or gradual the
development process, will be taxed beyond capacity within the first
two or three years of growth. The inherent lag time in meeting
water and sewerage requirements cannot be met without extraordinary
funding sources and major construction effort. The City Council

has recently (as of August, 1983) decided to proceed with the sewerage system already designed by calling for a $3 million bond election, although no funding sources have yet been seriously considered for expansion of the water system. City planners note, however, that if such funding becomes available construction of the system could be completed within two years. The economy of Unalaska would be subject to the profound influence of competing economic bases—in employment, services, product demand, and so on. Social distinctions based on occupation, income, and residence location will become even more prominent than those projected under the first scenario. Scarce revenues and deficient community facilities could generate increased levels of political conflict, especially between the OCS-related population and permanent and semi-permanent residents. Without additional sources of revenue, the size of city government will remain essentially the same as projected in the first scenario. Induced changes in the educational system will include rapid physical expansion of existing facilities and major changes in curricula. Health care provision, ironically, should improve as increased demand will push the community beyond the current marginal demand for services to the point where additional personnel and expanded facilities will have to be made available. The existing social service delivery system will require additional personnel but the subject population will remain relatively narrow; the character of the issues that will have to be handled by this service will increase in intensity and consequence. Recreational activities for the community at large will diversify as the character of the resident population changes. Resource utilization patterns in conjunction with recreation activities will place greater pressure on the limited subsistence resource base.

4.3.3 Regional Relationships

The character of economic, social and political relations between Unalaska and other communities in the Aleutian region should remain essentially the same as that projected in the first scenario. It is extremely difficult to assess the added economic impact of oil-related development of these relationships without knowing the specific impact this development will have on the other communities. However, community-specific impacts other than those projected for Unalaska are beyond the scope of this study. Nevertheless, with the projected increase in the population of Unalaska, it is very likely that the community's status as a regional center will be enhanced. This could serve to promote increased economic ties as residents of other communities come to Unalaska for shopping and seasonal employment. Enhanced political ties may result from the community's position as a regional administrative center. Social ties are expected to remain constant.

4.3.4 Population

As discerned from Table 4.9, in-community population at the peak of OCS activities, if major groundfish activity occurs at roughly the same time, will exceed 7,017 individuals. At peak activity groundfish-related population will add 4,521 permanent residents to Unalaska, to which must be added an additional 877 residents in association with petroleum activities. These figures are year-round population additions and must not be seen as analagous to the types of seasonal increases historically tolerated in response to herring, salmon or crab harvesting activities. To the above increased permanent population levels must be added the certain population ebbs and flows in response to major yearly fluctuations in resource levels of crab, salmon, shrimp, halibut, herring or other unpredictable changes in seasonal harvesting activities.

These changes can begin, peak and decline within 5-10 years (king crab and herring are excellent examples). If such a change were to coincide or overlap with groundfish and oil development the population of Unalaska could reach periodic peaks of 8-10,000. The growth of population directly in association with these two developments, in addition to the enduring nature of these developments, will strongly encourage secondary economic development and further population growth which will provide an additional population increase. The lag time associated with the types of development which must necessarily occur in order to support such rapid population increases would make a smooth transition very difficult.

The population would be distributed into three distinct employment categories with residence strongly conditioned by such employment. Amaknak Island would be the locus of groundfish activity with groundfish providing a source of year-round activity and crab processing acting to generate seasonal peak periods of activity and population. Captains Bay and portions of Amaknak's inner harbor will be locus of oil-related activity. Unalaska proper, and its periphery, will retain its existing residential orientation and will absorb the bulk of the permanent population growth associated with both groundfish and petroleum development.

This table, when compared with Table 4.2 indicates that the proportion of residents and non-residents in Unalaska through the forecast period is relatively consistent with the projections found under the first scenario. The composition of this population,

Table 4.10

Unalaska Resident and Non-Resident Population Projections:
Second Scenario,
1981-2000

Year	Residents		Non-Residents		Total	
	N	%	N	%	N	%
1981	1054	54.2	890	45.8	1944	100.0
1985	1492	57.5	1105	42.5	2597	100.0
1990	1699	62.4	1022	37.6	2721	100.0
1995	2941	70.5	1229	29.5	4170	100.0
2000	5398	76.9	1619	23.1	7017	100.0

however, by ethnicity, by employment, by education, and by other social variables will differ considerably from that suggested under the first scenario in the absence of petroleum-related development. The age and sex distribution of Unalaska's population under this scenario will remain essentially the same as that projected under the first scenario. By 1995, however, two notable differences in this projection will appear. The first will be that the mean age of the male population will slowly increase. Oil-related workers, as noted in the last chapter, tend to be older than other transient males. Second, as onsite commuters, many of these oil-related workers will bring their families with them to reside in Unalaska. The ratio of workers to dependents projected for the year 2000 is almost 1 to 4. The increase in families will contribute to an evenly balanced sex ratio and a pyramidal age distribution.

Table 4.11

Projected Ethnic Composition of the Population of Unalaska:
Second Scenario,
1985-2000

Ethnic group	1985		1990		1995		2000	
	N	%	N	%	N	%	N	%
Caucasian	1647	63.4	1565	57.5	2478	59.4	3729	53.1
Black	52	2.0	68	2.5	125	3.0	245	3.5
Aleut	254	9.8	322	11.8	409	9.8	519	7.4
Other	644	24.8	766	28.2	1158	27.0	2524	36.0
Total	2597	100.0	2721	100.0	4170	100.0	7017	100.0

The assumptions underlying these projections are similar to those in the primary scenario. With or without OCS development, the rates of growth of Blacks, Aleuts, and Others (primarily Vietnameses, Mexicans and Filipinos) will remain constant through the forecast period. The growth rate for Caucasians, however, will increase due to the fact that most of the oil-related workers are expected to belong to this group.

Under this scenario, Caucasians will continue to represent over one-half of the total population through the forecast period, a proportion greater than projected in the first scenario. Vietnamese, Mexicans and Filipinos will comprise a slightly smaller proportion of the total population than exists in the first scenario, but they will still represent over one-third the total population by the year 2000. The proportion of Aleuts will continue to decline until 1985, rise briefly for the next five years, and then decline at a rate of 3.7 percent per year, even though the absolute number of Aleut residents during this period will grow by the assumed annual rate of 5.4%.

4.3.5 Community Facilities

Public facilities, including water, sewage, electric, docking and airport facilities, within the first year or two of oil-development will reach critical demand levels. The established water supply and delivery system has (during the first quarter of 1983) proved inadequate to supply even current processor demand. At least one groundfish processor in Unalaska had to halt operations as a result of inadequate water supply. The sewage system will also require major renovation before significant additional demand can be tolerated. Available electrical power sources are currently adequate and can tolerate a significant increase in demand. However, access to service cannot be expanded at a rate sufficient to accommodate the projected increase in demand. Thus, the initial year or two of growth in demand will have to be satisfied by privately-owned electrical generation and only slowly reintegrated into the city system.

Airport renovation and expansion, currently proceeding with construction of a new terminal building but awaiting additional state funding for extension of the runway, will be seen as a critically limiting factor very early in the development sequence and urgent measures will need to be taken to assure that this facility is made adequate to the expected levels of development. Unlike the case in the primary scenario, the projected growth of OCS activity in Unalaska should generate revenue which could be used for airport renovation and expansion. However, given the assumed pace and cooccurence of the two development scenarios, it is not expected that this facility can be completed in time to facilitate the early development activities of either groundfish or OCS activities. Thus, the peak demand created by these two developments, if sufficient lead time is not available, could potentially result in severe air transportation inadequacies.

As reflected above, major projects will have to be initiated on an urgent basis and will have to rely on state and federal funding actions and, to an increasing extent on municipal bonds. The pace of growth will be unusually accelerated and will not allow adequate planning. The effort to meet urgent demands will have to be extraordinary and will result in altered priorities and unintended long-term consequences.

4.3.6 Housing and Real Estate

Permanent housing, regardless of which development scenario (excepting a non-OCS, non-groundfish scenario, not considered in our analysis) is implicated, will be incapable of absorbing expected precipitious growth without major dislocation. A lengthy period of residence in temporary bunk-house, trailer or pre-fab variety facilities will be unavoidable. Provision of services to those residences that are constructed will be subject to major delays.

As noted in the first scenario, real estate development within the city limits of Unalaska and in the immediate vicinity is limited by the lack of land suitable for development. Oil companies will undoubtedly make a concerted effort to purchase land or lease land from the Ounalashka Corporation in order to construct adequate housing for their employees. After 1991, unless the local Native corporation can protect the landownership rights of their stockholders through legal means, this concerted effort by the oil companies may extend to outright purchase of land from Aleut residents. This could result in the alienation of the Aleut population from their traditional territory.

4.3.7 Value System

Under this scenario, we expect to see an acceleration of the transition from a frontier to a modern value system as projected in the first scenario. This transition will depend on two factors: the character of the oil-related population and the character of economic growth. If oil-related workers and their families do begin to arrive in 1985 as projected, the period of social stability projected under the first scenario will not occur. It is expected that the oil-related employees, by virtue of their experience and education, will possess more of a modern value system than a frontier value system. If the economic growth associated with oil development in the region proves to be a stabilizing influence in the community and not another peak in the boom-bust cycle which has long characterized Unalaska's economy, then the modern value system will assume a larger role in influencing the attitudes, opinions and behavior of local residents than will the frontier value system. The world view of Unalaska residents will change in accordance with the predominance of the modern value system.

The role of kinship in the determination of social status will further decline as oil-related workers and their families will not be tied into extended kin networks during the forecast period. The economic prosperity associated with the oil-related segment of the population will enhance the importance of wealth as an index of social status while stratification of Unalaska society based on income and occupation will intensify much sooner than forecast under the primary scenario. Location of residence will also assume greater importance in the determination of social status under this scenario as residents who work in similar occupations will tend to reside in the same neighborhoods.

As the population grows and the percentage of non-Native residents increases, ethnic identity may decline in importance, especially if local Aleut residents are unable to retain property rights after 1991. The Aleut segment of the population will decline in proportion to the non-Native segment and while the community will assume a more ethnically diverse character, the importance of ethnicity as a marker of self and social identity will be no greater than any other community of comparable size in the United States.

4.3.8 Economic Subsystem

4.3.8.1 Output

4.3.8.1.1 **Employment**. The use of local services by oil development companies is constrained by several factors. Direct employment opportunities, often those considered by residents and local government to be of greatest benefit to the community, are likely to be minimal during all phases of oil development. Almost all direct employment oppportunities will be for skilled outsiders. Thus, this expectation will not be met and will negatively affect residents to the extent it is relied upon in community planning. It is, in essence, an unfulfillable expectation that will cause problems in the community. Local services may be required in the area of peripheral support services such as welding, machine shop, and commercial laundry, but even this is likely to occur on an incidental basis. For example, it is economically and logistically easier for ARCO and other petroleum operations to contract with outside firms for supply and maintenance requirements. These firms are familiar with the requirements of these facilities from long experience. For another example, local produce, usually of lesser quality because of lengthy transport and storage, is required only sporatically and even then there is substantial reluctance to purchase items locally because of the risk of "upsetting the deli-cate supply and demand balance already established." This too, has been learned from past experience in other communities of purchas-ing large quantities of goods from local commercial interests only to create severe local shortages and over-dependencies on continued purchase of such goods or services.

Nevertheless, with the anticipated residence of 222 OCS commuters and their families in Unalaska, the economic subsystem will be noticibly affected in all categories of impact measurement. Employment opportunities will increase markedly, and conversely, the absolute number (and rate compared to today) of unemployed individuals (at least temporarily unemployed) will also increase significantly. This is because in the current economy unemployment is structurally limited to only a certain category of resident. Transient and short-term residents will simply leave town once it becomes clear that suitable employment no longer exists, or if known employment opportunities exist elsewhere. Table 4.12 depicts the expected distribution of employment through the year 2000.

As characterized in this table, the major employment shift will occur between 1990 and 1995. The total employment increases during this period by approximately fifty-seven percent. Between 1995 and the year 2000 total employment increases by approximately sixty percent.

This employment level will generate major changes in the secondary economy as retail, construction, and other consumer acti-vities increase accordingly. The fact that both OCS and groundfish activities are expected to be relatively long term (when compared with the traditional fluctuations of particular fish species) and constant activities will provide a powerful incentive to establish additional commercial firms in the community. The rapid pace of these changes, however, will also result in shortages, underplan-

Table 4.12

Estimated Total Employment, City of Unalaska: Second Scenario, 1980-2000

Employment Sector	1980[a] (Actual)	1985	1990	1995	2000
Commercial Fishing	150	141	165	232	456
Mining-Oil	2	120	106	222	222
Contract Construction	12	67	84	151	194
Manufacturing	1166	1026	1011	1726	2910
Transportation, Public Utilities & Communications	57	56	58	106	192
Trade	60	89	100	192	334
Finance, Insurance and Real Estate	27	26	24	42	69
Services	44	64	70	135	236
Government	82	80	96	192	332
Total Employment	1600	1669	1714	2998	4945

a. Source: Alaska Consultants 1981:217.

ning and exaggerated expectations regarding profits and growth. The growth of population and of commercial opportunities, in turn, will generate a further population increase in relation to externally perceived options available in the community.

Table 4.13 below, describes the manufacturing and contract construction classifications by their component OCS and groundfish employment categories.

The anticipated decline in the relative strength of traditional fishery activity in Unalaska during the next decade is reflected in this table. We have not considered the potential growth of other traditional fisheries such as herring, halibut, or salmon in generating temporary or long-term growth in Unalaska. These are potential sources of fluctuations in the number of residents committed to particular fisheries adaptations. Given the current organization of the salmon, herring and, potentially, halibut commercial fisheries (e.g., ownership patterns, harvesting patterns, regulatory constraints, and so on) a major resurgence of any one of these in Unalaska during the next decade appears remote.

4.3.8.1.2 Income. The range of income distribution under this scenario is expected to remain essentially the same as that projected in the first scenario. In the short term, income levels of most current residents and the bulk of those employed in the processing sector will not increase appreciably in response to groundfish development. Income levels of local entrepreneurs will

182

Table 4.13

Estimated Basic Employment in Selected Sectors,
City of Unalaska:
Second Scenario,
1980-2000

Employment Sector	1980a	1985	Year 1990	1995	2000
Commercial Fishing	150	141	165	231	456
Traditional	(150)	(80)	(50)	(46)	(78)
Groundfish	(0)	(61)	(115)	(186)	(378)
Contract Construction	5	30	38	57	48
Traditional	(5)	(3)	(2)	(2)	(3)
Groundfish	(0)	(21)	(30)	(36)	(37)
OCS	(0)	(6)	(6)	(19)	(8)
Manufacturing	1166	1026	1011	1726	2910
Traditional	(1166)	(620)	(388)	(361)	(612)
Groundfish	(0)	(275)	(524)	(845)	(1725)
OCS	(0)	(131)	(99)	(520)	(573)

a. Source: Alaska Consultants 1981:219.

increase as the market demand associated with the oil-related
segment of the community results in increased business. The
incomes of oil workers and their families will represent the upper
end of the income scale in Unalaska.

4.3.8.1.3 Consumer Behavior. Consumer activity is expected
to increase much sooner and with greater intensity than was projected under the first scenario. The greater number of residents
and the relatively larger incomes of the oil-related segment of the
population will translate to more money spent on consumer purchases. During the first few years of this increase, most of the
consumer purchases will occur outside the community, due to the
familiarity of new residents with outside businesses and the relative lack of available stock on hand of local retail outlets. By
1990, however, the amount of money within the community available
for consumer purchases should stimulate the growth of retail businesses.

4.3.9 Social Subsystem

Periods of population stability tend to encourage closer
social ties and larger social networks. Major periods of seasonal
activity and high population broken by periods of inactivity and
low population tend to work toward very narrow and exclusive social
circles which endure the fluctuations. The prospective rapid
growth in population ultimately stablizing at several times the

current population will lead to development of new forms of social interaction which will compete with, disintegrate, and finally replace, earlier forms of social organization. After two or three years of rapid development this process of social change will be accepted as the normal course of events.

Social class distinctions will also emerge and gradually become tolerated as a normal consequence of growth. The increasing presence of residents of external origin, whose established patterns of social interaction are based on such a model, will accelerate this process. The indigenous and current long-term resident population of Unalaska will bear the brunt of these social changes. Residents of external origin traditionally form social groups on the basis of shared characteristics and they will likely share more in common with other such residents than with the local inhabitants. Many of those who take up permanent residence will be of the managerial and upper-level staff category and whose earnings, experience and orientation will tend to put them into a particular social classification though they will likely live in the community of Unalaska and interact socially and politically with other community members. Processor personnel, traditionally young and male, will form yet another social category but one which will not interact extensively with other residents of Unalaska, preferring instead to remain for the most part on Amaknak Island (Dutch Harbor). The bulk of the petroleum-related employees, on the other hand, will be mature, highly skilled, family men who will live in company-provided housing or in existing homes purchased or leased in Unalaska. As the experience in Valdez suggests, petroleum-related workers will not be strongly inclined, at least during the first few years of activity, to participate in formal community functions and will be even less inclined to participate in the political affairs of the city. Their involvement in other informal social activities will be largely determined by the number and age, and length of enrollment, of their offspring in the Unalaska school system. It is on the basis of the educational system (i.e., school-related activities) that many of the longer-term residents of the community have interacted and will continue to interact socially.

4.3.10 Political Subsystem

Community development and provision of services to increasing numbers of residents with limited revenues will be the primary political issue affecting the community under this scenario. The prospect of a sizeable increase of oil-related employees and their families residing in the community will intensify pressures to provide adequate housing and services. Without federal or state assistance, the local government may be unable to meet the demands of its constituents. The increased revenues associated with larger numbers of residents will be insufficient to provide these services, at least until 1991 when property held by Aleut residents can be subject to taxation. Even then, demand will have far outpaced the ability of the city government to provide adequate services.

Levels of political conflict will intensify much sooner than projected under the first scenario. As the new residents struggle for suitable housing and community facilities, they will be forced to compete with existing residents and projected groundfish workers for limited resources. The oil-related segment of the population could emerge as a distinct political force which will compete for revenues and positions on the city council with other segments of the population. Although oil workers have traditionally attempted to avoid such involvement in local affairs, as noted above, the sheer size of this segment and the difficulties in securing an acceptable quality of life may alter this pattern.

Conflict between the Ounalashka Corporation and the city council is also projected to intensify much sooner than expected under the first scenario. Inevitably, the pressure placed upon the city to provide adequate housing and services will conflict with the desire of the Ounalashka Corporation to protect the interests of their shareholders. As long as the Ounalashka Corporation retains control of most of the available land in the community, conflicts between the two political groups are bound to emerge. Some sort of compromise will be reached as long as the Ounalashka Corporation is able to profit by an agreement with the city.

The measures used by local residents to assess the efficiency of the city government will change in the manner projected under the first scenario. It is conceivable that community dissatisfaction with local government will be even greater than projected under the first scenario because of the latter's inability to provide adequate services to the increased numbers of residents. The expectations of oil-related workers will undoubtedly be greater than those of new residents expecting a frontier environment lacking in amenities common in other communities or of transients expecting to reside in Unalaska for a short time.

The crime rate is expected to increase at a greater rate than projected under the first scenario. This expectation is based on the belief that a diminished quality of life resulting from the strain of an increasing population of existing facilities and services could result in increased frustration and willingness to break the law. Moreover, increased social differentiation resulting from the presence of oil-related residents who are on the upper end of the income scale may stimulate greater criminal activity among residents at the lower end of the socioeconomic scale.

4.3.11 Religion

Both output and feedback impacts on the religious subsystem under this scenario will assume the forms described under the first scenario. By 1995, the Unalaska Christian Fellowship could be one of several different Protestant denominations operating churches in the community. A larger proportion of the community will be active members of churches than is currently the case and the role of churches in community affairs should approximate that of churches in communities of comparable size throughout the United States. As the number of Protestant churches increases, we should also expect an increase in the rate of fission among church congregations of

Protestant denominations.

4.3.12 Education

A projection of increases in the student population of Unalaska under this scenario is provided in Table 4.14. It is clear that during the early 1990s this population will surge dramatically, resulting in shortened construction lead-time, inadequate time for planning and informed decisionmaking, and major shifts in the content and focus of the school's curricula.

Table 4.14

Unalaska School Enrollment Forecast:
Second Scenario,
1985-2000

Year	Enrollment
1985	232
1990	265
1995	459
2000	842

The effect on education in Unalaska if both groundfish development and the peak of OCS activity occur simultaneously will be a major consideration for the community. The nature of the assumptions regarding permanent versus transient residency in association with groundfish development lead, independently of petroleum development assumptions, to the conclusion that the rapid expansion of present facilities will be required. If the projected curve of additional school population associated with oil development is considered, the current facility and staff will prove inadequate by the end of the first year of oil activity.

We foresee the need for the construction of at least two primary schools and the conversion of current facilities into a high school only. One of these two primary schools will have to be sited on Amaknak Island. This division will tend to accentuate existing social differences between the two segments (residents of Amaknak Island and Unalaska proper) of the community. An alternative plan outlined by Haeg and Bettis (1982) envisions the construction of a new junior high/high school facility adjacent to the existing facility which would itself be converted strictly into an elementary school. However, this plan does not seem to recognize the extent of residential growth which will in all probability occur on Amaknak island.

It is also conceivable that by the end of the projection period (1995-2000) a parochial school affiliated with the local Catholic church or some other religious institution could emerge. While much smaller in size and scope than the public schools, the

demand for some form of religious education, coupled with
dissatisfaction on the part of some residents with the quality of
education offered by the public schools, could provide an incentive
for the establishment of such a facility.

The organization of education, particularly the priorities
established in setting curricula, will shift according to the
relative percentage of OCS-related employees resident in Unalaska.
The petroleum-related employees are expected to push for higher
standards and create more pressure for college preparatory programs
in the high school. Increased achievement levels and a greatly
intensified level of extracurricular activities are projected after
1990.

4.3.13 Health Care

Under this scenario, the nature of health risks and disease
and mortality rates are expected to be similar to those projected
in the first scenario. While the number of diseases and illnesses
will increase, the morbidity and mortality rates are expected to
remain the same and perhaps show signs of decline as the quality of
health care available to local residents improves. The only devia-
tion from these projections are an increase in the number of
occupation-related accidents and injuries associated with the petroleum industry. Local health care providers will undoubedtly see
more of these types of conditions because they will be the most
available form of primary care in the short term.

Both the cost and the quality of health care will increase
dramatically under the assumptions of this scenario, especially
after 1990. It is likely that the additional tax revenues generated by petroleum activities will offset additional costs to the
community. The quality of care expected by the petroleum firms
will also serve to stimulate demand for additional health practitioners. One of two possible changes can be expected in the structure of delivery services. A second clinic may be constructed which
is at least partially funded by oil firms or the Iliuliuk Clinic
may be upgraded in a manner discussed in the first scenario. The
alternative possibility is that a small hospital (20-40) bed is
constructed in Unalaska by the early 1990s which provides primary
care to permanent residents and transient oil workers throughout
the region. Such a facility would provide services similar to
those provided by regional facilities in other Alaskan communities
such as Kanakanak or Bethel and could very well be administered by
the Aleutian/Pribilof Island Association.

4.3.14 Social Services

Because of the rapid increase of both economic growth and
population under this forecast, the need for social services will
increase--though probably not in direct ratio to the rate of
growth. While economic prosperity might serve to reduce social and
psychological tension in other contexts, the strain on the quality
of life resulting from increased population on limited utilities,

housing, increased socioeconomic status differentiation, increased income opportunities (which are unattainable for many), and so on, will mean a major increase in the severity and number of problems which will be encountered. A significant rise in the incidence of drug and alcohol abuse and domestic violence will be evident, particularly among the lower socioeconomic groups. This rise can be expected to occur much sooner than is projected in the first scenario, thus taxing existing personnel and facilities.

4.3.15 Recreation

The trend in recreational activities discussed under the first scenario will generally hold for this scenario with the following exceptions. First, there will be a general trend in recreational activities which are consumer oriented. Activities involving money (e.g., use of motor vehicles, planes, dining out, vacations, home entertainment systems) will increase most rapidly under this development scenario. Second, there will be a trend toward small-group activities as the population becomes more heterogeneous, with the exception of such community-wide events such as the Fourth of July and Crab Festival activities, community atheletic leagues, festivals, and school-related competitions.

Subsistence activities, to the degree they are tied to recreational objectives, will increase in intensity and in absolute number of participants. Where the actions of the newer residents, particularly the white oil-related employees, tend to reduce access to the traditional locations or resources of the long-term residents we expect to find increased conflict. The subsistence-related activities of Unalaska residents are particularly susceptible to disruption by newer residents and, because these activities are so closely tied to perceptions of identity, the likelihood of conflict is high.

5
The Physical and Social Environment of Cold Bay

5.1 THE PHYSICAL ENVIRONMENT

Cold Bay is located on the southwestern end of the Alaskan Peninsula on an inlet known as Cold Bay which nearly bifurcates the peninsula. The bay opens to the south and the Pacific Ocean. To the north, across an isthmus barely ten miles wide, lies the Bering Sea. The bay is about twenty-five miles long and nine miles wide. It is four miles wide at its mouth, and has a deep channel entrance marked at sixty feet. There are several reefs complicating entrance to the bay, including Kasolan Reef near the entrance and a group known as the Sandman Reefs a few miles off-shore.

Cold Bay's topography is predominantly tundra with few trees and many lakes, lagoons, and swamps. The most notable nearby physical features are Mt. Frosty to the southwest and the Pavlof complex (which includes several active volcanoes) to the northeast. There are several streams, including Trout Creek and Russell Creek, in the immediate vicinity. To the north of town the tundra gradually breaks up into a series of lakes and marshes, finally becoming the Izembek Lagoon which opens to the Bering Sea. The community itself is located on the western shore of the bay.

Cold Bay's climate is influenced by weather systems from both the Bering Sea and the Pacific Ocean. Weather is characterized by extreme cloudiness and fog, particularly in summer, averaging nine-tenths cloud cover year round. Wind is a major factor, averaging between fifteen and twenty miles per hour throughout the year with periods of sustained winds of thirty miles per hour not uncommon. Snow and precipitation are not heavy, although measurable precipitation occurs over 200 days per year. Snow falls from October to May and averages about eight to ten inches per month. In winter snow combined with high winds frequently result in blizzard-like conditions which severely reduce visibility. Temperature is relatively invariant, due to the moderating influence of the large ocean masses nearby. Maximum temperatures average fifty degrees in July and thirty degrees in December, and minimums average between twenty degrees in January and February and forty-five in August (National Oceanic and Atmospheric Administration, 1981).

Though Cold Bay is in a sub-arctic region, it is surrounded by abundant food resources, both marine and terrestrial. Particularly important are the marine resources, notably the several varieties of salmon which spawn in the region each summer and fall. The Cold Bay region is especially rich in fish and crab. There are five species of salmon which migrate through the Cold Bay region, including small numbers of king (chinook), and larger numbers of sockeye (reds), chum (dogs), pinks (humpies), and silvers (coho). Most fish bound for the Bristol Bay area pass within range of Cold Bay, and much of the fishing industry of King Cove, only a few miles to the south, is based on the intercept fishery created when the migrating salmon come close to shore to pass through Unimak Pass to the Bering Sea. There are several abundant varieties of groundfish including cod, halibut, pollock, and perch. There are also several varieties of crab (king, tanner, and dungeness in particular), and much of the economy of the surrounding region is, or has been, based on the crab fishery. Other marine resources include marine mammals such as seal (harbor, ringed, bearded, and fur), walrus, porpoise, beluga whale, and a resurgent population of pelagic sea otter. Abundant clam resources are also available but relatively unutilized.

The area surrounding Cold Bay is also rich in terrestrial fauna. The major animal food source is the barren ground caribou. A large herd of several thousand animals winters on the flanks of the Pavlof complex and, in late summer and early fall, migrates around the bay and through the immediate vicinity. The only other land animal exploited to any degree is the Alaskan Brown Bear but it is much less important than the caribou. There are also several varieties of fox in the area, most notably red fox, as well as weasels, wolverines, squirrels, and other smaller animals. Occasionally some of these latter species, particularly red fox, are trapped for their furs.

There is also a profusion of avian life. Many are actual or potential sources of food. The Izembek National Wildlife Refuge, north of town, serves as both stopover and home for an amazing range of birds. Birds using the area include several types of geese (Cackling Canada, Taverner's Canada, Emperor, and several varieties of brant), as well as numerous types of duck. The largest population of black brant in North America, over 250,000 birds, uses the lagoon on both the northern leg of their migration in spring and the southern journey in fall (Department of the Interior, 1973). A small population of the Aleutian Canada goose, at one time thought to be extinct, has been confirmed in the last decade. Other, more permanent, avian species include peregrine falcons and bald eagles. The latter can be seen in concentrations of fifty to a hundred during the summer and fall gathering at the edges of streams to feed on spawning salmon.

There are no plant resources of note in Cold Bay. The only flora which might be exploited is the tundra which, since it is composed of scores of separate plants, puts forth numerous types of berries in profusion in the late summer and fall. There are no trees in the immediate vicinity, although alder and shrub willow occur near streams and lakes.

The mineral potential of the immediate vicinity of Cold Bay is not known to be great. The area lacks any known deposits of commercial value, and the Izembek National Wildlife Refuge has been removed from the provisions of the mining laws. However, Cold Bay is in a region which is increasingly recognized as the locale of vast energy deposits, particularly petroleum, and leasing is scheduled for at least two major areas, the St. George and North Aleutian Shelf lease areas, in the near future.

Though Cold Bay is in proximity to potential oil deposits, there are no major power resources located in the immediate vicinity. The only exception is the possible development of wind power through the construction of a wind generator, which has not yet occurred on a large scale. The community is totally dependent on imported sources of energy, especially diesel oil, gasoline and natural gas.

There are several other resources which might be exploited commercially in the Cold Bay area, but as yet none have been developed. The most obvious are the salmon, crab and ground-fisheries. At least four varieties of salmon (reds, chum, pinks, and silvers) are present in large numbers from spring to fall, but Cold Bay residents do not exploit them commercially. Crab is also abundant, but they have also gone unexploited by Cold Bay resi-dents. At any rate, crab has been in decline as was noted in Chapter 2. The most prevalent groundfish is pollock, but this resource too has gone unexploited by locals. Other groundfish, including cod, perch, and halibut have also been relatively unuti-lized in the local area for sport or subsistence needs and almost totally ignored commercially.

5.2 EXTRASOCIETAL INFLUENCES

Cold Bay is remarkable in the degree to which it is implicated with external forces. There are three kinds of extrasocietal influence on the community. First is the presence of large state and federal government contingents. Second is the presence of a large external commercial sector. Third is the influence of an external sociocultural system, including outside values, techno-logy, and behavioral patterns. The community, as a transportation and communications center for the entire peninsula/insular region surrounding it, is dominated by external agencies and companies at the expense of local entrepreneurial activity. In this section we will briefly note these external forces and, in the following chapter, we will detail their operation at the local level.

5.2.1 External Government

External governmental agencies are prominent in Cold Bay. The community originated as a federal military site and the federal government has continued to maintain a major local presence, both civilian and military. State government, since the entrance of Alaska into the union, has also played a major role locally. Cur-rently total governmental employment has been outstripped by pri-vate employment, but both the federal and state governments remain major employers and play a large role in local life.

The federal government represents two-thirds of the public

sector in Cold Bay. The Federal Aviation Administration, which has
been in town from the 1950s, is concerned particularly with the
operation of the control tower and navigational facilities of the
Cold Bay Airport. The Fish and Wildlife Service of the Department
of the Interior has been in town from 1948 and is concerned with
the management of the Izembek National Wildlife Refuge and portions
of two other refuges (the Unimak Island Unit of the Aleutian
Islands National Wildlife Refuge and the Pavlof Unit of the Alaskan
Peninsula Refuge).   Other federal agencies represented in town are
the Post Office and the Air Force. Air Force personnel are located
at the Cold Bay Air Force Station approximately eleven miles northwest of town at Grant Point.

The State of Alaska is the second major governmental presence
in Cold Bay. It is spearheaded by the Department of Transportation
and Public Facilities which is in control of the vast majority of
land in the town. As the agent responsible for the airport, the
DOT is responsible for most of the town as well. The Department of
Fish and Game is responsible for overseeing commercial and subsistence fishery resources. A final state representative in town is
the single magistrate.

Although Cold Bay is heavily influenced by outside governmental agencies, many of the legislative impacts felt by the rest of
the region have gone almost unnoticed in Cold Bay. This is because
the population of Cold Bay is non-Native and almost exclusively
transient, consisting of people from outside the region who are not
permanent residents. The Alaska Native Claims Settlement Act,
which radically altered the political and economic power structure
of most of the region by placing a huge amount of land into the
hands of Natives, had little effect in Cold Bay. None of the
residents of Cold Bay have claimed land under the provisions of
ANCSA, and there is no Cold Bay Native Corporation. However, ANCSA
has had an impact as a result of the claims of the King Cove Native
Corporation of a significant portion of land within the city
limits.

A second legislative act with major region-wide impact has
been the Limited Entry Act of 1973 which restricted salmon fishing
to those able to qualify for a limited entry permit. The absence
of a fishing sector in the Cold Bay economy means that entry limitation has had no direct impact on the local economy or lifestyle.
No one in Cold Bay has a limited entry permit. Nor does Cold Bay
have docking or protected anchorage facilities, further retarding
development of a fishing sector.

Cold Bay is also relatively uninvolved with regional level
political organizations.   Again, this is a result of the lack of a
Native sector in the Cold Bay population, as most of the regional
political organizations are Native-oriented and sprang from the
legislative acts of the early seventies noted above. Just as there
is no local Native corporation or association, there is no involvement on the part of Cold Bay residents in region-wide Native corporations or associations. The only local impact of regional
Native corporations has been the intermittent presence of the
Thirteenth Regional Corporation, a major local landowner. The
Thirteenth Regional Corporation attempted to inaugurate a fish
processing sector in Cold Bay, but was unsuccessful.

5.2.2 External Commercial Influences

Though the governmental presence has dwindled in Cold Bay over the last decade, the community remains firmly in the grip of outside forces. Outside commercial corporations have usurped the role once filled by governmental employment. Currently these private corporations account for nearly two-thirds of Cold Bay employment, and they exert a tremendous amount of influence locally (especially given the near total absence of a local entrepreneurial sector). These private corporations have undermined the position held by external governmental agencies in the first two decades of the town's existence and are now the dominant forces in the Cold Bay economy. The structure of the private sector of the Cold Bay economy is very different from that of the surrounding communities.

Cold Bay, unlike almost every other village or town in the region, has an underdeveloped fisheries sector. There have been attempts in the past to develop this part of the economy, but thus far they have been unsuccessful. The only forms of fisheries activity in Cold Bay are modest. Seawest runs a small operation in which salmon eggs are shipped to Cold Bay from Nelson Lagoon (from the processor the Western Sea, which processes salmon for Seawest). Once the eggs are in Cold Bay Seawest packages and distributes them to Japan, Anchorage, or Seattle. The only other fisheries-related operation in town is the Northern Pacific Fisheries (Winky's), which operates in a building on the parking apron of the longer of the two runways. Northern Pacific also transships salmon from the northern side of the peninsula. The salmon is processed in Cold Bay and shipped out to Seattle or Anchorage. Both of these operations are small scale in comparison with fisheries activity in other villages or towns in the region.

The Cold Bay economy is unusual in its total dependence on a cash economy at the expense of subsistence activity. It is also unusual in that this cash economy is totally dependent on outside sources, with very little local entrepreneurial activity. Since there is no local economic activity, and the town is under the control of major outside firms and agencies, all consumer goods and services come into the town via air and/or sea and are carried by outside-based carriers. Also some individuals gain needed subsistence items through a government or company catalogue. Unlike other communities in the area, Cold Bay is totally dependent on links to the outside for survival. The residents of other communities on the peninsula and in the Aleutian Islands are more accustomed to exploiting the environment for their needs.

External commercial transportation and communications companies are central to the economic structure of the community. Cold Bay is both the transportation and communications hub of the entire region and is dominated in those sectors by major outside firms.

The major private transportation firms in town are Reeve Aleutian Airways and Peninsula Airlines. Both are outside-based corporations. Reeve is by far the larger, and operates the air terminal as well as flights into and out of Cold Bay six days a week (every day except Sunday). Peninsula serves as a feeder route for Reeve and takes Reeve passengers from Cold Bay to the smaller villages and towns in the area. Peninsula and Reeve also transport the U.S. mail for the entire region. Reeve flies routes among Cold Bay, Anchorage, Seattle, the Pribilofs as well as along the Aleutian chain.

The major communications firms are RCA, Alascom, and the Interior Telephone Company. RCA is by far the largest of the three, accounting for approximately ninety percent of all communications jobs. RCA operates at the Grant Point Air Force Base and maintains and operates the Distant Early Warning Station there. At one time RCA owned Alascom, which is responsible for bringing satellite television broadcasts into the community, but two years ago the subsidiary was sold to a Washington State-based utility. Alascom operates a satellite receiving dish and maintains transmission cables within the community. The Interior Telephone Company has only one part-time local representative and provides telephone service, including satellite service, to local residents.

There have been incipient oil-related developments already, and ARCO has a support facility designed to backup the exploratory oil rig in the Bering Sea. This is on land leased from the Thirteenth Regional Corporation, following their abortive attempt to establish a local fish processing industry. As of the latest report, Exxon is also interested in establishing such a support facility in Cold Bay. Cold Bay has been a staging area for many companies involved in the initial phases of exploration such as mapping and the setting up of navigational aids. However, despite these indications of possible future impact from oil-related development, the town has seen little real economic or social impact from these activities.

5.2.3 Larger Sociocultural System

Cold Bay is a centrifugal community. That is, local residents are much more interconnected with the larger sociocultural system of Alaska, the United States, and the western world than are residents in other towns in the region. The transience of local residents ensures that these connections will remain strong and, in most cases, dominant considerations. This means that the members of the community share the value and cultural system of the Euro-American population of the lower forty-eight states which sets them apart from the rest of the communities in this region of Alaska.

The domination of the community by Euro-Americans has led to the development of an essentially imported value system in the community which owes more to modern American standards and values than to the traditional Aleut values which inform most communities in the region. Thus there is an emphasis on individualism at the expense of group goals and action, the desire for individual control and acquisition of property and goods, and a commitment to "success" as measured through essentially instrumental means.

Connected with this imported value system is a commitment to the free enterprise cash economic system. It is through this system that the instrumental success of the individual is measured. The central belief here is the assumption that for a given amount of labor the individual has the right to expect an agreed upon

financial return. Connected with this is the belief that the
inhospitable environment of Cold Bay demands a higher return than
would similar work in a less removed and more benign environment.
Reciprocity is not generalized or based on primarily moral considerations, but is balanced and explicitly instrumental. As a
result of these factors the emphasis is on achieved position rather
than ascribed or inherited position, and on bettering that position
in ways which are measured more materially than morally.

The outer-directedness of Cold Bay is a two way process. The
people of the town are intimately connected to areas greatly
removed from the region and the state, but at the same time they
have all the conveniences and technology of that wider society.
The town is remarkably sophisticated in a technological sense.
Cold Bay has a highly developed technological infrastructure which
owes its origin to the connections of the community with the
western-oriented external environment.

The community is in close transportation and communication
touch with the rest of the state and nation. The airport assures
rapid connection with Anchorage, Seattle, California and points
even further removed. Its status as a major communications center
assures instantaneous contact with much of the world, and its
citizens almost universally have televisions and telephones with
satellite hookups, modern videotape equipment, automobiles, and so
on. Technology extends to the workplace as well, and the latest
electronic and navigational equipment is used by many of the town's
workers. RCA workers maintain sophisticated radar and other electronic equipment. RCA and the FAA are both in the process of
converting all their operations to solid state equipment which will
allow the remote control of nearly all functions at their respective facilities. Technologically Cold Bay is much more advanced
than most towns of comparable size in the lower forty eight.

Cold Bay owes this advanced technological position to its
domination by outside corporations and government agencies. This
externally imposed economic system, based on a wage labor
capitalist structure, is very different from the traditional subsistence system which is still strong in many of the surrounding
villages. The economic forces in the community are national or
international in scope, with little ultimate concern for Cold Bay
itself. Cold Bay is economically viable only as long as the return
from activities there contributes to the achievement of goals defined apart from the community itself.

The intimacy of the connections between Cold Bay and the
outside nation and world, not the least of which is the rapid
turnover in residents and company personnel, means that the town
can depend on outside sources for consumer goods to an unusual
extent. The airport, and the visits by Alaska state ferries, gives
access to a great variety of consumer goods. The single retail
outlet in town, upon which most people depend for the majority of
their consumer goods, is stocked with the same items one would find
in the corner store in a large city. Unlike other communities in
the region, there is little exploitation of subsistence resources,
making the residents that much more dependent on consumer goods.

5.2.4 Neighboring Communities

Cold Bay is one of several small communities on the Alaska Peninsula. The other communities, including King Cove, Pilot Point, Ugashik, Port Heiden, and Port Moller are dominated by ethnic Aleuts and, to a lesser extent, by Eskimos (Supiaq Eskimo). Cold Bay itself is almost totally Euro-American; literally a stronghold of whites in the midst of a nearly totally Native area. These ethnic differences have contributed to the pattern of relations between Cold Bay and the outside world. The fact that they are from such widely removed areas of the state and country means that they are not as intensely implicated in the social networks of the immediate vicinity as are the members of other villages and communities in the region. To our knowledge, there are few if any current kin ties between Cold Bay residents and residents of neighboring communities. Because of the limited involvement of Cold Bay in the commercial fisheries, there are few economic ties connecting it with other communities in the region. Cold Bay is also isolated in a political sense from other communities because it has no residents who are members of Native corporations or belongs to any regional or subregional entities.

Nevertheless, contact between local residents and residents from communities throughout the Alaska Peninsula and Aleutian Islands is frequent because of the community's role as a regional transportation center. Much of this contact occurs during stopovers in Cold Bay between the other communities and Anchorage. Travellers will frequent the Weathered Inn or visit with friends in town while waiting for connecting flights or breaks in the weather.

5.3 INTRASOCIETAL INFLUENCES

Cold Bay is interesting from the standpoint of intrasocietal forces for several reasons. First, the community presents a unique picture demographically with a very young population, heavily slanted toward single males, and with an absence of a significant Native population. Second, it has some difficult problems to be worked out concerning capacities and jurisdictions of several of the community facilities and utilities. Finally, there is remarkably little private development, largely because of the paucity of available private land.

5.3.1 Population

In discussing demography we will first come to an appraisal of the current structure of the community. This entails estimates based on 1970 statistics and on the changes which have occurred since then, as that is the most recent complete census of Cold Bay. Following this we will discuss the dynamic aspects of demography, particularly the processes of migration. We will be concerned with the processes by which recruitment and replacement of Cold Bay residents occurs in a process of repetitive change.

The 1980 national census provides only a gross estimate of the total aggregate population of Cold Bay. The most recent complete census is that of 1970. In that census the following general figures emerged:

Table 5.1

Population by Sex and Ethnicity,
Cold Bay, 1970

| Ethnic Group | Sex | | | |
	Male	Female	Total	Percent of Total
Caucasian	166	48	214	83.6
Black	9	0	9	3.5
Other	4	3	7	2.7
Total Non-Native	179	51	230	89.8
Aleut	9	7	16	6.2
Eskimo	2	3	5	2.0
Indian	3	2	5	2.0
Total Native	14	12	26	10.2
Total	193	63	256	100.0

Source: University of Alaska, ISEGR, 1973.

Several factors should be taken into consideration when assessing these figures. First, 1970 was at the height of the Vietnam War and the conflict had swollen the local population figures to one of their highest levels ever. In fact, some estimates put the population as high as 280 during the first half of the seventies, just before the war began to deescalate. Second, even the modest number of Natives enumerated in the census of 1970 (twenty-six out of a total of 256, or 10.2 percent of the total) is now far out of line with reality. In Cold Bay there has never been a large Native population, and even the small number in 1970 were there primarily as a result of the war effort and most left following the war. Today there are even fewer Natives. Third, there have also been changes in the female/male ratio since 1970. In 1970 the majority of the temporary population which swelled those figures to post-World War Two highs were single males, the bulk of whom left following the end of the war. In 1970, sixty-three or 24.6 percent of 256 inhabitants were female. Today those figures are much less disparate and females, while a long way from parity, are making a move in that direction.

The best and most recent estimates we have for the population of Cold Bay come from the current mayor of the town who estimates the total population at 226. The approximate age and sex distribution of this population is provided in Table 5.2. These figures illustrate some interesting demographic trends between 1970 and 1982, trends which, with certain qualifications, are continuing in the current decade. First, the percentage of the population repre-

Table 5.2

Population by Age and Sex,
Cold Bay, 1970-1982

Age	1970		1982	
	Males	Females	Males	Females
0-5	8	10	10	12
5-19	26	16	28	22
20-44	141	25	100	28
45-64	18	12	14	12
65+	0	0	0	0

Source: United States Census, 1972 and field estimates, 1982

sented by children aged nineteen and under has risen from 23.4 to thirty-two percent of the total, illustrating the growth of families as an important aspect of Cold Bay society. Women, of course, have also made a dramatic leap forward in the time since 1970 when they accounted for sixty-three out of 256 people, or only 24.6 percent of the total. Today, according to these estimates, they represent seventy-four out of 226 people, or almost thirty-two percent of the total. If we consider women over nineteen, we find the increase has been from 14.4 percent of the total (37 out of 256) to 17.7 percent (40 out of 226).

The most significant decline, of course, has been among males in general, and among the cohort aged twenty to forty-four in particular. Overall males declined from 75.4 to 67.3 percent of the total population. The overall sex ratio (expressed as number of males per female) has been altered in favor of females from 3.06 in 1970 to 2.05 in 1982, a dramatic shift though there are still over two males for every female in Cold Bay. Among adult males and females the disparity was, and remains, much greater. In 1970 the ratio of males to females was (for those aged 20 and above) 159:37, or 4.30. By 1982 this ratio had dropped to 114:40, or 2.85, still nearly three adult men for every adult woman. Finally, in the crucial category for families, the age cohort between twenty and forty-four, women made the greatest advances. In 1970 the ratio of men to women stood at 141 to 25, or 5.64 men for every woman, an extremely high figure. By 1982 this had shifted to 100 to 28, or 3.57, a strong advance but still an extreme ratio.

A final point should be made about the changes in the makeup of the population since 1970. The Native sector of the population has surely declined precipitously. The researcher only encountered five or six Natives in the time he was in the field, and the total is probably not over ten. We note as well that these individuals for the most part do not consider Cold Bay their permanent "home." In discussions with people in the community the researcher never received an estimate of more than a dozen Natives, and usually less than that. Even allowing for the higher of the estimates, this means a decline from twenty-six in 1970 to approximately ten in 1982, a drop of 69.7 percent. The Native population of Cold Bay today is negligible, and those the researcher met are either married to Euro-Americans or appear to have become essentially assimilated to Euro-American culture, so that effectively, from a cultural standpoint, there is no Native population in Cold Bay.

There also is a very low percentage of families in Cold Bay. At best only half the adult population is married. It is true that the ratio of married to unmarried, and the ratio of families to total population, has risen considerably from 1970, but a large part of this increase has to be seen as artificial since the high number of single males in Cold Bay during the Vietnam War was destined to be purely temporary. However, it is clear that the "stable state" of Cold Bay is still one in which there is a very low percentage of married people.

Finally, Cold Bay is, above all, a very young town in terms of the composition of its population. This is in line with the transience of the population, the low percentage of married couples, and the high ratio of males to females. There is no one in town over sixty-five, although there are a couple of permanent residents approaching that age who, if they indeed stay for another five to ten years, will change that picture somewhat. However, even in the age group from forty-five to sixty-four we find surprisingly few people. Of the total population of 226 only twenty-six are over forty-five years of age. Among males only fourteen, or 9.2 percent, are over forty-five.

Cold Bay is in a state of constant flux, but the kind of change which results is repetitive. That is, there is a constant change in personnel, but the structure of occupational and social relationships remains essentially unaltered. In order to understand the way in which this occurs we will detail the processes of in and out-migration.

Cold Bay has a consistent and steady rate of in-migration. This alone is distinctive for this region of Alaska. Most of the villages and communities in this area of Alaska experience seasonal variations in population, with many residents practicing an essentially transhumant pattern of presence in the village during fishing season and removal to Anchorage or other west coast urban areas during a major portion of the off season. However, in Cold Bay an individual migrates to the town, remains there with only short absences for two to five years, then leaves for good. One pattern is cyclical, the other lineal.

This pattern of immigration, residence and emigration is a result of the fact that the town is dominated by outside employers, particularly large governmental agencies and private transportation and communications corporations. Most of the companies and agencies therefore send people to Cold Bay for a specific tour of duty, and very few of these people ultimately become permanent residents, preferring rather to leave at the end of their tour than to stay. Other factors, such as seniority, open bidding of positions, promotions, and fixed contracts, also promote frequent turnover. This is further encouraged by the fact that there is simply no private land available in the community. Thus, even if an individual did desire to stay in Cold Bay he/she would be unable to do so unless they continued to work for an outside agency which provided them with housing. The result is that there is a gradual and steady turnover in population such that the vast bulk of the residents are replaced every five to ten years, with almost no one becoming a truly permanent resident.

The demographic characteristics of Cold Bay in-migration include an unusually young, male, and single population which is primarily Euro-American. Since Cold Bay is dominated by large outside employers almost everyone in town is brought from areas widely removed from Cold Bay. The result is that virtually all those coming into the community are white and non-Native. Those coming into Cold Bay do not come from the region immediately surrounding the town, but from such areas as Anchorage, Seattle, San Francisco, and other areas widely dispersed throughout the United States. Clearly the corporations and agencies which employ the people of Cold Bay recruit people to live there who are of working age, and just as clearly they are forced to leave should they no longer be of working age.

The other side of the coin of constant recruitment, and therefore constant immigration, is constant termination of residence in Cold Bay, or emigration. Emigration has historically more or less equalled immigration, since it is closely keyed to tours of duty served by individuals working for major outside agencies or corporations. Even during time of war when the town was more military site than community, the residents were serving tours of duty and would ultimately leave town for somewhere else.

This pattern of constant recruitment and replacement of the local population, and the distinctive pattern of in and out migration which it produces, is one aspect of Cold Bay structure which gives the community its centrifugal flavor. One result of this centrifugality is an unusual degree of interconnection with the world outside the community itself. Interestingly, Cold Bay residents have closer ties with people in much removed areas than they do with people in neighboring communities.

The fertility level in Cold Bay is very low. This is for several reasons. First, the high ratio of males to females means that there are relatively few families which means that the birthrate is correspondingly depressed. Second, the area is home for most residents only temporarily and they have little intention of starting a family and raising children in the community. Those who find that they are to have children, in fact, often leave the community in anticipation of the event, particularly as the level of medical attention available is not as good as outside.

The mortality rate is also very low in Cold Bay. This is largely a result of the combination of worker transience, the correspondingly young age of the population, the relative absense of physical occupational risks (e.g., fishing or processing), and the relatively more effective social controls on severe alcohol abuse. Since there is virtually no private land available in town it is almost impossible for an individual to retire in Cold Bay in that, upon retirement, his access to company housing would have to be terminated. The total absence in the population of people over the age of 65 supports this contention.

5.3.2 Community Facilities

5.3.2.1 **Electrical Power.** The electrical system is one area
in which Cold Bay appears well situated for the future, due to a
disastrous fire which led to the replacement of the old system with
a new one of greater capacity. This fire, on Easter morning of
1982, completely destroyed four generators and has led to the total
replacement of the power plant.

Cold Bay's electrical needs are filled by a powerplant
operated by the Northern Power Company. The company operates
generators which run on diesel fuel in a central location in the
built up section of town. Before the fire the community was served
by four generators, two of 600 kilowatts each, one of 400 kw, and
one of 100 kw, for a total generating capacity of 1700 kw
(although, in fact, since the company does not have the equipment
to parallel generators of unequal capacity, the most power which
could have been delivered simultaneously was 1200 kilowatts from
the two 600 kw generators operating together). Since the fire the
town has survived on an emergency generator with a capacity of 550
kw, which is sufficient for all the town's needs (as a rule summer
demand rarely exceeds 350 kw, and even during peak winter periods
demand is only 600 kw, only slightly more than the single generator
can deliver.)

Northern Power is currently involved in construction of a new
powerplant, consisting of three separate small buildings, each of
which will contain a generator. Two will be rated at 800 kw each,
and one will be rated at 600 kw, for a total capacity of 2200 kw.
This is far beyond the current needs of the community and should be
adequate for future needs, even in the event of significant growth.
However, even though the power capacity of the system has been, and
promises again to be, in excess of demand, there have been frequent
interruptions of service varying from a few minutes to several
hours. This has been particularly frequent since the fire reduced
capacity drastically. The situation is currently under investigation by the Alaska Public Utility Commission.

There are several private generators in town, most rated at
only a few kilowatts. One exception is the ARCO electrical system,
which is completely self-contained and is located on the property
leased by ARCO from the Thirteenth Regional Corporation. ARCO has
two generators, one rated at 50 kilowatts and one at 75 kilowatts.
Other private generators are owned by individuals, and the FAA has
an emergency generator to take over operation of most of the
crucial aspects of the airport in the event of power failure.
Plans also call for the new clinic to have an emergency generator.

5.3.2.2 **Sanitation.** The sewage system which serves almost
all of Cold Bay is owned and operated by the Federal Aviation
Administration. At some time in the future the city will be forced
to take over its operation. The system consists of a town-wide
pipe system which delivers sewage to a 22,500 gallon holding tank
where the sewage is aerated and chlorinated preparatory to its
expulsion into Cold Bay itself.

The system is already overloaded, with the facility asked to
process 30,000 or more gallons per day when its capacity is only
22,500 gallons. In addition, the system is operated by the FAA,

which is currently undergoing cutbacks in Cold Bay and hopes to divest itself of responsibility for sewer service. This has been given impetus by the recent incorporation of the town as a second class city.

Part of the problem in transferring the system from FAA to municipal control is that it currently falls short of Environmental Protection Agency standards, largely due to the overdemand on the system. The city and the FAA are currently involved in determining responsibility for bringing the system up to standard with the city wanting the FAA to do it before they transfer control and the FAA unclear as yet as to what its responsibilities are.

There are several privately owned cesspools in Cold Bay, including a large one at Winky's (Northern Pacific Fisheries), one of a thousand gallons planned for the clinic currently under construction, and one at the ARCO facility, as well as at least two built by people on land purchased in the 1979 land sale.

5.3.2.3 **Water.** The water system exhibits the same problems as the sewage system. The Cold Bay community water system is owned and operated by the Federal Aviation Administration. It consists of two wells which pump water to four storage tanks. Two of the tanks, with a capacity of 15,000 gallons each, are used for drinking water and two, with a capacity of 25,000 gallons each, are held in reserve for fire fighting. The FAA also maintains a delivery system consisting of a pipeline serving the whole of the built-up portion of Cold Bay as well as much of the outlying area.

The water system is now operating at capacity, and is often strained beyond capacity. It needs to be expanded, and at the same time the FAA would like to relinquish responsibility to the city. The incorporation of Cold Bay in conjunction with the scheduled FAA cutbacks, encouraged the FAA to begin negotiations with the city to switch control. As yet none of these negotiations are formal.

In the last year, there has been a sudden growth in the number of private wells in Cold Bay, due largely to the local presence of a well digger. In some ways, the community seems to have recognized the handwriting on the wall and begun to prepare for the future on an individual basis rather than trusting to the abilities of the central system.

5.3.2.4 **Communications.** Contrasting with the water and sewage systems is the telephone and communications system. Given the small size of the town and the fact that many villages and small towns in this, and other, regions of Alaska are dependent on a single village telephone the communications system in Cold Bay is surprisingly modern. The telephone system is adequate for present needs and has the capacity for expansion. This system, as well as the electrical system, is run by a private company and is in better condition than the government-run utilities.

Cold Bay's telephone system provides service to individual homes in the community. It is operated by the Interior Telephone Company. There are currently approximately 125 local subscribers as well as two pay telephones. The system has the capacity for satellite hookup for long distance calls. The system also has room for expansion and can handle approximately 400 lines, so it can accommodate at least three to four times as many users as it has currently. One problem, however, is service. Locals complain of

loud noises on the lines at times, and have difficulty in getting
repairs. The only local individual working for the company quit
recently and for a time there has been no representative of the
company in town.

5.3.2.5 **Transportation.** Fuel supply and transport are
crucial aspects of community capabilities. Fuel is readily
available in Cold Bay, since it is a major transportation link for
the region. Cold Bay has two kinds of fuel available, gasoline and
diesel. Gasoline is used predominantly for automobiles and other
motor vehicles, while diesel is used for generators, including the
power plant, and heating systems. Both gasoline and diesel are
provided by the Chevron facility located on the edge of the airstrip near the Reeve terminal. At the time of the fieldwork in the
summer of 1982 the cost of fuel was approximately $1.35 a gallon
for diesel and $1.46 a gallon for gasoline.

Fuel is brought into Cold Bay by both air and water, although
the former is a relatively expensive means of transport. Once in
town the fuel is stored in several large tanks. The largest complex of storage tanks is across the street from the Reeve Terminal
which includes one tank with a capacity of more than 2 1/2 million
gallons, owned by Chevron, one with a capacity of 500,000 gallons,
and several with capacities ranging from 40,000 to 167,000 gallons,
all owned by Reeve. Each of the major companies in town also has
storage facilities for their own supplies which are usually purchased from Reeve. The largest of these private complexes is near
the ARCO property and includes eleven 25,000 gallon tanks and two
which hold approximately 300,000 gallons each.

Fuel is delivered in town by tanker trucks owned by Reeve.
Individuals contract with Reeve to have diesel delivered, particularly for their furnaces, almost all of which run on diesel fuel.

Transportation is an area of community facilities in which
Cold Bay is both well and poorly situated. The town has a population of under 250, yet it has an international class airport with
sophisticated electronic navigational and control equipment. This
region of Alaska depends particularly on air transport, as well as
on boat transport. Cold Bay is very well situated with respect to
the former, and poorly situated with respect to the latter.

Cold Bay has the largest and most modern airport in the
region. It consists of two strips. The main strip is 10,400 feet
long and the crosswind strip is approximately 5,200 feet long. Both
are asphalt and concrete paved. The airport itself is the only
truly instrument controlled airfield in the region (almost every
other airport in the region is dirt and operates on visual flight
rules), and is almost never closed by weather. In 1981 the facility was open, despite at times brutal Alaskan winter weather,
every day of the year but one.

One problem the airport faces concerns jurisdiction. The
facility is run by the Department of Transportation, which maintains the airstrips and does most of the repair work. Recently the
Cold Bay City Council asked the state for a conveyance of some
state land and the state replied it would be happy to do so, but it
was all or nothing. This meant the City would have been left with
reponsibility for the airport and dock (see below) as well, an
intolerable burden for a town of just over 200 people. Once the

City made its concerns known, the state withdrew its offer. The City is considering a counter offer in which they agree to take some land now, the airport in two to three years, and, later, the dock, also run by the state. In this way the city could come gradually to control the major transportation facilities in town without attempting to assume the burden of all of them at once.

The major air carrier serving Cold Bay is Reeve Aleutian Airways. Peninsula Airlines also flies out of Cold Bay serving the smaller villages in the region not served by Reeve. Occasionally an Alaska Airlines or United States Air Force flight uses Cold Bay as a refueling stop.

The airport is maintained jointly by the Federal Aviation Administration and the State of Alaska Department of Transportation. The FAA is responsible for the operation of the navigation equipment, navigation aids, and the control tower. The DOT has responsibility for the maintenance of the airstrip itself and the apron areas adjacent to the airstrip.

Another aspect of transportation is land transport, which is dependent on a system of roads. As in most of rural Alaska, the regional road system is totally undeveloped, and roads exist only within the community and for a few miles out of town. Cold Bay has no road links to any other community in the region. There are approximately forty miles of unpaved road in and around town. The roads in town are gravel, as are most of those surrounding town. The major stretches of road are a section running from town eleven miles to the Air Force Station at Grant Point, and another of approximately seven miles running to Mortenson's Lagoon, a spur of which goes up Russell Creek to the Department of Fish and Game fish hatchery. This road is currently closed as a result of the collapse of the Russell Creek Bridge. There is also a road running several miles in the direction of Mount Frosty. The only paved section of road in the community is an approximately one mile section running around the eastern perimeter of the airport linking the Reeve Terminal, the hangars, and some businesses and agencies located on the edge of the airstrip itself.

The road system in Cold Bay is maintained by the State of Alaska Department of Transportation. The federal government maintains the roads in the Izembek Refuge and the military reservation.

There is a state owned dock in Cold Bay which was built in 1979. It is 1,824 feet long and 12 feet wide and is operated by the Department of Transportation. The dock has a "T"-section at the end which serves as a docking area for barges, replenishment vessels, and ferries which call four or five times a year with supplies. There are also several dolphins along the side of the dock which serve as docking sites for smaller ships, although in general docking facilities are inadequate for a fishing fleet or for use as a major point for shipping. The dock was designed primarily as a fuel unloading pier and is unsatisfactory for general cargo or industrial use. Major upgrading, or an entirely new dock, would be required for such uses. The state charges a docking fee of fifty dollars a day for the first three days and two hundred dollars a day for each day thereafter. The facility has pipeline hookups for the delivery of fuel and water to docked ships.

In general the marine facilities in Cold Bay are sparse and have constrained the development of fisheries-related economic activity. There is no small boat harbor, a necessity if Cold Bay is to attract fishermen to a local processor. As it stands now the nearest safe haven is King Cove, over twenty miles by water. A small boat harbor has been a subject of long-term discussion in the community, and the Army Corps of Engineers considered the feasibility of navigational improvements and the construction of small boat harbors for locations throughout coastal Alaska, one of which was Cold Bay, during the summer of 1982. A small boat harbor would encourage fishermen from the region to use Cold Bay as an offloading point, encouraging the development of a local fish processing industry. The presence of the airport is a strong incentive for such an industry, as it gives local processors the capability to rapidly deliver fresh or fresh frozen salmon or live crab. However, the findings with respect to Cold Bay were negative (Army Corps of Engineers, 1982).

Some have suggested that a good compromise would be a breakwater, which Cold Bay also lacks. At least a breakwater would provide a place for boats to anchor sheltered from bad weather. Though this has also been a major topic of discussion it has not progressed beyond discussion. At any event the development of a viable groundfish, crab, or salmon industry in Cold Bay will have to await the construction of some form of haven for fishing boats as well as for the installation of equipment with which to offload the product, neither of which can be projected for the next decade.

5.3.3 Housing and Real Estate Development

One of the effects of near total external control of the Cold Bay economy is a lack of private development. Private development is unusual in Cold Bay. The difficulty of getting private land restricts such growth, as does the difficulty of getting housing if not employed by a major local company. Most private development is at the instigation of those outside agencies and is designed for the use of their employees. In this section we will consider several aspects of private development, including housing, private investment, land purchase, and construction.

Almost all housing in Cold Bay is provided by the companies or agencies which operate in the town. Housing can be divided into that provided by the federal government, state government, private companies, and private individuals. Though the housing provided by the government may not be strictly private development, we include it here so an overall picture of local development can be presented.

There are three federal agencies which have constructed housing in Cold Bay: the Federal Aviation Administration, the National Weather Service, and the Fish and Wildlife Service. FAA housing consists of eleven homes located on St. Louis Road to the north of town and on the eastern edge of the longer of the two runways (Figure 5.1). These are modern woodframe homes with aluminum siding. The National Weather Service housing consists of six homes located to the immediate east of the FAA housing. The Fish

206

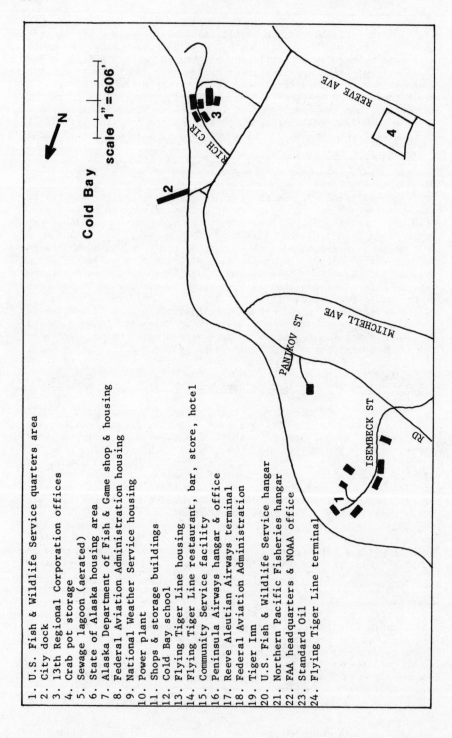

Cold Bay

scale 1" = 606'

N

REEVE AVE

RICH CIR

MITCHELL AVE

PANIKOV ST

ISEMBECK ST

RD

1. U.S. Fish & Wildlife Service quarters area
2. City dock
3. 13th Regional Corporation offices
4. Crab pot storage
5. Sewage lagoon (aerated)
6. State of Alaska housing area
7. Alaska Department of Fish & Game shop & housing
8. Federal Aviation Administration housing
9. National Weather Service housing
10. Power plant
11. Shops & storage buildings
12. Cold Bay school
13. Flying Tiger Line housing
14. Flying Tiger Line restaurant, bar, store, hotel
15. Community Service facility
16. Peninsula Airways hangar & office
17. Reeve Aleutian Airways terminal
18. Federal Aviation Administration
19. Tiger Inn
20. U.S. Fish & Wildlife Service hangar
21. Northern Pacific Fisheries hangar
22. FAA headquarters & NOAA office
23. Standard Oil
24. Flying Tiger Line terminal

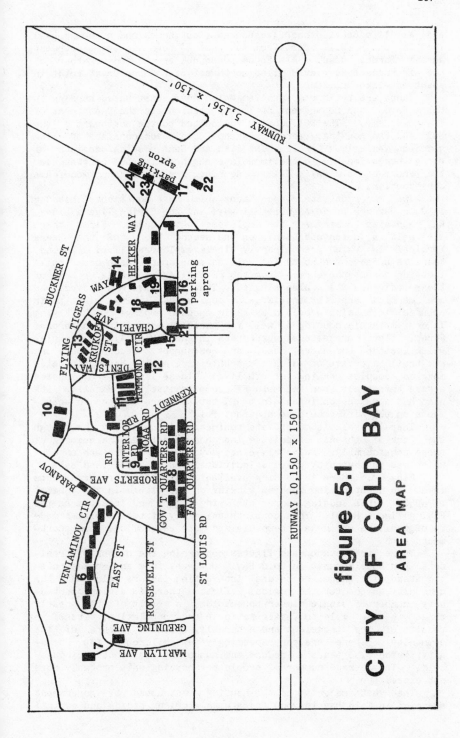

figure 5.1
CITY OF COLD BAY
AREA MAP

and Wildlife Service has five houses (four homes and a bunkhouse) located on a hill apart from the rest of town to the northwest across Baranov Road. Air Force personnel are housed together at the Air Force Base eleven miles northwest of town on Grant Point in apartment-like buildings.

There are two state agencies which have constructed housing in Cold Bay: the Department of Transportation and the Department of Fish and Game. The DOT housing is located to the northwest of the NWS and FAA housing, across Baranov Road, and consists of nine homes on Veniaminov Circle. The Fish and Game housing consists of three homes located to the immediate north of the DOT housing near the shore of Cold Bay. All these homes are of modern woodframe construction.

The major private corporations which have constructed housing in Cold Bay are Reeve Aleutian Airways and the Flying Tigers Lines. RAA maintains housing for its employees in two areas. First, there are half a dozen apartments on the second floor of the Reeve Terminal in which predominantly single employees live. Second, there is a Reeve bunkhouse (as well as a separate Reeve mess hall) located across the street from the Flying Tigers Lounge. Most of these individuals are also single. Those of Reeve's employees who are married are, by and large, local hires living with their spouses in housing provided by their spouses employer. The Flying Tigers maintain housing as well for their employees in two areas. First, there are several apartments in the Flying Tigers complex which includes the store, bar, and restaurant. Second, there are six trailers, five of which are double-wide mobile homes, in which married couples working for FTL live. These latter are located across the street from the main FTL complex itself. Finally, RCA also has a major contingent in town, but they are located in apartments on the Air Force Base at Grant Point.

There are also some private residences in Cold Bay, although the general absence of private land has restricted the number of these considerably. Privately-owned houses or trailers are on land which was purchased by private individuals in the 1979 land sale.

Finally, there is housing available for short term transients (such as construction workers working on the clinic in the summer of 1982). This lodging is run by Flying Tigers and is known as the Flying Tigers Hotel. This consists primarily of two complexes made up of trailers which have been divided into several one room apartments each.

There are no accurate figures concerning the number of residents per housing unit in Cold Bay. However, from an impressionistic standpoint there are several interesting factors which make the community unique for the region. First, there is a disproportionate number of single member households, a result of the nearly three to one male to female ratio in the population, itself a result of the transient and externally-oriented nature of the community. There are correspondingly few children in the community, which also tends to reduce the number of residents per household. The average number of people per housing unit probably does not exceed two.

The vast majority of the housing constructed by government agencies in Cold Bay is wood frame with aluminum siding and central heating which is run on diesel fuel. The trailers used by Flying Tigers, both for company housing and as the hotel, are standard mobile homes with insulated aluminum walls. Most of the housing in Cold Bay is therefore extremely modern and comparable to that to be found in any lower forty-eight suburban housing development or mobile home park. The housing provided by Reeve is old and small, but is still reasonably comfortable. The housing at the Air Force Base is modern and similar to apartments in a major urban area.

Though the housing in Cold Bay is generally of good quality, it is very difficult to find unless it is provided. All housing with the exception of the few private dwellings (at present there are only four private homes in all of Cold Bay) is allocated to individuals who work for an employer in town. This means it is impossible for an individual to come into town without a job and find housing. The situation is compounded by the general lack of available private land, which means that the individual is unable to get land on which to build even if he should be interested in doing so. The only place available for an "outsider" to stay is the Flying Tigers Hotel.

All of these factors--the domination of the community from outside, the general lack of available private land, and the occupational control of housing--result in a relatively low level of private investment overall in Cold Bay. Almost all private investment in Cold Bay is in terms of equipment or housing/buildings, rather than land. Since the land is controlled by the state the major private enterprises in town must lease the land on which they operate from the State of Alaska. Thus, Reeve, Flying Tigers, Peninsula, and all other private companies in town are operating on land leased for varying periods of time from the state.

In 1979 the State of Alaska held two land sales of 180 acres of waterfront and uplands near the dock. These were the only opportunities local residents have had to purchase land in the last fifteen years. However only some half dozen residents actually were able to purchase land due to the inflation of sales prices by outside speculators who purchased land on the assumption that it would skyrocket in value if oil development came to the region. The major purchasers in that sale were the Thirteenth Regional Corporation, King Cove Native Corporation, Reeve Aleutian Airways, and three cannery representatives. The Thirteenth Regional corporation had plans for development of the land but has since run into extreme financial difficulties. A portion of their land is now being leased to ARCO, and the rest remains essentially undeveloped.

The fact that the state owns virtually all the land in the developed area of town, and that the majority of the land alienated in the land sale of 1979 was purchased by outside interests with speculative purposes in mind has meant that very little construction or development of that land has occurred. Cold Bay is, to a large extent, on "hold" from the standpoint of construction until it becomes more clear the extent to which oil development will impact on the area.

Though private development has been stunted in Cold Bay through the lack of private land, there has been some development. The most substantial investment has been by the Flying Tigers Lines (FTL), which holds an exclusive twenty-five year lease from the

State of Alaska for the operation of, among other things, a hotel, bar, restaurant, and store. FTL also has a substantial investment in trailers and living quarters for its employees. Living quarters for employees is one investment shared by all major Cold Bay employers. However, beyond these living quarters most employers have only modest investments at best. The other exception to this, along with FTL, is Reeve Aleutian which has a substantial investment in aircraft and ground support facilities. Nonetheless, all private corporations in town do not own land but lease it from the State of Alaska. This lack of substantial local investment by outside firms which, nonetheless, control the local economy means it is possible for these corporations to leave town if necessary without being concerned over major losses in local investments. This may, in some instances, be seen as a weakness in the Cold Bay economic structure.

This lack of available private land, and the resultant low level of private investment is reflected in a low level of local construction activity. Cold Bay changes slowly, and there has rarely been a period of major construction which has not resulted from military necessity, and most such construction has been temporary in nature. However, though construction is usually inactive, it does seem to have accelerated somewhat in the last year. The powerhouse, destroyed in a fire on Easter Day 1982, is being reconstructed. The clinic has just been constructed (September, 1982) by RoyCo, Inc. of Anchorage, at an estimated cost of $297,000, which included an attached generator room and septic system (RoyCo cost statement, 1982). ARCO has carried out some construction in providing facilities for its workers, though this consisted mainly of moving trailers onto the land for living space and construction of a large garage and recreational building. There are plans for a new multi-purpose room which will be added onto the school, and two local residents are planning to construct a new hangar on the airport apron. Construction of the multi-purpose room is scheduled for the spring of 1983 and should be completed by fall of 1983. The implications of this new community facility are significant as far as social cohesion and interaction are concerned and are discussed in the scenarios following this ethnography.

6
The Community Structure
of Cold Bay

In this chapter we will detail the structure of Cold Bay. As with our discussion of the structure of Unalaska in Chapter Three, we will begin with the value system of the residents of Cold Bay. Next we will discuss the organization of the basic subsystems of Cold Bay social structure, including the local economy, social networks, political organization, religion, education, health care, social services, and recreational activities. At most points we will find the local inhabitants remarkably outer-directed in their concern with status and prestige and in their actions in the various subsystems. In many ways Cold Bay is secondary as an arena in which residents, as transients, are interested in competing or interacting.

6.1 VALUE SYSTEM

Cold Bay inhabitants share certain aspects of a frontier ethic. The town is overwhelmingly male. Virtually all the inhabitants of the community come from outside the area and are in Cold Bay for only a relatively brief and fixed period of time. There is a strong sense of independence and self-reliance. There is a feeling of challenging a difficult environment which is fundamentally different from the modern, often urban, environment which has been left behind. Connected with this is an emphasis on physical prowess and self-sufficiency rather than dependence on others for the provision of services in particular. Almost everyone in Cold Bay maintains and repairs their housing, vehicles, and other technological devices rather than depend on often non-existent technicians or repairmen.

Connected with this frontier ethic is the belief on the part of the vast bulk of the population that their sojourn in Cold Bay is only temporary, and that they are not committed to a permanent stay in the community. Most people are sent to Cold Bay by their employers, and most see it as an opportunity to make and save substantial sums of money for the future. Moreover, the benefits of a stay in Cold Bay are expected to be enjoyed somewhere else in Alaska or, more often, in the lower forty-eight. The most important result of this is the lack of commitment to Cold Bay itself,

211

with the result that there is little civic spirit or sense of community. Again, the community shares little of the sense of an intense moral community which we are used to associating with small towns.

Also connected to the fact that the members of the Cold Bay community are essentially transient and lack commitment to Cold Bay per se is the external orientation of the community. The lack of commitment to the community should not be interpreted as a complete lack of concern about what goes on in the community. Cold Bay residents are concerned about their community, nonetheless, they see their stay primarily as temporary and are therefore understandably less concerned about long term development in the community than would be the case if they were permanent residents. Cold Bay is a quintessentially centrifugal community. It is made up of people who as often as not have more intense, long-lasting, and strong social connections to people outside the community than they do to other residents. This is also a result of the transient nature of the community which has resulted in an unusual situation in which there are no kinship relations among the members of the community. Kinship is traditionally the informing matrix through which social relations in small scale communities are ordered, but in Cold Bay there are no operative kinship relations beyond the nuclear family. Any kinship relations which exist link members of the community and people outside the community, again serving to weaken the multiplex nature of social relations and, by extension, the sense of community itself.

Finally, most of the factors noted above are also influenced by the male orientation of the community. Adult men outnumber adult women by a ratio of almost three to one (2.85 to 1, and for adults aged twenty to forty-four the ratio is a very high 3.57 to 1). This heightens the emphasis on physical prowess and reinforces the sense of a frontier ethic in which the individual submits to a difficult and trying environment in the hopes of future returns which are to be enjoyed outside of Cold Bay—when the individual returns "home."

Status in Cold Bay is very much an individualistic measure. The relatively low proportion of families, along with the transience of the residents, means that status is not measured in terms of family prestige or lineage depth, but in very pragmatic and relatively instrumental terms. The fact that recruitment and replacement occurs so readily and involves nearly all residents means there is little time for individuals to institutionalize a status hierarchy.

There is, in essence, no local generational depth to the families in Cold Bay. The vast majority of people in Cold Bay are single or they are in town as short term transients and do not have their families present with them. This means there is not only little prestige attached to specific families, but there is little knowledge of the families of the people living in town.

Another means of distinguishing status is wealth. Those who are in Cold Bay are all roughly on a par from the standpoint of social class and income. There is no one in Cold Bay who can be called wealthy, with the exception of one or two people who are in town only occasionally. There is no owner class in the community since all local employers are outside agencies and companies. Thus the occupational and social scale is collapsed to encompass only the middle ranges. Almost everyone in town is in the middle class. They are middle- and lower-level management and white collar employees or skilled blue collar employees. Ultimately, no one is particularly interested in displaying their wealth in the context of Cold Bay. If an individual becomes wealthy it is displayed in other venues, such as Anchorage or Seattle. Another factor is the tendency, in bush Alaska, for those who have become at least moderately wealthy to continue to act and live as they did before they came into money. It is often cited as a source of pride by bush Alaskans that one can walk into a bar and not tell the paupers from the millionaires. The latter still wear blue jeans, may have a somewhat unkempt appearance, and, in general, do little overtly to call attention to the fact of their wealth.

The belief system of most Cold Bay residents is one which includes a desire for the amenities of modern, twentieth century American life, while not expecting to become wildly rich. The residents are realists, and the one church in town is only modestly subscribed. They are willing to work hard for what they get, but they expect to be properly remunerated for their labor. Cold Bay residents, by and large, have more faith in science and technology than religion. There is a respect for religious beliefs, but most do not feel bound by a particular set of denominational canons. This, of course, is variable and is not meant to imply that there are no deeply religious people in the community, only that most do not fall into that category.

There are, in effect, no operative ethnic relations in Cold Bay. This is a result of the fact that the community is nearly 100 percent Euro-American, with very few Native residents. There is, therefore, no situation in which ethnic identity comes into play in social relations. There is some latent sense of ethnic relations in that a few locals feel the Alaskan Native is gaining an undue advantage over them in general as a result of legislation in the last several years. However, this is not a widespread perception in the community.

A final aspect of the value system revolves around recriprocity and redistribution. Small communities are often characterized by intense reciprocal and redistributive networks. Several factors work against extensive redistribution in Cold Bay. First, redistribution is often an economic reflection of social status or political power, with goods flowing to a central, powerful figure who then redistributes them to the population. The rough equivalence of economic position of all members of Cold Bay society means there is no individual who is able to assume this position. Second, the strength of ecconomic and social links between residents of Cold Bay and the external world means that there is little redistribution which occurs within the community itself because the local arena is not the most important one for the residents. Much of the money earned by individuals in Cold Bay is used for aims defined external to the community. Since the establishment of prestige within the community is relatively unimportant to the residents, there is little incentive to build up a network of obligation through the establishment of a redistributive system.

Where redistribution reflects a social and/or political hierarchy, reciprocity is an expression of social equality. Reciprocity does exist within the Cold Bay system. As in much of bush
Alaska individuals feel a certain kinship simply as a result of
sharing the burden of facing an objectively challenging and difficult environment. Meals are often shared, with individuals establishing a rough balance between giving and receiving over time.
Aid is generally quickly forthcoming for home improvements, repairs, or construction, and it is generally recognized that the
individual calling for such help has incurred a debt which can be
called due when needed by those who rendered the aid. Again,
however, the transience of the community means that only those who
have been in town for a certain minimum period of time are really
involved in such networks.

2.2 ORGANIZATION

Though Cold Bay has a small population it lacks the insularity
we are accustomed to finding in small communities. It is a cosmopolitan, open society—that is, the people who make it up are
cosmopolitan and have experience far beyond the confines of Cold
Bay itself.
The central facility of Cold Bay is the Cold Bay Airport, the
raison d'etre for the town's existence. The economic structure,
as we will see below, is dominated by the transportation and communications sectors and by the federal and state government; it is
above all a transient community, and this presents problems of
coordinated, long-term planning as well as problems of community
integration. Socially the community is characterized by the unusual extent to which kinship beyond the family is inoperative as a
principle of social organization, by the overriding importance of
friendship as the locus of social activity, and, finally, by the
central role played by occupation in determining friendship and
associational networks. Politically the community is fragmented.
Political relations are, as are all other social relations, transi-
tory and dominated by transients. The town has recently incorporated, insuring more control than would otherwise be possible over
the future course of events in the community. Nonetheless, those
who are there to witness those changes are likely to be very different from those currently planning for them, with attendant
problems in preparation and outcome. Religious activity is relatively low. The one chapel in town is ostensibly interdenominational, but in fact, in terms of liturgy and ritual tends to be
Baptist. Health care is an area in which Cold Bay is currently
upgrading itself considerably through the construction of a modern
clinic/hospital which will provide well for the health needs of the
community, although there are currently no plans for stationing a
medical doctor permanently in the community. Social services are
an area in which Cold Bay is sadly lacking, unless we count the
services provided by the individual employers in the community.
The fact that Cold Bay is a full employment, transient (and therefore extremely young) community obviates the need for many social
services which are required in other small towns of comparable

size. Recreational activities revolve around socializing at one of two local bars and outdoor activities such as fishing and hunting. Families do get together and have fish fries and the like, but the social interaction is not as intense as one would expect in a small town.

We will see throughout this chapter that the dominant considerations explaining the nature of Cold Bay social structure have to do with, first, the fact that the town is dominated by a few outside employers, both private and governmental; second, that the result of this form of employment is the transience of the population such that individuals rarely remain in town more than a few years and thus have little time for the establishment of social ties; third, that another result of this is the youth and single-male-orientation of the community; and finally, that the community is almost completely devoted to airport related activities, transportation, and/or communications sectors being particularly prominent in the local economic environment with very little local entrepreneurial activity. All these factors encourage strong intercommunity networks and weak intracommunity networks.

6.2.1 Economic Organization

There are five particular characteristics which distinguish the economic organization of Cold Bay. First, it is one of the few communities in the Aleutian Chain and Alaska Peninsula region not directly dependent on marine resources, particularly salmon and/or crab, for its economic survival. The fisheries-related sector is extremely small as a proportion of total economic activity, and indeed has undergone contraction in recent years. There is the potential for considerable development in this area, and this is a crucial sector bearing on the future economic vitality of the town, but at present fisheries activity is a minor consideration in the town's economic life.

The weakness of the fisheries sector is a result of several factors. The airport has dominated the economic life of the town and led it away from large-scale participation in the fisheries. The town originated as an Euro-American settlement. Thus, when the early seventies saw the introduction of Limited Entry salmon fishing, Cold Bay had extremely few residents who were interested in or able to gain permits, with the result that the development of an indigenous fishing community was foregone. Although this does not preclude fish processing, the few attempts at this have so far been ill planned or relatively small scale.

The second economic generalization that can be made about Cold Bay concerns the kind of economic activity which characterizes and dominates the community. Cold Bay is dominated by three sectors in particular; transportation, communications, and government. The nature of these sectors is, again, largely attributable to the central position assumed by the community as a result of its airport.

A third economic characteristic of Cold Bay revolves around the nature of the workers. The majority of local employees are transient, remaining for a period running from six months to between three and five years. This is because most workers are not hired locally but are already work for a company outside Cold Bay and are sent there for tours of duty of varying lengths. This means there is a tremendous turnover of employees every few years, as well as a large turnover in population as a whole since the economy is dominated by a few employers, almost all of whom practice some form of the tour of duty.

Fourth, Cold Bay's economy is not only dominated by a handful of employers, almost every one of these employers, and all the major ones are corporations or government agencies which are external to Cold Bay itself. There is little local entrepreneurial activity, and that which is present is, at least so far, on a very modest scale. This means the aims of these firms are defined externally to Cold Bay, and that major economic fluctuations and changes are responses to aims and goals outside the community.

The fifth economic characteristic of Cold Bay has to do with land tenure. The process by which Cold Bay originated suddenly and fully developed as a transportation center of strategic national importance guaranteed property would be under the control of the national government. This was facilitated by the lack, currently or historically, of a permanent indigenous settlement in the area. Subsequent to World War II the federal government no longer felt the need to maintain control, but they nevertheless did so until 1959 when, with the entrance of Alaska as a state in the union, control of much of the property in town was transferred from the federal to the state structure. The state now owns virtually all land in Cold Bay, with the exception of small holdings of the federal government and a handful of private individuals. Thus, the dominant factor of land tenure in Cold Bay is the near-total lack of private land or land available for private development (with the exception of a small amount alienated by the State Department of Natural Resources in the 1979 land sales and an estimated 100 acres north of the city limits). The lack of an indigenous population has meant that Cold Bay residents were unable to lay claim to land in their community. The one major exception to this lack of private land ownership paradoxically involves Cold Bay land but does not involve Cold Bay residents. The Native Corporation of King Cove has selected, as part of its conveyance of land under the provisions of ANCSA, a stretch of prime residential land between Russell Creek and Mortensen's Lagoon, a tract occupying nearly a third of the total city limits on the southeast side.

Cold Bay, then, is economically influenced by a combination of a lack of a preexistent Native community in the area, the subsequent development of a major airport by external powers, and the resultant lack of available private land. A closer examination of the economic structure of the town will verify this.

6.2.1.1 **Cash Economy**. As noted above, the commercial harvesting and processing sectors are minor in Cold Bay, at least at present. There was an attempt on the part of the Thirteenth Regional Corporation to develop a harvesting and processing capability, revolving around salmon, groundfish, and crab, but this was short lived as the Thirteenth Corporation ran into financial difficulties and was forced to retrench—the Cold Bay operation was one of several victims of this retrenchment. Currently there is almost no commercial harvesting in Cold Bay.   The town lacks a small boat harbor or breakwater, so there are no fishing boats which identify Cold Bay as their home port.   The local dock is ill-equipped to efficiently off-load large quantities of product, and has not attracted widespread use by fishermen from neighboring villages.

There is, however, considerable potential for commercial harvesting in the area, as evidenced by the success of fishermen out of King Cove, only twenty-five miles away.   The area is in the center of a vast crab fishery; the groundfishery is characterized as one of the most abundant in the world, though it is essentially unexploited by domestic fishermen; and the area sits astride one of the most productive salmon fisheries in the world.   None of these options are currently utilized,however, nor are they likely to be in the near future.

The processing sector would seem to hold more promise for Cold Bay as it does not require resident fishermen.   Nonetheless, the only real processing activity in Cold Bay is the operation of the Northern Pacific Fisheries (locally known as Winky's, after the owner).   This firm processes salmon and sometimes crab and other marine resources.   However, the total employment is usually five people, though it fluctuates between as few as two and as many as fifteen.   Winky's has only been in town for a couple of years, and it is still too early to be certain whether it will prove to be a long-term operation or not.

The only other processing activity in town is a local representative of Seawest Corporation.   Seawest has an agreement with the Tokyo Overseas Trading Company of Japan to deliver salmon eggs for export to Japan, and earlier in the year there were two Japanese workers who lived at Winky's and took delivery of the salmon eggs, packaged them, and sent them to Japan.   However, the rate of delivery was so slow that by the end of July they had been instructed by their company to move their operation to Pilot Point and take delivery of eggs there.   Currently there are no representatives of the Trading Company in Cold Bay.

Entrepreneurial activity of local origin is very limited in Cold Bay.   Few individuals remain in Cold Bay long enough to initiate such activity.   This lack of a significant sector of truly permanent residents has stunted the development of a genuinely local economic sector.   There are only two, possibly three if we stretch the definition, local entrepreneurial activities which can even be considered small scale.

The largest local business is Cold Bay Truck Rental.   This business is owned and operated by two men who consider themselves to be permanent residents.   The two owners are also the only two employees of the business.   They have between fifteen and twenty vehicles which they rent out to both locals and short-term transients (the number of vehicles varies, as local conditions are very hard on vehicles and a good number are in a constant state of disrepair).   Vehicles are rented at a rate of forty dollars a day—there are no weekly rates, although several local residents have been allowed to rent vehicles by the month at a considerably reduced rate.   This is currently the most ambitious and successful local entrepreneurial effort.   However, neither of the individuals operating the business depend on it for their sole source of income and both hold other jobs in the community as well.

The second local entrepreneurial effort involves two individuals who are attempting to build an airplane hangar on the parking
apron of Cold Bay Airport. Their intent is to rent out hangar
space to local pilots and, possibly, initiate an air taxi service,
similar to, but smaller in scope than that run by Peninsula Airlines. They have currently contracted for the final surveying of
the property on which they will build the hangar, after which they
will be free to begin construction. They are also currently having
a well dug on the property which should be completed by the end of
September (1982). Construction is expected to be completed by fall
of 1982.

These local businesses account for only four people (three if
we count the individual involved in both as a single person), or
less than three percent of total Cold Bay employment. The only
other local operation which generates income is a single backhoe
owned by a local citizen which he rents out to those who need to
use it. However, most residents know this individual well enough
that they are able to gain use of the backhoe for little or no
payment. As often as not the use of the backhoe is based on the
return of the favor in another form at a later date, rather than on
a cash basis.

Alternative forms of employment constitute the vast majority
of all economic activity in Cold Bay. No more than an average of
twelve people are involved in employment in the processing, harvesting, and local support sectors together. Thus, considerably more
than ninety percent of all jobs in Cold Bay fall under the state
government, federal government, or external commercial agencies.

The federal sector has historically been the dominant economic
force in Cold Bay. Although this is no longer the case, and the
sector continues to undergo contraction, it is still an economic
force in the community. The federal agencies which operate in Cold
Bay are, in order of size of labor force, the Federal Aviation
Administration, the National Weather Service, the Fish and Wildlife
Service, and the Post Office.

The Federal Aviation Administration has a long history of
involvement in Cold Bay, and at one time had sole responsibility
for the operation of the Cold Bay Airport. It has since relin-
quished most of this responsibility to the State of Alaska Department of Transporation, although it retains responsibility for the
operation of the control tower and air controllers, and for maintenance of the navigation aids and other equipment associated with
the tower. The FAA currently employs sixteen people.

The National Weather Service is the second largest federal
employer in Cold Bay with a workforce of five. The Weather Service
is responsible for augmenting the FAA in the operation of the
control tower through the provision of updated weather forecasts
and for the monitoring of conditions at the airport itself. The
NWS in Cold Bay is also an "upper atmosphere station" and releases
weather balloons daily which transmit data from the upper atmosphere to a Rawinsonde Dome.

The last two federal civilian employers are the Fish and
Wildlife Service of the Department of the Interior, and the Post
Office. The Fish and Wildlife Service currently employs four

people in Cold Bay. The Post Office employs two people who are
local hire. The final federal employer in Cold Bay is the Air
Force. There is a contingent of approximately sixteen men located
at the Air Force Base on Grant Point. They both work and live on
the base.

The state is the other governmental employer in Cold Bay.
Historically this sector has represented a minority of government
employees, far outnumbered by federal employees. However, during
the last decade state employment has slowly increased while federal
employment has dropped. Currently federal employees still outnumber state employees by approximately two to one, but the gap continues to narrow and if federal retrenchment plans are realized
state employees may come to equal or surpass federal employees by
the end of the decade. There are four state employers: the Alaska
Department of Transportation and Public Facilities (the DOT), the
Alaska Department of Fish and Game, the Aleutians Rural Education
Attendence Area (REAA), and the Magistrate.

The major state employer is the Department of Transportation.
Currently the DOT employs six people in Cold Bay.. The DOT takes
primary responsibility for the maintenance of the airport and the
area surrounding it, and for emergency and safety procedures at the
airport. This latter includes the maintenance and operation of the
airport firefighting equipment which includes six vehicles (1 Go-
Track, 1 attack vehicle, two standard trucks, one tanker, and one
converted jeep).

The second state agency in Cold Bay is the Department of Fish
and Game. This department takes primary responsibility for the
monitoring of commercial fishing in the entire western peninsula
region, keeping records of catch levels, escapement levels, keeping
streams cleared for spawning salmon, and so on. The Cold Bay
office works closely with the Unalaska and Sand Point offices in
monitoring shellfish activity as well. The Fish and Game Department also operates a salmon hatchery on Russell Creek, several
miles to the southeast of Cold Bay. The Department has seven
employees. Of these usually two or three are located at the Russell Creek Fish Hatchery, while the bulk are located at the Fish
and Game headquarters in town. Several of the employees are in
Cold Bay only seasonally, approximately half the year from late
spring to early fall, after which they return to the regional or
state Fish and Game offices to collate and analyze the data from
the previous year while the other employees are here year round.

A third major state employer is the Aleutian Islands R.E.A.A.
which employs the teachers at the Cold Bay School. The school,
which has recently been extended from K-9 to K-12, has four
teachers and a maintenance man, for a total of five employees.
They are employed for nine months out of the year, and have the
summer off.

The final state employee in town is the magistrate, who is
responsible as the legal representative of the State of Alaska for
Cold Bay. The magistrate is also responsible for a considerable
number of villages and towns in the surrounding region, and makes
frequent trips during the year to outlying areas to serve the needs
of those residents.

There is one other area of government recently inaugurated in

Cold Bay.   This is municipal government which employs one clerk on
a half-time basis.

Altogether government employees account for approximately
forty percent of the Cold Bay workforce, a figure which has
declined steadily in the last decade and which promises to continue, perhaps even accelerate, its decline over the next decade.
The majority of these employees (in particular the FAA, National
Weather Service, the DOT and, to a certain extent, the Fish and
Game Department) are in Cold Bay for a limited time only.   The FAA
and the Weather Service have tours of duty of two years, or, in
some cases, of one year, while the Department of Transportation
and, in some cases, the Fish and Game Department have tours of duty
of eighteen months.   Thus, among the government employees in Cold
Bay there is little likelihood that one would find many individuals
who have been in town more than a few years, and those who have
been in town over five years are rare.   In many instances this is
because the government agency provides for what is known as "return
rights".   That is, the individual is helped with his moving
expenses, and those of his family, when he leaves Cold Bay to
return to where he came from or to take another position with his
employer in another town.   However, it is often the case that these
return rights are good only if exercised within a certain period of
time, generally allowing no more than three renewals of the tour of
duty before they are lost.   Thus, though the time varies considerably, it is difficult for most government workers to remain in Cold
Bay much beyond five years before they are faced with the choice of
staying on indefinitely or exercising their return rights and
leaving Cold Bay for another assignment.   Most choose the latter.
This, of course, means that the working population is in constant
flux, with people leaving and arriving on a regular basis.

External commercial agencies form the largest single cohort of
employers in Cold Bay.   Historically this position has been held by
the government sector, but in the last decade, particularly with
the de-escalation of the Vietnam War, the private sector has
outstripped the government sector, a process which continues to
gather momentum today.   The private sector now outnumbers government workers (with the exclusion of federal military personnel at
the Air Force Base) by about 1.5 to one.   The largest contributors
to the private sector are the fields of transportation, communications, and service, in that order.   There are also small numbers of
processing, covered earlier, and construction workers.

The two largest external commercial entities in the transportation sector are Reeve Aleutian Airways and Peninsula Airlines.
Reeve has been in Cold Bay since World War II, and currently maintains the only regularly scheduled passenger service into and out
of Cold Bay.   Reeve has a total of twenty-two employees, maintains
several facilities in town, including the Reeve Terminal building
in which there is a passenger waiting room, baggage and ticket
counter, offices, and the post office.   They also have a bunkhouse
in town for employees and an employee mess hall next to the bunkhouse.   Reeve provides housing for many of its employees in the
bunkhouse and in rooms on the second floor of the terminal.

In addition to being the largest employer in town, Reeve also
has the highest percentage of "local hires" of any major employer

in Cold Bay. Fourteen of the twenty-two people who work for Reeve were hired in Cold Bay rather than brought in from outside. This is because many of the Reeve employees are married to people who work for other agencies, particularly governmental, in town. This works to Reeve's advantage in several ways. First, it means they do not have to provide housing for all their employees as do most of the other major employers in town. Second, it means they do not incur the expense involved in helping with the costs of relocation to bring an employee to Cold Bay to work. Finally, it means they do not have to worry about guaranteeing return rights, since their workers were already in Cold Bay when they were hired.

Reeve also provides some important economic services for the community. They sell diesel oil from their terminal next to the passenger terminal in a cooperative venture with Chevron. This is the source of diesel heating fuel for most of the townspeople. They also provide gasoline for most of the vehicles in town. Finally, they provide fuel for the non-Reeve planes in the area which use the Cold Bay airport frequently.

The second major transportation company in town is Peninsula Airlines. Peninsula is based in King Salmon, but the Cold Bay office is a relatively large and independent one. Peninsula provides three kinds of service. First, under contract to Reeve, they fly to Nikolski on Monday, King Cove on Tuesday, Thursday, and Friday, Akutan on Wednesday, and False Pass on Thursday. These are passenger flight continuations of Reeve flights which originate in Anchorage or Seattle. Second, they fly charters whenever they are hired to do so. Generally these are to someplace on the west peninsula or in the Aleutian Islands. Finally, they have contracts for mail runs to Atka, False Pass, and King Cove. Peninsula now has six planes which are used for these various purposes, two Grumann Gooses and Piper Navajos, with one Piper Saratoga and one DC3. They employ ten people, including six pilots, two secretaries, the manager, and one line person. Peninsula's physical plant includes one large hangar which also has office space in it, and one slightly smaller hangar devoted completely to housing airplanes. Peninsula also leases hangar space to ARCO which is in town pursuing offshore surveying and oil exploration.

In the communications sector there are three concerns, one of substantial size and two relatively small. These are, in order of number of employees, RCA, Alascom, and the Interior Telephone Company. This sector, communications, represents nearly as large a proportion of the Cold Bay labor force as the transportation sector. All together (including in the number the employees of the Cold Bay Truck Rental Company) transportation accounts for thirty-four jobs in Cold Bay, or approximately twenty-two percent of all Cold Bay employees. The communications sector, on the other hand, accounts for some thirty-one employees, or approximately twenty percent. These two sectors alone account for well over forty percent of the Cold Bay labor force.

RCA is the largest firm in the communications sector. They employ approximately twenty-eight people, making them the largest employer in Cold Bay. Until recently they employed over thirty people, but this was before they divested themselves of Alascom, and began their retrenchment program. RCA maintains and operates most of the radar equipment at the air force base, and has taken increasing responsibility for its operation in the last few years from the military.

Alascom is another private communications company in Cold Bay. Alascom provides satellite broadcasts for the entire community, including the Air Force Base. This includes both radio and television. Alascom was divested by RCA about a year and a half ago (early 1980) and is now owned by Pacific Power Company of Washington State. They employ two people full time. They offer a cable television service which is subscribed to by most households.

The final external commercial agency in the communications sector is the Interior Telephone Company. This is a regional telephone company employing only one person in Cold Bay. This individual is responsible for installation and service, and often works only part time, as is currently the case.

The service sector consists of two major companies, Flying Tigers Lines and the Northern Power Company. The Flying Tigers has been an historically important force in the shaping of modern Cold Bay. They entered the area in the 1960s and became particularly important in the seventies. At one time they flew freight and cargo in and out of Cold Bay regularly, but in the last ten years this has declined considerably. In fact, only about one Flying Tiger flight a month comes through Cold Bay. Nonetheless, the Tigers remain a major influence in Cold Bay because of their involvement in the community service and support sector.

Flying Tigers operates the major shopping and entertainment complex in Cold Bay. They operate the only store in town; the only place where purchases of food, dry goods, sporting goods, medical needs, and so on can be made. They operate the only restaurant in town. They also operate the only bar in town, the primary meeting place and literally only place to socialize in Cold Bay proper. "The Weathered Inn" is by far the most popular social venue in Cold Bay. It is particularly popular among the singles in town, and the unusual demographic makeup of Cold Bay includes a large proportion of single people, almost completely single men. Flying Tigers also operates the only public hotel in town. Altogether Flying Tigers has about sixteen employees (though they may drop as low as twelve employees during the off season) working in the store, the bar, the restaurant and overseeing the operation of the hotel. Most of these were hired by Tigers outside of Cold Bay and subsequently transported there, as is the pattern for most of the large employers in town. However, like Reeve, Flying Tigers has a certain percentage of employees who were hired subsequent to moving to Cold Bay.

Flying Tigers is particularly crucial to the current character of Cold Bay and to the possibilities for future development of the city for one reason above all others. In 1960 they signed a lease with the state which gave them exclusive rights to operate a bar, hotel, restaurant, and store, among other facilities, in Cold Bay for the next twenty-five years. This lease expires in 1985, but at that time Tigers has the option of renewing it for another twenty-five years or letting it lapse. This lease has already had important effects on local development. Some years ago an outside firm came to the city with an offer to build a hotel and restaurant in

town. Local residents were generally receptive to the idea, but
when the central office of the Flying Tigers was contacted and
permission requested of them, per their lease, it was flatly
denied.   Thus, any future growth of the city will have to contend
with the wishes of this externally oriented group of businessmen,
which will determine the direction taken by the commercial sector
of Cold Bay. At this writing it appears that the Flying Tigers are
leaning toward not renewing their lease, which would open Cold Bay
to other commerical interests, but it is too early yet to be certain what will transpire.

Table 6.1

Cold Bay Labor Force by Sector, 1982

Economic Sector	Total employees	Percent of Total Workforce
Government	63	40.9
Federal	43	27.9
Federal Aviation Administration	16	
National Weather Service	5	
Fish and Wildlife Service	4	
U.S. Post Office	2	
U.S. Air Force	16	
State	19	12.3
Department of Transportation	6	
Department of Fish and Game	7	
Aleutians R.E.A.A.	5	
Magistrate	1	
Municipal	1	0.7
Clerk	1	
Private Employers	91	59.1
Transportation	34	22.1
Reeve Aleutian Airways	22	
Peninsula Airlines	10	
Cold Bay Truck Rental	2	
Communications	31	20.1
R.C.A.	28	
Alascom	2	
Interior Telephone Company	1	
Service	18	11.7
Flying Tigers Lines	16	
Northern Power Company	2	
Manufacturing/Processing	6	3.9
Northern Pacific Fisheries	5	
Seawest	1	
Construction	2	1.3
Well Digger	1	
Laborer	1	
TOTAL	154	100.0

This completes the employment structure of Cold Bay. With these data we can now detail the overall structure of the Cold Bay labor force. This is done in Table 6.1.

6.2.1.2 **Subsistence**. The cash economy exercises almost total dominance over the Cold Bay economic organization, despite the fact that it is directed in large measure outside the town. Subsistence economic activity has no history and is relatively little practiced—beyond recreation. This is despite the fact that the area provides for an abundance of subsistence needs. However, many of the local residents do take some advantage of the fish and game resources in the area.

There are several spots around Cold Bay where one can fish very successfully for salmon. All of the major southern peninsula runs come into Cold Bay to some extent, including reds, kings, chum, and silvers. A fair proportion of the local residents do fish each year to provide a supplement to their diet, some fewer depend on salmon for a major part of their diet during the season and some freeze salmon for the winter.

A Cold Bay resident is eligible for a subsistence salmon permit which allows him or her to take up to two hundred salmon with a set net. There are several streams in the vicinity which provide excellent fishing. Mortensen Lagoon is also very popular for setnetting. Although salmon is the major fish taken, both for subsistence and with a sportfishing license which most residents purchase, there are also good quantities locally of cod, halibut and crab which are harvested in moderation by residents.

Hunting is also a pastime of some popularity in Cold Bay, and a large number of residents utilize it to supplement their diets. The most popular game animal is the Barren Ground Caribou. Caribou season is in the fall of each year, and the animals are so plentiful that one is literally guaranteed the animal of his choice. Caribou is often frozen and put away for winter. Bear is also hunted occasionally, though almost always as a game animal rather than as a source of sustenance. Duck and geese are hunted in season (September and October) and are also frequently frozen for the winter. Trapping is limited and generally confined to red fox, weasel and wolverine. In general, however, Cold Bay probably utilizes the biological resources of its environment for subsistence less than any town or village in the region.

Cold Bay, then, is a community dominated by a cash economy, and one in which the subsistence sector plays a minor role at best. There has never been a need to depend on the subsistence sector, as there was never a time when Cold Bay was in any sense isolated or out of touch with consumer products.

6.2.1.3 **Non-Labor Force**. Cold Bay is also unusual in that there is virtually no non-labor force. That is, each household has at least one gainfully employed individual who is able to support the household, and many have two such individuals. Almost every "local hire" is the spouse of someone who already has a job. There is no unemployment in Cold Bay. The idea simply does not make sense in the context of the community. The town both attracts those with jobs already and purges itself of those who lose their job or are unable to find one. One does not go to Cold Bay to live except at the instigation of an employer who "sends" the individual

or his spouse there.   By the same token, it is impossible to survive there, even to find a place to live, unless one has a job, so
those who lose their job invariably move on to another community
very quickly.
There are also no retired people in Cold Bay.   The primary
reason for this is that most people, while working, live in housing
provided by their employer in town.   There is almost no private
land available for the individual to purchase and on which he can
build a home.   This means that once the individual is no longer
working for a company represented in town it is impossible for him
to find an alternative place of residence. People do not retire in
Cold Bay, they retire from Cold Bay.   In several discussions with
people living in employer-provided housing we noted that they would
enjoy retiring here, but it is simply impossible for them to find a
place to live, much less purchase, once they no longer have access
to employer-provided housing.   Thus, there are no social security
or pension beneficiaries in town, although most people in town are
building up a pension fund which will be utilized on retirement—
but retirement to some place other than Cold Bay.
Finally, just as there are no unemployed and no retired residents of Cold Bay, neither are there any people drawing Aid for
Dependent Children or welfare payments (Public Assistance Recipient
and Expenditures Study, 1981).   Cold Bay is a relatively young,
full employment town. There is no one here who is not supported by
someone with a job or who does not have a job of their own.   This
somewhat rosy picture of a town of full employment with no welfare,
AFDC or other non-productive activity is, unfortunately, purchased
at the expense of a sense of community and civic identity.
6.2.1.4 Conclusion. This discussion of the sectors of Cold
Bay employment gives an indication of the kind of marketplace
relations which exist in the city. The most important features are
the relative importance of external versus local businesses, and
the ratio of transportation, communication, and government employment to service and construction. There are only two locally owned
and operated businesses, and one of these has yet to open its
doors. On the other hand major corporations, such as Flying Tigers
and RCA, and both federal and state governments dominate the
employment picture.
The result in the marketplace is that Cold Bay has little
secondary and tertiary employment—there are no television stores,
or plumbing businesses, or electrical repair stores. The focus is
outward, rather than inward. A great many people in town work
every day to assure the passage of goods and people _through_ the
town rather than into it.   Distribution is a key element of Cold
Bay, but it is distribution in the context of a region, not in the
context of the town itself. Most goods, especially major ones, are
simply imported through the airport or on ships which call at Cold
Bay several times a year (such as the ferries _Western Pioneer_ and
Dolphin).   Produce cannot be grown locally and must be imported,
and the one Cold Bay concession to a retail business is the store
at the Flying Tigers. But even the locals purchase many of their
dry goods outside, either when they make trips to Anchorage, which
may be several times a year, or, especially in the case of government workers, through a catalogue providing commisary-like privi-

leges, or, in the case of RCA and the military, at the commisary on
the Air Force Base.

The result of this system of distribution and consumption is
that there is little interaction by local residents with other
residents in the marketplace. The greatest proportion of expenditure for goods and services is directed outward, and there is
little multiplier effect of local capital in the local marketplace.
There is no local production; even the few retail outlets (the bar
and the store) depend on outside supply for their inventory. In
Cold Bay the only place one can spend money is in the Flying Tigers
complex.

In many ways this centrifugal tendency in the Cold Bay economy
presents problems when we come to talk about an economic structure
of Cold Bay. The boundaries of such a system are difficult to draw
because the network of cash economic relations is unusually sparse
among the residents while it is unusually dense between Cold Bay,
as a depot, and the other towns and villages in the region. Without a doubt Cold Bay is closest, in terms of volume of economic
goods exchanged, to Anchorage to the east and Dutch Harbor/Unalaska
to the west. Very strong ties also exist with, especially, King
Cove, False Pass, and Nelson Lagoon. There are also substantial
ties with the entire Aleutian chain as far west as Attu. Interstate ties are particularly strong between Cold Bay and Seattle.

6.2.2 Social Organization

We have seen the effects of the emphasis on transportation,
communications, and the government in economic terms above. The
essential factor which emerged there, as illustrated by several
features of the economic structure of Cold Bay, was the centrifugal
nature of the town's economic structure. This general characteri-
zation can also be applied to the social and political structure of
Cold Bay.

There are six major tendencies which lend Cold Bay its unique-
ness of social structure. First, the importance of kinship is
minimal, and in no case that we know of does its importance extend
beyond the family unit itself. Extended kinship networks, usual
for this part of Alaska, simply do not exist.

Second, even though the importance of kinship has been
restricted to the family unit itself, it is even less important
than that would imply. This is because of the predominance of
single individuals in the community. Families are in a distinct
minority, so, from the standpoint of kinship, the most frequent
occurrence is the individual as a social isolate.

Third, the most important matrix for social relations in Cold
Bay is friendship. The lack of kin co-residence in town, beyond
the family level, means that extra-familial relations are almost
exclusively friendship relations.

Fourth, friendship relations themselves are strongly conditioned by workplace relations. This is particularly true of residence patterns since most employers provide housing in a centralized area for all or a major portion of their workers. Thus,
one's neighbors are also one's workmates, and the ease of estab-

lishing friendship ties with one's immediate neighbors is reflected
in the influence of occupation on associational networks.

Fifth, the importance of friendship as a basis of social
relations is further enhanced by the paucity of voluntary associations, itself at least partly a result of the transience of the
population. This lack of voluntary associations means that friendship must fill much of the gap in the possibilities for social
interaction.

Finally, and underlying much of the preceding, local residents
have unusually strong outside links and relatively tenuous links
within the community. Cold Bay residents are on intimate terms
with people from all over the region, state, and nation. From a
social, as well as economic standpoint, Cold Bay is a community in
a condition of stable flux. It is strongly centrifugal with a
fairly rapid replacement rate. Thus, the individual actors change
rapidly, but the overall structure remains fairly stable. A
closer look at specific aspects of the social structure of the
community will illustrate these contentions.

Primary social networks are those consistent relations among
individuals which carry a particularly heavy moral load. Primary
social relations may be divided into four separate spheres,
although to some extent there is inevitably overlapping among some
of these areas. These spheres are those of kinship, family, neighborhood, and friendship. In essence, of course, familial relations
are only a restricted and specialized instance of kinship relations, but the difference is important enough to justify their
treatment as separate categories. Thus kinship here refers primarily to extra-familial relationships. By the same token there is
inevitably a greater or lesser degree of overlap between neighborhood networks and friendship networks. Indeed, as we will see,
this is particularly true in Cold Bay for several reasons.

Cold Bay is interesting in terms of primary relations for a
number of reasons. First, the family is virtually the extent of
kinship relations. Extra-familial kinship relations simply do not
exist as there are no families within the community related to one
another either consanguineally or affinally. Therefore, familial
relations are particularly important and families are somewhat
isolated. Neighborhood relations are interesting in that they are
almost totally determined by workplace relations, since most of the
major employers provide housing, thereby determining the physical
location of their employees. The further result of this is the
strong conditioning of friendship relations by occupation, since it
is naturally more likely that strong associational ties will be
formed with someone physically proximate rather than more distant.

6.2.2.1 __Kin-Based Relations__. The importance of extra-
familial kinship relations in Cold Bay is negligible. The nature of
the community as an enclave which is controlled by external corporations and agencies, and the choice to live in the town is
governed more by occupation than by locale. Thus, even though the
individual might desire to remain in a town where he has extensive
kinship relations, his company may request that he go to Cold Bay
for reasons unrelated to his residential preferences. By the same
reasoning, it is very unlikely that related individuals will both
be working with corporations with interests in Cold Bay, and even

less likely that both would end up drawing an assignment which put
them in Cold Bay simultaneously.

Most villages in this region, such as King Cove, Nelson
Lagoon, and False Pass, are dominated by less than half a dozen
kindreds. Kinship is the basic matrix of all activity in such
villages—not alone of social relations, but also extending to
include economic, political, religious, and all other relations.
In Cold Bay this is not the case. Not only is kinship, in the
extended sense of the term used here, not operative "horizontally"
(that is, across the current structure of social relations), it is
not even a consideration "vertically" (that is in terms of intergenerational transmissions of, e.g., descent, inheritance, and/or
succession). To our knowledge, there has not been, in the history
of the city, a single family group which has given birth to,
raised, and brought to maturity children who have, subsequently,
themselves established permanent residence in Cold Bay.

The family is an important locus of social action in Cold Bay.
The absence of more extended kinship networks means that the family
is the major operative kinship system in the town. Families which
reside in Cold Bay are close knit units who depend heavily on other
family members for social interaction. However, the transient
nature of the Cold Bay community has operated to minimize the
number of families present and, therefore, to minimize the importance of familial relations in the total field of social relations.

A fair proportion of the residents of Cold Bay are short-term
transients. This group, even if married (and they are dominated by
single men), does not bring its family to Cold Bay to reside
because the nature of their work is such that they will be there
for only a year or less and the economic and social cost of such a
move is prohibitive. Even among the long-term transients, a group
which makes up the majority of Cold Bay's population, there are an
unusual number of single males. From the standpoint of kinship,
Cold Bay is dominated by social isolates, primarily single males,
who have no kinship links at all, either consanguineal or affinal,
in Cold Bay.

Nonetheless, this should not be construed to mean that the
family is inoperative as a social matrix in Cold Bay. The family
does assume some important functions among some segments of the
population. Two groups in particular are the locus of most of the
familial activity in Cold Bay. One is the long term transients who
work for the major outside companies or agencies with interests in
Cold Bay. These people are there for such a lengthy period of time
that, if they are married, they bring their families with them.
This is abetted by the fact that most of these firms provide com-
pany-owned housing, usually of a high quality, to their employees.
The family is also fairly important among the permanent residents,
which is the smallest of the social groups determined by length of
residence.

Both groups of families interact heavily with one another and
form a social group essentially removed from the other, larger
social groups in Cold Bay. Visiting is intense among these groups,
and the longer the period of residence of the entire family the
more extensive the associational links among the families. However, in discussing this point we are moving beyond the realm of

the family itself and into the importance, and structure, of associational networks. We will cover this topic in some detail below.

6.2.2.2 <u>Neighborhood Relations</u>. As in most towns and cities,
neighborhood is an important element of social relations in Cold
Bay. The simple fact of geographical proximity makes the establishment of social ties, other things being equal, easier among
neighbors than among those more widely removed from one another.
However, in Cold Bay there are two factors which complicate (some
might say simplify) the situation and result in an unusual structure in associational networks.

First, neighborhoods are anything but haphazard. Just as with
the decision to come to Cold Bay initially, the decision concerning
where one resides is under the control of external agencies rather
under the control of the individual. Almost all of the residents
of Cold Bay live where they do as a result of the provision of
housing by their employer, and not as a result of personal choice.
As was noted in the last chapter, housing provided by each government agency or business comprise distinct neighborhoods throughout
the community. The result of this structure is that in Cold Bay we
have a remarkable example of the determination of geosocial structure by occupation. One's place of residence is determined by the
company for which one is an employee, and since the vast majority
of Cold Bay residents are here as a result of working for, or being
married to someone who works for, major outside firms, this geosocial structuring is remarkably pervasive. Cold Bay is what might
be thought of as a "multi-company town", different from the traditional company town in that there are several companies each of
which regimentalizes its workers in terms of residential location,
and that most of the workers are transient, even if long term
transient, rather than permanent residents.

Neighborhood, then and the character of one's neighbors, is a
direct reflection of occupation, and like so much of the nature of
Cold Bay's organization, be it economic, social, political, or
otherwise, it illustrates the overriding importance of external
agencies in the life of the town. There are some permanent residents of Cold Bay who have managed to gain their own land and build
homes on it, thus breaking out of the occupation/neighborhood
equation. However, to this date there are really only three, four
if we stretch it, such cases. With these few exceptions all the
long-term transients and permanent residents live in places determined by occupation/residence. This predisposes these individuals
toward certain patterns of associational relationships likewise
based on residence.

6.2.2.3 <u>Friendship Relations</u>. Friendship forms the most
salient context of social relations in Cold Bay. Since there are
very few extra-familial kinship relations, associational ties are
the dominant focus of social interaction. However, these associational ties differ depending on three factors: length of time in
Cold Bay, neighborhood location, and marital status (or, more
accurately, presence or absence of co-residence with a spouse
and/or children) interact in each case to produce a predisposition
toward one kind of associational network or another.

The first factor is length of residence. We distinguish among
short-term transients (those who are in Cold Bay for a year or

less), long-term transients (those who are in Cold Bay for considerably more than a year, but not permanently), and permanent
residents (those who have made Cold Bay their home). Again, the
categories are not as rigid as they might first seem. A person who
has been in Cold Bay less than a year might conceivably have bought
property (from someone who, for example, had themselves bought
property in the 1979 land sale), begun the construction of a house,
and, in short, made the decision to become a permanent resident.
By the same token, an individual might have lived in Cold Bay for
five years or more, yet still be alert for an opportunity to go
elsewhere, having no intention of remaining in town any longer than
necessary. In such a case the individual who had been here less
than a year could be considered a permanent resident, while the
individual who had been here five or six years, or even longer,
might be seen as a transient. Nonetheless, these categories, given
the caveats expressed here, can be useful for a mapping of associational networks.

In essence the associational networks parallel the categories
determined by length of residence, with some exceptions. The
short-term transient group interacts primarily with members of its
own group. This group is almost exclusively single males who are in
town for a specified project and who will be here a year at the
most. They therefore do not come to be heavily involved in the
social networks of the long-term transients and/or permanent residents. Most of them are housed either in the Flying Tigers hotel,
the Reeve bunkhouse, or a similar structure near the center of
town, so they are arranged roughly in an "inner-town neighborhood"
which makes it most convenient to interact with one another,
especially as they know few people outside that area of town and
have little time to establish such relations. Even those of this
group who are married are invariably not accompanied by their
spouse or their children, placing them structurally in a position
equivalent to that of a single person. Moreover, this group almost
universally lacks local transportation, which generally restricts
them to the "inner town" area.

For this group the major center of social activity is the
Flying Tigers complex in the heart of town. It is there that they
take all of their meals, since they only rarely have appliances for
cooking in their rooms and since this is the only restaurant in
town. However, the dominant focus of their social activity is the
Weathered Inn, the bar in the Flying Tigers complex. This is the
only true social spot in Cold Bay, and each night it is filled with
a mixture of people, a large number of whom are short-term transients. As these people rarely have vehicles or a means of transportation, they are restricted to the Flying Tigers complex for
entertainment and are unable to get out to the Air Force Base
except occasionally to take advantage of the recreational possibilities there.

Among this group, then, residential location, length of residence and marital status all reinforce one another to encourage
formation of strong associational ties within the group and relatively tenuous ties outside the group. For the other two groups
determined by length of residence in Cold Bay these three factors
produce somewhat more complex patterns of associational networks.

Among the long-term transients there are at least two major associational patterns. Long-term transients may be in Cold Bay anywhere from a year to five years or more--indeed the upper limit of long-term transience is difficult to define explicitly as even people who have been in town for more than five years are often avowedly transient and have no intention of living permanently in Cold Bay. However, in basic form we can say that the nature of the associational network for the long-term transient depends on the interplay of our three basic factors: residential location, marital status and time. The interesting aspect is that as the third factor increases, that is as the individual comes to have been in Cold Bay for a longer period of time, the determinative balance of the other two factors, area of residence and marital status, shifts accordingly.

When the long-term transient comes to Cold Bay he finds himself placed involuntarily in a neighborhood which is composed of others who also work where he works, along with the families, if any, of these people. The long-term transient is immediately, even though he has not been in town for more than a week, distinguishable from the short-term transient by several factors. The availability of a decent home in a nice neighborhod is one of these factors. The establishment of a "permanent" household is another, including, if he is married, the presence of his wife and/or family. The individual is naturally assimilated, barring unforeseen problems, into the social networks which revolve around his workplace. This is because he becomes acquainted with his fellow workers much faster than he is able to get to know anyone else in town, and because this intimacy is reinforced strongly on a daily basis by the fact that he, and his family if he has one, are located on the same street residentially as those people he has come to know at work.

Thus, the first step in the assimilation of the long-term transient is the establishment of an associational network based primarily on occupation. However, once the long-term transient has been in town for at least several months, and perhaps as long as a year, he begins to shift those associational links in a way which can be attributed more to marital status than geosocial structure. Thus, once the individual is comfortable in Cold Bay he will, if he is single, begin to establish relations with other single individuals who are also in Cold Bay for extended periods, either long-term transients or permanent residents. This group then grows to become his primary social network, replacing or augmenting that based on neighborhood/occupation. To a certain extent this network, or networks, also revolves around the Flying Tigers complex, and it is usual to see the group of long term singles in the bar quite often, at least several times a week and sometimes every evening (particularly at happy hour). However, although they are similar to the short-term transients in this respect, they are different in that the bar does not exhaust their social relations. This group also involves themselves in extensive social interaction outside the Flying Tigers complex. This interaction takes several forms.

First, the fact that this group usually works for one of the major companies in town for an extended period means that they have much nicer residential accommodations than is the case for the short-term transients. They therefore have frequent get togethers and parties at one another's homes to which most of the long-term singles in town come. Almost every evening the chances are fair that someone will be doing something which will serve as an excuse for a get-together. This invariably includes dinner, drinking, listening to records, and so on. This is particularly true in the summer, when there are always large stocks of fish like salmon or crab to serve as a basis for a meal and a party. However, although the pace of such parties slows in the off-season, it is rare for a week to go by without someone having a party or get-together of some kind. Of course, there are also many sub-groups among this general group, and frequently only a portion of the general group will come together for a smaller gathering. Also included in the activities of this group is a percentage of the married group, but almost always these are the younger marrieds who generally have no children--it is unusual for anyone over thirty or thirty-five to be included in this group unless they are single.

The second major social activity of this group which occurs outside the Tigers complex involves hunting or fishing. Most of the people who remain in Cold Bay for any length of time come to involve themselves in either one or both of these activities. Each weekend a substantial group of these people are involved in the outdoor activity appropriate to the season. Effectively this means fishing during the spring and summer, hunting (especially caribou, but occasionally red fox or bear) in the summer and fall, and hunting geese in the fall. These activities usually include the same group which parties together, and indeed these activities often provide the food which is the basis for the meal at the party. These individuals, as residents of Alaska, also have the right to subsistence licenses to fish for salmon and hunt caribou, and these are generally group activities. This is particularly true of fishing because a subsistence permit allows one to take up to fifty salmon at a time with a set net, and this activity requires several people in order to be done properly.

A final activity which members of this group often pursue together, though in smaller groups as a rule than those activities mentioned above, involves taking time from Cold Bay and going to "town." Town is Anchorage, and it is unusual for one of these individuals to make a trip to town alone. Such a trip usually lasts for at least a weekend, and often for as long as a week or more, and is seen as a chance to kick up one's heels, interact with women (since most of this group consists of single males), and generally partake of the excitement of the city. Once an individual announces that he is planning a trip to town it is almost inevitable that one or more people from his associational network will decide to go along, and the event is turned into a festive occasion.

The second major subgroup of the long-term transients are those who are married and older or married with children. When they arrive in Cold Bay initially their occupation is central in determining their associational networks. They live and work with the same group of people. This occupational group forms the initial basis of their social networks. However, with an increase

in time the rationale for their social networks undergoes a change
from occupation to marital status with important implictions for
the nature of that network.

Once a married couple with children has been in town for a
fairly long period of time they begin to interact with other
married couples with children, or with older married couples who
are childless. This proceeds regardless of the occupational
affiliations of those involved in this emerging network. Thus, the
associational network comes to cross-cut occupation as the individuals remain in town for increasing period of time. This occurs as
several simultaneous processes. The couple may need people with
whom they can share childcare responsibilities, and the nature of
reciprocation makes other married couples with children the logical
choice. Children, of course, also imply attendance at school, and
involvement in school-related activities also brings together
groups which cross-cut occupational affiliation.

There are several social venues which characterize this
married group with children among the long-term transients. They
do not take advantage of the bar at the Flying Tigers with the
regularity of the single and young married group, although they do
visit it occasionally. Most of their social activity, however, is
spent in visiting other members of their social network and in
parties and get togethers with other members of their group.
Usually these events take place at the home of another older
married couple, and they involve dinner, music, and conversation.
This group also involves itself in outdoor activitites such as
hunting and fishing, particularly among the men of the group.

The final group based on length of time resident in Cold Bay
is the permanent residents. Though there is no necessary correla-
tion between length of time in Cold Bay and permanency, in general
these are people who have been in town at least five years and
often much longer. Of course there are a number of people who have
been in Cold Bay for longer than five years who still do not see
themselves as permanent residents and who continue to actively
search for acceptable alternatives to living in Cold Bay. The
permanent resident group is the smallest of any of the groups we
have discussed here.

The permanent resident group contains within it a certain
proportion of people who violate the rule equating occupation and
residential location. These are the permanent residents who have
managed to gain some land of their own and may even have been able
to build a home on that land. There are not many of these people,
however. In the last fifteen years there have only been two opportunities for local residents to purchase or homestead land. The
first was prior to 1968 when it was possible for residents to
homestead some land to the north of Trout Creek which was, at that
time, held by the Bureau of Land Management. Two local residents
took advantage of that possibility and homesteaded sites. Neither
of these sites has been developed yet. The second opportunity came
in the 1979 sales of state-owned land by the Department of Natural
Resources. Of the half-dozen local residents who were able to get
land three have actually moved onto their land and a fourth has
allowed a friend to move a cabin onto his land. Thus about four of
the permanent residents have moved onto land not controlled by the

state, and another four or so have land onto which they can move when they are able to afford to develop it.

The fact that at least a portion of the permanent resident group does not live in occupationally determined housing means that occupation exerts less influence on the structure of their social networks than is the case among the other groups in town. This group is therefore more free to determine their social network by choice rather than by the influence of the workplace. In fact, by the time an individual has been in town for five years or more this process, as we saw above with reference to the long-term transients, is likely to have occurred at any event. However, in the case of the permanent residents this aids in establishment of another of the characteristics of their social networks - isolation. It is among the permanent residents that we find the greatest tendency toward restriction of the social network to the family with very little interaction with those outside the household. They are in some cases living in areas more removed from the built up portion of town, particularly those who have built on land they own themselves, and this allows them to reduce interaction at their option, something which is much more difficult for those living in company provided housing which resembles an extremely small tract home development.

This tendency toward isolation is abetted among the permanent resident group by their minority status within the community. In a sense they see themselves as a small in-group while everyone else about them, even the long-term transients, is passing through. They see themselves as committed and concerned with the future of Cold Bay, while those who will inevitably leave the town eventually may become involved for a brief time but will finally abandon the enterprise. This is not to say that this group is totally isolated, but the tendency is stronger here than in any other group. In fact the married couples among the permanent residents do tend to be involved most strongly with one another, but are also involved with the married couples among the long-term transients. However, the people with whom the permanent residents establish the most intense social relations are not long-term transients but other permanent residents.

6.2.2.4 **External Relations**. One aspect of the social networks of the permanent residents has to do with relations with people outside of Cold Bay. People who have been here ten years or more, almost all of whom are permanent residents, have established contacts with other permanent residents in towns and villages all over the region, and there is an inter-community network of considerable vitality. This is particularly true of connections with King Cove, Unalaska/Dutch Harbor, Nelson Lagoon, and other villages in the immediate vicinity.

Short-term transients, on the other hand, have their major social networks in areas removed from Cold Bay, whether it be other parts of Alaska or the lower forty-eight. These people are only in town for a brief time and both friendship and kinship networks are much stronger outside the town than within it. The long-term transients also have very strong outside networks, also in areas often far removed from Cold Bay. Though they are in town for a considerable time, and they do develop associational networks

within the community, the fact that they know they will eventually
leave and that they do not have any kinship relations in town means
that they are careful to maintain outside connections in anticipation of the time when those networks will be reactivated on their
passing from Cold Bay.

The community is very tenuously held together with internal
social networks and is remarkably outer directed. This is largely
a result of the nature of the community as a transportation and
communications center and the resultant transience of its population. It makes it very difficult to exactly define the limits of
the Cold Bay social system, since it is so extensively interlinked
with outside structures. In this sense Cold Bay approaches a
limiting case for small towns. In spite of the fact that we are
accustomed to small towns which are tightly knit moral communities
with a highly insular quality, Cold Bay illustrates that this is
not a necessary correlate of small size. Through the unusual
series of events which spawned the town and the continuing role it
has been called on to play a social structure has emerged which
draws individuals outside the community itself and makes the establishment of a strong community network, a strong sense of community, very difficult and highly unlikely. To a certain extent
these characteristics are probably shared by other communities
which find themselves occupying a central role as communication
and/or transportation centers. The very nature of those enterprises forces interaction with and awareness of the outside world
to a greater extent than do many other kinds of activity.

6.2.3 Political Organization

6.2.3.1 Local Affairs. Until recently there was no internal
political structure in the sense of a formalized political entity
which could be said to be concerned solely with Cold Bay at the
expense of outside interests. This has changed with the incorporation of the community as a second class city in January of 1982.
Prior to this, however, political power was synonymous with state
power. The major force in town has been, for past twenty years or
more, the State of Alaska, particularly as represented by the
Department of Transportation.

Prior to incorporation the Department of Transportation was
the most powerful institution in town and took, almost by default,
major responsibility for political decisions. The department was
responsible for airport security, and since the town itself is
almost completely located on airport property this naturally en-
tailed responsibility for the town as well. What minor problems of
law enforcement arose were generally handled by the security man
from the DOT.

With the incorporation of the town this situation changed in
law but less so in fact. The town is now constituted as a mayor-
council form of government with seven council members from which a
mayor is selected by the council. Ostensibly political power is
vested in these individuals. The members of the council tend to be
long-term transients with some permanent residents. Effectively
this means that those who are in particular positions of power in

the major companies or agencies in the community have transfered
this power to the political arena. The mayor of the community is
also the head of the FAA contingent and as such combines two of the
most powerful positions in the community. It is interesting that
long-term transients form a majority of the council, both because
they represent a majority of the voters and because of the reti-
cence on the part of some permanent residents to become actively
involved in community affairs. However, there are several permanent residents who have become involved and who are represented on
the council, and they form a sizeable minority of members.

Paradoxically, the incorporation of the community, which would
appear to be an act of political consolidation, has served as a
mechanism through which political power in the town has become
decentralized. No longer is there a single authority in the community, since it is now headed by a group of seven people from
somewhat diverse backgrounds. Nonetheless, too much can easily be
made of this redistribution of political power. Despite the council, the city has very little real power yet. It controls no land,
has a very limited income (the entire year's budget for 1982 is
$26,000, and all revenues thus far are a result of state revenue
sharing), and is dominated by long-term transients who will ultimately pass from the scene. Much of the political power in the
community remains in the Department of Transportation.

6.2.3.2 Social Control. Means of social control in Cold Bay
are essentially informal. The major means of controlling social
behavior which is considered to be offensive is through gossip,
ridicule, censure, and other informal means. There is very little
crime, and and what crime does exist is relatively small scale.

The community has as yet not hired a patrolman, nor is there a
trooper stationed in the community. When the community incorporated it gained the right to have a patrolman stationed in the
town, but it has not taken advantage of this right yet. Many in
the community express concern over hiring a patrolman as they feel
that such a step would be a tacit admission that the community has
a crime problem which, so far, it does not. People prefer to
resort to less formal means of conflict resolution and will probably continue to resist institution of a patrolman's position as long
as crime continues to be essentially petty and infrequent as it is
now. This means that the DOT security is still the only form of
permanent law enforcement in the community, and reinforces the
perception of the DOT as the true locus of effective political
power.

6.2.4 Religious Organization

There is a small chapel in Cold Bay located in a quonset hut
across the street from the Flying Tigers complex. The church is
ostensibly interdenominational, but in fact it has a definite
Baptist cast to its liturgy and services. The church is not heavily subscribed, but it does attract a fairly regular following for
Sunday services. Usually about twenty people are in attendance.
The church has made several attempts to become more involved in the
community including the establishment of a Sunday school program

and a teen program, but these have been intermitent and have aroused relatively little interest in the community. Essentially most people in Cold Bay have little interest in church or church activities.

Most of those who do attend church services are long-term transients or permanent residents. As such, even though there are relatively few people involved, the church does perform a function as a means of social integration, one of the few such structures in the community.

6.2.5 Education

Education is an area in which Cold Bay has been upgraded in the last few years, with generally positive results for the residents of the town. Cold Bay has an elementary and a secondary school, both located in the same building. The school was expanded from K through 9th grade to K through 12th grade in 1978, and now offers a high school diploma (Alaska Department of Community and Regional Affairs, Community Profile, 1982). This has been greeted with pleasure by local residents who now feel no pressure to leave the community when their children come of age for high school. The school is part of the Aleutian Region School District which is a state-funded Rural Education Attendance Area headquartered in Anchorage.

The Cold Bay school was originally built in 1961, and has since been renovated and expanded twice, once in 1967 and again in 1980. The school now consists of four classrooms, one media center/library, and several smaller utility rooms. In addition the community has recently received state approval for an expansion which will consist of a multi-purpose media room to be funded with 1.3 million dollars. The community feels that the most favorable form of expansion would be the construction of an entire new school facility, but had to settle for more modest plans for expansion.

The area served by the school is strictly local. The Cold Bay School takes its students exclusively from Cold Bay itself, although it also serves the Cold Bay Air Force Base at times when there are married couples resident there, particularly those who work for RCA.

There are currently four teachers to serve the students of the Cold Bay School. The grades for which the teachers are responsible vary from year to year with the school population. In general two are responsible for the high school students and two for the elementary school students.

As Table 6.2 indicates, enrollment varies somewhat from year to year, which is to be expected in a community as transient as Cold Bay. Nonetheless, there has been a gradual but steady increase in the student population over the last decade. Current estimates of enrollment are between forty-eight and fifty-five students.

One of the teachers serves as overall administrator (principal) for the facility. All funding, school improvements and changes, hiring of teachers, and so on, are under the control of the REAA.

Table 6.2

Total Cold Bay School Population (K-12),
1969-1980

| School Year | Grade Level | | |
	K-8	9-12	Total
1969-70	28	0	28
1970-71	25	0	25
1971-72	21	0	21
1972-73	16	4	20
1973-74	28	0	28
1974-75	24	5	29
1975-76	23	2	25
1976-77	24	0	24
1977-78	21	4	25
1978-79	30	8	38
1979-80	24	11	35

Source: Alaska Consultants 1981:134.

There are several incentives for the children of Cold Bay to pursue post-secondary education as well as disincentives to leaving early. First, as noted above, they do not have the significant option of a high paying fishing job on leaving high school (or during high school) which some others in the region have. Second, the parents of these students are generally much better educated than the people in the surrounding villages. Most of them have had an extensive education and a good deal of technical, white collar experience. This is a group to whom education seems natural and desirable, and these attitudes are inculcated in their children. Third, most of the residents of Cold Bay will not remain in the community for more than a few years, and therefore they are likely, by the time the child is ready for college, to move to an area in which post-secondary education is much more generally available.

The school is not as central a facility in Cold Bay as might be expected, partly because there are relatively few families with school-age children, so interest is not high. The school does act as a venue for social activities at times and occasionally sponsors a basketball or baseball game with neighboring communities, but has not become a genuine focus of the community. The school has, however, changed in the perceptions of local residents in the last few years as a result of its expansion from kindergarten through ninth grade to kindergarten through twelfth grade. This has meant that families with children do not feel the need to leave town when their children come of age for high school, and families can, on the average, stay in town longer than was previously the case.

6.2.6 Health Care

Health care has never been perceived as adequate in Cold Bay. However, in the summer of 1982 a clinic was constructed which promises to greatly improve the level of health care in town.

The major facilities in Cold Bay are the clinic, which is only just being completed, and the facilities at the Air Force Base. Beyond these the residents must depend on transport out of town for serious or emergency medical attention. Currently the service capacity of medical facilities in town is extremely limited. There are at least four Emergency Medical Techicians who provide basic service to the residents. For more serious matters the only current local alternative is the medic at the Air Force Base. There is a small and modern clinic at the base which is able to provide a wide range of basic medical care. There is currently no local facility for serious medical problems or surgery, and residents must depend on air transport to other parts of the state, particularly to Anchorage, in such an eventuality. This situation is in the process of change with the opening of the clinic which should be in operation by winter of 1982-1983. The clinic will have facilities for three examination rooms, an emergency room, a laboratory, a pharmacy, and a kitchen. It will be able to accommodate approximately four to five people at one time.

The city is currently considering negotiation with a doctor, from either Kodiak or Unalaska, to provide intermitent care through regular visits to the clinic in town.

Up to now there has been little charge for what health care has been available, but with the opening of the clinic this situation is likely to change. The use of the EMTs by residents of Cold Bay is generally free of charge. Any medication or equipment required is generally paid for. With the opening of the clinic charges will be made for the use of clinic facilities, although as yet the schedule of payment has not been worked out.

Provision of health care to the residents of Cold Bay has thus far been of little direct cost to the government. EMT training is usually subsidized by the state, but this has not represented a major expense. The government did make a substantial investment in the construction of the clinic, almost all of which was paid for through state funds. The total investment in the clinic will eventually be approximately $300,000 ($296,785.00 according to the Contractor Pay Estimate provided by RoyCo and dated August 23, 1982), almost all of which will be state provided.

Health issues are of relatively little concern to people in town. The population of Cold Bay is unusually young and in good health. The nature of the town as a transient center, full employment of the population, and youth all contribute to good mental and physical health. Medical and psychological issues are generally relatively minor.

Though alcohol abuse is potentially a problem throughout rural Alaska, it has not become one in Cold Bay. One of the few contexts for social interaction available to local residents, particularly single males, is the local bar. However, all these people manage to hold a job and assume the responsibilities associated with providing for oneself. No one can let alcohol take

precedence over work, for if they did they would end up terminated
and, in that case, would have to leave town. In this sense the
community is self-purging. Those with a serious alcohol problem
simply cannot survive in town. Another factor which retards the
abuse of alcohol somewhat is the fact that the only bar in town
does not open until four o'clock in the afternoon. This is per-
fectly logical since everyone in town is working until that time
anyway, but it also helps to reduce the daytime abuse of alcohol.

There are few serious psychological or stress-related problems
in Cold Bay. There has been no reported suicide in the history of
Cold Bay as far as our research could ascertain. Depression does
not appear to be a major problem in the community, at least partly
because of the full employment conditions. Anyone suffering from
depression of such magnitude that it would lead to suicide would
probably run into job and personal difficulties which would preclude his staying in the community.

There appear to be very few accidents of a serious nature in
Cold Bay. The only exception to this are automobile accidents and
an occasional accident involving the crash of an airplane. However, rarely do automobile accidents result in injury since it is
uncommon to travel at more than thirty miles per hour in town.

As with physical health, the residents of Cold Bay are
generally in good mental health. Once again, the ultimate factor
in this mental health is the self-purging nature of the community.
Those who have such severe psychological problems as to be debili-
tating simply cannot remain in town if they cannot hold a job
responsibly.

The people who have come to Cold Bay are generally prepared
for the difficulties which they will face. Cold Bay is relatively
isolated, but this isolation is mitigated substantially by the
airport and the daily traffic which comes through the community.
Alienation does not have a chance to become a chronic problem since
most are only in town for a set period of months or years and know
they will eventually be leaving.

Just as with mental and physical illness, and for much the
same reasons, mortality rates are unusually low in Cold Bay. This
is especially a result of the fact that the town is a full employment town, controlled by external companies and agencies, and with
no private land available for building. This means that the individual remains in Cold Bay only as long as he or she or one's
spouse can hold a job with one of the major employers in town.
Therefore there are no retired people in town and there are very
few elderly citizens, which reduces the level of mortality greatly.

Accidental death is the only form of death which is important
statistically in Cold Bay, and even this is very low. The major
source of accidental death is plane crashes, since the town has a
major airport and serves as the air center of the entire region.
Most often these are crashes of private planes, although there have
been less than half a dozen of these in the last twenty years.
Auto accidents could also potentially be lethal, though we heard no
reports that such had occurred. Finally, occasionally someone may
be attacked by a bear, as one individual from outside the community
was several years ago, but this is very rare.

6.2.7 Social Services

6.2.7.1 Facilities and Personnel.

The level of available social services in Cold Bay is very low. Partly this can be explained by the fact that the community is a relatively young and healthy one and partly by the fact that these people are "preselected" by their companies before they arrive in town.

There are no facilities in Cold Bay devoted to social service per se. The only places in which even rudimentary social work occurs is through the church, which occasionally offers discussion groups covering various topics, and the Air Force Base. There is no one in Cold Bay who has been trained specifically to extend social services and provide counseling for individuals needing it. No professional help is available. The pastor of the church does provide voluntary aid upon request.

What social services are available are provided by volunteers with little but practical experience in dealing with such issues. There is no one in town with professional experience in such issues.

6.2.7.2. Social Issues.

Social problems are not marked in Cold Bay. Again, this is partly because of the built-in guarantee of full employment and the relative youth of the population. Though certain social problems are acknowledged, in no cases are they seen as so serious as to require professional care or counseling.

Alcoholism is not a social issue in Cold Bay. The people of the town realize there is little else to do of a social nature, and they accept drinking as appropriate as long as it does not interfere with the performance of one's duties, both to employer and to family. Alcohol is primarily consumed by young, single males. This is a result of the general absence of other social activities, particularly involving women.

The issue of social disintegration is an interesting one in Cold Bay. In fact the community is very loosely integrated to begin with as a result of the transience of the population. However, the people who come to Cold Bay expect this to be the situation when they arrive. The result is a social structure which appears to be disintegrative, but without the attendant psychological and social consequences we are accustomed to associate with such situations. The social structure of the town is extremely atomistic, particularly with reference to the unusually high number of single males in the community, but the members of the group see this as a necessary sacrifice for what most define as a future goal which justifies that sacrifice. What appears, then, to be social disintegration resolves itself into an extremely centrifugal community. Cold Bay is not so much disintegrative as it is integrated into a much larger social world than the town itself. The people, then, do not suffer lack of social integration as a result of the disintegrative aspects of Cold Bay, but gain much of their needed sense of belonging from networks outside the community. They do not lack social integration, they simply do not depend on Cold Bay for it.

Violence does not appear to be a problem of any magnitude in Cold Bay. There is very little violence in the bar or as a result of drinking. In the time the researchers spent in the town the incidence of violence was extremely low. There was also no example of wife beating to our knowledge. The small number of families reduces the possibility of such activity.

Stress is somewhat of a problem among certain elements of the Cold Bay population, particularly among the women. Almost all the women in town are married and came to town with their husbands when they were transferred by an outside agency. The husbands have extensive social networks immediately as a result of their job, but many of the women find it more difficult to establish a viable social network. There are few families in town, and the opportunities for social activity are severely limited. Many women try to find work with Reeve, which is the largest hirer of local help, and Tigers, both to supplement income (and usually savings) and to keep active. Although we mention this as a problem, we saw no instance in which stress had advanced to such a degree that it became a behavioral problem.

There is no regular provision for treatment of social problems in Cold Bay. The only available outlet is the pastor of the church, and this is on an irregular basis. Nor are there any provisions for regular or professional counseling for social problems. Therapeutic intervention is also lacking in town. It is unclear at this time whether the completion of the clinic will lead to the provision of some psychological or social counseling. As of now there are no plans for such programs, nor an apparent need.

6.2.8 Recreation

In this section we will discuss recreational vehicles, music and electronic means of recreation, subsistence-related activities, and visiting and vacation patterns.

6.2.8.1 **Activities** **Involving** **Vehicles.** Cold Bay residents utilize many kinds of recreational vehicles. Particularly noteworthy is the number of airplanes in the community, symptomatic of the status of the town as an air crossroads of the region. Cold Bay, with a large and thoroughly modern airport, is the location of a large number of aircraft. A number of people have pilots licenses and fly primarily for recreational purposes. There are also, of course, numerous people who are in Cold Bay often and who fly for a living but also fly recreationally when they get the opportunity.

Boats are much less utilized for recreational or subsistence purposes. The major problem is the lack of any facilities, such as a small boat harbor, for docking and for protection during rough weather. There is not even a breakwater for shelter during heavy weather. Cold Bay also lacks a fishing infrastructure so there are few boats available for recreational purposes in the first place.

Another popular kind of vehicle is the pickup truck. Cold Bay has a large variety of trucks, many of which are utilized recreationally. Pickup trucks are owned by a great number of people, perhaps by half the households in town. A large percentage of these are four wheel drive vehicles. Trucks are by far the most popular type of vehicle in town, both for working and for

recreation.
Trucks are also an important adjunct to other recreational
activities in which the driving of the vehicle is not the primary
aim. When traveling to streams for fishing or to Frosty Mountain
for hunting it is nearly mandatory to have a four wheel drive
vehicle. Such trips often involve driving over stretches of
tundra, fording small streams, and other activities which demand a
four wheel drive vehicle.
There are also a number of three wheel motorcycles in Cold
Bay, at least as many as a dozen. They are a very popular and
convenient mode of transportation around town since the built up
portion of the community is not large. There are considerably
fewer snowmobiles as the winter conditions in Cold Bay are not as
conducive to snowmobiles as they are in much of the surrounding
region.
6.2.8.2 Home Entertainment. Cold Bay residents take full
advantage of modern electronic means of recreation. Video recor-
ders are very popular. Since the number of television stations is
limited videotape movies are very popular forms of entertainment.
Almost every household in town has a betamax or other video
recorder. When visiting Anchorage, it is a popular pastime to take
along one's video recorder and tape movies shown on closed circuit
systems in motels. These are then taken back to Cold Bay where
they are a staple of local entertainment. Video games are also
increasingly popular. These are found in an increasing number of
homes and are particularly popular among families with children.
Television is limited to two stations, one cultural and educational and the other entertainment, beamed into town via satellite
by Alascom. Radio is limited as well, and is generally restricted
to the Armed Forces Radio Network which is transmitted by satellite
from Anchorage. The limited availability of television and radio
entertainment results in an emphasis on stereo and other recording
systems as means of entertainment. Very few houses do not have a
sophisticated phonograph system, and most have both a record player
and a tape recorder.
6.2.8.3 Outdoor Activities. Subsistence-related activities
are less important means of recreation in Cold Bay. Residents do
not involve themselves in such activities with nearly the frequency
of the surrounding communities. They do take some advantage of the
excellent opportunities for such activity in the area around the
town, however.
Fishing is the most pursued of these activities. From early
June, when chinook (king) salmon begin running (in only modest
numbers in this area), through the large red runs of July and
August and to the pink, chum, and, finally, silver runs toward the
end of summer Cold Bay residents take advantage of subsistence
permits to take these fish.
Hunting is also a pastime of some importance among Cold Bay
residents. By far the most important resource here is the Barren
Ground Caribou. Cold Bay residents, as residents of the State of
Alaska, have the right to subsistence permits which allow them to
take up to five caribou per year at virtually no cost. Several
people in town take advantage of this each year and caribou is a
major source of food from fall onward. "Boo Burgers", ground

caribou made like a hamburger, are a popular local fare.
These subsistence activities, as noted above, are not only a
means of getting food, but also serve as a focus of social interaction.   A fishing trip usually consists of at least three or four
men who spend the day together enjoying one another's company as
much as the fishing itself.   The same is true of hunting and other
subsistence activities.

6.2.8.4 **Visiting and Vacations.** Visiting and vacations are
also popular forms of recreation among local residents.   Visiting
is particularly popular within the community, while vacations take
residents to far flung areas of the globe.   Visiting is popular
among the residents and is a daily activity for many. The proximity of all residents within a small, circumscribed area of town
makes such visiting relatively effortless.   Intercommunity visiting
and vacations are also popular among Cold Bay residents, but does
not occur extensively with the surrounding communities.   Since it
is a non-Native enclave in the midst of Native settlements, and
somewhat more involved in more extensive and distant social networks, Cold Bay residents visit more distantly removed areas most
frequently when they take trips.

Interestingly, though Cold Bay residents visit other settlements in the region relatively little (except for the visits which
are a result of official capacity), there is almost nobody in the
region who has not been in Cold Bay.   This is a result of the
airport.   Therefore, many people, particularly businessmen and
official representatives, know a great many people from other
communities at least casually.

Cold Bay residents visit interregionally and interstate as
often as regionally.   The major destination for both visiting and
vacationing in the state is Anchorage.   Many people consider themselves permanent residents of Anchorage, not Cold Bay.   Anchorage
is also the nearest "real city", and as such is the favorite destination for those who simply want to take a week or weekend and "do
the town".   The most popular states for vacationing and visiting
both are Washington and the west coast in general.   Hawaii is also
very popular as it is close to the Aleutians and airfare is modest.

6.2.8.5 **Community Activities.**   Finally, the Cold Bay School
is the venue for social occasions.   It is used for movies and
potlucks as well as PTA meetings and other school functions.   The
school also has a program of intramural athletics, and on occasion
fields a team for competition with other schools in the region.
Basketball is particularly popular in this region of Alaska, with
softball a close second.   In the near future the school will be
expanding its role as a community center with the addition of a
multi-purpose room.   The room will allow for expanded space in
which to show movies, hold meetings, and so on.

7
Forecast Scenarios
for Cold Bay

7.1 INTRODUCTION

In this chapter, two forecast scenarios will be examined. The first or primary scenario examines the course of change given current trends and conditions without the possibility of OCS development in or within the vicinity of Cold Bay. The second scenario examines the likely consequences of OCS development within the vicinity of Cold Bay on the community itself. This scenario is based on the possibility of construction of a major oil and gas facility on the south side of the Alaska Peninsula with no direct road link to Cold Bay.

Before proceeding with these scenarios, it should be pointed out that projections are made based on existing information, proposed changes in the environment (such as changes in government or corporate policies), and existing levels of technology. It should be recognized that the parameters used to make these forecasts could themselves change in ways which are not projected by the systems model itself. Hence decisions affecting numbers of employees or proposed sources of revenues could be affected by factors independent of the sociocultural and socioeconomic systems of the community and thus alter the entire forecast.

It will become evident that this chapter is structured in a manner similar to that of Chapter Four. However, given the different requirements of the Minerals Management Service for projections of change in Unalaska and Cold Bay, as well as the differences in sociocultural structure and organization, the amount of attention devoted to each particular section in this chapter will not be identical to that of similar sections in Chapter Four.

7.2 FIRST SCENARIO

7.2.1 Assumptions

The first scenario for the future course of change in Cold Bay assumes no OCS-related development. This scenario will provide us with a baseline against which the effects of future OCS development, should it occur, can be assessed.

The major assumption under this scenario is that the Federal Aviation Administration and RCA will carry out their efforts to reduce the number of personnel and level of activity in Cold Bay by "remoting" the airport such that air traffic can be directed from a central location in the region other than Cold Bay. Other employers also have made plans or are exploring the possibility of reducing their labor force and the forecasts made under this scenario assume that these plans will be carried out.

7.2.2 Summary of Effects

Even without OCS development certain long-term trends will be apparent in the community. In general the changes which will occur in Cold Bay will be most dramatic in the areas of the economy, politics, and social relations. Most of these will result from demographic changes projected for this period. Cold Bay's population will undergo a substantial contraction, primarily as a result of the remoting of FAA and RCA functions which will reduce the Cold Bay workforce by one-third. Economically this will mean a decline in the relative importance of both external government and communications as sectors of the Cold Bay economy. Once again, as in World War Two, the Korean War, and Vietnam, Cold Bay will become almost purely a transportation enclave, although the agencies will be civilian rather than military. Politically the major questions over the next decade have to do with the acceptance of responsibility for the operation of several municipal facilities, particularly the water and sewer systems, road maintenance, and the airport and the dock, all in the face of a diminished revenue base. These needs will inevitably lead to another political problem, the decision whether or not to institute a system of taxation in the community. However, as always, the major political problem will revolve around the attempt to acquire some municipal land for private sale. Socially the contraction of the economy and resultant decline in population will have the paradoxical effect of increasing the sense of community as the permanent residents come to represent a greater proportion of all residents. We will now examine each of these areas in detail.

7.2.3 Regional Relationships

7.2.3.1 Economic Relations. The primary basis for economic relations between Cold Bay and other communities in the region is the airport and the community's role as a regional transportation center. This role is not expected to change during the forecast period under this scenario. If groundfish industry development does occur in the region, as projected under the first scenario in Chapter 4, or if OCS development occurs elsewhere in the Aleutians region, air traffic through Cold Bay could increase, resulting in more revenue for the community. However, as noted below, this may be offset by a decline in air traffic terminating in Cold Bay itself.

If the community is able to initiate developments in the commercial fisheries, particularly the processing sector, economic ties between Cold Bay and other communities in the region where many of the local fishermen reside could increase. However, for reasons discussed in Chapter Six, the prospect of development of a commercial processing sector in the community appears unlikely under this scenario.

7.2.3.2 **Political** **Relations.** No significant changes in political relations involving Cold Bay and other communities in the region are expected under this scenario. Cold Bay will remain politically isolated from other communities in the region. Where other communities in the Alaska Peninsula are part of the Aleut Corporation or Bristol Bay Native Corporation, Cold Bay is a non-Native community and thus not involved with either Native corporation. Some involvement has occured between the community, the Thirteenth Regional Corporation, and the King Cove Native Corporation, but existing relations involving these communities are not expected to change within the next ten years.

7.2.3.3 **Social** **Relations.** Currently the majority of Cold Bay residents have their strongest social relationships with people living either in different regions of Alaska, most often a major urban area, or in other parts of the United States. This is because most residents are recruited from outside the community and outside the region as a whole. Since most residents work for major state or national government agencies or for national or international corporations very few of the local workers are actually from southwestern Alaska. Thus, the only people who have extensive intraregional networks are the permanent residents, who currently make up a very small minority of the total Cold Bay population.

If the population of Cold Bay declines, and the proportional contribution to the population of the permanent residents does increase there will also be an increase in the proportional importance of regional ties, since this group is most heavily implicated in purely regional networks. At the same time the relative importance of interregional and, particularly, interstate networks will also decline.

7.2.4 Population

Projected alterations in the structure of the Cold Bay economy, to be discussed below, will have direct effects on the demographic structure of the community. These effects include a contraction in total population, an improvement in the male/female ratio resulting primarily from a proportional increase in the number of families, and an older average age of the population.

Total population will decline considerably as a result of the cutbacks in the number of employment positions in the community. There will be a direct decline of fifty-six workers between 1982 and 1990. Of these sixteen will be single military employees (or married employees who do not have their families with them in Cold Bay). This leaves forty other workers who may or may not have their families present. Assumptions provided by the MMS Office are that half of the non-military employees in Cold Bay will have families, and that those families average 2.5 people. If this is the case, then these forty people would represent a total population loss of approximately seventy people. We can therefore expect a total population decline of approximately eighty-six people between 1982 and 1990. This would reduce the estimated 1982 population of 226 to about 140 to 145. We expect the total population, therefore, to decline to somewhere in the range of 135 to 150 people by 1990. After 1990 we expect population to begin a gradual rise once again as regional groundfish and/or oil-related development begin to affect the community, so by 2000 we expect the population to reach between 160 and 180 people.

One result of the decline in population will be a slight improvement in the ratio of males to females. Currently this ratio stands at approximately 2.05:1 (approximately 2.85:1 among adults). With the loss of the Air Force contingent a major group of single males will be removed from the community. Though less extremely, RCA is also an employer which has a somewhat high ratio of single men. Partly this is a result of the removed location of RCA operations at the Air Force Base, and partly it is a result of the fact that most RCA employees are housed in relatively small apartments unsuitable for families. This means that the ratio of men to women could drop to between 1.5 and 1.75:1 (and perhaps as low as 2:1 among adults). However, this will have minor social implications, as there has traditionally been relatively little contact between workers at the Air Force Base and the community itself, since the two are separated by eleven miles.

At the same time the ratio of males to females is moving closer to parity, the proportion of the total population consisting of families will also increase, again because of the removal of a major group of single individuals with the withdrawal of the Air Force personnel. However, again, too much should not be made of these changes in sex and family/single ratios. In fact the level of interaction between the Air Force Base and the city itself has been only moderate, and the lasting social implications in the city of these statistical changes will not be great.

Finally, the reductions discussed here will cause some changes in the age structure of the Cold Bay population. Currently the population is a very young one. This is for several reasons, including the fact that there are no retired people in the community, the location is fairly isolated and requires at least a certain element of physical hardiness, and there are a large number of single males, generally in their twenties to early thirties. However, with the withdrawal of the military and RCA, both of which have employees who are, on the average, younger than those employed by other companies or agencies in the community, the average age of the Cold Bay population will rise somewhat. Though specific figures concerning the age structure of the community are unavailable, it is clear that there will be a major reduction in the single male group between the ages of twenty and thirty-five.

to be achieved by 1989, at which time the only manpower requirements will be for two or three technicians to maintain the equipment. Thus, within seven years plans call for a reduction of the
FAA personnel from sixteen to two.

Remoting will also be the cause of major reductions in the
number of personnel employed at the Air Force Base. A process
similar to that occurring in the FAA is also occurring with the
federal military and RCA (the latter is discussed below under
communicatons). Plans are to remote all operations at the base
(location of a DEW station and other military radar and navigational facilities) to King Salmon. Military personnel have already
been reduced at the base over the last few years as a result of the
subcontracting of operations of most base facilities to RCA.
Within two years it is projected that there will be no military
personnel at the base.

Discussions with personnel in other federal agencies revealed
no similar plans for retrenchment on the part of the Fish and
Wildlife Service, the National Weather Service, or the Post
Office. However, the cuts noted above would result in a reduction
of the federal sector of the Cold Bay economy from forty-three of
154 jobs in 1981, or 27.9 percent of total employment, to approximately thirteen of 124 jobs in 1990 (this does not take into
account other non-federal cutbacks which will be discussed below),
or 10.5 percent of total employment, a reduction of almost two-
thirds. This means the labor force will shrink, from federal
cutbacks alone, by over twenty percent in the next eight years, and
that the federal contribution will be cut by almost two-thirds.
This is a direct and serious threat to the current economic structure of the community, as these employees account not only for a
major portion of local employment, but as well are important sup-
porters of the small service sector which will also be threatened
by their withdrawal.

With these projections we can estimate the total decline in
the federal sector. Though we cannot be certain that the time-
tables set by the various agencies will be adhered to exactly,
Table 7.1 represents what would occur if these schedules are followed and if no other events intervene.

Other government employment will also drop, though less dramatically, over the next decade. State government currently accounts
for a total of nineteen out of 154 jobs, and there are plans for
cutbacks in this number. The agency which will account for most of
this decline is the Alaska Department of Fish and Game. According
to latest reports (personal communication, June, 1983) the ADF&G
has plans to lay off the local biologist, and the future of the
Russell Creek Salmon Hatchery, which employs two to three people,
is in serious jeopardy. If these plans eventuate, it will mean a
loss of between three and four positions, reducing the ADF&G contingent in town to two or three people total. This would represent
a reduction of twenty to twenty-five percent in the number of state
employees in town.

These trends in government employment will alter the Cold Bay
economy fundamentally. Federal and state employment will, for the
first time, be roughly equal in the community. Overall, government
employment will probably drop from the current sixty-three (in

otherwise be the case. Second, the availability of a certain amount of private land will mean that the permanent population of the community could potentially increase significantly. However, we expect that this will have little effect during the projection period due to the contraction of employment possibilities in the community. Nonetheless, this will probably have more serious consequences for the community's social organization.

In the last chapter we noted the domination of the 1979 land sale by oil and fisheries speculators. Several suggestions have been tendered concerning strategies to avoid the domination of any future sale by speculators. It appears that the most efficient way of doing this would involve two aspects. First, the land could be zoned either residential or utility. The former would guarantee that the land would be of little use to speculators hoping for future oil- or fisheries-related development. Land might be zoned utility in order to allow those who purchase it to run small businesses out of their homes, while it would still preclude major commercial operations of the sort in which speculators would be interested. Second, the land could be sold in relatively small lots which would also make it less palatable to large speculators.

Even though there is little land currently available, housing will pose no problems for the community during the forecast period. All housing, with the exception of less than a half-dozen homes, is now provided by outside employers. Thus, there is never a housing shortage, but neither is there a glut. With the reductions by several of the major companies and agencies operating in Cold Bay, and subsequent population reductions, there will be an oversupply of housing in the community. It is unclear at this time the potential uses to which that housing might be put, but it is possible it might be rented or leased by individuals who hope to stay in Cold Bay. In this way the reduction in the labor force may paradoxically contribute to an increase in the number of permanent residents. However, even if individuals are successful in renting or leasing these homes, permanent residency will ultimately depend on the availability of some land for purchase.

7.2.7 Value System

While significant changes are expected in the economic and demographic structure under this scenario, relatively few changes are expected in terms of the value systems adhered to by local residents. As will be discussed in greater detail below, the retrenchment of the labor force and the resultant decline in population will result in the increased prominence of a permanent segment of the local population. These residents might possibly adopt a value orientation comparable to the "frontier" value system of non-Natives of Unalaska described in Chapter Three. However, because of the community's status as a transient employment center and a non-Native community, we do not expect that the values of permanent residents will be as influenced by the values of the Native residents of surrounding communities as has been the case in Unalaska. Rather, their orientation will continue to be largely determined by the Euro-American value system of the outside world.

With respect to the transient residents who continue to work in Cold Bay, their value system will essentially remain similar to that described in the last chapter. Assessment of social status, world view, ethnic identity, and forms of exchange will continue to be based on a combination of the "frontier" and "modern," urban-oriented, Euro-American value systems.

7.2.8 Economic Subsystem

7.2.8.1 Output. The immediate outlook for the Cold Bay economy appears bleak. A combination of retrenchment by major local employers, lack of a fisheries infrastructure to take up the slack, and a general lack of local entrepreneurial activity combine to present a serious threat to the future of the Cold Bay economy. The picture is made worse by the current lack of available private land, although it is likely that this situation will be ameliorated to some extent in the near future.

However, on the positive side is the presence of a major international-class airport which will at least guarantee the survival, even if at a reduced level of activity, of the local economy. There is also the possibility, though it is extremely remote at present, that the fisheries-related sector may be developed. This development would be particularly likely if a closer link were established between Cold Bay and King Cove. Finally, for reasons detailed below, the economic contraction will not result in a growth of the non-labor forces as it would in most other communities. In the following economic discussion we will consider likely patterns in income distribution/disparities, employment patterns, unemployment and non-labor force patterns, economic class distinctions, and housing and real estate.

7.2.8.1.1 Employment. Employment patterns will change radically in the future, even without OCS-related development in the area. The next decade will see a severe contraction of both communications and government as employers, with a resultant relative increase in the importance of the transportation sector. The workforce will shrink by approximately one-third, the contribution of transportation as a percentage of the workforce will rise from 22.1 percent in 1982 to about thirty-four percent in 1990, and the combined contribution of communications and government will shrink from sixty-one percent to about thirty-seven percent.

There are several indications of the extent to which the federal sector will decline in the next ten years. First, the Federal Aviation Administration has continuing plans for retrenchment of its Cold Bay personnel, a process which has already begun. The FAA cutbacks are scheduled to occur in three stages. The first, scheduled to be completed in 1983, will involve switching over all Cold Bay equipment to solid state, reducing the manpower requirements in Cold Bay from the present sixteen to approximately thirteen. The next phase, scheduled to occur between 1983 and 1986, would see all flights out of Cold Bay remoted into one of a series of "hub control centers" (probably King Salmon or Bethel), reducing manpower requirements to less than half the 1983 figure, or approximately six people. Finally, total remoting is scheduled

to be achieved by 1989, at which time the only manpower requirements will be for two or three technicians to maintain the equipment. Thus, within seven years plans call for a reduction of the
FAA personnel from sixteen to two.

Remoting will also be the cause of major reductions in the
number of personnel employed at the Air Force Base. A process
similar to that occurring in the FAA is also occurring with the
federal military and RCA (the latter is discussed below under
communicatons). Plans are to remote all operations at the base
(location of a DEW station and other military radar and navigational facilities) to King Salmon. Military personnel have already
been reduced at the base over the last few years as a result of the
subcontracting of operations of most base facilities to RCA.
Within two years it is projected that there will be no military
personnel at the base.

Discussions with personnel in other federal agencies revealed
no similar plans for retrenchment on the part of the Fish and
Wildlife Service, the National Weather Service, or the Post
Office. However, the cuts noted above would result in a reduction
of the federal sector of the Cold Bay economy from forty-three of
154 jobs in 1981, or 27.9 percent of total employment, to approximately thirteen of 124 jobs in 1990 (this does not take into
account other non-federal cutbacks which will be discussed below),
or 10.5 percent of total employment, a reduction of almost two-
thirds. This means the labor force will shrink, from federal
cutbacks alone, by over twenty percent in the next eight years, and
that the federal contribution will be cut by almost two-thirds.
This is a direct and serious threat to the current economic structure of the community, as these employees account not only for a
major portion of local employment, but as well are important sup-
porters of the small service sector which will also be threatened
by their withdrawal.

With these projections we can estimate the total decline in
the federal sector. Though we cannot be certain that the time-
tables set by the various agencies will be adhered to exactly,
Table 7.1 represents what would occur if these schedules are followed and if no other events intervene.

Other government employment will also drop, though less dramatically, over the next decade. State government currently accounts
for a total of nineteen out of 154 jobs, and there are plans for
cutbacks in this number. The agency which will account for most of
this decline is the Alaska Department of Fish and Game. According
to latest reports (personal communication, June, 1983) the ADF&G
has plans to lay off the local biologist, and the future of the
Russell Creek Salmon Hatchery, which employs two to three people,
is in serious jeopardy. If these plans eventuate, it will mean a
loss of between three and four positions, reducing the ADF&G contingent in town to two or three people total. This would represent
a reduction of twenty to twenty-five percent in the number of state
employees in town.

These trends in government employment will alter the Cold Bay
economy fundamentally. Federal and state employment will, for the
first time, be roughly equal in the community. Overall, government
employment will probably drop from the current sixty-three (in

Table 7.1

Changes in Federal Employment in Cold Bay, 1982 to 1990

Year Employer	1981	1983	1986	1990
Federal				
Federal Aviation Ad.	16	13	6	2
National Weather Ser.	5	5	5	5
Fish and Wildlife	4	4	4	4
U.S. Post Office	2	2	2	2
U.S. Air Force	16	10	0	0
State				
D.O.T.	6	6	6	6
Fish and Game	7	6	3	3
Magistrate	1	1	1	1
R.E.A.A.	5	5	4	4
Municipal	1	1	1	1
Total	63	53	32	28
Percent Change from 1982		15.9	49.2	55.6

Source: Field Interviews, 1982.

1982), or over forty percent of all employment, to approximately twenty-eight, or about twenty-five percent of all employment.

Government is only one of three sectors which have traditionally dominated the Cold Bay economy. Transportation and communications are the largest private sectors, and there are plans for some cutbacks in these areas as well. The most important company in this regard is RCA. RCA is heavily implicated in the retrenchment occurring at the Air Force Base through remoting operations at King Salmon. Indeed, most of the work of this transition is being done by RCA employees, which is why the Air Force contingent is being reduced faster and earlier than the RCA work force.

RCA plans to cut its work force from approximately twenty-eight (in 1982) to less than fifteen within two years. This will be a major cut in both the communications sector of the Cold Bay economy, since RCA is the dominant employer accounting currently for some twenty-eight out of thirty-one employees in this sector, and in the Cold Bay economy overall, since RCA is the largest single employer in town.

Other employers in the communications sector will maintain steady employment levels over the next decade. However, the other two companies, Alascom and Interior Telephone Company, currently account for only three jobs (indeed, with the resignation of the single Interior Telephone employee during the summer of 1982 these two companies accounted for only two employees). Overall, then, communications will drop from a total of approximately thirty-one positions to approximately fifteen or sixteen positions.

Cold Bay, then, is confronted with massive employment reductions. From a total of ninety-four jobs in these two sectors, or over sixty percent of total employment, the end of the decade will see them accounting for approximately thirty-eight jobs, a reduction of sixty percent. This will represent an overall reduction of local employment from a total of 154 in 1982 to approximately ninety-eight from these two areas alone.

With these reductions in the communications and government sectors there will also be pressure on the support sector. The heart of this sector is the Flying Tigers complex of restaurant, bar, hotel, and store. Flying Tigers currently employs between twelve and sixteen people depending on the season, with summer the season of highest employment. We project that this number will undergo a small cutback in response to the overall cutback of a third in the Cold Bay labor force. If this occurs, then, we can expect Flying Tigers employment to drop to approximately ten to fourteen.

Though the drop in the support sector might be expected to be greater, given the size of other local cutbacks, in fact the local support sector depends much more heavily on regional traffic, through the airport, and regional marketing, through the Flying Tigers Store, than on local demand. Therefore, major local cutbacks will not result in correspondingly large cutbacks in the support sector.

Another factor which will affect the level of employment of Flying Tigers is the outcome of the lease renewal process. Flying Tigers has a twenty-five year lease which was signed in 1960 and is due to expire in 1985. This lease gives Flying Tigers exclusive rights to operate a store, bar, restaurant, package store, and several other businesses. If this lease is not renewed, and current evidence suggests that it will not be (personal communication, May, 1983), the result could be a termination of Tigers' presence in town. However, even if the lease is not renewed, this is not likely to result in any immediate major changes in the local employment picture for two reasons. First, no other firm has such an infrastructure yet which could compete with the existing Tigers operation. Second, even after a period of time during which it would be possible for other companies to establish competing activities the overall reduction in the Cold Bay labor force, and therefore population in general, means that there will be no need for an expansion of support services. Thus, even if Flying Tigers terminates its operations and is replaced by another firm the ultimate impact on local employment is likely to be small.

This drop in government, communications, and support/service sectors will, in all probability, not be matched by a corresponding drop in the private transportation sector. This is because Cold Bay will continue to be a major transportation center for the entire region, and very little of the traffic which comes through the community is destined for Cold Bay per se. Reeve Aleutian Airways in particular should be insulated from these local economic fluctuations. Peninsula Airlines, which currently employs ten people locally, depends heavily on carrying Reeve passengers to other regional destinations not served by the latter, and should suffer little decline in business as a result of local population

declines. In essence these companies depend much less on local
business than they do on transshipment of people and material.

While it is true that there are likely to be developments in
other parts of the region which will increase the amount of traffic
through Cold Bay, we expect this to be offset by the reduction in
traffic to Cold Bay itself. Some developments which might act to
increase traffic, at least seasonally, are the growth of a groundfishing industry, particularly in Akutan and Unalaska, and the
growth of tourism in, for example, the Pribilofs. However, the
current number of employees in Cold Bay should prove sufficient to
accommodate this seasonal increase.

The sectors discussed here represent a total of 141 out of the
154 jobs held in Cold Bay in 1982. If the cutbacks occur as we
have projected here, these sectors would represent a total loss of
fifty-six jobs, distributed as shown in Table 7.2.

Table 7.2

Cold Bay Labor Force Reductions, 1982 to 1990

	1982	1983	1986	1990
Government	63	53	32	28
Communications	31	24	18	12
Support Services	16	14	14	14
Transportation	32	32	32	32
Other	13	13	13	13
Total	154	135	108	98
Reduction from 1982 (percent)		5.8	34.8	39.4

The overall effect of these reductions will be a growth in
the importance of the transportation sector at the expense of
government and communications. This is ironic in a sense as Cold
Bay originated as a transportation enclave, and it appears that it
will once again become dominated by that sector. This process
should not be seen as unique or irreversible, however. The history
of Cold Bay has been precisely one of the expansion and contraction
of the workforce in very wide fluctuations, but always with the
transportation sector as a stable and persistent core. Cold Bay is
now involved in another period of contraction, but this time it is
the result of technological changes rather than political or military decisions.

7.2.8.1.2 Income. The Cold Bay labor force, in the absence of
a fisheries sector, is dominated by middle-level white collar
workers and skilled laborers, producing an income scale which is
remarkably compressed. Almost all those working in Cold Bay make
between twelve and thirty thousand dollars per year. There is no
one who makes the hundred thousand plus a year which some fishermen
make, nor is there anyone who is indigent as a result of having,

256

for example, been left out of the limited entry system as has been the case in other communities (Petterson, Palinkas, and Harris 1982).

In the absence of OCS development there is no reason to assume that the character of the Cold Bay income structure will change appreciably. There are essentially no economic classes in the community, as all are on roughly a par from the perspective of income, and it is expected that the future of the community will remain characterized by this remarkable absence of economic distinctions.

7.2.8.1.3 **Consumer Behavior.** Even though the number of employed positions in the community are expected to decline under this scenario, no major changes in patterns of consumer behavior are projected. This is because the income levels of those who remain in the community will remain constant or increase with the rising cost of living and because of the expected continuity in existing means of consumer purchase. Most consumer items will continue to be purchased outside the community.

7.2.8.2 Feedback

7.2.8.2.1 **Cash Economy.** The structure of the Cold Bay economic system is expected to become dominated once again by the transportation sector at the expense of the governmental and communications sectors. Throughout the 1980s the Cold Bay economy will be characterized by contraction as the corporations and agencies which have retrenchment plans at present carry those plans out. However, by the 1990s some regional and local events may have occurred which will begin to reverse this trend.

The first shift in the 1990s concerns the development of new economic capabilities in the region which will have an impact on Cold Bay's position as a transportation and communications center. The most dramatic of these concern two areas of development. First, the groundfish industry is expected to develop rapidly from 1990 on in Akutan and Unalaska. This would result in increased traffic through Cold Bay, and in an increased role for the community as a supply point for the groundfish industry which would in turn lead to expansion in transportation and support services in Cold Bay directed outside the community. The second regional development is OCS-related development. If Unalaska or any other regional center becomes the focus for oil-related development Cold Bay will become a major staging area for both personnel and material. In this case we would also expect a modest expanson of the support sector and of the transportation and communications sectors. This should be sufficient to reverse the decline in the Cold Bay economy and population and the community would grow slowly throughout the decade of the 1990s.

The second possible shift in the 1990s would affect Cold Bay more deeply. This is the possibility of the establishment of a road link between Cold Bay and King Cove. This is not expected during the 1980s, but it is possible such a link may be established in the 1990s. If this occurs it would finally give impetus to the development of a local fish processing sector, particularly given the convenience of the airport and the possibilities for distribution which it presents. In this event the Cold Bay economy would be given both a lift and a new direction. This would lead to much more rapid growth than the regional development of a groundfish or oil-related industry.

7.2.8.2.2 **Subsistence**. No changes in the economic organization of subsistence activities are projected under this scenario.

7.2.8.2.3 **Non-Labor Force**. Cold Bay is, by definition, a full employment community. That is, no one can remain in town unless they have a position. This is a result of the difficulty of finding land for private purchase, and the near impossibility of finding a position in town without working first for a major company in another location and only then being sent to town. The cutbacks which Cold Bay will experience are only local, and do not necessarily represent overall reductions in the agency or corporation. Most of these employees will continue to work for the company or agency, but in another location. Nonetheless, they will be forced to leave town, whether they still have a job or not. Therefore there will be no growth in the Cold Bay non-labor force. Again, this is an example of the self-purging nature of the Cold Bay system. The town is so organized that it is virtually impossible for it to suffer from unemployment of any kind.

The only possible exception to the equation of residence and job is among the permanent residents. It is possible, if permanent residents come to represent a greater proportion of the population, that eventually some of them may retire in Cold Bay. This depends on the availability of land. A few already own land, and if more becomes available for private purchase the number of permanent residents may increase. This will be a slow process throughout the forecast period, but could well accelerate sometime after the end of that period.

7.2.9 Social Subsystem

The changes projected above in the Cold Bay economic system will have effects on the social structure of the community as well. In this section we note the probable course of social change over the projection period. Included in our discussion are kinship patterns, neighborhood patterns, friendship networks, and extended regional, state, and national networks.

7.2.9.1 **Output**. If land becomes available, and at present it appears likely it will in the next few years, and the proper circumstances prevail, the community could see the emergence, for the first time, of genuine kinship networks. The availability of a certain amount of housing, particularly that abandoned by the FAA, could also encourage the settlement of people related by kin ties should it prove possible for them to rent, lease, or buy those houses. However, we feel that this is likely to be restricted to only one or two instances and will, in no case, become widespread during the projection period. This is for several reasons.

First, the shrinking economy will simply not encourage large numbers of people to remain in town, and the town, as we noted above, will inevitably experience a net out-migration during the projection period. Second, even if land does become available there is no guarantee that local individuals, or individuals who would like to reside permanently in Cold Bay, will be able to gain to such land. This was certainly the case in the 1979 sale of land by the Department of Natural Resources.

Over the long term, however, if the attempt to gain land and reserve it for the use of local residents is successful it could result in an increase in the importance of kinship as a basis of social interaction. However, even in the event of a "successful" effort in terms of land acquisition, the importance of kinship is not likely to increase dramatically during the projection period. The increase in importance will be very gradual, but if the permanent population does in fact grow steadily, even if slowly, eventually kinship may come to play a much larger role in the community than is currently the case.

An important aspect of kin relations is family patterns. These are particularly important in the Cold Bay kinship system since familial relations actually constitute the extent of kinship. Over the forecast period we anticipate that family patterns will remain essentially unchanged from their current structure with one exception. The agencies and corporations cutting back on their levels of employment in Cold Bay, with the exception of the Federal Aviation Administration, are those which tend to employ somewhat younger men who are less likely to be married and have families than many others in the community. It is probable, then, that families will increase as a percentage of the total population during the next few years, even though absolutely they will experience no growth. However, if land does become available and affordable for local residents, then it is possible that in the longer term families will grow in absolute numbers as well as proportionally. Therefore, over the forecast period we expect families to grow as a proportion of total population, and toward the end of the forecast period we expect to see the beginnings of a slow increase in the absolute number of families. If this occurs it is possible that, in the longer term, kinship may become important not only horizontally (that is, across the field of social relations) but also vertically (that is, across generations). It is possible that some families may have offspring who will themselves remain in Cold Bay, thus establishing for the first time in the history of the community an intergenerational kinship network.

Neighborhood patterns will also change gradually under this scenario. Currently neighborhood patterns are almost totally determined by occupation, as nearly everyone in town is working for a major outside agency which provides employee housing. However, with the retrenchment of several of these major employers and the potential availability of land, these patterns may change so that neighborhood structure is not so completely determined by occupation. If individuals are able to buy land on which to build they will not be restricted to company housing. By the same token, the potential availability of some housing in the community, notably that left behind by the FAA in its retrenchment, may also contribute to a breakdown of the equation between occupation and residence as people working for various employers move into the empty units.

We noted above in the discussion of income levels and dis-

parities the remarkably compressed nature of the Cold Bay income
scale. Most of the people in the community are white collar workers or skilled blue collar workers. This means that there are
very few social or economic class distinctions based on income. We
expect this to continue to be the case throughout the projection
period. Even though there will be a severe cutback in total Cold
Bay employment, those positions left in the community will remain
white collar or technical positions, which means the incomes of
those remaining in the community will remain approximately equal.
This lack of income differentials is abetted by the lack of social
venues. Since there is effectively only one place in the community
to which one can go for social activity it is impossible to establish a public segregation of social classes, even if they did
exist. With the drop in population we expect the number of social
venues to remain constant, with the effect that social segregation
will remain unimportant in the community.

Should land become available it is possible that the number of
permanent residents will begin to slowly increase. The availability of the FAA housing could also encourage the growth of this
group. However, even if the number of permanent residents does not
increase absolutely, current permanent residents will come to form
an increasingly larger proportion of the total population as that
population continues to shrink. If we take the current permanent
population as between twelve and fifteen people they represent
approximately six percent of the total population. This same set
of permanent residents would represent ten percent of the total
population of 130 to 150 projected for the end of the forecast
period. If, in fact, the availability of land and housing provokes
an increase in the number of permanent residents, then for the
first time the permanent population will then represent a substantial proportion of the total population.

As the permanent population comes to represent an increased
proportion of total population the chances for the formation of an
integrated community increase. As more people are resident for a
longer period of time social links become more intense; more moral
and less instrumental. Paradoxically, then, it is possible that as
Cold Bay declines in population and economic activity it may at
last develop into a social system in which a genuine sense of
community becomes increasingly well developed.

7.2.9.2 **Feedback**. Over the next decade the social patterns
of Cold Bay will be affected by the contraction of both employment
and population. This will lead to several social changes before
the year 2000. First, the permanent residents will continue to
grow as a percentage of total population until 1990, and absolutely
from 1990 to 2000. Total population itself will reverse its contraction around 1990 and begin to grow slowly during the following
decade. Second, with this growth kinship will finally come to play
an important role in Cold Bay social structure. Third, the importance of occupation as a determinant of friendship networks will
weaken steadily during the late eighties, and more rapidly in the
nineties as permanent residents build and live in areas not defined
by occupation. Fourth, the number of families will gradually
increase, especially during the late eighties and the 1990s, which
will result in an increase in social activities. Fifth, inter-

regional and interstate networks will begin to suffer at the expense of intraregional networks as people who have been in the community and region for a long while come to form an increased share of total population.

Finally, the growth of the permanent population and the construction by them of private housing will, particularly following 1990, encourage the growth of a community spirit. As the population comes to be made up of an increasingly large proportion of permanent residents and families social relations will become more intense, commitment to the community more general, and a sense of community will begin to emerge strongly for the first time.

7.2.10 Political Subsystem

7.2.10.1 Output. The course of political activity through the remainder of the decade of the eighties will be one of consolidation. The municipal government will slowly come into control of the major utilities in the community, particularly the water and sewage systems, and the major local facilities, including the airport and the dock. These will present major problems of operation and revenue generation. Negotiations will continue for several years between the city and the state regarding, in particular, the airport and the dock. The structure of municipal government and responsibilities will be established as well during this period.

The most important issues facing the community during the forecast period revolve around the acquisition of sufficient land for private use and the provision of adequate community infrastructure and facilities. The city is currently in negotiation to gain land from both the state and federal governments. We feel, based on the most recent information, that this effort will be at least partially successful within the next two to five years, and that a certain amount of land will be under the control of the city.

The city has recently acquired an ally in its attempts to gain land, among other goals. The Aleutians East Coastal Management and Regional Planning Program has recently been initiated and has been involved in an attempt to identify local needs and help in planning for the future. The AECMRPP is funded by the Division of Community Planning of the Department of Community and Regional Affairs of the State of Alaska. It is currently involved in Cold Bay in an attempt to define particular local needs, including housing, public works, and utilities, and may have a major long-term impact in the community. This development can only be encouraging to the long-term prognosis for both gaining land and effectively dealing with utility and community infrastructure issues.

At the same time the Bristol Bay Cooperative Management Plan study group (Nebesky, Langdon and Hull 1983) projects that Cold Bay will acquire, through state land disposals from any of several sources, approximately one thousand acres of land over the next twenty years. The BBCMP expects this process to begin by 1987 with approximately seventy-five acres of land coming to Cold Bay each year from 1987 to 2002.

The most difficult political decisions facing the city have to do with the provision and maintenance of an adequate community infrastructure. Currently most of the infrastructure is operated by outside agencies rather than the city. The city will be faced with increasing responsibility for the operation of the sewer and water systems in particular as the FAA retrenches and pulls most of its personnel out of town.

The operation of these utilities will force the city to come to terms with problems of revenue generation. There will be increased pressure to institute a property and/or sales tax in order to finance improvements in these systems, several of which are currently substandard. It is also unclear the extent to which these systems, even once brought up to standard, will be self-supporting. In order for them to generate enough revenue to pay for their own operation changes will either have to be made in the rate structure for delivery of service or other forms of municipal taxation will have to be considered. People will also have to be hired to oversee operation of the facilities. In any event these will be important political issues during the projection period.

The municipality, which was incorporated in January of 1982, has the right as a second class city to levy both a sales tax and a property tax. However, this has not yet been done and there is a good deal of sentiment against it. The city is also in a position to collect a portion of the state fish tax from the government should fisheries development occur in the community. However, since there is literally no offloading of fish in Cold Bay currently this will remain only a possibility unless dramatic changes (such as the construction of a small boat harbor and an adequate dock) occur. We therefore project that the fish tax will not be a major source of income since there will be little if any development of the fisheries sector. We also project that, despite local resistance, the city will eventually be forced into establishing a tax structure. In all probability both a sales and a property tax will be enacted.

Cold Bay is a community remarkably free of social or political conflict. There are, however, two areas of potential conflict which should be considered by those in power. The first involves the political split between the municipal government and the state, particularly as the state actually owns most of the land in the community. The second potential area of conflict is between the permanent residents and the bulk of the community.

The major potential problem area is between the jurisdictions of the State of Alaska and the City of Cold Bay. While the city has incorporated and has formed a municipal power structure, the fact is that it still lacks any significant local leverage. That is, despite the fact that the city is now incorporated, the state remains in contol of almost all local land and a good deal of the local infrastructure. The state provides street maintenance, and operates the airport and the dock.

Over the next decade the transfer of power from the state to the municipality in all these areas will be the major issues confronted by the municipal government. The city is currently in negotiation to gain some land, and is beginning to consider the mechanics of taking over responsibility for the operation of several utilities and facilities operated by the state or federal governments.

The airport and dock present special problems. It will be necessary for the city to effect a gradual transfer of responsibility from the state so that the municipality is not overwhelmed by having to take over operation of too much too soon. The city and state will have to cooperate in establishing a system whereby the former is able to operate those facilities without risking its financial solvency.

In Cold Bay the level of community debt is very low. Until the community incorporated the idea of municipal debt was meaningless. In the time since the community has incorporated the municipal government has shown little inclination to bind the city to long-term debt and has generally avoided doing so. We expect this to be true for the duration of the projection period as there will be little need for local bond issues or related revenue measures since the community will be shrinking in size rather than growing. The revenues needed for operation of utilities and community facilities should be generated by local taxes, and state and federal revenue sharing.

Community satisfaction levels are high in Cold Bay. Actually, there are few expectations of Cold Bay when the individual arrives in the community, and the residents make few demands for social or other activity while in the community. The fact that almost all residents know they will not be permanent residents of Cold Bay means that they are able to adapt to what might otherwise seem to be a difficult environment. The major expectations held of Cold Bay concern the opportunity to earn a good salary, put some money away for the future, and perhaps enjoy some outdoor recreation. Thus, the low level of expectations on arrival in Cold Bay results in a high level of satisfaction on the part of the populace.

Means of social control have traditionally been predominantly informal in Cold Bay, and we foresee no change in this pattern during the projection period. Though there has recently been some sentiment for the introduction of a patrolman, to which the city has a right as a second class city, we project that this sentiment will diminish over the next few years. As the population shrinks, and as permanent residents become a higher proportion of total population, the perceived need among residents for formal means of social control will probably decline. As a social sense of community begins to develop informal mechanisms of social control, such as gossip or censure, will prove to be even more effective in most situations. Incidence of violent crime is extremely low, almost nonexistent, and as the population shrinks such events will become even more rare.

7.2.10.2 **Feedback**. From the perspective of political structure, Cold Bay has recently embarked on a path which will lead to continued change during the projection period. With the incorporation of the community as a second class city in January of 1982 the possibility of the exercise of local political power emerged. This political structure, particularly the city council, will be faced with several important decisions over the next decade which will determine the nature and direction of change for that period.

We do not expect that the political structure will change appreciably over the first half of the forecast period. The positions will remain unremunerated, and will continue to be filled by individuals whose primary involvement in Cold Bay is related to employment by major outside firms, at least through 1990. From 1990 to 2000 there will be a gradual increase in the participation levels of permanent residents as their numbers grow slowly. This structure should be adequate to deal with the issues facing the community over the projection period.

The only exception to this concerns the acceptance of responsibility for the operation of some of the community infrastructure, such as the sewer and water systems. It will clearly be necessary for the city to hire people to oversee the operation of these facilities. In all probability this will entail at most two or three people, but they will have to be salaried or hired on a commission basis and will entail some municipal expenditure.

7.2.11 Religion

7.2.11.1 Output.
Over the next decade religious activity in Cold Bay will remain at present levels. Over the period from 1990 to 2000 religious activity will gradually become more important once again in the community, and the chapel should become more of a center of social and recreational activity. This will be a result of the growth in the permanent population of the community and will be a reflection of an increasingly tightly knit social community.

If the permanent population of the community increases we would expect to see some reflection of this in an increase in religious activity. However, with the overall decrease in population which will occur over the next decade, the result will be a slightly reduced level of activity until 1990.

7.2.11.2 Feedback.
The religious structure of Cold Bay is not currently well developed, and we project that there will be little change in this state of affairs over the forecast period. Cold Bay's single interdenominational chapel is moderately subscribed at best and is the focus of few social activities. However, this has fluctuated somewhat in the last few years, and the chapel has often attempted recreational or social programs.

7.2.12 Education

7.2.12.1 Output.
Cold Bay currently has a school offering instruction from kindergarten through high school. Over the projection period there will be little need for expansion of this facility, and we see the current facility as adequate for future needs.

There is currently sentiment in the community for expansion of the school. Cold Bay has recently been granted $1.3 million for the construction of a multi-purpose room, but many residents were disappointed the grant was not substantially greater in order to support construction of an entirely new and larger facility. However, given the projections of future population decline, we feel this sentiment will soon change and that local residents will realize over the next several years that the facility as it currently exists is adequate for local needs. If enrollment figures

264

drop at approximately the same rate as the population itself there
will be little need for expansion. Current enrollment averages
around fifty students, but we project that future enrollment will
gradually drop until it averages around thirty students by 1990
then once again rise slowly to perhaps forty students by the year
2000. The current facility is adequate for that number.

The curriculum of the Cold Bay School is a fairly challenging
and modern one. The students have almost all had experience in
other schools in widely removed areas of the United States, often
in major urban areas. They are therefore accustomed to the demands
of such an educational environment. We do not foresee any major
changes in curriculum over the forecast period.

Cold Bay students are well motivated to achieve in school.
Much of this is a result of the fact that they have, as a rule, had
experience in other educational facilities in major urban areas.
They are completely familiar with the educational environment, and
the fact that their parents are, by and large, white collar or
skilled blue collar workers means they have been raised with a
positive value on education. Most students assume they will go on
to college. We project that these high achievement levels will
continue through the forecast period.

7.2.12.2 Feedback. There will be little change in the Cold
Bay educational system over the period to the year 2000. The
expansion of the facility which is now occurring will be sufficient
for needs well into the 1990s as population, and by extension
enrollment, continues to drop. The current curriculum is adequate
as preparation for continued education and, with the exception of
periodic upgrading, will be satisfactory for the future needs of
the students.

The student population itself will change somewhat over the
next two decades. Primarily it will become a more permanent population, and it will be much more frequent, for example, for a
student to remain in the Cold Bay School for much longer periods of
time. It is also likely that some of the teachers will become more
permanently committed to the community and this will result in an
additional sense of continuity on the part of the students. Finally, social patterns will be more focused on the school than is
currently the case as students become more long term.

7.2.13 Health Care

7.2.13.1 Output. Cold Bay is in a fortunate position from the
perspective of health care provision in that the town has recently
completed construction of a modern health clinic which will provide
for the health needs of the community during the projection period.
Rates of illness are low in Cold Bay, as those who become seriously
ill and are unable to continue working are invariably removed from
the community to an urban area where they can receive more expert
medical care. We see no change in this situation over the projection period.

One area in which there will be a potential problem in health
care delivery is in the availability of a doctor for the community.
The city is currently considering the possibility of having a

doctor from Unalaska or Kodiak pay regular visits to the community
to minister to the health care needs of the population for a fixed
fee. It appears likely some such arrangement will be concluded and
that the community will, for the first time, have at least intermittent care available from a physician.
   The Cold Bay population is remarkably healthy. This is a
result of the fact that the population is unusually young and
physically oriented. Over the next decade, there will be a gradual
increase in problems related to aging as the population comes to
consist increasingly of permanent residents who will be, on the
average, older than the transients who currently dominate the
community. In general, however, over the next decade there should
be little change in the general absence of stress-related illness,
alcoholism, and the other physical and mental maladies which are
fairly common in rural Alaska.
   7.2.13.2 **Feedback.** The health care situation in Cold Bay has
been resolved to a great extent with the recent construction of a
modern clinic in the community. With the projected decrease in
population this clinic should suffice for local needs well into the
nineteen nineties and probably to the year 2000.
   Over this time there will be a gradual shift towards two kinds
of medical need. Both will result from the growth in the permanent
population, and will become particularly noticible during the
second half of the projection period. First, problems of aging
will, as noted above, become more salient. Second, problems of
child development and childhood illness will become more important
as the permanent population, along with their school age children,
comes to represent a greater proportion of total population. These
issues may call finally for the permanent presence of a medical
doctor in the community. If this occurs behavioral patterns will
change such that people increasingly seek medical attention within
the community rather than outside it.

7.2.14 Social Services

   7.2.14.1 **Output.** The number of social problems prevalent in
Cold Bay are not expected to significantly increase over projection
period. Because of the relative lack of rigid social class
distinctions and the structure of employment, there are very few
cases of domestic violence, welfare, alcoholism, and drug abuse in
the community. With the projected decline in population and
employment positions projected under this scenario, it is possible
that the number of social problems exhibited by those who remain in
the community, especially the permanent residents, may increase
because of feelings of isolation and alienation from the larger
society. However, it is unlikely that this will become a major
problem for the community as a whole.
   7.2.14.2 **Feedback.** Even if the contraction of the
community's labor force and population does result in a greater
feeling of isolation and alienation, given the anticipated reduced
levels of commitment to Cold Bay on the part of government agencies
and private corporations, we do not expect that a social service
system will be established under this scenario.

7.2.15   Recreation

7.2.15.1   **Output.**   We have already discussed visiting, vacation and related patterns in the section on social cohesion and
will not repeat that discussion here.   This section will concentrate on hunting, fishing, and other outdoor activities.

We project little change in recreational activities over the
forecast period.   Currently Cold Bay residents utilize the subsistence resources available in the area to a modest extent as a means
of recreational activity.   This includes particularly fishing for
salmon and Dolly Varden, and hunting for game birds, caribou, and,
in relatively rare instances, bear.   The one change which could
occur in this area concerns the proportion of people involved in
such activities.   As the population slowly contracts, and comes to
be made up of proportionately more permanent residents, the amount
of such activity per capita is likely to increase.   This is a
direct result of the fact that the permanent residents tend to be
involved in such activity more frequently than are the transients.
Other than this, we foresee little change in the kind and level of
recreational activity.

7.2.15.2   **Feedback.**   Recreation in Cold Bay will remain social
and leisure-oriented.   In addition to brief vacations to Anchorage
and extended vacations to Hawaii and other parts of the United
States, recreational activity will be organized by two major
venues.   First is the exploitation of the subsistence resources in
the region.   This will take place, but to a much lesser extent than
is characteristic of the surrounding communities which consist of
groups used to a long history of subsistence exploitation.   The
second kind of activity will involve technological devices such as
four wheel vehicles and three wheeler motorcycles.   These latter
will often be used in concert with hunting and fishing.

7.3   SECOND SCENARIO

7.3.1   Assumptions

The second scenario provided by the MMS Office for Cold Bay
assumes the construction of a major gas and/or oil facility on the
south side of the Alaska Peninsula with no direct road link to Cold
Bay itself.   Despite the presumed distance between the community
and such a facility, it is assumed that Cold Bay will become affected by such development because of its role as a regional transportation center.   It is also assumed that a U.S. Coast Guard facility
would be established in the community and that a certain percentage
of the oil facility employees will reside in Cold Bay.

7.3.2   Summary of Effects

The most dramatic changes which would occur in Cold Bay over
the forecast period are in the areas of economic activity, political structure, and social structure.   Economically, the community

would come increasingly under the influence of oil-related
activity, representing a partial shift from the traditional status
of Cold Bay as a government, transportation, and communications
center. Support and service sector employment would also increase
substantially. Politically, the rapid growth of the Cold Bay
economy would provoke several difficult issues. The city would be
faced with the need for revenue generation as it takes over operation of local utilities and facilities and is forced to expand
them. It would be faced with the need to overhaul the political
apparatus of municipal government itself as the operation of the
city becomes a full-time job. Several new bureaucracies would have
to be established to oversee the expanded scope of municipal operations. Socially the consequences of these economic and political
changes would be a strengthening of the transient nature of the
community, a further submergence of permanent residents, and a
formalization of means of social control. In the following sections we consider each of these areas in detail.

7.3.3 Regional Relationships

7.3.3.1 Economic Relations. Intraregional networks would
become more intense under this scenario. This would result from
the implication of the entire region in the operation and supply of
the refinery and terminal. Such a facility would draw the surrounding area closer together as the terminal is partially supported, both with material and personnel, by the region. Direct
employment opportunities, indirect support and service employment,
and other effects of a major facility would increase regional
interaction. Cold Bay would be the focus of this process since the
bulk of men and material would come through the airport.

If the development of an oil refinery in the region results in
the growth of a support sector of wholesale and retail outlets in
Cold Bay, as discussed below, residents from surrounding communities may possibly spend more time and money in the community for
consumer expenditures. Currently, such purchases are either made
through bulk shipments to these communities, or residents throughout the region must travel to Anchorage in order to purchase necessary or desired items. An expanded support sector in Cold Bay
could result in an enhanced role as a regional commercial center as
well as employment center.

7.3.3.2 Political Relations. The development of an oil and
gas facility in the region would spur the development of regional
political relations. Currently, Cold Bay is isolated from surrounding communities in the region because it is an non-Native enclave
and is not dependent upon commercial fishing industry or local
subsistence resources for its economic livelihood. However, with
the prospect of increased revenues and employment opportunities, as
well as possible negative impacts, it is conceivable that greater
efforts will be made by either the Aleut Corporation, Bristol Bay
Native Corporation, or an alliance of communities on the Alaska
Peninsula to develop political ties to Cold Bay. These ties would
serve to insure that surrounding communities share in the positive
aspects of oil-related development and jointly avoid some of the

negative aspects.

7.3.3.3 **Social Relations.** Most of the intraregional networks would remain essentially instrumental in nature. Social interaction between residents of Cold Bay and surrounding community would increase with greater frequency of contact and increased opportunities for visits to Cold Bay for shopping and/or employment opportunities. Because the community would remain a non-Native enclave in a region dominated by Native Alaskans, purely social visiting or information exchange would undoubtedly be limited and occur primarily with permanent residents of Cold Bay. Nevertheless, social interaction between local residents and residents of surrounding communities will rise considerably under this scenario.

7.3.4 **Population**

The effects on population of a development in the general region of Cold Bay would be much less substantial than if the facility was constructed in Cold Bay itself. Although there would be a great increase in the number of people passing through the community, all these people would not live in Cold Bay itself. The exact proportion of people working on the construction and operation of the oil or LNG facility living in the community depends largely on the distance of the facility from the community.

Population effects should be divided into those during the construction period and those during the operational period. In general construction is projected to take two years, during which time the greatest number of people are in the region. From year three onward the facility would be in operation, and the number of people would drop rather precipitously between years two and three, after which it would once again begin a gradual rise.

There are certain assumptions which involve the relationship between employment changes and population changes which were provided by the MMS Office. Under these guidelines we are assuming the following: (1) of the direct employees of the facility ten percent would live in Cold Bay, and half of these would have families; (2) of the support service personnel fifty percent would live in Cold Bay, and half of these would have families; (3) all of the US Coast Guard personnel would live in Cold Bay, half of whom would have families; and (4) the average family would consist of 2.5 people. With these assumptions we can estimate employment and population levels for the community over the projection period.

The forecast for population in Cold Bay as a result of oil-related development is shown for the third, fourth, and fifth years in Tables 7.3 - 7.5. These tables begin in the third year, which is the first year of operation, because it is only then that permanent population effects will begin to be felt.

If we take the current population of Cold Bay as 226 (the summer of 1982), the changes in population for the first five years are shown in Table 7.6.

These estimates reflect two major periods of population increase. First, at the start of the first year of construction there would be a minimal increase in population as some support and direct personnel locate in Cold Bay. However, this number would,

Table 7.3

Population Increase, Cold Bay: Regional Facility, Year 3

	Commuters	Employees in C.B. With	Without Families	Population Family	Total
Direct Employment	270	15	15	38	53
Special Services	25	12	13	30	43
U.S. Coast Guard	0	25	25	63	88
Total	295	52	53	131	184
Induced Employment	(7)		(1)	(10)	
Effect of Induced Emp.		9	9	23	32
Total					216

Table 7.4

Population Increase, Cold Bay: Regional Facility, Year 4

	Commuters	Employees in C.B. With	Without Families	Population Family	Total
Direct Employment	405	22	23	55	78
Special Services	38	18	19	45	64
U.S. Coast Guard	0	25	25	63	88
Total	443	65	67	163	230
Induced Employment	(11)		(2)	(12)	
Effect of Induced Emp.		12	13	30	43
Total					273

Table 7.5

Population Increase, Cold Bay: Regional Facility, Year 5+

	Commuters	Employees in C.B. With	Without Families	Population Family	Total
Direct Employment	540	30	30	75	105
Special Services	50	25	25	63	88
U.S. Coast Guard	0	25	25	63	88
Total	590	80	80	201	281
Induced Employment	(15)		(2)	(15)	
Effect of Induced Emp.		16	16	40	56
Total					337

Table 7.6

Cold Bay Population: Regional Facility, Years 0 through 5

Year	Population	Percent Annual Population Growth
0	226	
1	245	8.4%
2	245	0.0%
3	442	80.4%
4	499	12.9%
5	563	12.8%

as our earlier estimates reflect, be small. The next major jump occurs with the onset of the operational phase at the start of the third year. This is by far the largest increase in the population of the community itself, as many of those associated with the facility locate in the community. Once this has occurred there would be only gradual growth since the majority of those residing in Cold Bay would have done so at the beginning of the operational period. Ultimately the rate of population increase would once again decline as the operational phase is brought fully on line. We expect total population to be approximately 600 to 700 by 2000.

7.3.5 Community Facilities

The area of utilities is one which would also pose serious problems for the municipality over the next decade. The fact of development of a major facility in the region would in itself probably put little additional strain on these facilities. During the construction period there would be a small increase in the population of the community, as we noted above. However, this increase would in all probability be offset by the losses we project as a result of a contraction in the labor force in the transportation, communications, and government sectors. The net result would be little additional demand on the community infrastructure. It is during the operational period that the major demand would be placed on community infrastructure as the population of Cold Bay begins to rise steeply. This is particularly true during the first year of the operational phase, which is when the bulk of the population increase is expected to occur.

The city is in a way fortunate that there would be little population increase during the first two years, that is, during the construction period. This would create a lag time of two years during which preparations can be made for the population increase expected to occur from the third year on. With careful planning the city could avoid the overtaxing of the infrastructural system through expansion and upgrading before the need is apparent.

Even with no major increase in demand, however, the city faces important decisions with reference to operation of the major utilities. As we noted in the first scenario, the next decade will see the city taking responsibility for the operation of the water and sewage systems, and these both pose problems even at current use levels. Both systems are overworked with the current population of 226, and both are currently operated by the Federal Aviation Administration. The FAA, in concert with its plans for retrenchment of its Cold Bay office, is eager to divest itself of responsibility for the operation of these systems. However, there are two problems associated with this process. First, the systems themselves, and particularly the sewage system, are substandard. The sewage system does not currently meet Environmental Protection Agency standards and who should be responsible for bringing the system up to standard has not clearly been established. The second problem concerns the ability of the city to operate the systems once they are transferred to municipal control. This will be particularly crucial immediately following the transfer of control to the city. At that stage the city will have very few revenues (the current total city income per year is less than $30,000) and will be asked to assume the operation of two major infrastructural systems. This will call for a decision concerning revenue generation.

Ultimately, the city would be forced into one of two courses of action. First, the city may decide to raise rates for delivery of water and/or sewage service to those utilizing the services. In this way it may be possible to generate enough revenue to both bring the systems up to standard and to fund their continued operation following their upgrading. The second alternative would be for the city to generate revenue by introducing a taxation schedule, either property tax, sales tax, or both. We will discuss this alternative at length under political activity.

Other infrastructural systems are in somewhat better condition to accommodate a large increase in population. The electricity generation system is currently being expanded to a delivery capability of 1200 kilowatts, which is over twice the current peak demand on the system. This system can therefore nearly accommodate the projected total population at the end of five years from the beginning of construction. The telephone system also has adequate room for expansion.

7.3.6 Housing and Real Estate

In the event of a major development in the region of Cold Bay, there would be additional problems which must be faced by the municipality in the areas of housing and utilities. This would become particularly crucial after the facility has begun its operational phase, which is the time during which we expect the greatest increase in the number of people living in Cold Bay itself. The problem of land acquisition would also be major, and underlies to a great extent many of the other economic problems facing the community.

The first group which would have to be housed is the Coast Guard. We have assumed a total of fifty Coast Guard personnel, half of whom would have families, for a total of eighty-eight people. Housing for this cohort would be provided by the Coast Guard and constructed during the first two years, or during the construction period itself.

Housing must also be provided for those personnel living in Cold Bay itself employed in both support and direct services. This number includes, by the fifth year, fifty-five single individuals and fifty-five with families, for a total of 193 people. Housing for this group would probably be provided by the companies which employ them.

7.3.7 Value System

With the projected increase in population resulting from the construction of an oil and gas facility in the region, the community should become more socially heterogeneous. While the large majority of the new residents will be non-Native and adhere to a Euro-American value system, the range of values represented in the community will expand, reflecting a broader segment of attitudes and opinions than is currently the case. Differences in values will be based on socioeconomic differences. While the value system as a whole will continue to be characterized as "modern" Euro-American, more community members, especially the permanent residents, many of the construction workers, and individuals on the lower end of the income scale in the community, will possess elements of a "frontier" value system. These elements include emphasis on individual initiative, male domination in social relations, lack of concern for income and occupational prestige, and respect for enterprise and physical labor.

One of the more noticible aspects of this diversity in values would be in the assessment of social status by local residents. Transient professionals and skilled workers would continue to evaluate social status of fellow workers and residents on the basis of income, occupation, and education. Permanent residents would begin to use length of residence, extent of community involvement, and political power as measures of social status, as has been the case among non-Native residents of Unalaska.

The belief system of Cold Bay residents would continue to be characterized as secular. However, as more residents move into the community, values shaped by strong religious belief systems would grow in importance.

With the increasing social heterogeneity of the population, it is also likely that different views regarding the course of future development would emerge. Those who view the environment as something to be exploited would come into conflict with those seeking to preserve the quality of life and minimize the negative impacts of economic growth. These opposing views could have important implications for social relations and political activities.

Despite the emergence of differing attitudes towards economic development, opinions regarding the assessment of social status, and perspectives on the importance of community relations, it is expected that a definite sense of community spirit would emerge in Cold Bay under this scenario. Even among those who expect to live in the community for a short period of time, Cold Bay should eventually be seen as something more than a transient enclave, isolated from the rest of Alaska. Economic and population growth would foster a sense of community and promote the integration of the community with the outside world in a psychological as well as social sense.

7.3.8 Economic Subsystem

7.3.8.1 Output. The economic subsystem of Cold Bay would be among those areas most dramatically affected by the development of an oil refinery and an LNG plant in the vicinity of the community. These effects would include the following. There would be the emergence for the first time of income distribution disparities. There would be a shift in employment patterns from a nearly equal division among government, transportation, and communications sectors to dominance by refinery and terminal workers with a large expansion of the labor force. This would result from the large growth in population.

7.3.8.1.1 Employment. Employment can be divided into direct and indirect employment. The former includes those people actually working on the construction of the facilities during the first two years and those involved in the direct operation of the facilities from year three onward. Indirect employment includes support services and the employees of the United States Coast Guard. Support services can be further broken down into fire equipment operators, helicopter pilots and crews, food services, housekeeping services, recreation services, facilities maintenance, and business office personnel. In general the first two years would see by far the greatest number of people in each of these categories. We project the numbers of these personnel to be approximately the following for the first six years of activity, including two years of construction and four years of the operational period.

Table 7.7

Employment in Cold Bay Region: Regional Facility, Years 1 to 6

Year	Oil Terminal	LNG Terminal	Support Services	USCG	Total
	Construction				
1	940 (235)	3200 (800)	196 (49)	200 (50)	4340 (1085)
2	940 (235)	3200 (800)	196 (49)	200 (50)	4340 (1085)
	Operations				
3	100 (25)	200 (50)	50 (12)	50 (12)	400 (99)
4	150 (38)	300 (75)	75 (19)	50 (12)	575 (144)
5	200 (50)	400 (100)	100 (25)	50 (12)	750 (187)
6	200 (50)	400 (100)	100 (25)	50 (12)	750 (187)

Note: Numbers in parentheses indicate the number of employees

on shift at any time at the facilities. This is one quarter of
the total labor force (on the assumption that one half of the
force is off rotation for a set period - perhaps two weeks -
and of the half remaining only one half is at the site at any
one time).

The support service figures for the first two years are high
because this number of people would be needed to provide support
services for the construction personnel. Following the first two
years these numbers drop precipitously because the number of permanent personnel in the area would be considerably less than the
temporary highs of the construction period. The U.S. Coast Guard
personnel figures are also high during the first two years to
reflect construction activity at the Coast Guard Station site.
Once this facility is constructed the number of permanent personnel
required would be reduced by seventy-five percent.

Support services can be further broken down into kinds of
support offered, both during the construction and operational
phases. We estimate these numbers to be approximately as shown in
Table 7.8.

Table 7.8

Support Services Employment, Cold Bay:
Regional Facility, Year 5+

Support Services	Construction	Operations
Fire Equipment Operators	16 (4)	16 (4)
Helicopter Pilots and Crew	20 (5)	16 (4)
Food Services	60 (15)	20 (5)
Housekeeping Services	60 (15)	24 (6)
Others	40 (10)	24 (6)
Total	196 (49)	100 (25)

The economic effects of the construction of such a facility in
the general vicinity of Cold Bay depend on several factors. The
first factor is timing. Effects on Cold Bay would vary depending
on whether the time concerned is the pre-construction, construction, or operation period. The second factor which must be considered has to do with the possibility of Cold Bay being utilized as
a port for the transshipment of oil and/or gas. The third factor
concerns the distance from Cold Bay to the oil facilities themselves.

The construction of a major oil or LNG facility in the general
region of Cold Bay would affect the economy in two general ways.
First, the balance among Cold Bay economic sectors would be radically changed, with refinery workers becoming the dominant local

group of employees. Second, Cold Bay's position as the regional transportation and communications center would be enhanced as a result of the increased activity involved in the operation of the oil and LNG facility.

Table 7.9

Cold Bay Labor Force: Regional Facility, Years 0 through 5

Year	0	1	2	3	4	5
Employer						
Government	63	52	41	45	45	45
Federal	43	31	17	17	17	17
State	19	17	18	20	20	20
Municipal	1	4	6	8	8	8
Communications	31	26	20	20	20	20
Support/Serv.	18	28	28	43	55	68
Transportation	34	36	40	42	42	42
Man./Process.	6	6	6	6	6	6
Construction	2	2	2	2	2	2
Refinery/Terminal	0	0	0	30	45	60
Coast Guard	0	0	0	50	50	50
Total	154	150	137	238	265	293

Table 7.10

Cold Bay Labor Force: Regional Facility, Years 0 through 5, by Percent of Total

Year	0	1	2	3	4	5
Employer						
Government	40.9	34.7	29.9	18.9	17.0	15.4
Federal	27.9	20.7	12.4	7.3	6.4	5.8
State	12.3	11.3	13.1	8.4	7.5	6.8
Municipal	0.6	2.7	4.4	3.4	3.0	2.7
Communications	20.1	17.3	14.6	8.4	7.5	6.8
Support/Serv.	11.7	18.7	20.4	18.1	20.8	23.2
Transportation	22.1	24.0	29.2	17.6	15.8	14.3
Man./Process.	3.9	4.0	4.4	2.5	2.2	2.0
Construction	1.3	1.4	1.5	0.9	0.8	0.7
Refinery/Term.	0.0	0.0	0.0	12.6	17.0	20.5
Coast Guard	0.0	0.0	0.0	21.0	18.9	17.1
Total	100.0	100.0	100.0	100.0	100.0	100.0

In Tables 7.9 and 7.10 we outline our projections for the Cold Bay labor force over the first five years of refinery related activity, including two years of construction and three years of operation. In Table 7.9 we have expressed employment of each sector by actual number employed, while Table 7.10 contains the same information but in terms of percentage of total workforce represented by each sector.

Table 7.9 clarifies the number of workers who would arrive in Cold Bay over the first five years of construction and operation of an oil terminal and an LNG refinery. The major expansion would occur in the areas of oil-related workers and support and service functions (as well as a large percentage growth in municipal employees). The overall changes in the proportional contribution of various sectors are very large, and are clarified in Table 7.10.

These tables indicate the overall changes which are likely to occur in the Cold Bay labor force and economy. As we noted in the first scenario, both communications and government employment are currently scheduled to contract significantly over the next decade. However, we project that the development of a major refinery in the region would slow this reduction in employment, and this slowing is reflected in Tables 7.9 and 7.10.

Overall we project that Cold Bay employment would drop slightly in the first two years during which construction is occurring, then rise substantially as permanent personnel are introduced both at the refinery and at the Coast Guard Base. The drop during the first two years is the result of retrenchment in the government and communications sectors in particular, although as we noted this drop is projected to be less precipitous than otherwise if a refinery is constructed and operated nearby. In the third year the introduction of refinery and Coast Guard personnel would fundamentally alter the Cold Bay economic structure.

This drop in government employment would not be evenly distributed across all government sectors. The federal civilian branch will be the most severely affected. From a total of twenty-seven employees in year 0 federal civilian employment would drop to seventeen at the end of year five. However, state government would actually increase its number of employees by one. This would occur through a drop in state employment in the first year as the Russell Creek Hatchery is closed and the biologist is let go from the Department of Fish and Game, followed by a rise in employment as more teachers are hired by the R.E.A.A. as the population of the community increases. We project that the number of people (including maintenance) employed by the R.E.A.A. would rise from five in year 0, to six in year 1, eight in year two, and ten in years three through five. Municipal government would also increase as an employer from the current one person to, eight by the end of five years.

A second sector which will experience at least relative contraction is the communications sector which will drop from over twenty percent of all employment to less than seven percent. The reduction in importance of the government and communications sectors is not so much a result of retrenchment in that sector as it is a result of the rapid expansion of other sectors. This great increase in total employment means that any sector which simply maintains stable levels of employment would nevertheless drop sharply as a proportion of overall employment.

At the same time these areas of the Cold Bay economy are contracting other areas would be expanding. The most notable are the support/ service, transportation, teaching (which we have already noted), terminal/refinery, and Coast Guard sectors. Support and service would necessarily expand, first in response to needs of the construction personnel, later in response to the increased permanent population of the community. We project that this sector would grow from the current eighteen employees to approximately sixty-eight employees after five years, which represents a percentage increase from 11.7 percent to 23.2 percent of all employment. Some of this support sector would doubtless reflect local entrepreneurial efforts as the community comes for the first time to have an endogenous economic capability.

The transportation sector is also projected to undergo modest increases. We estimate that increased transportation demands would result in an increase in Reeve employees, and in all likelihood result in the initiation of at least one other charter service in town. Overall this suggests an increase from the current thirty-two transportation employees to approximately forty-two by the end of the five years.

Finally, the major growth in the Cold Bay economy would be a result of the operation of the refinery and the Coast Guard Station which would be constructed in the community. Permanent refinery personnel would not begin to locate in Cold Bay until after the construction period is over, that is in the third year. This group will grow rapidly from thirty employees in the third year to forty-five in the fourth year and finally to sixty in the fifth year, and will ultimately represent 20.5 percent of all Cold Bay employment. The Coast Guard Base would experience all its growth at the conclusion of construction in the third year. From that point on approximately fifty employees would be stationed in Cold Bay, representing 17.1 percent of all employment in the fifth year.

Even though, under this scenario, some oil and LNG workers will live in Cold Bay, the major effects on Cold Bay would result from its position as a transportation, communications, and support center. Cold Bay would be the logical choice for a staging area for any facility in the area, primarily as a result of its excellent airport. Cold Bay would therefore be the community through which most personnel associated with such a project, both in the construction and operational phases, would have to pass. Much of the material for the project, and for its continuing operation, would also pass through Cold Bay.

7.3.8.1.2 **Income.** Under this scenario, total income and total per capita income are both expected to increase. As the community grows rapidly there would be an increasing range of incomes represented. The refinery and terminal would attract middle and upper management personnel as well as a large population of laborers. Even though most of these people would not live in Cold Bay, enough would make the town home to affect the current structure of incomes. For the first time there would be at least two distinct groups of employees, management and laborers.

7.3.8.1.3 <u>Consumer Behavior</u>. With the projected development of a support sector in the community, two specific changes in consumer behavior can be anticipated under this scenario. First, there will be more consumers in the community to purchase wholesale and retail items. Especially among new permanent residents requiring household items, the demand for consumer goods by the community as a whole will increase. With the projected increase in per capita income, more money will be available for consumer purchases as well. This will further encourage the growth of the support sector through the multiplier effect. Finally, as the support sector grows, more goods will become available for purchase in Cold Bay. This will encourage consumer purchases in the community itself rather than in Anchorage which is currently the case. Thus, increased spending on consumer goods and purchases in the community rather than elsewhere are anticipated under this scenario.

7.3.8.2 <u>Feedback</u>

7.3.8.2.1 <u>Cash Economy</u>. According to this scenario, then, Cold Bay will, over the first five years of construction and operation of the refinery, undergo a shift from a government-dominated economy to one dominated by private enterprise. For the first time in its history Cold Bay will be a non-government town, although government will remain important. While all levels of government currently account for approximately forty percent of Cold Bay employment, we project that by the end of year five government will represent only 15.4 percent of all employment.

The areas of the cash economy which would be most heavily affected by such developments are the support sector and the transportation and communications sectors. The support sector would receive a substantial boost as the demand for food, dry goods, and so on rises steeply. The Flying Tigers store is already well-suited to fill such a need as it currently operates in the same capacity as a supplier to many of the smaller villages in the region. The direct air links between Cold Bay and Anchorage facilitate the shipment of goods through the community and make it the logical "halfway house" for such goods. The presence of Peninsula Airlines insures delivery capabilities to any nearby site with an airstrip. The transportation sector would be affected as the number of people passing through Cold Bay on the way to the facility, particularly during the construction phase, increases. This will call for additional personnel in many phases of airport operation. It will also provide an opportunity for additional charter flights from Cold Bay to the construction site itself. Currently Peninsula is the only charter operation out of Cold Bay, but in the event of such construction it is likely that at least one other such operation would be introduced.

In the support area the development of a major facility within the region could alter the current plans of the Flying Tigers Lines. Tigers has at present a twenty-five year lease which gives them exclusive rights to the operation of several businesses in town, most importantly a restaurant, bar, store, and hotel. At present it appears that Tigers is uninterested in renewing that

lease, which expires in 1985, particularly as it seems unlikely
that the state will consider renewing it as an exclusive lease.
However, if it appears that there will be development in the region
then Tigers would have an incentive to remain in town, even in the
absence of an exclusive lease. We expect that this will depend to
a large extent on timing. If it becomes obvious to people in town,
and to Tigers in particular, that such development is imminent
within the next year or so Tigers will probably remain in town
since they have already established the infrastructure necessary to
service such a facility. However, if the awareness of development
does not occur for several years we expect that Tigers will go
through with its plans to relinquish its Cold Bay holdings and that
some other company will take over that position in the community.

Whether the major support company in town remains the Tigers
or becomes another company which takes over the local Flying Tigers
operation, we expect the support sector to gradually expand over
the next decade, as reflected in the figures we have presented
above. Supplying a major facility in the region would provide a
boost to such support businesses, and that demand, in conjunction
with ongoing demand from the villages in the region which have
traditionally been served by Tigers, would insure the vitality of
that sector of the Cold Bay economy. Several other retail and
wholesale outlets of various kinds can be expected after the expi-
ration in 1985 of the FTL lease.

7.3.8.2.2 Subsistence. Subsistence currently plays no major
role in the Cold Bay economy because the community is largely non-
Native and heavily involved in the cash economy. Even with the
proposed increases in population, subsistence activities will continue to be primarily for recreational purposes.

7.3.8.2.3 Non-Labor Force. The construction of a major facility in the region of Cold Bay will probably not alter the full
employment nature of the community. This will be insured if the
community requests that the companies working on the construction
phase of the oil or LNG facility do their hiring in Anchorage
rather than in Cold Bay or one of the surrounding communities. The
citizens of Valdez found that the most visible and one of the most
troublesome contingents were those who came to the community hoping
to find a job but without work guaranteed. This group has no means
of income and can be involved in petty theft and other kinds of
crime. If hiring was done in Anchorage and this was widely publi-
cized, and no interviewing or hiring was done at the site, Cold Bay
could avoid the problems associated with a group of unemployed
laborers.

7.3.9 Social Subsystem

7.3.9.1 Output. In general the development of such a facility would serve to maintain the outline of Cold Bay social structure. This will be true both during the construction period and
during the period of actual operation of the facility. Cold Bay is
long accustomed to transient workers passing through the community.
Thus, the introduction of the construction crews, who would be
involved in the establishment of the facility, would be easily

assimilated by the community. Few of the workers would be
stationed in Cold Bay itself, so they would be relatively uninvolved in Cold Bay social life. Following the construction period
Cold Bay would serve as the staging area for the facility, and
would be utilized as a place of residence by some workers and
management personnel, and it is at this time that the major social
impacts would begin to be felt.

We have noted the general lack of importance of kinship in
Cold Bay. The effects of a major oil-related development in the
region on the lack of kinship networks in Cold Bay would be negligible. There are two reasons for this. First, the majority of
workers would be on tours of duty, residing elsewhere on a permanent basis. The extent of kinship links contributed by this group,
then, would probably be siblings who happened to work for the same
or related companies with operations in Cold Bay.

The second reason kinship links would not be in evidence among
the oil-related workers actually explains the first. As in almost
every other instance of a worker in Cold Bay these men would be
working for a major outside corporation or agency. They would have
worked several other places for the same company, and probably
expect to work in yet other places. That is to say, just as with
the rest of the people of Cold Bay, these are transient workers for
outside agencies. Therefore, for the vast majority of those who
settle in Cold Bay the kinship system would not extend beyond the
nuclear family, and many would not even have their family present.

Neighborhood patterns would change to some extent given our
assumptions. We assume there will be some retrenchment on the part
of the FAA and RCA, even if it is eventually less than presently
anticipated. In that event some housing would be opened in Cold
Bay, a relatively rare occurrence. This means there may be room,
if the homes can be leased, rented, or bought, for some people to
move into a neighborhood who do not share occupations with others
in that neighborhood. This would break the strict geosocial equation of occupation and neighborhood and contribute to cross-occupa-
tional social ties. However, among the existing neighborhoods of
Cold Bay this is expected to occur on a small scale.

In addition to changes among existing neighborhoods, there
would be new neighborhoods in Cold Bay. That percentage of people
working at the oil and LNG facilities who choose to live in Cold
Bay would provoke a minor housing boom. This, of course, assumes
that land becomes available for private purchase. Two kinds of
building would occur. First, existing hotel accommodations would
be expanded and new accommodations built. This would probably
occur in the existing downtown area. Second, housing would begin
to appear on the periphery of the existing community. This housing
would be dominated by oil and LNG workers and constitute another
example of residence determined by occupation.

With the option of additional social locations, such as bars
and restaurants, it is likely that social distinctions would
develop as different places are frequented by different segments of
the population. The emergence of these groups would depend on the
number of managerial class workers who establish residence in Cold
Bay, the number of blue collar workers, and the number of successful local entrepreneurs who are able to profit from the arrival of

the companies. We expect these groups to all make an appearance in Cold Bay, and to introduce and encourage new social distinctions. However, as long as the facilities are located at a distance from the city these effects should not be overwhelming. These social effects would vary in speed and duration. During the initial two year period of construction there would be extremely heavy traffic through the community to the site and from the site back to Anchorage. However, very few of these people would take homes in Cold Bay. They would not become long-term members of the community, and their relations with the majority of community members would be essentially instrumental.

Once construction is over some small percentage of the workers and managers at the refinery and terminal would probably take up residence in Cold Bay. This is the period when incipient social distinctions would make themselves felt as certain groups begin to frequent certain social areas while others patronize different locations.

In addition to changes in intraregional social networks, discussed above, interregional, and interstate networks would also be altered under this scenario. In general interregional networks would become stronger, while interstate networks become somewhat weaker. The extent to which each of these occurs depends primarily on the number of oil-related personnel who live in Cold Bay itself. If we assume approximately ten percent this will have a significant, though not overpowering, effect. The people working on both the construction and operation of the facilities will in many cases be those who gained experience in such work during the pipeline construction and the construction in Valdez. This means there will be a higher proportion of Alaskans than was the case in Valdez, so ties to other parts of Alaska will be particularly strong. Also, as the increased demand for supplies and services is felt in the region Cold Bay would find itself in more intense interaction with Anchorage and other regions of Alaska. Cold Bay would be the transportation and communications center of these activities and Cold Bay merchants and service workers will be in closer and more frequent contact with Anchorage than previously.

7.3.9.2 Feedback. The effects of these developments on Cold Bay social structure would be important but not pervasive. The growth of the population in the event of a regional facility, as opposed to one located in Cold Bay itself, would be more gradual and peak at a much lower threshold. Nonetheless, there would be several important effects. In general the structure of Cold Bay social networks would gradually diversify and become more complex.

First, the traditional determination of residence by occupation would begin to break down to some extent. As homes become available with the retrenchment of several government agencies it may be possible for people to get homes which are not directly owned by their employer. However, this should not be overstated, since even the oil-related workers who live in Cold Bay would probably be living in housing provided by their employer.

There would also be effects on the nature of social networks. As occupation comes to determine residential location less it would exert less influence on social networks, and other associational factors than occupation would become important. Associated with this change would be the introduction of social class distinctions based on the economic distinctions discussed above. With more social venues and increased socioeconomic distinctions among the segments of the population, groups would emerge which socialize primarily with one another and less with others.

The extent to which these processes occur will depend largely on the success of the city and individuals in gaining land. If land becomes generally available then the options for residence would increase considerably, making possible the development of non-occupationally determined residence. If enough land becomes available it is possible that neighborhoods may actually become at least partially determined by income, rather than occupation alone.

7.3.10 Political Subsystem

7.3.10.1 **Output.** With the growth in economic activity and population associated with the establishment of a major facility in the region Cold Bay would come under pressure to expand municipal government in several areas. The municipal government itself would undergo a change from essentially volunteer to salaried labor. The forces of change confronting the city would be too great to be met by a cadre of people who are able to devote only part time to the administration of the city. The city council positions will probably remain unsalaried, but it would be necessary to institute a municipal infrastructure which can oversee community development and plan for the future. The city would probably hire a city manager to run the bureaucracies necessary to oversee the processes of municipal development. There would be a need for a formal law enforcement division of the government, consisting of at least one patrolman and perhaps several. There would be a need for a City Planning Department, a City Treasurer's Office, and a Public Utilities and Facilities Office at a minimum. Municipal government would become a significant local employer.

The expansion of municipal government would increase the possibility of local political conflict. As those now in control of municipal government are confronted with these changes it would be necessary for them to relinquish much of their current power in favor of the professionals hired from outside. This means that the city would have to engage in a search for qualified personnel to fill many of the appointed positions in municipal government. Most of the people who are hired to operate the municipal structure would be outsiders who are not committed to Cold Bay on a long-term basis. This process presents the community with several challenges which should be made explicit in advance of the process itself.

The control of municipal government would inevitably be assumed by people who have relatively little experience of Cold Bay itself. With the influx of population would come a whole new group of voters who may well return their choices to the city council. A danger here is the possibility that this group of officials may be tempted to bond the city into long-term debt in order to meet short-term needs.

Most of these problems revolve around the danger of taking the construction period as diagnostic of the long-term effects of oil-related development. It must be clearly understood that the influx and demand of the construction period is only temporary and would reduce considerably during the operational period.

Beyond the restructuring of municipal government there would be several other political issues to be addressed over the projection period. These include the assumption of responsibility for utilities and facilities, the administration of community development in general, the decision whether or not to institute a tax structure, changes in the means of social control, and, underlying much of this, the ongoing attempt to gain control of some land for private or municipal ownership.

One of the most immediate problems to be faced by the city has to do with the operation of community utilities and facilities. The sewage and water systems will be taken over by the city in the next few years. We have already noted the economic problems presented by these utilities, but there are political aspects to this situation as well. The water system is currently operating at capacity and will have to be expanded in the event of any significant population increase. The burden for financing this expansion would probably fall to the city and would be a major issue in the near future. The political situation with the sewage system is somewhat more complex. The city will probably attempt to negotiate with the FAA to have the latter bring the system up to standard before it is transferred to the municipality. Once this occurs the system will still have to be expanded. The assumption of responsibility on the part of the city for these utilities will therefore involve a delicate series of negotiations for which the local officials should plan well in advance.

Much the same political process will occur between the city and the state. The state currently operates the airport, the dock, and does street maintenance. The latter will pose the least problems. It appears that the state will probably, in the event of a transfer of power, excess some of its equipment which the city could then purchase for the purpose of continuing with street maintenance. As essentially all the streets in the community are currently dirt or gravel, this generally involves grading and the spreading of oil and/or gravel. We expect this responsiblity to be transferred to the city within a few years.

The airport and the dock pose more serious problems. The operaton of these facilities is very expensive and is currently beyond the scope of the municipal government. Nonetheless, these facilities will eventually be turned over to the city, and preparation must be made for this eventuality well in advance. Successful resolution of this process will take, from the standpoint of the city, adroit political maneuvering. It would be preferable for the city to reach an arrangement with the state whereby transfer of control could occur gradually over several years. The airport in particular is currently far beyond the means of a community to operate. In order for the city to take responsibility, then, for these major facilities there will have to be several other major changes, particularly in the revenue generating capacity of the municipality. This brings us to a discussion of possible changes in the tax structure of the community.

The problem of revenue generation will be an acute one for the

city over the duration of the projection period, but particularly
during the first few years during construction and initial operations. During this period the demand on community services of
various sorts, from the water and sewage systems to the airport and
the dock, would be greatly increased. However, this increase would
be only temporarily at the levels achieved during the construction
period and eventually fall back to more moderate levels during the
operational phase. The city must therefore institute a means of
collecting municipal revenues while being careful not to overextend
itself during this initial period. During construction revenues
may be relatively high, but they would once again drop off once the
operational period begins.

These demands on the city would almost surely force it into
instituting a system of local taxation. The possibilities of
revenue from both property and sales tax would be too enticing to
resist, particularly given the additional burdens which the city
would be asked to assume. The city should also plan carefully to
make the airport and the dock profitable. If this process is
handled correctly it should be possible for the municipality to
generate considerable revenue from the operation of those facilities. Indeed, on the assumption that the oil-related facilities
are situated at some distance from Cold Bay it would be crucial for
the city to make the airport and the dock money-making facilities.
This is because there would be few direct revenues from oil-related
property taxes. Therefore, other means of income generation must
be considered. While property and sales taxes would take some of
the burden, it is unrealistic to assume that a community the size
of Cold Bay, even with the additional population expected as a
result of oil-related development, would be able to generate enough
in tax revenue to support the greatly increased demands on municipal government. Therefore, the airport and the dock must generate
a considerable amount of this revenue. It is only at those two
facilities that Cold Bay would be able to realize substantial
income from the companies operating in the region, since the facilities themselves would be outside the taxation jurisdiction of the
community.

Cold Bay is currently free of any marked social or political
conflict. The community is relatively homgeneous economically and
socially, and there are few overt expressions of social conflict.
However, with the changes which are projected for the next two
decades there are some areas in which the potential for such conflict exists and which should be planned for in advance.

The first possible area of conflict may be between the municipal government and the oil-related companies which will move into
the area. There would be an understandable desire on the part of
the oil-related firms to have the municipal government assume much
of the cost of the upgrading and construction of housing, utilities, and related activity which will have to take place with the
development of a regional facility. It would be important for the
municipal government to come to an early and clear understanding of
relative responsibilities in these areas. If the municipal government is careful in planning for these developments it should be
possible to gain several important concessions from the companies
locating in the area in terms of aid in upgrading local utilities

and facilities used, in part, by oil-related personnel.

A second possible area of conflict is between the permanent residents and the influx of new transients. However, in all likelihood this should not become overt as the permanent residents may simply reduce their levels of social interaction as they are overwhelmed by the population influx. Nonetheless, the end result of this process would be a further reduction in the sense of community which characterizes Cold Bay as the permanent residents become an ever smaller proportion of total population.

Finally, an ongoing theme during this period would be the relationship between the state and the municipal government. At several points there are crucial issues to be resolved between the two, including the issues of land acquisition and the assumption of responsibility for the operation of the dock and the airport.

The level of community debt is something which would have to be carefully monitored and controlled by those who are in positions of power in the municipal government. As noted above, the temptation would be to overextend the city in terms of loans or bond issues during the construction period. However, if this is avoided, the long-term situation should be favorable for the city as it begins to generate revenue from the operation of the airport and dock and avoids large short-term debt.

Community satisfaction levels should remain essentially unchanged with one possible exception. In general, those who go to Cold Bay are satisfied with relatively little in the way of social or cultural life. They do not expect to find such opportunities and are not disappointed when they are not present. The period of time spent in Cold Bay is seen as a hiatus during which the important activity should be to make some money and prepare for the future in another location. Therefore, since expectations are not high before arrival in Cold Bay the general lack of social and cultural activities is not seen as a burden.

However, there is one group which may experience a definite decline in levels of satisfaction. This is the permanent resident group. This group is not in Cold Bay for instrumental reasons, that is, to make money or because they were sent. They have made a choice to live in Cold Bay because of the isolation, the natural resources available, including hunting and fishing, or for any of several other reasons which revolve around the advantages of an isolated, rural existence. The influx of population which would attend oil-related development would in all probability be seen as a deterioration in the quality of life by these permanent residents. This could provoke either increased social isolation on the part of the permanent residents or might even lead to their abandonment of the community.

Finally, as we noted briefly above, the means of social control would also have to be adjusted during this period. The growth of the population would cause several changes necessitating the formalization of social control. Where currently the community relies almost exlcusively on informal means of social control, we expect that the projection period would see the institution of a local police department. The movement of large numbers of construction workers through the community would demand formal law enforcement capabilities. As more social venues, particularly

286

bars, are opened, and more people come into, or at least through,
town there would be increases in petty crimes such as public drunk-
eness, assault, and so on. Once the construction period is over
there would be less need for law enforcement officers. We expect
that the community would probably need two or three officers during
the construction period, and that this number can be reduced to one
or two once the operational period begins.

7.3.10.2 **Feedback**. Overall the major preoccupation of the
municipal government over the projection period would be the
management of the diverse processes which together constitute community development. In the widest sense this would be the task of
the city over the next ten to twenty years: managing the development of the community in the face of large scale oil-related
development in the region. This would take professional administrators with experience in city planning and operation. The ultimate result of this would be the transfer of political power from
part-time officials to full-time municipal employees, and the formalization of many aspects of political structure.

The most important political decisions would revolve around
negotiations between the city and the oil companies concerning
responsibility for the upgrading and building of housing, community
infrastructure, and so on. The most elementary aspect of this
would again be attempts on the part of the city to gain some land,
particularly from the state. The city would also come into control
of the airport and the dock and, through judicious planning, should
be able to convert those facilities into substantial revenue generators. However, the process of assumption of power should be
carefully orchestrated to insure that the municipality does not
come under too heavy a burden too rapidly. The effect of this
would be to establish the city at last as a viable and powerful
local entity which must be consulted and accounted for by major
external powers.

The most fundamental changes, then, would be twofold in the
political arena. First, the structure of municipal government
would be overhauled with professional administrators in positions
of considerable power. Second, the city itself would become a
strong fiscal entity as it gains the means to generate substantial
revenues for the first time. Both of these processes are signs of
the maturation of Cold Bay as a political entity.

7.3.11 **Religion**

7.3.11.1 **Output**. If a major oil-related facility is located
in the region of Cold Bay, but not in the community itself, we
project little change in the religious structure of the community.
The city currently has one interdenominational chapel which fills
the religious needs of the citizens. However, this chapel is only
moderately utilized by residents.

During the rest of this decade we expect the chapel will prove
to be adequate for the religious needs of the community. At most a
small expansion of the facility may prove to be in order to accommodate the increased population. However, as the chapel is now
undersubscribed we expect it will be able to meet this slightly

increased demand. In the decade from 1990 to 2000 increased population will probably result in inauguration of at least one other
explicitly denominational church.

7.3.11.2 **Feedback.** Over the next two decades religious activity should first remain fairly stable then begin to increase
gradually among Cold Bay residents. During the first decade there
would be little change, but during the second decade the possible
increase in families and the overall increase in population would
be felt to some extent at the level of religious activity. By the
1990s it would probably be necessary to expand the existing chapel,
and it is likely that other religious sects or movements may enter
the community. The structure of religious activity would likely
change at this time as the denominational affiliations of other
churches forces the currently interdenominational chapel to become
more obviously associated with a particular belief system. However, no matter how large the community becomes the level of religious activity would remain fairly low.

7.3.12 Education

7.3.12.1 **Output.** Education is an area which would also feel
the effects of major oil-related development in the region. In
general the major effects would be an eventual need for expansion
of the physical facilities. However, the curriculum and achievement levels on the part of the students are expected to remain
stable. We expect that there would eventually be a need for expansion of the school facilities to be able to accommodate approximately seventy-five to one hundred students. However, this would
probably not be done until the long-term demand is clear. This is
expected to occur only during the operational period.

We expect achievement levels to remain constant over the
projection period. Cold Bay students are relatively achievement
oriented and this is largely a result of the fact that most of them
come from other parts of the state or country in which they have
had extensive experience with the larger sociocultural system.
They therefore share the values placed on individual achievement,
success, and so on. We expect this to continue throughout the
projection period.

We also expect few changes in the current curriculum of the
Cold Bay School. The present curriculum is similar to that operating in a typical urban school in the rest of the United States.
It is intended to prepare the students for further education, on
which a high value is placed. Vocational skills receive less
emphasis than do academic skills, and we expect this to continue to
be the case as most students would still be the children of white
collar professionals or skilled blue collar workers who place a hgh
value on academic achievement.

7.3.12.2 **Feedback.** Throughout the forecast period there
would be a need for a gradual expansion of the school facilities
and increase in the number of teachers. Beyond this, however, we
expect little change in the nature of educational activity. The
community is unusually committed to education and most believe that
it is important for their children to go beyond the secondary

level. There are few disincentives to continuing this education, and this would continue to be the case with the possible exception that some students would be tempted to work at the oil facilities rather than complete their education. However, this in itself would require the acquisition of certain skills necessary for such employment. For this reason we do not expect the oil faciliites to significantly affect the student educational aspirations.

7.3.13 Health Care

7.3.13.1 Output. Cold Bay is in a relatively good position with reference to health care as the community has only recently completed construction of a modern clinic. We expect this clinic will accommodate the health care needs of the community over the projection period, even with the expected increases in population. It is possible that the clinic may establish a relationship with a doctor from outside the community to come into the city on a regular basis to provide more professional health care for the local population.

The major demand on health care facilities would be during the construction period, for two reasons. First, this is the period during which the most people would be in the region, thereby logically calling for greater levels of health care. Second, the construction phase is the most dangerous from the standpoint of accidental injury. The city should insist that the construction and oil companies provide a good deal of their own medical and emergency care or share in the increased burden placed on the clinic.

7.3.13.2 Feedback. Health care is an area in which Cold Bay is relatively well prepared for the development of oil facilities in the region. The clinic can handle most problems which might arise, and it is likely that the city would, in concert with the oil companies, arrange for a doctor to be at least intermittently present in the community. This should provide sufficient health care for the needs of the community over the projection period.

The kinds of health issues may well change during the forecast period. During the construction period, in addition to accidental injury, it is likely that issues of alcoholism and stress-related illness may become more important. This could result from the fact that many of the construction and/or operational workers who are "off rotation" may remain in Cold Bay to socialize, drink, and spend their time while they are not working at the facilities. The presence of a group of people who are not working for a period of a week or two would be novel for Cold Bay, necessitating some adaptation on the part of local health care delivery personnel.

In general the structure of health care would change in two ways. First, with a doctor visiting, and perhaps eventually residing in, Cold Bay health care would be professionalized. Second, with the presence of major oil companies health care delivery would become a joint government/private enterprise activity.

289

7.3.14 Social Services

7.2.14.1 Output. Under this scenario the frequency of social problems requiring professional assistance is expected to increase throughout the forecast period. Alcohol and drug abuse and domestic violence would probably emerge as social issues. The resettlement of large numbers of individuals, even those who are short-term transients, the changes to the environment associated with economic growth, and the demands placed on an inadequate infrastructure, may all combine to increase levels of stress in the community. These stressors would not affect all segments of the community to the same degree. Residents with relatively little education working in lower-paying jobs would be at greater risk for exhibiting these problems than transient professionals or permanent residents in managerial positions.

7.2.14.2 Feedback. Under this scenario, the organization of social services are expected to change significantly. Social problems which are currently minor or nonexistent would become a noticible part of social life in the community. Pressure would be placed on state agencies and municipal government to provide adequate personnel and services to address issues of alcoholism and domestic violence. With the projected decline in state revenues in the 1990s, however, access to qualified social service personnel may be limited. Informal services provided by local residents would be increasingly relied upon.

7.3.15 Recreation

7.3.15.1 Output. With an expansion in the number of people in the community of Cold Bay would come some changes in the patterns of recreational activity engaged in by those inhabitants. The number of people would lead to an increased utilization of the subsistence and sport resources in the region, which are considerable. This would pose little problem for the resources themselves, as they are among the most abundant on the continent. The only potential problem is the overuse of the physical facilities.

The major concern of the Fish and Wildlife Service with additional demand on the area concerns Izembek Refuge. The concern is not with the game per se, but with the potential overuse of the trails and roads and the refuge. These roads are kept in a purposely primitive state, and the Service fears that too many people would begin to despoil the environment. However, we do not project that the number of people who would come to Cold Bay under this scenario will necessitate extreme measures.

Other, technological, means of recreation would also increase in popularity. These include four wheel drive vehicles and three wheeler motorcycles which are used to explore the region around town and as transportation for other sporting activities. Flying would also remain a popular form of recreation, encouraged by the excellent airport.

7.3.15.2 Feedback. As the population of the community grows the level of use of the fishing and game resources in the community would rise. However, these levels would still be considerably lower, per capita, than is characteristic of the surrounding villages and communities. Cold Bay residents would still be largely transient, and they are unaccustomed to depending on subsistence resources for a major part of their diet. They hunt and fish primarily for sport, and there is not the added incentive of affirmation of ethnic identity which exists for many in the surrounding region.

Bibliography

Alaska Consultants
1981   St. George Basin Petroleum Development Scenarios: Local
        Socioeconomic Systems Analysis. Alaska OCS Socioeconomic
        Studies Program Technical Report No. 59. Anchorage: Bureau
        of Land Management, Alaska Outer Continental Shelf Office.

Alaska Department of Community and Regional Affairs.
1979   Community Planning and Development for the Bottomfish
        Industry. Phase I Report. Juneau.

Alaska Department of Community and Regional Affairs.
1982   Cold Bay Community Profile. Juneau.

Alaska Department of Labor
1980   Alaska Fisheries Statistics Bottomfish Labor Study, Part
        IV. Juneau.

Alaska Department of Labor, State Demographer
1981   Special Census of Unalaska. Juneau.

Alaska Office of Information Services
1981   Public Assistance Recipient and Expenditures Study Semi-
        annual Report, Volume 6. Juneau: Statistical Support Unit,
        Alaska Office of Information Services.

Albrecht, S.L.
1978   Socio-cultural factors and energy resource development in
        rural areas in the west. Journal of Environmental
        Management, 7:73-90.

The Aleutian Eagle
        A Bi-Weekly Newspaper, Published in Unalaska, Alaska.
        Various issues from Vol. 1, No. 1, September 1981.

Aleutian/Pribilof Islands Association
1978   Tribal Specific Health Plan: Aleutian-Pribilof Islands
        Association Health Department. Prepared by Don Bantz and
        Associates. Anchorage.

291

292

Bailey, F.G.
1969   Strategems and Spoils: A Social Anthropology of Politics.
       New York: Schocken Books.

Bee, Robert
1974   Patterns and Processes: An Introduction to Anthropological
       Strategies for the Study of Sociocultural Change. New
       York: Free Press.

Berger, Louis & Associates, Inc.
1983   Social Indicators for OCS Impact Monitoring. 3 Volumes.
       Alaska OCS Social and Economic Studies Program Technical
       Report No. 77. Anchorage: Minerals Management Service,
       Alaska Outer Continental Shelf Region.

Berreman, Gerald D.
1956   Drinking patterns of the Aleuts. Quarterly Journal of
       Studies on Alcohol, 17:503-514.

1964   Aleut reference group alienation, mobility, and accultura-
       tion. American Anthropologist, 66:231-248.

Beyer Engineering
1981   Water System Master Plan: City of Unalaska, Alaska. Pre-
       pared for the City of Unalaska. Anchorage.

Black, Lydia
1980   Early history. In Lael Morgan (ed.) The Aleutians. Alaska
       Geographic, 7 (3):82-105.

Campbell, Angus, Converse, Philip E., and Willard L. Rogers
1976   The Quality of American Life: Perceptions, Evaluations,
       and Satisfactions. New York: Russell Sage.

Carley, Michael J. and Ellen O. Derrow
1980   Social Impact Assessment: A Cross-Disciplinary Guide to
       the Literature. London: Policy Studies Institute.

City of Unalaska
1972   City council census. unpublished.

1981   Department of Public Safety Annual Report, 1981. mimeo.

1982   Aleutian Regional Airport Project Documentation. Prepared
       by Dames & Moore. Anchorage: Dames & Moore.

Cluett, C., Mertaugh, M.T., and M. Micklin
1977   Demographic model for assessing the socioeconomic impacts
       of large-scale industrial development projects. Paper
       presented at the 1977 annual meetings of the S. Reg.
       Demogr. Grp. Virginia Beach, Virginia, October 21-22.

Earl R. Combs, Inc.
  1981   St. George Basin and North Aleutian Shelf Commercial Fish-
         ing Analysis. Alaska OCS Socioeconomic Studies Program
         Technical Report No. 60. Anchorage: Bureau of Land Manage-
         ment, Alaska Outer Continental Shelf Office.

Cortes, Fernando, Przeworski, Adam, and John Sprague
  1974   Systems Analysis for Social Scientists. New York: John
         Wiley and Sons.

D.E. Raven Associates
  1982   An exploration of the readiness of Unalaska to support a
         hospital. Unpublished manuscript.

Dames & Moore
  1980   Site, Design, and Cost Studies for Feasibility Assessment,
         Offshore Runway Extension at Unalaska Airport, Alaska.
         Prepared for Alaska Department of Transportation and Pub-
         lic Facilities, Division of Aviation Design and Construc-
         tion. Anchorage.

Dames & Moore Norgaard (USA) Inc.
  1982a St. Paul Harbor Development Plan. Prepared for the Alaska,
         Department of Transportation & Public Facilities.
         Anchorage.

Dames & Moore Norgaard (USA) Inc.
  1982b Chernofski Harbor Development Plan. Prepared for the
         Alaska Department of Transportation and Public Facilities.
         Anchorage.

Denver Research Institute
  1979   Socioeconomic Impacts of Western Energy Resource Develop-
         ment, Volume IV: Computer Model Documentation. Washington
         DC: U.S. Council on Environmental Quality.

Dixon, Mim
  1978   What Happened to Fairbanks?: The Effects of the Trans-
         Alaska Oil Pipeline on the Community of Fairbanks, Alaska.
         Boulder CO: Westview.

Easton, David
  1965   A Framework for Political Analysis. Englewood Cliffs, NJ:
         Prentice Hall.

Finsterbusch, Kurt
  1980   Understanding Social Impacts: Assessing the Effects of
         Public Projects. Beverly Hills CA: Sage.

Ford, A.
  1976   User's Guide to the BOOM 1 Model. LA-6396-MS. Los Alamos,
         NM: Los Alamos Scientific Laboratory.

294

Freudenberg, William R.
1983   Theoretical developments in social and economic impact
        assessment. pp. 8-18. In S. Yarie (ed.) Proceedings of the
        Alaska Symposium on the Social, Economic, and Cultural
        Impacts of Natural Resource Development. Alaska Pacific
        University, Anchorage: August 25-27, 1982. Fairbanks:
        University of Alaska.

Geertz, Clifford
1973   The Interpretation of Cultures. New York: Basic Books.

Gilmore, J.S.
1976   Boom towns may hinder energy resources development.
        Science, 191:535-540.

Haeg Bettis Associates
1982   Unalaska City School District Facility Survey and Analysis.
        Anchorage.

Hallowell, A.I.
1955   Culture and Experience. New York: Schocken Books.

Hrdlicka, Ales
1945   The Aleutian and Commander Islands and Their Inhabitants.
        Philadelphia: Wistar Institute of Anatomy and Biology.

Huskey, Lee and Jim Kerr
1980   Small Community Population Impact Model. Alaska OCS Socio-
        economic Studies Program Technical Report No. 4. Anchor-
        age: Bureau of Land Management, Alaska Outer Continental
        Shelf Office.

Jones, Dorothy M.
1969.   A Study of Social and Economic Problems in Unalaska, an
        Aleut Village. Unpublished Ph.D. Dissertation. Berkeley:
        University of California.

Kirtland, John C. and David F. Coffin, Jr.
1981   The Relocation and Internment of the Aleuts During World
        War II. Prepared for the Aleutian/Priblof Islands Asso-
        ciation.

Kleinfield, J.S.
1971   Sources of parental ambivalence toward education in an
        Aleut community. Journal of American Indian Education,

Lantis, Margaret
1970   The Aleut social system, 1750 to 1810, from early
        historical sources. pp. 139-301. In: Margaret Lantis (ed.)
        Ethnohistory in Southwestern Alaska and the Southern
        Yukon: Method and Content. Lexington KY:University of
        Kentucky Press.

Leistritz, F.L., Hertsgaard, T.A., Senechal, D.M., Murdock, S.H., Toman, N.E., Wiig, K., and G. Schaible
1978 The REAP Economic-Demographic Model: Background, Structure and Applications. Bismark ND: North Dakota Regional Environmental Assessment Program.

Leistritz, F.L. and S.H. Murdock
1981 The Socioeconomic Impact of Resource Development: Methods for Assessment. Boulder CO: Westview Press.

Mountain West Research, Inc.
1978 Bureau of Reclamation Economic Assessment Model (BREAM) Technical Description. Denver: U.S. Bureau of Reclamation.

Murdock, S.H. and F.L. Leistritz
1980 Selecting socioeconomic assessment models: a discussion of criteria and selected models. Journal of Environmental Management, 10:241-252.

Murdock, S.H., Leistritz, F.L., Hamm, R.R., and S. Hwang
1982 An assessment of socioeconomic assessments: utility, accuracy, and policy considerations. Environmental Impact Assessment Review, 3 (4):333-350.

Muth, Robert M.
1983 Identifying social effects in forestry decisionmaking: lessons from the past and prospects for the future. pp. 167-179. In S. Yarie (ed.) Proceedings of the Alaska Symposium on the Social, Economic, and Cultural Impacts of Natural Resource Development. Alaska Pacific University, Anchorage: August 25-27, 1982. Fairbanks: University of Alaska.

Nebesky, Will, Langdon, Steve, and Hull, Teresa
1983 Economic Subsistence, and Sociocultural Projections in the Bristol Bay Region. Volume I: Analysis and Projections. Prepared for the Bristol Bay Cooperative Management Plan and Refuge Comprehensive Plans. Anchorage: Institute of Social and Economic Research, University of Alaska.

North Pacific Fisheries Management Council and U.S. Department of Commerce, National Oceanic and Atmospheric Administration, National Marine Fisheries Service.
1980 Draft Environmental Impact Statement for the Groundfish of the Bering Sea and Aleutian Islands Area. Anchorage.

Petterson, John S.
1982 Limited entry and the Native American fishermen: a case study of the Bristol Bay, Alaska salmon fishery. Prepared for the National Science Foundation, Washington D.C.

296

Petterson, John S., Palinkas, Lawrence A., and Bruce M. Harris
1982   North Aleutian Shelf Non-OCS Forecast Analysis. 2 Volumes.
        Alaska OCS Socioeconomic Studies Program Technical Report
        No. 75. Anchorage: Minerals Management Service, Alaska
        Outer Continental Shelf Region.

Petterson, John S., Palinkas, Lawrence A., Harris, Bruce M., Downs,
Michael A., and Beverly Holmes.
1983   Unalaska: Ethnographic Study and Impact Analysis. Alaska
        OCS Social and Economic Studies Program Technical Report
        No. 92. Anchorage: Minerals Management Service, Alaska
        Outer Continental Shelf Region.

Petterson, John S., Harris, Bruce M., Palinkas, Lawrence A. and
Steve Langdon
1983   Cold Bay: Ethnographic Study and Impact Analysis. Alaska
        OCS Social and Economic Studies Program Technical Report
        No. 93. Anchorage: Minerals Management Service, Alaska
        Outer Continental Shelf Region.

R&M Consultants, Inc.
1981   Sand Point Harbor Master Plan. Prepared for the Alaska
        Department of Community and Regional Affairs. Anchorage.

Redfield, Robert
1952   The Primitive World and its Transformations. Berkeley:
        University of California Press.

Retherford, R.W. Associates
1979   City of Unalaska Electrification Study. Prepared for the
        City of Unalaska. Anchorage.

Rogers, George W.
1979   Critique of the Arthur D. Little, Inc., analysis and
        recommendations for state policy and directions for
        developing a bottomfish industry for Alaska. Juneau:
        Alaska Legislative Affairs Agency, Juneau.

Sekora, P.
1973   Aleutian Islands wildnerness study report. Draft reprint.

Shields, Mark A., Cowan, J. Tadlock, and David J. Bjornstad
1979   Socioeconomic Impacts of Nuclear Power Plants: A Paired
        Comparison of Operating Facilities. NUREG/CR-0916.
        ORNL/NUREG/TM-272. Oak Ridge TN: Oak Ridge National
        Laboratory.

Stenehjem, E.J.
1978   Summary Description of SEAM: The Social and Economic
        Impact Assessment Model. Argonne IL: Argonne National
        Laboratory.

Tikhmenev, P.A.
1940   Historical Review of the Origin of the Russian- American
       Company and its Activities up to the Present Time. Michael
       Dobrynin, trans. Washington, DC: U.S. Government Printing
       Office.

Tryck, Nyman & Hayes
1977a Census of population, September 26 - October 8, 1977.
       Prepared for the City of Unalaska. mimeo.

1977b City of Unalaska, Alaska; Recommended Community Develop-
       ment Plan. Prepared for the City of Unalaska. Anchorage.

Tutiakoff, P.
1981   The Aleut world war II relocation and internment: an
       overview.   IN The Aleut Relocation and Internment During
       World War II: A Preliminary Examination. Anchorage: Aleu-
       tian/Pribilof Islands Association.

Unalaska Rural Education Center, University of Alaska.
1982   Fourth Quarter and Annual Report. mimeo.

United States Council on Environmental Quality
1978   Regulations for Implementing the Procedural Provisions of
       the National Environmental Policy Act. Reprint 43 FR
       55978-56007, 40 CFR Parts 1500-1508. Washington DC: U.S.
       Government Printing Office.

United States Department of the Army, Army Corps of Engineers,
Alaska District
1982   Bottomfish Interim Study Reconaissance Report. Anchorage.

United States Department of Commerce, Bureau of the Census
1960   Number of Inhabitants, Alaska. Final Report PC(1)-3A.
       Washington DC: U.S. Government Printing Office.

1972   Alaska Final Population and Housing Unit Counts, 1970.
       Washington DC: U.S. Government Printing Office.

1981   Alaska Final Population and Housing Unit Counts, 1980. PH
       C 80-V-3. Washington DC: U.S. Government Printing Office.

United States Department of Commerce, National Oceanic and
Atmospheric Administration
1981   Local Climatological Data: Annual Summary with Comparative
       Data, Cold Bay Alaska. Asheville NC: Environmental Data
       and Information Service, National Climatic Center.

United States Department of the Interior
1973   Birds of the Izembek National Wildlife Refuge. Washington
       DC: Fish and Wildlife Service, Bureau of Sport Fisheries
       and Wildlife.

298

University of Alaska, Alaska Sea Grant Program
  1980 Western Alaska and Bering-Norton Petroleum Development
        Scenarios, Commercial Fishing Industry Analysis. Alaska
        OCS Socioeconomic Studies Program Technical Report No. 51.
        Anchorage: Bureau of Land Management, Alaska Outer Conti-
        nental Shelf Office.

University of Alaska, Institute of Social, Economic, and Government
Research
  1973 Age and race by sex characteristics of Alaska's village
        population. Alaska Review of Business and Economic
        Conditions, 10 (2).

Unwin, Scheben, Korynta, and Huettl
  1982 Airport Master Plan, Unalaska Airport 1982-2000. Prepared
        for the City of Unalaska. Anchorage.

Veltre, Douglas W. and Mary J. Veltre
  1982. Resource utilization in Unalaska, Aleutian Islands, Alaska.
        Prepared for Alaska, Department of Fish and Game, Subsis-
        tence Division. mimeo.

Veniaminov, Ioann
  1840 Notes on the Islands of the Unalaska Division. Translated
        by R.H. Geoghegan. Fairbanks, 1915. Ann Arbor MI:
        University Microfilms, originally published in Russian in
        St. Petersburg.

Index

300